THE FATHERS
OF THE CHURCH

MEDIAEVAL CONTINUATION

VOLUME 2

THE FATHERS OF THE CHURCH

MEDIAEVAL CONTINUATION

EDITORIAL BOARD

Thomas P. Halton
The Catholic University of America
Editorial Director

M. Josephine Brennan, I.H.M.
Marywood College

Kathleen McVey
Princeton Theological Seminary

Elizabeth Clark
Duke University

Daniel J. Sheerin
University of Notre Dame

Hermigild Dressler, O.F.M.
Quincy College

Robert D. Sider
Dickinson College

Robert B. Eno, S.S.
The Catholic University of America

Michael Slusser
Duquesne University

Frank A. C. Mantello
The Catholic University of America

David J. McGonagle
Director
The Catholic University of America Press

FORMER EDITORIAL DIRECTORS

Ludwig Schopp, Roy J. Deferrari, Bernard M. Peebles,
Hermigild Dressler, O.F.M.

Cynthia Kahn, Warren J. A. Soule
Staff Editors

PETER DAMIAN
LETTERS
31–60

Translated by
OWEN J. BLUM, O.F.M.
Quincy College
Quincy, Illinois

THE CATHOLIC UNIVERSITY OF AMERICA PRESS
Washington, D.C.

Copyright © 1990
THE CATHOLIC UNIVERSITY OF AMERICA PRESS, INC.
All rights reserved

LIBRARY OF CONGRESS CATALOGING-IN-PUBLICATION DATA
Peter Damian, Saint, 1007?–1072.
[Correspondence. English]
Letters / translated by Owen J. Blum.
    p. cm.—(The Fathers of the Church, Mediaeval Continuation v. 2)
Translation of the Latin Letters of Peter Damian.
Bibliography: p.
Includes index.
Contents: [1] 1–30—[2] 31–60
ISBN 0–8132–0707–X [Vol. 2] ISBN 978-0-8132-2637-8 (pbk.)
  1. Peter Damian, Saint, 1007?–1072—Correspondence.
2. Christian saints—Italy—Correspondence.
I. Blum, Owen J., 1912– . II. Title. III. Series.
BX4700.P77A4 1990   270.3—dc19   88-25802

CONTENTS

Preface	vii
Abbreviations	ix
Select Bibliography	xi
Concordance	xix
Letter 31	3
Letter 32	54
Letter 33	56
Letter 34	59
Letter 35	61
Letter 36	64
Letter 37	71
Letter 38	73
Letter 39	98
Letter 40	111
Letter 41	215
Letter 42	216
Letter 43	218
Letter 44	221
Letter 45	244
Letter 46	250
Letter 47	252
Letter 48	263
Letter 49	272
Letter 50	289
Letter 51	335

Letter 52	341
Letter 53	343
Letter 54	344
Letter 55	355
Letter 56	361
Letter 57	369
Letter 58	390
Letter 59	394
Letter 60	404

Indices
    Index of Proper Names   409
    Index of Sacred Scripture   417

PREFACE

Volume 2 of the English translation of *The Letters of Peter Damian* includes Letters 31–60, written during the years 1049 to 1059. Letters 1–30 included in Volume 1 of the series were written before 1049. The bibliography of the sources and literature, the list of standard abbreviations, and the concordance of the new letter numbering are printed in both volumes. When new sources and literature occur, they will be cited in full in the appropriate footnote, from which an abbreviated citation, used later, will be readily understood. Short forms introduced into Volume 1 will continue to be used in Volume 2.

Herewith, the translator wishes to extend his thanks once again to the individuals and institutions named in the preface to Volume 1, without whose generous aid and encouragement his work would not have come to fruition. On this occasion he also thanks the Director of the Catholic University of America Press, David J. McGonagle, for his role in inaugurating *The Fathers of the Church: Mediaeval Continuation*, and Cynthia Kahn and Warren J. A. Soule, staff editors at the Press, for their expertise in guiding these letters through the editorial process.

Quincy College, Spring 1989   Owen J. Blum, O.F.M.

ABBREVIATIONS

AA SS	*Acta Sanctorum.* 70 vols. Paris, 1863–1940.
Abh B	*Abhandlungen der Preussischen Akademie der Wissenschaften*
AUF	*Archiv für Urkundenforschung*
Beuron	*Vetus Latina. Die Reste der altlateinischen Bibel,* ed. Archabbey of Beuron, 1949–.
BHL	*Bibliotheca Hagiographica Latina*
Biblia sacra	*Biblia sacra iuxta Latinam vulgatam versionem iussu Pii Papae XI ... edita,* 1926–.
CC	*Corpus Christianorum, Series Latina.* Brepols, 1954–.
CCCM	*Corpus Christianorum, Continuatio Mediaevalis.* Brepols, 1971–.
CSEL	*Corpus Scriptorum Ecclesiasticorum Latinorum.* Vienna.
DA	*Deutsches Archiv für Erforschung des Mittelalters*
DACL	*Dictionnaire d'archéologie chrétienne et de liturgie.* Ed. Fernand Cabrol. 15 vols. Paris, 1907–1953.
DHGE	*Dictionnaire d'histoire et de géographie ecclésiastiques.* Ed. Alfred Card. Baudrillart. Paris, 1912–.
DTC	*Dictionnaire de théologie catholique.* 15 vols. Paris, 1903–1950.
DuCange	*Glossarium mediae et infimae Latinitatis.* Ed. Charles de Fresne DuCange. 10 vols. Paris, 1883–1887.
FOTC	The Fathers of the Church. New York and Washington, D.C., 1947–.
Gaetani	*S. Petri Damiani ... Opera omnia.* 4 vols. 1606–1640. Later editions will be cited by year of publication.
HJb	*Historisches Jahrbuch.*
HV	*Historische Vierteljahrschrift*
HZ	*Historische Zeitschrift*
Itala	*Itala: Das Neue Testament in altlateinischer Überlieferung.* Ed. A. Jülicher. 4 vols. 1963–1976.
ItPont	*Italia Pontificia*
JE	Jaffé-Ewald }
JK	Jaffé-Kaltenbrunner } Regesta Pontificum Romanorum
JL	Jaffé-Löwenfeld }
LThK	*Lexikon für Theologie und Kirche*
Mansi	*Sacrorum conciliorum nova et amplissima collectio.* Ed. Joannes Dominicus Mansi. 53 vols.

MGH	Monumenta Germaniae Historica
Auct.ant.	Auctores antiquissimi
Capit.	Capitularia regum Francorum
Conc.	Concilia
Const.	Constitutiones et acta publica imperatorum
D—DD	Diploma—Diplomata
Epp.	Epistolae (in Quarto)
Ldl	Libelli de lite
LL	Leges (in folio)
Necr.	Necrologia Germaniae
Poetae	Poetae Latini medii aevi
SS	Scriptores (in folio)
SS rer. Germ.	Scriptores rerum Germanicarum in usum scholarum
SS rer. Merov.	Scriptores rerum Merovingicarum
MIÖG	Mitteilungen des Instituts für Österreichische Geschichtsforschung. 1923–1942.
Muratori	Rerum Italicarum Scriptores. Ed. Muratori. 2d ed. 1900ff.
NA	Neues Archiv der Gesellschaft für ältere deutsche Geschichtskunde
NCE	New Catholic Encyclopedia
PL	Patrologia Latina. Ed. J. P. Migne. Paris, 1844–1855.
RE	Real-Encyclopädie der Classischen Altertumswissenschaft. Ed. Pauly-Wissowa
RHE	Revue d'Histoire Ecclésiastique
Sabatier	Bibliorum sacrorum Latinae versiones antiquae. Ed. P. Sabatier. 3 vols. 1743.
SBA	Sitzungsberichte der Bayerischen Akademie der Wissenschaften
SC	Sources chrétiennes. Paris, 1942–.
StMGBO	Studien und Mitteilungen zur Geschichte des Benediktiner-Ordens und seiner Zweige
TU	Texte und Untersuchungen zur Geschichte der Altchristlichen Literatur. Berlin, 1882–.
Vulg	Biblia sacra iuxta vulgatam versionem. Ed. Robert Weber. 2 vols. 2d ed., 1975.
ZKG	Zeitschrift für Kirchengeschichte
ZRG	Zeitschrift der Savigny-Stiftung für Rechtsgeschichte, Kanonistische Abteilung

SELECT BIBLIOGRAPHY

Sources

Altercatio aecclesiae contra synagogam et synagoge contra aecclesiam, ed. Blumenkranz, "Altercatio aecclesiae contra synagogam. Texte inédit du Xe siècle," *Revue du moyen âge latin* 10 (1954), 5–159 (here 53–123).
Ambrose. *Exameron*, ed. C. Schenkl. CSEL 32, 1 (1887), 1–261.
Anastasius papa II. *Epistolae et decreta*, ed. A. Thiel. Epistolae Romanorum pontificum genuinae 1 (1867–1868), 614–639.
Augustine. *De civitate Dei*, ed. B. Dombart and A. Kalb, CC 47 and 48 (1955).
———. *Enarrationes in Psalmos*, ed. E. Kekkers and J. Fraipont, CC 39 (1956).
———. *In Iohannis evangelium tractatus CXXIV*, ed. R. Willems, CC 36 (1954).
———. *Tractatus adversus Iudaeos*, PL 42, 51–64.
Auxilius. *De ordinationibus a Formoso papa factis*, (PL 129, 1059–1074).
Benedicti Regula, ed. R. Hanslik, CSEL 75 (1977). 2d ed.
Burchard of Worms. *Decretorum libri XX* (PL 140, 537–1058).
Canones apostolorum, ed. C. H. Turner. In *Ecclesiae occidentalis monumenta iuris antiquissima. Canonum et conciliorum Graecorum interpretationes latinae* (1899), 1–32.
Collectio Dionysio-Hadriana (PL 67.39–346).
Constitutiones apostolorum, ed. F. X. Funk. In *Didascalia et constitutiones apostolorum* 1 (1905).
Cyprian. *Ad Quirinum testimoniorum libri tres*, ed. R. Weber, CC 3 (1972), 1–179.
Euagrius. *Altercatio legis inter Simonem Iudeum et Theophilum Christianum*, ed. E. Bratke, CSEL 45, 1 (1904).
Gregory I. *XL Homiliarum in Evangelia libri duo* (PL 76, 1075–1312).
———. *Registrum epistolarum*, ed. P. Ewald and L. M. Hartmann, 2 vols., MGH Epp. 1 and 2 (1891, 1899).
Herman of Reichenau. *Chronicon*, ed. G. H. Pertz, MGH SS 5 (1844), 67–133.
Humbert of Silva Candida. Ed. E. G. Robison, *Humberti Cardinalis libri tres adversus simoniacos*, Ph.D. diss. Princeton (1971).
Innocent I. *Epistolae et decreta* (PL 20, 463–638).
Isidore of Seville. *De fide catholica ex Veteri et Novo Testamento contra Iudaeos ad Florentinam sororem suam* (PL 83, 499–538).
———. *Etymologiarum sive originum libri XX*, ed. W. M. Lindsay. In *Scriptorum Classicorum Bibliotheca Oxoniensis* (1911).
———. *Liber de variis quaestionibus adversus Iudaeos seu ceteros infideles vel plerosque haereticos iudaizantes ex utroque testamento collectus*, ed. A. C. Vega and A. E. Anspach. In *Scriptores ecclesiastici hispano-latini veteris et medii aevi*, vols. 6–8 (1940).

Jerome. *Commentariorum in Abacuc prophetam libri duo*, ed. M. Adriaen, CC 76A (1970), 579–654.
———. *Commentariorum in Esaiam libri duodeviginti*, ed. M. Adriaen, CC 73 (1963), 1–799.
———. *Commentariorum in Hiezechielem libri quatuordecim*, ed. F. Glorie, CC 75 (1964).
———. *Epistulae*, ed. I. Hilberg, CSEL 54 (1910).
———. *In Hieremiam prophetam libri sex*, ed. S. Reiter, CC 74 (1960).
———. *Liber interpretationis hebraicorum nominum*, ed. P. Lagarde, CC 72 (1959), 57–161. (Cited as Jerome, *Nom. hebr.*)
John the Deacon. *Sancti Gregorii magni vita* (PL 75, 59–242).
John of Lodi. *Vita B. Petri Damiani* (PL 144, 113–146).
Justinian. *Institutiones*, ed. P. Krueger. In *Corpus iuris civilis* 1 (1911). 12th ed.
Leo I. *Epistolae* (PL 54, 551–1218).
Liber pontificalis, ed. L. Duchesne. *Le liber pontificalis*, 3 vols. (1886–1957).
Nicholas II. *Concilium Lateranense posterius*, ed. L. Weiland, MGH Const. 1 (1893), 549ff.
Ordines Romani, ed. M. Andrieu. *Les Ordines Romani du haut moyen âge* 2 (Spicilegium sacrum Lovaniense. Études et documents 23, 1960).
Papias. *Vocabularium latinum* (1491; reprint 1966).
Pascasius Radbertus. *De corpore et sanguine Domini*, ed. B. Paulus, CCCM 16 (1969).
Peter Damian. *Die Briefe des Petrus Damiani*, ed. K. Reindel, MGH Die Briefe der deutschen Kaiserzeit, 4 (1983).
———. *Sancti Petri Damiani sermones*, ed. G. Lucchesi, CCCM 57 (1983).
———. *Vita Beati Romualdi*, ed. G. Tabacco, Fonti per la storia d'Italia 94 (1957).
Poenitentiale Egberti, ed. F. W. Wasserschleben, Die Bussordnungen der abendländischen Kirche (1851), 231–247.
Pontificale Romano-Germanicum, ed. C. Vogel and R. Elze. *Le pontifical Romano-Germanique du dixième siècle*, 2 vols. (Studi e testi 226–227, 1963).
Pseudo-Alcuin. *De divinis officiis liber* (PL 101, 1173–1286).
Pseudo-Augustine. *De altercatione ecclesiae et synagogae dialogus*, ed. G. Sequi and J. N. Hillgarth, La "altercatio" y la basilica paleocristiana de Son Bou de Menorca, *Boletin de la sociedad arqueologica Luliana* 31 (1954), 1–60.
Pseudo-Isidore, ed. P. Hinschius, *Decretales Pseudo-Isidorianae et capitula Angilramni* (1863). (That the edition of Hinschius does not fully reproduce Pseudo-Isidore is pointed out by Fuhrmann, *Fälschungen*, 153ff. and 168ff.).
Quodvultdeus. *Contra Iudaeos, Paganos et Arrianos*, ed. R. Braun, CC 60 (1976), 225–258.
Regino of Prüm. *Libri duo de synodalibus causis et disciplinis ecclesiasticis*, ed. F. G. A. Wasserschleben (1840).
Rufinus. *Historia ecclesiastica*, ed. Th. Mommsen. In Eusebius, *Werke*, vol. 2, ed. E. Schwartz, Die griechischen christlichen Schriftsteller der ersten drei Jahrhunderte 9 (1903–1909).
Tertullian. *Adversus Iudaeos*, ed. E. Kroymann, CC 2 (1954), 1337–1396.
———. *Adversus Marcionem*, ed. E. Kroymann, CC 1 (1954), 437–726.

SELECT BIBLIOGRAPHY   xiii

Literature

Amadesius, Josephus Aloysius. *In antistitum Ravennatum chronotaxim ab antiquissimae ejus ecclesiae exordiis ad haec usque tempora perductam disquisitiones perpetuae dissertationibus ad historiam et nonnullos veteris ecclesiae ritus pertinentibus illustratae* 2 (1783).

Balboni, Dante. "San Pier Damiano, maestro e discepolo in Pomposa," *Benedictina* 22 (1975).

———. *L'abate Constantino Gaetani (1568–1650) editore delle opere di S. Pier Damiani (1606–1640)*. In *Ascetica cristiana e ascetica giansenista e quietista nelle regioni d'influenza avellanita*. Atti del I Convegno del Centro di studi avellaniti, 1977 (1978), 111–125.

Bartoccetti, Luigi. "Serie dei vescovi delle diocesi marchigiane," *Studia Picena* 12 (1936), 105–123; 13 (1938), 61–73; 14 (1939), 129–147; 15 (1940), 97–124; 16 (1941), 57–74.

Benson, Robert L. *The Bishop-elect. A Study in Medieval Ecclesiastical Office.* 1968.

Berschin, Walter. *Bonizo von Sutri. Leben und Werk.* In *Beiträge zur Geschichte und Quellenkunde des MA* 2 (1972).

Blum, Owen J. *St. Peter Damian: His Teaching on the Spiritual Life* (The Catholic University of America. Studies in Mediaeval History N.S. 10. 1947).

Borino, Giovanni Battista. "L'elezione e la deposizione di Gregorio VI," *Archivio della Reale Società Romana di Storia Patria* 39 (1916), 141–252 and 295–410.

Bultot, Robert. *Pierre Damien*. In *Christianisme et valeurs humaines. A. La doctrine du mépris du monde, en occident, de S. Ambroise à Innocent III*, 4.1 (1963).

Burchi, Pietro. *Cronotassi dei vescovi di Cesena*. (Bibliotheca ecclesiarum Italiae 1, 1965), 135–266.

Cantin, André. *Pierre Damien. Lettre sur la toute-puissance divine.* SC 191 (1972).

———. "Les sciences séculières et la foi. Les dieux voies de la science au jugement de S. Pierre Damien (1007–1072)," *Centro Italiano di studi sull'alto medioevo* 5 (1975).

Capitani, Ovidio. *San Pier Damiani e l'istituto eremitico*. In *L'eremitismo in Occidente nei secoli XI e XII*. Pubblicazioni dell'Università Cattolica del Sacro Cuore. Miscellanea del centro di studi medioevali 4 (1965), 122–163. (Cited as Capitani, *L'istituto eremitico*).

———. *Immunità vescovili ed ecclesiologia in età "pregregoriana" e "gregoriana." L'avvio alla "restaurazione."* (Biblioteca degli Studi medievali, 3, 1966).

———. *Episcopato ed ecclesiologia nell'età gregoriana*. In *Le instituzioni ecclesiastiche della "societas christiana" dei secoli XI–XII: Papato, cardinalato ed episcopato*. (Miscellanea del centro di studi medioevali 7, 1974), 316–373.

Conrat, Max. *Geschichte der Quellen und Literatur des römischen Rechts im frühen MA* 1, (1891).

Davidsohn, Robert. *Geschichte von Florenz* 1 (1896).

Della Santa, Mansueto. *Ricerche sull'idea monastica di San Pier Damiano.* Studi e testi Camaldolesi 11 (1961).

Dressler, Fridolin. *Petrus Damiani. Leben und Werk.* (Studia Anselmiana 34, 1954).

Falce, Antonio. *Bonifacio di Canossa, padre di Matilda*, 2 vols. 1926–1927.

Firminger, W. K. "St. Peter Damian and Auxilius," *Journal of Theological Studies* 26 (1925), 78–81.

Fliche, Augustin. *La réforme grégorienne*, 3 vols. (Spicilegium sacrum Lovaniense. Études et documents 6, 9, and 16. 1924–1937).
Fois, Mario. "I compiti e le prerogative dei cardinali vescovi secondo Pier Damiani nel quadro della sua ecclesiologia primaziale," *Archivum historiae pontificiae* 10 (1972), 25–105.
———. "La sede apostolica e la riforma della chiesa secondo Pier Damiani," *Civiltà Cattolica* 123.4 (1972), 320–336.
Fornasari, Giuseppe. "Prospettive del pensiero politico di S. Pier Damiani," *Miscellanea. Raccolta di saggi storici e linguistici a cura della facoltà di magistere dell'università di Trieste* 1 (1979), 463–516.
———. "Pier Damiani e Gregorio VII: dall'ecclesiologia monastica all'ecclesiologia politica," *Fonte Avellana nel suo millenario. 1. Le origini.* Atti del V convegno del centro di studi avellaniti (1982), 151–244.
Fournier, Paul. "Un groupe de recueils canoniques italiens des Xe et XIe siècles," *Mémoires de l'institut national de France. Académie des inscriptions et belles-lettres* 40 (1916), 95–213.
Fuhrmann, Horst. *Einfluss und Verbreitung der pseudo-isidorischen Fälschungen von ihrem Auftauchen bis in die neuere Zeit* (Schriften der MGH 24, 1972–1974).
Gaudenzi, Augusto. "Lo svolgimento parallelo del diritto longobardo e del diritto romano a Ravenna," *Memorie della regia accademia delle scienze dell'istituto di Bologna, Classe di scienze morali, sezione giuridica* I, 1 (1906–1907), 37–164.
Giabanni, Anselmo. "Lo spirito della regola di S. Benedetto e la vita monastico-eremitica secondo S. Pier Damiano," *Benedictina* 1 (1974), 135–156.
Gibelli, Alberto. *Monografia dell'antico monastero di S. Croce di Fonte Avellana* (1896).
Gilchrist, John. "*Simoniaca haeresis* and the Problem of Orders from Leo IX to Gratian," *Proceedings of the Second International Congress of Medieval Canon Law*, ed. S. Kuttner and J. J. Ryan (Monumenta iuris canonici C 1, 1965), 209–235.
Giorgetti Vichi, Anna Maria and Sergio Mottironi, *Catalogo dei manoscritti della biblioteca Vallicelliana* 1 (Indici e cataloghi N.S. 7, 1961).
Granata, Aldo. "Contributo alla conoscenza del lessico in S. Pier Damiani: Dispensatio," *Istituto Lombardo. Rendiconti. Classe di lettere e scienze morali e storiche* 108 (1974), 715–755.
Grillantini, Carlo. *Storia di Osimo. Vetus Auximon* 1 (1957).
Hauck, Albert. *Kirchengeschichte Deutschlands* 3 (4th ed. 1920).
Hefele, Carl Joseph and Henri Leclercq. *Histoire des conciles*, 11 vols. (1907–1952).
Herrmann, Klaus-Jürgen. *Das Tuskulanerpapsttum (1012–1046)*. (Päpste und Papsttum 4, 1973).
Hoesch, Henning. *Die kanonischen Quellen im Werk Humberts von Moyenmoutier. Ein Beitrag zur Geschichte der vorgregorianischen Reform.* (Forschungen zur kirchlichen Rechtsgeschichte und zum Kirchenrecht 10, 1970).
Hoffmann, Hartmut. "Zur mittelalterlichen Brieftechnik," *Spiegel der Geschichte. Festgabe für Max Braubach zum 10. April 1964*, ed. K. Repgen and S. Skalweit (1964), 141–170.
Kolping, Adolf. *Petrus Damiani. Das Büchlein vom Dominus vobiscum* (1949).
Krause, Hans-Georg. *Das Papstwahldekret von 1059 und seine Rolle im Investiturstreit* (Studi Gregoriani 7, 1960).

SELECT BIBLIOGRAPHY

La Bigne, Marguerin de. *Appendix bibliothecae sanctorum patrum* (1579).
———. *Sacra bibliotheca sanctorum patrum* 3 (2d ed. 1589).
Ladner, Gerhart. *Theologie und Politik vor dem Investiturstreit. Abendmahlstreit, Kirchenreform, Cluni und Heinrich III.* (Veröffentlichungen des österreichischen Instituts für Geschichtsforschung 2, 1936).
Laqua, Hans Peter. *Traditionen und Leitbilder bei dem Ravennater Reformer Petrus Damiani (1042–1052).* (Münstersche Mittelalter-Schriften 30, 1976).
Lassus, L.-Albert. "Solitude et communion dans l'église d'après saint Pierre Damien," *Revue Thomiste* 76 (1976), 22–33.
Leclercq, Jean. *Saint Pierre Damien, ermite et homme d'église* (Uomini e dottrine 8, 1960).
Leonardi, Corrado. "Di s. Vincenzo vescovo e martire di Bevagna e della chiesa di s. Vincenzo del Furlo," *Bollettino della deputazione di storia patria per l'Umbria* (1970), 5–29.
Lindemans, S. "Auxilius et le manuscrit Vallicellan Tome XVIII," *RHE* 57 (1962), 470–484.
Little, Lester K. *The Personal Development of Peter Damian,* (Order and Innovation in the Middle Ages: Essays in Honor of Joseph R. Strayer, ed. W. C. Jordan, B. McNab and T. F. Ruiz [1976]), 317–341, 523–528.
Lokrantz, Margareta, *L'opera poetica di S. Pier Damiani* (Studia Latina Stockholmensia 12, 1964).
Lucchesi, Giovanni, "L'*Antilogus contra Judaeos* di S. Pier Damiano e Pomposa," *Analecta Pomposiana* 1 (1965), 89f.
———. *Clavis S. Petri Damiani (1970);* rev. reprint from *Studi su S. Pier Damiano in onore del Cardinale Amleto Giovanni Cicognani* (Biblioteca Cardinale Gaetano Cicognani 5, 1961), 249–407.
———. *Per una vita di San Pier Damiani. Componenti cronologiche e topografiche.* In San Pier Damiano nel IX centenario della morte (1072–1972) 1 (1972), 13–179 (No. 1–153) and 2 (1972), 13–160 (No. 154–231).
———. *I viaggi di S. Pier Damiani,* in: S. Pier Damiani. Atti del Convegno di studi nel IX centenario della morte. Faenza, 1972 (1973), 71–91.
———. *Giovanni da Lodi, il discepolo.* In San Pier Damiano nel IX centenario della morte (1072–1972) 4 (1978), 7–66.
———. "Sull'antica tradizione manoscritta di S. Pier Damiani," *Benedictina* 24 (1977), 209–223.
Maassen, Friedrich. *Geschichte der Quellen und der Literatur des canonischen Rechts im Abendlände* 1 (1870).
Mabillon, Johannes. *Annales ordinis sancti Benedicti occidentalium monachorum patriarchae* 4 (1707).
Mähl, Sybille. *Quadriga virtutum. Die Kardinaltugenden in der Geistesgeschichte der Karolingerzeit* (Beihefte zum Archiv für Kulturgeschichte 9, 1969).
Massa, Eugenio. *I manoscritti originali del beato Paolo Giustiniani custoditi nell'eremo di Frascati* (1967).
———. *Paolo Giustiniani e gli antichi manoscritti avellanesi di San Pier Damiani.* In Fonte Avellana nella società dei secoli XV e XVI. Atti del IV Convegno del Centro di studi avellaniti (1980), 77–160.
Meier-Welcker, Hans. "Die Simonie im frühen Mittelalter," *ZKG* 64 (1952–1953), 61–93.
Mercati, Giovanni. "Parmensia II. La lettera di sottomissione d'un arciprete di Parma a Pasquale II.—L'autore delle Collectanea ex opusculis Petri

Damiani," *Studi e documenti di storia e diritto* 23 (1902), 6ff.; reprinted in *Opere minori* 2 (Studi e testi 77, 1937), 353–356.
Miccoli, Giovanni. "Il problema delle ordinazioni simoniache e le sinodi Lateranensi del 1060 e 1061," *Studi Gregoriani* 5 (1956), 33–81.
———. *Due note sulla tradizione manoscritta di Pier Damiani* (Note e discussioni erudite 8, 1959).
———. "Théologie de la vie monastique chez Saint Pierre Damien (1007–1072)." In *Théologie de la vie monastique* (*Théologie* 49, 1961), 459–483.
———. *Chiesa Gregoriana. Ricerche sulla riforma del secolo XI* (Storici antichi e moderni N.S. 17, 1966).
Michel, Anton. *Papstwahl und Königsrecht oder das Papstwahl-Konkordat von 1059* (1936).
———. "Die antisimonistischen Reordinationen und eine neue Humbert-Schrift," *Römische Quartalschrift* 46 (1938; published 1941), 19–56.
———. *Die Sentenzen des Kardinals Humbert, das erste Rechtsbuch der päpstlichen Reform* (Schriften der MGH 7, 1943).
Mittarelli, Johannes-Benedictus and Anselmus Costadoni. *Annales Camaldulenses ordinis sancti Benedicti*, 9 vols. (1755–1773).
Neukirch, Franz. *Das Leben des Petrus Damiani* (1875).
Palazzini, Pietro. "Note di diritto romano in S. Pier Damiano," *Studia et documenta historiae et iuris* 13–14 (1947–1948), 235–268.
———. "Il diritto strumento di riforma ecclesiastica in S. Pier Damiani," *Ephemerides iuris canonici* 11 (1955), 361–408 and 12 (1956), 9–58.
———. (Ed.) *Dizionario dei concili*, 6 vols. (1963–1967).
———. *San Pier Damiani al centro della riforma della chiesa Marchigiana nel secolo XI*. In San Pier Damiano nel IX centenario della morte (1072–1972) 2 (1972), 161–232. (Cited as Palazzini, *Chiesa Marchigiana*).
———. "S. Pier Damiani eremita e priore a Fonte Avellana," *Studi Gregoriani* 10 (1975), 69–110.
———. *Influssi damianei ed umbertini nell'azione e legislazione dei papi pregregoriani contro la simonia da papa Clemente II a Nicolò II*. In Fonte Avellana nella società dei secoli XI e XII. Atti del II Convegno del Centro di studi avellaniti (1978), 7–41.
Payer, Pierre J. *Book of Gomorrah. An Eleventh-Century Treatise against Clerical Homosexual Practices*. Waterloo, Ontario, 1982.
Pelster, Franz. "Die römische Synode von 1060 und die von Simonisten gespendeten Weihen," *Gregorianum* 23 (1942), 66–90.
Petrocchi, Massimo. *Note su Fonte Avellana*. In Aspetti dell'Umbria dall'inizio del secolo VIII alla fine del secolo XI. Atti del III Convegno di Studi Umbri. Gubbio (1966), 243–254.
Picasso, Giorgio. *La tradizione libraria di Fonte Avellana nella società dei secoli XI e XII*. Atti del II Convegno del Centro di studi avellaniti (1978), 345–366.
Pierucci, Celestino and Alberto Polverari. *Carte di Fonte Avellana* 1 (Thesaurus ecclesiarum Italiae 9, 1, 1972).
Pierucci, Celestino. *La vita eremitica secondo S. Pier Damiano*. In San Pier Damiano nel IX centenario della morte (1072–1972) 4 (1978), 67–122.
———. "La struttura edilizia di Fonte Avellana al tempo di San Pier Damiano," *Studi Gregoriani* 10 (1975), 131–139.
———. *Inventari dell'antica biblioteca di Fonte Avellana*. In Fonte Avellana nella società dei secoli XIII e XIV. Atti del III Convegno del Centro di studi avellaniti (1979), 141–234.

SELECT BIBLIOGRAPHY xvii

Prete, Serafino. "San Pier Damiani le chiese marchigiane la riforma nel secolo XI," *Studia Picena* 19 (1949), 119–128.
Reindel, Kurt. "Studien zur überlieferung der Werke des Petrus Damiani I–III," DA 15 (1959), 23–102; 16 (1960), 73–154; 18 (1962), 317–417.
———. *Die Handschriften der Werke des Petrus Damiani*. In S. Pier Damiani. Atti del Convegno di studi nel IX centenario della morte. Faenza, 1972 (1973), 93–113.
———. "Petrus Damiani und seine Korrespondenten," *Studi Gregoriani* 10 (1975), 203–219.
———. "Neue Literatur zu Petrus Damiani," DA (1976), 405–443.
Repetti, Emanuele. *Appendice al Dizionario geografico fisico storico della Toscana* (1846).
Robison, Elaine Golden, ed. *Humberti Cardinalis libri tres adversus simoniacos*. Ph.D. diss. Princeton (1971).
Roschini, Gabriele M. *La mariologia di s. Pier Damiano*. In San Pier Damiano nel IX centenario della morte (1072–1972) 1 (1972), 195–237.
Ruysschaert, José. *Constantino Gaetano, O.S.B., chasseur de manuscrits*. In Mélanges Eugène Tisserant 7 (Studi e testi 237, 1964), 261–326.
Ryan, J. Joseph. *Saint Peter Damiani and His Canonical Sources. A Preliminary Study in the Antecedents of the Gregorian Reform* (Pontifical Institute of Medieval Studies. Studies and Texts 2, 1956).
Saltet, Louis. *Les réordinations: étude sur la sacrement de l'ordre* (1907).
Samaritani, Antonio. "Gebeardo di Eichstätt, arcivescovo di Ravenna (1027–1044) e la riforma imperiale della chiesa in Romagna," *Analecta Pomposiana* 3 (1967), 109–140.
———. "Sui destinatari degli opuscoli 2–3, 29, 42/2, 48 di S. Pier Damiano," *Analecta Pomposiana* 3 (1967), 141–147.
Sarti, Mauro. *De episcopis Eugubinis* (1755).
Schmidt, Tilmann. *Alexander II (1061–1073) und die römische Reformgruppe seiner Zeit*. (Päpste und Papsttum 11, 1977).
Schwartz, Gerhard. *Die Besetzung der Bistümer Reichs—Italiens unter den sächsischen und salischen Kaisern mit den Listen der Bischöfe 951–1122* (1913).
Schwarzmaier, Hansmartin. *Lucca und das Reich bis zum Ende des 11. Jahrhundert*. (Bibliothek des Deutschen Historischen Instituts in Rom 41, 1972).
Seekel, Friedrich. *Geistige Grundlagen Petrus Damianis untersucht an liber Gratissimus*, Ph.D. diss. (Berlin, 1933).
Sohm, Rudolph. *Das altkatholische Kirchenrecht und das Dekret Gratians*, in: Festschrift der Leipziger Juristenfakultät für Dr. Adolf Wach zum 16. November 1915 (1918), 1–674.
Spinelli, Giovanni. "La data dell'ordinazione sacerdotale di S. Pier Damiani," *Benedictina* 19 (1972), 595–605.
Steindorff, Ernst. *Jahrbücher des Deutschen Reichs unter Heinrich III.*, 2 vols. (Jahrbücher der Deutschen Geschichte, 1874–1881).
Tabacco, Giovanni, ed. *Petri Damiani vita Beati Romualdi* (Fonti per la storia d'Italia 94, 1957).
Theiner, Augustin. *Disquisitiones criticae in praecipuas canonum et decretalium collectiones* (1836).
Ughelli, Ferdinando. *Italia sacra* 2 (2d ed. 1717).
Vernarecci, Augusto. *Fossombrone dai tempi antichissimi ai nosti* 1 (1907).
Vitaletti, Guido. "Un inventario di codici del secolo XIII e le vicende della biblioteca, dell'archivio e del tesoro di Fonte Avellana," *La Bibliofilia. Rivista*

di storia del libro e delle arti grafiche, di bibliografia ed erudizione 20 (1918–1919), 249–264 and 297–315; 21 (1919–1920), 42–76, 117–156, 291–338; 22 (1920–1921), 30–41.

———. *La biblioteca di Fonte Avellana* (1925).

Wilmart, André. "Une lettre de S. Pierre Damien à l'impératrice Agnès," *Revue Bénédictine* 44 (1932), 125–146.

Woody, Kennerly Merritt. *Damiani and the Radicals*, Ph.D. diss., Columbia University (1966).

———. "Sagena piscatoris: Petrus Damiani and the Papal Election Decree of 1059," *Viator* 1 (1970), 33–54.

CONCORDANCE

Since the new edition of Damian's letters in Kurt Reindel, *Die Briefe des Petrus Damiani*, MGH Die Briefe der deutschen Kaiserzeit (München, 1983) has assigned new numbers in chronological order, the old system of numbering for *epistolae* and *opuscula* is now outmoded. To correlate the new with the old, the following concordance is herewith provided. There is no longer a distinction between "letters" and "works," and *Letters* 171–180 are placed at the end of the series because they are undatable.

MGH (Chronological) Numeration in Earlier Editions

Reindel	Migne Number	Reindel	Migne Number
1	opsuc. 2 and 3	23	epist. 8, 9 = opusc. 58
2	epist. 7, 15	24	epist. 6, 14 = opusc. 29
3	epist. 3, 2	25	epist. 8, 7 = opusc. 42/2
4	epist. 3, 3	26	epist. 1, 3
5	epist. 4, 2	27	epist. 6, 24 = opusc. 48
6	epist. 6, 6	28	opusc. 11
7	epist. 3, 5	29	epist. 6, 15
8	epist. 5, 12	30	epist. 4, 4
9	epist. 6, 28	31	opusc. 7
10	epist. 6, 23	32	epist. 4, 13
11	epist. 2, 19	33	epist. 1, 4
12	epist. 4, 6	34	epist. 4, 10
13	epist. 1, 1	35	epist. 5, 6
14	epist. 4, 7	36	epist. 5, 17 = opusc. 8/2
15	epist. 8, 4	37	epist. 6, 7
16	epist. 1, 2	38	opusc. 16
17	opusc. 10	39	epist. 5, 9 = opusc. 27
18	opusc. 14	40	opusc. 6
19	opusc. 8/1	41	Ad Heinricum
20	epist. 7, 2	42	Ad Odalricum
21	epist. 8, 8	43	epist. 7, 1
22	epist. 4, 5	44	epist. 6, 30 = opusc. 51

Reindel	Migne Number	Reindel	Migne Number
45	epist. 5, 8	88	epist. 1, 20
46	epist. 1, 5	89	epist. 1, 21 and opusc. 4
47	epist. 4, 14 = opusc. 26	90	epist. 2, 13
48	epist. 2, 1	91	epist. 3, 1 = opusc. 38
49	epist. 2, 5	92	epist. 6, 16 = opusc. 59
50	opusc. 15	93	epist. 8, 13
51	epist. 7, 14	94	epist. 8, 14
52	epist. 2, 4	95	epist. 2, 11
53	Ad Iohannem	96	epist. 1, 15
54	epist. 6, 18 = opusc. 46	97	epist. 2, 2 = opusc. 31
55	epist. 6, 19	98	epist. 1, 18 = opusc. 24
56	epist. 6, 27	99	epist. 3, 6
57	epist. 1, 10 = opusc. 20	100	epist. 6, 5
58	epist. 3, 4	101	epist. 3, 7
59	epist. 3, 9 = opusc. 25	102	epist. 2, 15 = opusc. 34/1
60	epist. 1, 7	103	epist. 6, 2
61	epist. 1, 6 = opusc. 17	104	epist. 7, 5 = opusc. 56
62	epist. 4, 11	105	epist. 6, 8 = opusc. 21
63	epist. 2, 9	106	epist. 2, 14 = opusc. 33
64	epist. 7, 9	107	epist. 1, 16
65	opusc. 5	108	epist. 1, 17 = opusc. 23
66	epist. 7, 19 = opusc. 50	109	epist. 1, 19 = Vita Rodulphi et Dominici
67	epist. 7, 11 = opusc. 57/1	110	opusc. 9
68	epist. 7, 12 = opusc. 57/2	111	epist. 3, 8 = opusc. 39
69	epist. 2, 3 = opusc. 22	112	epist. 4, 3 = opusc. 18/2
70	epist. 5, 16 = opusc. 42/1	113	epist. 6, 4
71	epist. 7, 4	114	epist. 7, 16 = opusc. 18/3
72	epist. 1, 9 = opusc. 19	115	epist. 4, 16
73	epist. 4, 1	116	epist. 6, 10
74	epist. 4, 12	117	epist. 6, 17 = opusc. 45
75	epist. 2, 8	118	epist. 6, 35 = opusc. 55
76	epist. 6, 31 = opusc. 53	119	epist. 2, 17 = opusc. 36
77	epist. 5, 5	120	epist. 7, 3
78	epist. 6, 11 = opusc. 44	121	epist. 5, 1
79	epist. 1, 8	122	epist. 1, 11
80	epist. 4, 17 = opusc. 40	123	epist. 6, 21 = opusc. 47
81	opusc. 1	124	epist. 7, 6
82	epist. 2, 12	125	epist. 6, 3
83	epist. 8, 5	126	epist. 2, 20 = opusc. 37/1
84	epist. 5, 7	127	epist. 2, 21 = opusc. 37/2
85	epist. 8, 3	128	Ad Ambrosium et Liupardum
86	epist. 2, 18 = opusc. 52		
87	epist. 4, 9	129	epist. 5, 14 and 5, 15

CONCORDANCE   xxi

Reindel	Migne Number	Reindel	Migne Number
130	epist. 7, 7	156	epist. 2, 6
131	epist. 6, 13	157	epist. 4, 8
132	epist. 6, 26 = opusc. 49	158	epist. 6, 22
133	epist. 6, 34	159	epist. 2, 16 = opusc. 35
134	epist. 6, 36	160	epist. 2, 7 = opusc. 32
135	Ad Cinthium	161	epist. 6, 1 = opusc. 43
136	epist. 8, 12	162	epist. 2, 10 = opusc. 18/1
137	epist. 6, 33 = opusc. 54		and epist. 5, 4
138	epist. 5, 2	163	epist. 5, 3
139	Ad Tebaldum	164	epist. 1, 12
140	epist. 1, 13	165	opusc. 12
141	epist. 5, 13	166	epist. 6, 29
142	epist. 6, 32	167	epist. 1, 14
143	epist. 7, 18	168	epist. 3, 10 = opusc. 34/2
144	epist. 7, 8	169	epist. 6, 25
145	epist. 8, 1	170	epist. 8, 10
146	epist. 8, 11 = opusc. 30	171	epist. 8, 15
147	epist. 5, 10	172	epist. 5, 11 = opusc. 41
148	epist. 7, 13	173	Ad Bucconem
149	Ad Agnetem	174	epist. 4, 15
150	epist. 6, 20	175	Ad Honestum
151	epist. 7, 17	176	epist. 6, 9
152	epist. 6, 12	177	epist. 5, 18
153	opusc. 13	178	Ad abbatem A.
154	epist. 7, 10	179	epist. 8, 6
155	epist. 8, 2	180	Ad episcopum W.

Numeration of Earlier Editions in MGH

Migne Number	Reindel	Migne Number	Reindel
epist. 1, 1	13	epist. 1, 15	96
epist. 1, 2	16	epist. 1, 16	107
epist. 1, 3	26	epist. 1, 17 = opusc. 23	108
epist. 1, 4	33	epist. 1, 18 = opusc. 24	98
epist. 1, 5	46	epist. 1 19 = Vita Rodul-	109
epist. 1, 6 = opusc. 17	61	phi et Dominici	
epist. 1, 7	60	epist. 1, 20	88
epist. 1, 8	79	epist. 1, 21	89
epist. 1, 9 = opusc. 19	72	epist. 2, 1	48
epist. 1, 10 = opusc. 20	57	epist. 2, 2 = opusc. 31	97
epist. 1, 11	122	epist. 2, 3 = opusc. 22	69
epist. 1, 12	164	epist. 2, 4	52
epist. 1, 13	140	epist. 2, 5	49
epist. 1, 14	167	epist. 2, 6	156

PETER DAMIAN

Migne Number	Reindel	Migne Number	Reindel
epist. 2, 7 = opusc. 32	160	epist. 5, 3	163
epist. 2, 8	75	epist. 5, 4 = part of opusc. 18/1	162
epist. 2, 9	63		
epist. 2, 10 = opusc. 18/1	162	epist. 5, 5	77
epist. 2, 11	95	epist. 5, 6	35
epist. 2, 12	82	epist. 5, 7	84
epist. 2, 13	90	epist. 5, 8	45
epist. 2, 14 = opusc. 33	106	epist. 5, 9 = opusc. 27	39
epist. 2, 15 = opusc. 34/1	102	epist. 5, 10	147
epist. 2, 16 = opusc. 35	159	epist. 5, 11 = opusc. 41	172
epist. 2, 17 = opusc. 36	119	epist. 5, 12	8
epist. 2, 18 = opusc. 52	86	epist. 5, 13	141
epist. 2, 19	11	epist. 5, 14	129
epist. 2, 20 = opusc. 37/1	126	epist. 5, 15	129
epist. 2, 21 = opusc. 37/2	127	epist. 5, 16 = opusc. 42/1	70
epist. 3, 1 = opusc. 38	91	epist. 5, 17 = opusc. 8/2	36
epist. 3, 2	3	epist. 5, 18	177
epist. 3, 3	4	epist. 5, 19 = opusc. 28	spuria
epist. 3, 4	58	epist. 6, 1 = opusc. 43	161
epist. 3, 5	7	epist. 6, 2	103
epist. 3, 6	99	epist. 6, 3	125
epist. 3, 7	101	epist. 6, 4	113
epist. 3, 8 = opusc. 39	111	epist. 6, 5	100
epist. 3, 9 = opusc. 25	59	epist. 6, 6	6
epist. 3, 10 = opusc. 34/2	168	epist. 6, 7	37
epist. 4, 1	73	epist. 6, 8 = opusc. 21	105
epist. 4, 2	5	epist. 6, 9	176
epist. 4, 3 = opusc. 18/2	112	epist. 6, 10	116
epist. 4, 4	30	epist. 6, 11 = opusc. 44	78
epist. 4, 5	22	epist. 6, 12	152
epist. 4, 6	12	epist. 6, 13	131
epist. 4, 7	14	epist. 6, 14 = opusc. 29	24
epist. 4, 8	157	epist. 6, 15	29
epist. 4, 9	87	epist. 6, 16 = opusc. 59	92
epist. 4, 10	34	epist. 6, 17 = opusc. 45	117
epist. 4, 11	62	epist. 6, 18 = opusc. 46	54
epist. 4, 12	74	epist. 6, 19	55
epist. 4, 13	32	epist. 6, 20	150
epist. 4, 14 = opusc. 26	47	epist. 6, 21 = opusc. 47	123
epist. 4, 15	174	epist. 6, 22	158
epist. 4, 16	115	epist. 6, 23	10
epist. 4, 17 = opusc. 40	80	epist. 6, 24 = opusc. 48	27
epist. 5, 1	121	epist. 6, 25	169
epist. 5, 2	138	epist. 6, 26 = opusc. 49	132

CONCORDANCE xxiii

Migne Number	Reindel	Migne Number	Reindel
epist. 6, 27	56	opusc. 1	81
epist. 6, 28	9	opusc. 2	1
epist. 6, 29	166	opusc. 3	1
epist. 6, 30 = opusc. 51	44	opusc. 4	89
epist. 6, 31 = opusc. 53	76	opusc. 5	65
epist. 6, 32	142	opusc. 6	40
epist. 6, 33 = opusc. 54	137	opusc. 7	31
epist. 6, 34	133	epist. 8/1	19
epist. 6, 35 = opusc. 55	118	opusc. 8/2 = epist. 5, 17	36
epist. 6, 36	134	opusc. 9	110
epist. 7, 1	43	opusc. 10	17
epist. 7, 2	20	opusc. 11	28
epist. 7, 3	120	opusc. 12	165
epist. 7, 4	71	opusc. 13	153
epist. 7, 5 = opusc. 56	104	opusc. 14	18
epist. 7, 6	124	opusc. 15	50
epist. 7, 7	130	opusc. 16	38
epist. 7, 8	144	opusc. 17 = epist. 1, 6	61
epist. 7, 9	64	opusc. 18/1 = epist. 2, 10	162
epist. 7, 10	154	opusc. 18/2 = epist. 4, 3	112
epist. 7, 11 = opusc. 57/1	67	opusc. 18/3 = epist. 7, 16	114
epist. 7, 12 = opusc. 57/2	68	opusc. 19 = epist. 1, 9	72
epist. 7, 13	148	opusc. 20 = epist. 1, 10	57
epist. 7, 14	51	opusc. 21 = epist. 6, 8	105
epist. 7, 15	2	opusc. 22 = epist. 2, 3	69
epist. 7, 16 = opusc. 18/3	114	opusc. 23 = epist. 1, 17	108
epist. 7, 17	151	opusc. 24 = epist. 1, 18	98
epist. 7, 18	143	opusc. 25 = epist. 3, 9	59
epist. 7, 19 = opusc. 50	66	opusc. 26 = epist. 4, 14	47
epist. 8, 1	145	opusc. 27 = epist. 5, 9	39
epist. 8, 2	155	opusc. 28 = epist. 5, 19	spurium
epist. 8, 3	85	opusc. 29 = epist. 6, 14	24
epist. 8, 4	15	opusc. 30 = epist. 8, 11	146
epist. 8, 5	83	opusc. 31 = epist. 2, 2	97
epist. 8, 6	179	opusc. 32 = epist. 2, 7	160
epist. 8, 7 = opusc. 42/2	25	opusc. 33 = epist. 2, 14	106
epist. 8, 8	21	opusc. 34/1 = epist. 2, 15	102
epist. 8, 9 = opusc. 58	23	opusc. 34/2 = epist. 3, 10	168
epist. 8, 10	170	opusc. 35 = epist. 2, 16	159
epist. 8, 11 = opusc. 30	146	opusc. 36 = epist. 2, 17	119
epist. 8, 12	136	opusc. 37/1 = epist. 2, 20	126
epist. 8, 13	93	opusc. 37/2 = epist. 2, 21	127
epist. 8, 14	94	opusc. 38 = epist. 3, 1	91
epist. 8, 15	171	opusc. 39 = epist. 3, 8	111

Migne Number	Reindel	Migne Number	Reindel
opusc. 40 = epist. 4, 17	80	opusc. 50 = epist. 7, 19	66
opusc. 41 = epist. 5, 1	172	opusc. 51 = epist. 6, 30	44
opusc. 42/1 = epist. 5, 16	70	opusc. 52 = epist. 2, 18	86
opusc. 42/2 = epist. 8, 7	25	opusc. 53 = epist. 6, 31	76
opusc. 43 = epist. 6, 1	161	opusc. 54 = epist. 6, 33	137
opusc. 44 = epist. 6, 11	78	opusc. 55 = epist. 6, 35	118
opusc. 45 = epist. 6, 17	117	opusc. 56 = epist. 7, 5	104
opusc. 46 = epist. 6, 18	54	opusc. 57/1 = epist. 7, 11	67
opusc. 47 = epist. 6, 21	123	opusc. 57/2 = epist. 7, 12	68
opusc. 48 = epist. 6, 24	27	opusc. 58 = epist. 8, 9	23
opusc. 49 = epist. 6, 26	132	opusc. 59 = epist. 6, 16	92

Letters That Are Not Found in Migne

To abbot A.	178	To Henry	41
To Agnes	149	To Honestus	175
To Ambrose and Liupardus	128	To John	53
		To Odalricus	42
To Bucco	173	To Tebaldus	139
To Cinthius	135	To bishop W.	180

LETTERS
31–60

LETTER 31

Peter Damian to Pope Leo IX. This letter, known as the *Book of Gomorrah*, is prefaced in many MSS by Leo's letter to Damian, praising the author for his work and prescribing penalties for clerics who are guilty of the crimes therein discussed. After distinguishing the four classes of unnatural vice to which many of the secular clergy of his region were addicted, Damian deplores the degradation of the priesthood thereby effected, and indicates the consequences for the spiritual life of the Church. He begs the pope to take counsel with wise and prudent men and, with the force of his authority, to educate and purge the clergy in accord with the sacred canons.

(Second Half of 1049)[1]

EO THE BISHOP,[2] servant of the servants of God, to his beloved son in Christ, Peter the hermit, the joy of everlasting happiness.[3]

(2) The short book which you have written against the fourfold defilement of carnal pollution in becoming prose, but with still more becoming reasoning, most dear son, manifests with obvious evidence that the concentration of your mind with loving zeal has arrived at the resplendent bed of sparkling purity. For one like you who has so raised the arm of the spirit against the obscenity of lust, has surely subdued the savagery of the flesh. This execrable vice sets one far apart from the author of virtue who, since he is pure, admits of nothing that is impure. Nor can one who will subject himself to sordid pleasure share in his company. Clerics, indeed, whose most impure life you in your prudence have lamentably and also intelligently discussed, verily and most assuredly will have no share in his inheritance, from which by their

---

1. For the date here assigned, see Lucchesi, *Vita* no. 84.
2. Leo IX became pope on 12 February 1049.
3. This prefacing letter of Pope Leo IX (JL 4311; *ItPont* 4.94f., no. 2) is not found in all the MSS of the *Book of Gomorrah*.

voluptuous pleasures they have withdrawn. If they lived purely, they would be called, not only the holy temple of the Lord, but also his very sanctuary, in which with snow white splendor the illustrious Lamb of God is offered, by whom the foul corruption of all the world is washed away. Such clerics, indeed, profess, if not in words, at least by the evidence of their actions, that they are not what they are thought to be.

(3) For how can one be or be called a cleric, who of his own free will has no fear of defilement by his own hands, or by the hands of another, touching carnally his own private parts or those of others, or with detestable unnaturalness fornicating within the thighs or from the rear. Concerning such men, since you were motivated by sacred fury to write what seemed appropriate to you, it is proper that we intervene, according to your wishes, with our apostolic authority, so that all anxiety and doubt be removed from the minds of your readers. So let it be certain and evident to all that we are in agreement with everything your book contains, opposed as it is like water to the fire of the devil. Therefore, lest the wantonness of this foul impurity be allowed to spread unpunished, it must be repelled by proper repressive action of apostolic severity, and yet some moderations must be placed on its harshness.[4]

(4) And thus, all those who are defiled in any way by the four types of filth which have been mentioned, are, in consideration of due censure, deposed by our judgment and that of the sacred canons from all ranks of the Church which is immaculate. But acting more humanely, and relying on divine mercy, it is our wish and also our command that those who

---

4. At this point Leo decided that a somewhat "more humane" approach would be taken in punishing offenders in this matter. See P. S. Payer, *Peter Damian: Book of Gomorrah. An Eleventh-Century Treatise against Clerical Homosexual Practices* (1982), 18–19. Payer's work is prefaced by an excellent introduction, and contains the first English translation of the *Liber Gomorrhianus*. Unfortunately, he was compelled by circumstances to translate the edition of Gaetani (PL 145.161–190), which is a bowdlerized text, purposely altered either by Gaetani, or even by one of the medieval "editors." J. Boswell, *Christianity, Social Tolerance, and Homosexuality* . . . (1980), 213, assumes that Damian's book, sequestered by Pope Alexander II in 1069, was the *Book of Gomorrah* (see Peter Damian, Letter 156). This opinion has received little support.

will with their own hands or with one another have practiced masturbation, or have sinned by ejecting semen within the thighs, but have not done so for any length of time, nor with many others, if they shall have curbed their desires and have atoned for their infamous deeds with proper repentance, shall be admitted to the same grades to which, while they were practicing these crimes, they had not devoted their lives. We remove all hope of recovering their order from those who alone or with others for a long time, or for even a short period or with many, have defiled themselves by either of the two kinds of filthiness which you have described, or, which is horrible to hear or to speak of, have sunk to the level of anal intercourse. Should anyone dare to criticize or attack this decree bearing apostolic sanction, let him be aware that he does so with the risk of losing his rank. For he who does not attack vice, but deals lightly with it, is rightly judged to be guilty of his death, along with the one who dies in sin.

(5) But, dearest son, I rejoice indescribably that you promote by the example of your life whatever you have taught by your eloquence. For it is greater to teach by action than by words. Wherefore, with the help of God may you attain the palm of victory and rejoice with the Son of God and of the Virgin in our heavenly home, abounding in as many rewards, and crowned, in a sense, with all those who were snatched by you from the snares of the devil.

The Book of Gomorrah by the Humble Monk, Peter Damian.

(6) To the blessed Pope Leo, Peter, the monks' least servant, sends the homage of his proper devotion.

(7) Since we know from the mouth of Truth itself that the Apostolic See is the mother of all churches, it is proper that if any doubt should arise in matters pertaining to the welfare of souls, one should have recourse to her as to the teacher and, as one might say, to the source of heavenly wisdom, so that from this unique principle of ecclesiastical discipline a light may go forth by which the entire body of the Church is

bathed in the utter brilliance that Truth imparts, once the darkness of uncertainty has been dispelled. In our region a certain abominable and most shameful vice has developed, and unless it be prevented as soon as possible by the severest punishment, it is certain that the sword of divine fury will be unsheathed, leading in its unchecked violence to the destruction of many. One is nauseated with shame and embarrassment to speak of things so disgracefully foul, or even to mention them within earshot of Your Holiness. But if a physician is appalled by the contagion of the plague, who is likely to wield the cautery? If he grows squeamish when he is about to apply the cure, who will restore health to stricken hearts? The befouling cancer of sodomy is, in fact, spreading so through the clergy or rather, like a savage beast, is raging with such shameless abandon through the flock of Christ, that for many of them it would be more salutary to be burdened with service in the world than, under the pretext of religion, to be enslaved so easily under the iron rule of satanic tyranny. It would be better for them to perish alone as laymen than, after having changed their attire but not their disposition, to drag others with them to destruction, as Truth itself testifies when it says, "But if anyone is a cause of stumbling to one of these little ones, it would be better for him to be drowned in the depths of the sea with a great millstone round his neck."[5] Unless immediate effort be exerted by the Apostolic See, there is little doubt that, even if one wished to curb this unbridled evil, he could not check the momentum of its progress.

On the Variety of Sodomites

(8) But that the matter be completely clear to you and be properly presented, there appear to be four varieties of this criminal vice.[6] There are some who pollute themselves; there

---

5. Matt 18.6. The text varies somewhat from the *Vulgate*.
6. According to Ryan, *Sources* 28, no. 15, the four types here described depend on Burchard, *Decretum* 19.5 (PL 140.967D). Authors have had varied reactions to these deplorable practices reported by Damian. Neukirch 55, thinks that Damian might have exaggerated the situation; A. Dresdner, *Kultur- und Sit-*

LETTER 31   7

are others who befoul one another by mutually handling their genitals; others still who fornicate between the thighs; and others who do so from the rear. Of these, as we proceed through the various degrees, the two latter are to be judged more serious than the others. Certainly a greater penance must be imposed on those who sin with others than on those who masturbate alone; and a more severe judgment is to be passed on those who corrupt others by anal intercourse than on those who couple between the thighs. The ingenious artifice of the devil contrived these stages of corruption, so that the higher the unhappy soul rises in the scale of vice, the deeper it is likely to be buried in hell.

That Improper Leniency on the Part of Prelates Does Not Check Those Who Deviate from Right Conduct

(9) It often happens that those who are guilty of this abandoned behavior come to their senses through the generosity of divine mercy, are led to repentance, and devoutly submit to public penance, no matter how severe, but dread to face the loss of ecclesiastical status. Some prelates, however, acting perhaps more leniently than they should, in respect to this vice flatly decide that no one need be deposed from orders because of the first three degrees we listed earlier; they do not refuse to degrade only those who are known to have committed anal intercourse. In other words, should one prompt an ejaculation by his own effort, or pollute another by manipulating him with his hands, or lie with another between the thighs in the manner of the different sexes, so long as he avoids violating his partner from the rear, he should be given a penance commensurate with his crime, but not deprived of clerical status. Thus it happens that a man who is known to have committed this sin with eight or even ten equally foul

---

tengeschichte der italienischen Geistlichkeit im 10. und 11. Jh. (1890), 325, states that "it is more probable that the majority of the clergy lived peacefully as married men, and that only a small fraction was given over to loose living and debauchery." Dressler, *Petrus Damiani* 100f. was of the opinion that Damian could well have acquired the data for his indictment from his experience as a confessor, while Little, *The Personal Development* 333f., 526f. considers the possibility of Damian's homosexual experiences in his youth.

companions, is still permitted to continue in his rank. Without a doubt, such permissive indulgence hardly excises the lesion but only stimulates its growth; it does not promote in the culprit bitter regret over his daringly illicit acts, but rather grants him freedom for future ventures. It would seem that an erotic cleric, whatever his rank in orders, dreads more to be despised by men than to be condemned under the scrutiny of the divine Judge. As a result, he prefers any penance, no matter how severe or enduring, to the danger of losing his status. And while because of this imprudent discretion he does not fear to lose his benefice, he is challenged both to dare novel sins and to persist the longer in deeds for which he has come off unscathed. And so, to put it another way, so long as he is not struck in the place where his illness is more severe, he sensuously wallows in the foul slough of obscenity into which he has fallen.

That Those Who Are Addicted to Impure Practices Should Be neither Promoted to Orders nor, if Already Ordained, Be Allowed to Continue

(10) On the other hand, it seems to me to be utterly preposterous for those who are habituated to the filth of this festering disease to dare present themselves for orders, or to remain in them if already ordained. It is clearly contrary to reason and opposed to the canonical decrees of the Fathers. I state this, not to render a definitive opinion in your august presence, but only to make my own position clear. It is not without cause that this shameful deed is considered to be the worst of crimes, seeing that Almighty God is always read to have detested it; even when he had not yet curbed other vices, he already kept condemning this one with the precepts of the Law, under pain of the strictest penalty. Passing over the fact that with sulphurous fire from heaven he destroyed the two eminent cities of Sodom and Gomorrah and all the surrounding country-side;[7] he struck down Onan, the son of Judah, because of this enormity and brought him to an untimely

---

7. Cf. Gen 19.

death, as Scripture relates: "But Onan, knowing that the offspring would not be his, spilt his seed on the ground every time he slept with his brother's wife, to avoid providing children for his brother. And therefore, the Lord killed him because he did a detestable thing."[8] In the Law it also says, "If a man lies with a man in the same way as with a woman, both have done a hateful thing; they must die, their blood shall be on their own heads."[9]

(11) He, moreover, who has committed this crime for which the Old Testament prescribes the death penalty, should not be promoted to ecclesiastical orders. This is borne out in the letters of blessed Pope Gregory, writing to Passivus the bishop: "You, my brother," he says, "are well aware how long the Abruzzi has been without pastoral care. For a long time we have sought for someone worthy of ordination from that district, and were totally unable to find one. But since Importunus[10] is highly recommended to me because of his moral life, his zeal for chanting the psalms, and his love of prayer, and is reported to lead a holy life, I wish that you, my brother, would have him visit you and that you would provide him spiritual advice so that he may progress in virtue. And if it is clear that he is innocent of any sins that according to the tenor of the Law are punishable by death, let him be ordained,[11] either to become a monk, or raised by you to the subdiaconate, and after some time, God willing, let him be promoted to the cure of souls."[12]

(12) Notice that in this context it is clearly understood that any man who sins with a man by intercourse as with a woman, that is, between the thighs, which crime, as we stated above, was punishable by death in the Old Law, even though he en-

---

8. Gen 38.9–10. 9. Lev 20.13.
10. Gregory I, *Reg.* 12.4.2, 350, here has *Oportunus*, but the form, *Importunus*, used by Damian, frequently appears in the variant MS readings of the *Register*. John the Deacon, *Sancti Gregorii magni vita* 3.12.137B, uses the form *Oportunus*.
11. The phrase, "let him be ordained," is unique to Damian, and is not found either in the MS tradition of the *Register* or in John the Deacon's *Vita*.
12. Gregory I, *Reg.* 12.4.2, 350; JE 1855; John the Deacon, *Sancti Gregorii magni vita* 3.12.137B; Ryan, *Sources* 28f., no. 16.

joys a good reputation, is zealous in promoting psalmody, is preeminent for his love of prayer, and is held in high esteem for his holy life; such a man can indeed receive full forgiveness of his guilt, but nowise can he be permitted to aspire to ecclesiastical orders. At the same time that Importunus, a venerable man, is praised and acclaimed, is honored and highly regarded for his upright and holy life, and esteemed for his many virtues, it is, nonetheless, later written of him, "If it is evident that he is innocent of any sins which, according to the tenor of the Law are punishable by death, then let him be ordained." It is perfectly clear that when a capital crime has degraded a man, no subsequent holy life will reform him to the point where he might receive orders and ecclesiastical status. No one may aspire to reach the heights of preferment who has surely fallen into the depths of mortal sin. Hence, it is as plain as day that anyone proven guilty of fornicating with a man between the thighs, which, without a doubt is a mortal sin, will be promoted to ecclesiastical orders in total opposition to the norms of Holy Scripture and in complete disregard of the regulations ordained by God.

*Whether Such Men May Be Permitted to
Discharge This Office if Ecclesiastical Necessity Demands*

(13) But perhaps someone will say that necessity demands and that no one is present who can celebrate divine services in the Church; consequently, the decision, which, as justice required, was at first appropriately severe, is now softened in the face of practical necessity. I am going to reply to this in a summary way: Was it not a pressing matter, and one fraught with necessity, at the time when the Apostolic See was without a shepherd? Shall we wipe out a rigorous judgment to benefit an individual, but retain it unchanged even to the deprivation of an entire people? If we do not sacrifice a principle to benefit a vast multitude, shall we violate it to promote one man's advantage? Let the eminent preacher come forward and explain what he thinks about this vice. In his letter to the Ephesians, he says, "For you can be quite certain that no one who indulges in fornication or impurity or avarice can inherit any-

thing of the kingdom of Christ and of God."[13] Therefore, if an unclean man has no inheritance at all in heaven, how can he be so arrogant as to presume a position of honor in the Church, which is surely the kingdom of God? Will he also fear to despise the Divine Law, which he disregarded by steeping himself in crime, when he assumes the dignity of ecclesiastical office? Indeed, he saves nothing for himself, because at every turn he was not afraid to be in contempt of God.

(14) This Law was imposed especially on those who violated it, as Paul attests when writing to Timothy: "The Law is not framed for people who are good, but for criminals, for the irreligious and for sinners, for the sacrilegious and defiled; it is for people who kill their fathers or mothers and for murderers, for those who are immoral with women or with men, for slavers, for liars and perjurers, and for everything else that is contrary to sound teaching."[14] Hence, as we have demonstrated, since this Law was instituted for those who are immoral with men to prevent them from daring to dishonor holy orders, by whom, I ask, should it be observed if it is despised in particular by those upon whom it was enjoined? No doubt, if he is such a capable person, it is obvious that the more prudent he is in choosing means to an end, the more careful he should be in observing the precepts of valid law. The more aware a person is, the more reprehensible is his offense, because anyone who, had he wished, could prudently have avoided sin, will inevitably deserve punishment. For as James says, "Everyone who knows what is the right thing to do and does not do it commits a sin."[15] And Truth itself says, "Everyone to whom much is given, of him more will be required."[16] If a learned man violates the right order of ecclesiastical law, it would be surprising if an ignorant man observed it. If, however, just any educated man were irregularly or-

---

13. Eph 5.5.
14. 1 Tim 1.9–10. For Damian's variation from the *Vulgate*, see *Beuron* 25.6.409f.
15. Jas 4.17. See *Beuron* 26.1.54f.
16. Luke 12.48.

dained, it seems that he is, in a sense, paving the way to error, which he so arrogantly set out to tread, for those who follow him who are, I am sure, less gifted. Moreover, he is to be condemned, not only because he sinned, but for the further reason that by the example of his own presumption he has invited others to emulate his sin.

That Those Who Desire Ordination After Incurring This Vice Have Become Depraved

(15) Who can turn a deaf ear, or, more to the point, who does not tremble through and through at the words that Paul, like a mighty trumpet, blasts at such as these? "God abandoned them to their hearts' desire and to the practices with which they dishonor their own bodies."[17] And almost immediately following, he said, "That is why God has abandoned them to degrading passions. For their women have turned from natural intercourse to unnatural practices, and their menfolk likewise have given up natural intercourse with women to be consumed with passion for each other, men doing shameless things with men and getting an appropriate reward for their perversion. And since they refused to see that it was rational to acknowledge God, God has abandoned them to their depraved ideas to do that which was reprehensible."[18] Why is it that they are so eager to reach the top in ecclesiastical rank after such a grievous fall? What should we think, and what conclusion should we draw but that God has abandoned them to their depravity? While they are slaves to sin he does not permit them to see what they need to do. Since the sun, that is, he who rises over death,[19] has set for them, and after losing the sight furnished by their conscience, they are unable to judge the malice of the filthy acts that they perform, and to conclude that it is even worse that they desire ordination uncanonically, against the will of God. Accordingly, as is usually the case according to God's decrees, they who defile themselves with this corrupting vice are smitten

---

17. Rom 1.24.   18. Rom. 1.26–28.
19. Cf. Ps 67.5. This translation uses "the west" as a symbol for death.

with a due judgment of punishment and incur a benighting blindness. Thus we read of the primitive originators of this foulness: "They were about to use violence against the upright Lot and were at the point of breaking down the door. But then," Scripture says, "the men reached out, pulled Lot back into the house, and shut the door. And they struck the men outside the house with blindness, from the youngest to the oldest, so that they could not find the doorway."[20] It is evident, moreover, that the two angels who, we read, were sent to blessed Lot, aptly represent the persons of the Father and the Son. This becomes clear from what Lot said to them: "I beg you, my lord, your servant has won your favor and you have shown great kindness to me in saving my life."[21] Certainly, one who speaks in the singular to two people as you would to one, is surely honoring one substance in two persons.

(16) Consequently, sodomites attempt violently to break in on angels when impure men attempt to approach God through holy orders. Surely, they are struck with blindness, because by the just decree of God they fall into interior darkness. They are thus unable to find the door because in their separation from God by sin they do not know how to return to him. One who tries to reach God by the tortuous road of arrogance and conceit, rather than by the path of humility, will certainly fail to recognize the entrance that is obviously right before him, or even that the door is Christ, as he himself says: "I am the door."[22] Those who lose Christ because of their addiction to sin, never find the gate that leads to the heavenly dwelling of the saints.

(17) They have become confirmed reprobates, since in failing to measure the exact weight of their guilt in the balance of personal judgment they conclude that the leaden burden of their punishment is but light and trivial. Now, the Apostle clearly explains what was previously said, viz. "They struck

---

20. Gen 19.9–11. The expression "the upright Lot," is not found in any biblical text.
21. Gen 19.18–19.   22. John 10.9.

the men who were outside the house with blindness,"[23] when he states, "God abandoned them to their reprobate ideas."[24] He obviously comments on the following phrase: "And they could not find the doorway," when he continues, "To do that which is reprehensible," as if he were saying that they were trying to enter a door that was closed to them. To be sure, one who is unworthy of holy orders and tries to break into the service of the altar does the same as he who abandons the obvious gateway and tries to enter through some impassable obstacle of the wall. Since such persons, moreover, are denied free access, while promising themselves that they will enter the sanctuary, they are forced instead to remain in the forecourt, frustrated in their presumption. They can go ahead and bang their head against the rocks of Sacred Scripture, but they will never be able to enter by way of this divine authority. And while attempting to break in where they are not permitted, they can do nothing but vainly grope their way along the hidden walls. To such as these one may aptly apply the words of the prophet: "They grope their way along at noon day as if it were night."[25] Since they are unable to cross the threshold in straightforward fashion, they wander about in circles, dizzied by the maddening rotation. Of such the psalmist says, "My God, make them like a wheel,"[26] and again, "the wicked walk in a circle."[27] Paul also speaks of them in the passage cited above, as he continued, "Those who do such things deserve to die, not only they who do them, but they also who approve those who practice them."[28]

(18) Unquestionably, one who is not awakened by this aweful thunder of apostolic invective must be thought more likely to be dead than asleep. And since the Apostle makes such an effort to intensify the severe punishment of this sentence, and that, not for the faithful among the Jews, but for gentiles and for those ignorant of God, what, I ask, would he have said had he beheld this deadly wound reeking in the very body of

23. Gen 19.11.
24. Rom 1.28.
25. Job 5.14.
26. Ps 82.14.
27. Ps 11.9.
28. Rom 1.32.

the Holy Church? And especially, what grief, what fire of compassion would kindle his devout heart upon learning that this destructive plague was raging even among those in sacred orders? Listen, you do-nothing superiors of clerics and priests. Listen, and even though you feel sure of yourselves, tremble at the thought that you are partners in the guilt of others; those, I mean, who wink at the sins of their subjects that need correction and who by ill-considered silence allow them license to sin. Listen, I say, and be shrewd enough to understand that all of you alike "are deserving of death, that is, not only those who do such things, but also they who approve those who practice them."[29]

Of Bishops Who Practice Impure Acts with Their Spiritual Sons

(19) What an unheard of crime! What a vile deed, deserving a flood of bitter tears! If they who approve of these evildoers deserve to die, what condign punishment can be imagined for those who commit these absolutely damnable acts with their spiritual sons? Who can expect the flock to prosper when its shepherd has sunk so deep into the bowels of the devil? What man will continue to be under his authority, knowing that he is so hostilely estranged from God? Who will make a mistress of a cleric, or a woman of a man? Who, by his lust, will consign a son whom he has spiritually begotten for God to slavery under the iron law of satanic tyranny? If a man violates a woman for whom he has stood as godfather, will anyone hesitate in deciding that he be deprived of Holy Communion, or in ordering that he undergo the ordeal of public penance according to the norms of the sacred canons?[30] For it is written that "spiritual begetting is greater than physical."[31] Indeed, there is scarcely any difference between

---

29. *Ibid.*
30. See Burchard, *Decretum* 17.8.920C–921A; see also Ryan, *Sources* 29, no. 17.
31. See Walafrid Strabo, *Libellus de exordiis et incrementis quarundam in observationibus ecclesiasticis rerum* 27, ed. A. Boretius and V. Krause, MGH Capit. 2 (1897) 512, II ". . . that there be a distinction between spiritual and carnal generation."

receiving a person from the lay state into the clerical order and thus begetting a spiritual son to God, and baptizing or standing as godfather for one baptized. To be sure, the canonical institution of orders is a renunciation of the world and as such is, in some way, a second baptism.[32]

(20) It follows, therefore, that the same sentence is rightly inflicted on him who assaults his own daughter, or who by sacrilegious intercourse abuses his spiritual daughter, and on him also who in his foul lust defiles a cleric whom he has ordained. Perhaps we should distinguish here the quality of both crimes: in the two prior cases, even though he practices incest, he is sinning naturally, because he sinned with a woman; in the latter case, by his shameful action with a cleric he commits a sacrilege on a son, is guilty of the crime of incest on a man, and violates the law of nature. It seems to me that it is more excusable to indulge in lustful acts with an animal than with a man for one should be judged less severely for losing his own soul than for dragging another with him to destruction. What a sorry state of affairs that one's ruin depends on another, so that when one dies, the other must necessarily follow.

Of Those Who Confess Their Crimes to the Same Persons with Whom They Have Sinned

(21) So that we are not unaware of the devil's clever devices, let me put before you some of the tools that he and his council have designed in his ancient laboratory of evil. I would be remiss if I allowed the fact to be hidden, that some of those who are shot through with the poison of this crime, when their conscience begins to trouble them, confess to one an-

---

32. The last two sentences of this paragraph do not appear in PL 145, 166D, or in Gaetani 3 (1615), 69D, and consequently escaped all commentary, including that of Ryan, *Sources*. In the last sentence, however, and from the context in which it appears, it is quite clear that Damian is not speaking of religious profession, but of entrance into the clerical state. Because the latter is also a renunciation of the world, like religious profession it is also in some way a second baptism. While it is a patristic commonplace to equate religious profession with baptism (see Damian, Letter 38, and Letter 90), his statement on the clerical state may well be unique.

other lest their guilt come to the attention of others. Despite the fact that, as actual culprits, they are ashamed to look others in the eye, they themselves become judges and each happily grants to the other the blanket forgiveness that he aspires to acquire for himself. It follows, then, that they have become penitents involved in great crimes, and still their lips are not pale from fasting nor are their bodies wasted by self-denial. Moreover, since they do not hesitate to gorge themselves, their passions are basely aroused to their usual lust. Thus it happens that he who has yet to weep for the sins he has committed, is guilty of still more lamentable crimes.

(22) The Law commands, however, that when one has contracted leprosy, he should show himself to the priests.[33] But when an unclean man confesses to another, defiled by evil that they have committed in common, it is a case of a leper showing himself to a leper and not to the priests. Now, since confession is by definition a revelation, what does he reveal, I ask, who tells his hearer something already known? Or, in what sense can this be called a confession, where nothing is revealed by the penitent but what the hearer already knows? By what right or what law can one bind or loose the other when he is constrained by the bonds of evil deeds common to them both?[34] He who is himself held in chains, labors in vain to release another from his shackles. He who would guide a blind man on his way must himself have sight, or he will be the cause of his client's fall, as the voice of Truth declares when it says, "If one blind man leads another, both will fall into a pit."[35] And again "Observing the splinter in your brother's eye, you never notice the plank in your own." Hypocrite! take the plank out of your own eye first, and then you will see how to take out the splinter that is in your brother's eye."[36]

(23) By these texts from the Gospels it becomes perfectly

---

33. Cf. Lev 14.1–32; Matt 8.4; Luke 5.4.
34. See J. Cavigioli, "De sententia s. Petri Damiani circa absolutionem complicis in peccato turpi," *Apollinaris* 12 (1939), 35–39, esp. 36.
35. Matt 15.14; Luke 6.39. For the variant reading, see Sabatier 3.904.
36. Luke 6.41–42; cf. Matt 7.5.

clear that he who is oppressed by the same guilty darkness tries in vain to invite another to return to the light of repentance. While he has no fear of extending himself to outstrip the other in erring, he ends up accompanying his follower into the yawning pit of ruin.

That He Who Prostitutes a Monk Is to Be Legally Deposed Just like One Who Violates a Nun

(24) But now we meet face to face, you sodomite, whoever you may be. Do you refuse to confess your deeds to spiritual men because you are afraid to lose your clerical status? Yet, how much more salutary it would be to suffer passing shame in the community of men than to undergo eternal sentence before the tribunal of the heavenly Judge? Perhaps you will tell me: If a man sins with a man only by femoral intercourse, he is certainly in need of penance, but from motives of human compassion he should not unalterably be denied sacred orders. But I ask you: If a monk should have relations with a nun, in your judgment, should he remain in the order? There is hardly any doubt that you would agree that he should be dismissed from the order.[37] It follows, therefore, that what you admit as reasonable for the nun, you should also logically allow as applicable to the monk. And since you apparently concur in this judgment regarding monks, by the same token you must include clerics in your determination. As I said before, however, we must be discriminating: your case should be judged the worse in that, since both are of the same sex, it is palpably contrary to nature. Since, moreover, in passing judgment on sins one rightly always inquires into the free decisions of the sinner, it follows that he who fouls a man's thighs would, if nature so allowed, achieve with the man with the same act of insane, unbridled lust as he would with a woman. He did what he could, going as far as nature would allow. And so he was unwilling in setting a limit to this crime, in that the law of nature had placed a functionally impassable barrier. Therefore, because the same law obtains for monks

---

37. See Burchard, *Decretum* 8.29 (797AB).

of both sexes, we must conclude that since one who violates a nun is rightly deposed, so also one who corrupts a monk must absolutely be prevented from exercising his office.

That Both He Who Sins with His Daughter or Goddaughter, and He Who Defiles His Son by the Sacrament of Penance, Is Guilty of the Same Crime

(25) But now let us go back in our discussion to those holy, I mean, those cursed confessors. If any diocesan priest should sin with a woman whose confession he has heard even once, no one would doubt that he deserves to be degraded by synodal decree. However, if he should sin with a priest or with a cleric in major orders, whose confession he had heard or to whom he had gone as a penitent, shall he not in justice be deprived of the benefice attached to his status? For it is the common expression to call him a "son by penance," just as we also say "son by baptism." Thus we read of blessed Mark the Evangelist, "He is Peter's son in baptism."[38] And the famous preacher who said, "For Christ did not send me to baptize but to preach the Good News,"[39] also said on another occasion, "What is it that we are proud of before the Lord, if not you? It was I who begot you in Christ Jesus by preaching the Good News."[40] And again he said this to the Galatians: "My children, I must go through the pain of giving birth to you all over again, until Christ is formed in you."[41] Therefore, if he who was sent not to baptize but to preach the Good News and, in so doing, to incite to penance, begot and endured the pains of childbirth, then he is properly called a son who receives penance, and a father who administers it. Now, then, if we pay close attention to what was said above, it will become perfectly obvious that both he who seduces his own daughter or his daughter by baptism, and he who sins shamefully with his son begotten in sacramental penance, are guilty of the same crime. And just as it is proper in law that he, who sinned with a woman whom he had begotten, or of whom he

---

38. Cf. 1 Pt 5.13.
39. 1 Cor 1.17.
40. Cf. 1 Thess 2.19; 1 Cor 4.15.
41. Gal 4.19.

is godfather, or to whom he had administered sacramental penance, should be kept in every way from exercising his office; so too should he be treated who commits unclean acts with his son by the same sacrament.

On Spurious Canons Which Mislead Completely Those Who Rely on Them

(26) But since a certain amount of nonsense is found mixed in with the sacred canons, and on this nonsense desperate men presumptuously rely, let me here quote some of it that I might clearly prove that these and similar documents, wherever they turn up, are false and completely apocryphal. Among other items, note the following:[42] A priest, not in monastic vows, who sins with a girl or with a prostitute, shall do penance for two years[43] and three lents, always fasting on dry bread on Mondays, Wednesdays, Fridays, and Saturdays; if he sins with a nun or with a man, and if this is habitual, a fast of five years should be added.[44] In like manner, deacons who are not monks, as well as monks who are not ordained, must do penance for two years. A few lines down one reads this: A cleric, not in monastic vows, who has intercourse with a girl, shall do penance for half a year;[45] if he sins frequently, let him do penance for a year. Likewise, if he is a canon; if he sins frequently, two years.

(27) Again, if one should sin like a sodomite, some say he should do penance for ten years; he who is habituated in this sin must be more severely punished; if he is ordained, let him be degraded and do penance as a layman. One year of penance is assigned if a man should fornicate between the thighs; if he repeats the act he must do penance for two years; if he should practice anal intercourse, he must do penance for

---

42. Burchard, *Decretum* 17.39.926B–927A; see *Poenitentiale Egberti* 5, 236f.; Ryan, *Sources* 29, no. 18; see also F. W. H. Wasserschleben, *Die Bussordnungen der abendländischen Kirche* (1851), 94f. Damian differs from his sources in shortening the periods of penance.
43. Burchard, *Decretum* 17.39.926C has three years; the *Poenitentiale Egberti* 5.3, 236 assigns three or four years.
44. Both Burchard and Egbertus have seven years.
45. The two sources have one year of penance.

three years; if a boy, the penance is for two years. Whoever fornicates with cattle or draught animals must do penance for ten years. A bishop who sins with quadrupeds must do penance for ten years and be deprived of his office; a priest, five; a deacon, three, a cleric, two. Many other deceitful and sacrilegious elements can be found interpolated into the sacred canons by the devil's cunning, which I would rather destroy than copy, rather contemptuously spit upon than make lists of such wanton claptrap. Now it is on these fantasies the sodomites rely, they place their trust in them as if in revelations given in dreams, and thus delude themselves with an illusory, assured hope. But let us see whether these documents agree with canonical authority and demonstrate textually and in real life whether they should be accepted or rejected.

A Conclusive Rejection of the Aforementioned Canons

(28) Now, to go back to the beginning of this deceptive chapter. It states that a priest not in monastic vows, who sins with a girl or with a prostitute, shall do penance for two years. Who is there so stupid or so irrational as to think that a penance of two years is a fitting penalty for a priest convicted of fornication? Anyone who has only a smattering of canonical science, or who has been barely introduced to the subject would obviously know that the penance assigned for a priest who sins by fornication is at least ten years, to say nothing of more severe penalties. A penance of two years for fornication should be considered too light, not only for priests, but even for laymen, for whom the sentence is three years if, after their fall they are willing to make amends. Next, it is said: If one (that is, if a priest) should sin with a nun or with a man, and if this is habitual, a fast of five years should be added. In like manner, deacons who are not monks, as well as monks who are not ordained, must do penance for two years. There is an item at the beginning of this senseless statement which I am explicating, that caught my eye and thoroughly interested me, namely, where it says, "If . . . with a nun or with a man." Now, my good sodomite, look closely at this passage of yours that you love so dearly, embrace so eagerly, and thrust forward as

a shield for your defense, and notice that it does not matter whether one sins with God's handmaid or with a man, for the sins are equated and the sentence imposed is the same. So now there is nothing over which you can contend with me, nothing in which you can rightly dissent from my allegations.

(29) But who would be so insanely foolish or become so utterly blind that he would decide to impose a penance of five years on a priest who sinned with a handmaid of God, that is, with a nun, or a penance of two years on a deacon or a monk? Is this not the noose awaiting those who are about to die? Is this not the snare for erring souls? Who indeed could censure such a statement as this: "That a cleric not in monastic vows, who has intercourse with a girl, shall do penance for half a year"? And who is such an expert in the science of Sacred Scripture or so resourceful in the subtle art of dialectic that he would presume to condemn such a penalty imposed by the law, or the judicial decision of an authority so deserving of contempt? What is the source that prescribes three years for a layman while deciding that a cleric is to do penance for six months? Clerics who commit fornication are indeed fortunate if they are subject to the decision of sodomites, for the very same amount that they measure out to others they seek to measure out to themselves.[46] This author of error is so hungry to win souls for the devil that, while attempting to cause the destruction of monks, he expands his perverse doctrine to include the clerical ranks. This murderer of souls, unable to glut his vicious appetite only by the death of monks, lusts to stuff himself also at the expense of the other order.

(30) But now let us see what follows: "If one should sin like a sodomite, some say he should do penance for ten years; he who is habituated in this sin must be more severely punished; if he is ordained, let him be degraded to do penance as a layman. One year of penance is assigned if a man should fornicate between the thighs; if he repeats the act he must do penance for two years; if he should commit anal intercourse,

---

46. Cf. Matt 7.2.

he must do penance for three years." But since sinning like a sodomite, as you yourselves assert, is the same as having anal intercourse, how is it that your canons in just one line show such disparity, enjoining a penalty of ten years for those who sin like sodomites, but restrict penitential practices to a short three years on those who have anal intercourse, which is the same thing? Are they not rightly to be compared to those monsters, not produced by nature but devised by human craft, some of which have the head of a horse and the hooves of a goat? With which canons or decrees of the Fathers do these ridiculous ordinances agree, in that they are so self-contradictory and leap about like horn-headed creatures? If they do violence to one another, by which authorities will they be supported? "Every kingdom divided against itself is heading for ruin, and a house divided against itself shall fall. And if Satan is divided against himself, how can his teaching stand?"[47] At one point, indeed, they seem to inflict a severe sentence, at another they display a certain cruel mercy. Like some chimerical monster it will roar frightfully in the form of a menacing lion, and then humbly bleat like a poor little she-goat. By such variety of forms they cause a person to laugh rather than feel penitential compunction.

(31) The items that follow are also similarly marred by error: "Whoever fornicates with cattle or draught animals must do penance for ten years. Also, a bishop who sins with quadrupeds must do penance for ten years and be deprived of his office; a priest, five; a deacon, three; a cleric two." Since first of all it says that anyone who fornicates with cattle or draught animals will be punished with ten years of penance, how do we arrive at the statement that follows, that for lying with animals a priest should be assessed five years of penance, a deacon three, and a cleric two? The source that holds everyone, also every layman, to a penalty of ten years, is the same that imposes five years on a priest, that is, that remits half of the total punishment. Now, I ask, with what page of Holy Writ

---

47. Luke 11.17–18. For the variant readings in this citation, see Sabatier 3.315.

are these lightheaded dreams that are so obviously self-contradictory in agreement? Who does not realize, does not see at a glance that these and similar texts, falsely inserted into the sacred canons, are forgeries of the devil, cleverly manipulated to deceive unsuspecting souls? Just as poison is deviously mixed with honey or with any other more delicious foods, so that while their flavor entices one to eat,[48] the deadly potion is disguised to enter more readily into one's system; so too these cunning and deceitful fictions are inserted into the Sacred Writings to avoid the suspicion of forgery. They are covered over, as it were, with honey, in that they are supplied with the flavor of feigned piety. But beware of them, whoever you are, lest the Sirens' song[49] allure you with its deadly sweetness and your soul, like a ship, go down in the whirlpool off the Scyllaean rock.[50] Do not be terrified by the sea of exaggerated austerity found in the holy councils, and do not allow the shallow Syrtian sandbanks[51] of apocryphal canons to attract you by the promised gentleness of their waves. A ship avoiding rough water often suffers shipwreck by coming too close to the sandy shore, while, on the other hand, by plowing through heavy seas, it sails out safely without loss of cargo.

That These Ridiculous Statutes, Because They Seem to Have No Certain Author, Are Rightly to Be Excluded from the List of Canons

(32) But who is responsible for forging these canons? Who has dared to sew sharp-spined thorns and thistles in the purple grove of the Church? Everyone knows that every authentic canon is found either in the revered decrees of the councils or in the pronouncements of the holy fathers, the pontiffs of the Apostolic See. No man on his own authority is allowed to publish canons, for this privilege belongs to him

48. See Leo I, *Epistola* 15, 688A.
49. On the sirens, see Isidore, *Etym.* 11.3.30–31.
50. On the Scyllaean rocks, see Isidore, *Etym.* 11.3.32; 13.18.4.
51. See Isidore, *Etym.* 13.18.6.

alone who is currently presiding in the chair of Blessed Peter. But these spurious canonical suckers to which I refer are obviously unrelated to the holy councils and are demonstrably foreign to the decrees of the Fathers. It follows, therefore, that since they clearly derive neither from the decretals of the Fathers, nor from the sacred councils, they are in no way to be included among the canons.[52] Accordingly, whatever is not included among the species is without doubt also alien to the genus. Now if we inquire about their author, he cannot be named for certain, since there is no uniformity of authorship in the various codices. In some it is written, "Theodore says"; in others, "The Roman penitential says"; in another, "The Apostolic Canons." In some places they are entitled in one way, and elsewhere, in another, and while they are not credited with having one author, they doubtlessly lose all authority. Since they totter on such flimsy authorship, they demonstrate nothing with clear authority.[53] And so it is necessary that these forgeries, which produce in their readers the darkness of doubt, stop basking in the light of sacred writings, where all doubt has been removed. Now, therefore, that we have eliminated from the canons this dramatic nonsense on which the sodomites have relied, and having clearly convicted them with reasonable arguments, I will now set before you canons about whose fidelity and authority there can be absolutely no doubt. In the Council of Ancyra is found the following:[54]

52. See A. Michel, *Sentenzen* 2 n. 2, where he refers to the two authentic sources of canon law that Damian stresses.
53. Ryan, *Sources* 30, no. 20, believes that Burchard, *Decretum* 17.39, is the source of Damian's suspected authorities. Blum, *St. Peter Damian* 173 and idem, "The Monitor of the Popes: St. Peter Damian," *Studi Gregoriani* 2 (1947), 459–476, esp. 473, accepts Damian's labeling of the *Canones Apostolorum* as spurious. But see H. Fuhrmann, "Studien zur Geschichte ma. Patriarchate," ZRG Kan. 39 (1953) 112–176; 40 (1954), 1–84 and 41 (1955) 95–183, esp. 131f. n. 117.
54. The title here is also a part of Damian's citation. Ryan, *Sources* 30f., no. 21, states that the *Collectio Dionysio-Hadriana* (PL 67.154CD), *Regulae Ancyrani Concilii* 35 must be the source of this quotation.

*"Of Those Who Commit Fornication Irrationally,
That Is, Who Commit Immoral Acts with Animals,
or Who Defile Themselves with Men"*

(33) "Of those who have acted irrationally, or who are now acting in this way: Whoever have committed such a crime before their twentieth year, after spending fifteen years as penitents, may then participate in common prayer; then after five years in this state, they may finally receive the Eucharist. Their manner of life during the years they are penitents must also be examined, and only after that may they be pardoned. But if they were grossly addicted to these crimes, they must submit to a longer period of penance. Those who are over twenty years of age and are married, and have fallen into this sin, may participate in community prayers after spending twenty-five years in penance. Following five years in this state, they may then finally receive the Eucharist. If married men over the age of fifty should sin in this fashion, they may receive Holy Communion at the end of their lives."

(34) Notice that in the very title of this revered authority we see clearly that not only those who practice anal intercourse, but also those who sin with men in any form are compared throughout with those who practice bestiality. Moreover, if we look to the choice of words, we observe that they are used cautiously and with great discretion, as when it is said, "Those who have intercourse with animals or who defile themselves with men." Now, if by the phrase, "those who defile themselves with men," the council had meant those who practice anal intercourse, it would have been necessary to use two words, since it could have expressed the idea well enough with the one phrase, "to have intercourse." Indeed, for economy of style it would have sufficed to express the whole sentence in one word, namely, "those who have intercourse with animals or with men." For those who fornicate with animals and those who have anal intercourse with men copulate in the same way. But since he speaks of some who have intercourse with animals, and of others who do not have intercourse but who are defiled with men, it is obvious that at the

end of the sentence he is speaking of those who defile men and not of those who corrupt them. It should be noted, however, that this conciliar regulation was directed especially to laymen, which by inference can easily be gathered from what follows: "Those who are over twenty years of age and are married, and have fallen into this sin, having spent twenty-five years as penitents, may participate in community prayer, in which state they must remain for five years. Then finally they may receive the Eucharist."

(35) Now, if laymen guilty of this crime, who after performing twenty-five years of penance are to be admitted to common prayer, but not as yet to the reception of communion, how can a priest be judged worthy, not merely of receiving but of offering and consecrating these sacred mysteries? If the former is scarcely permitted to enter a church and pray with others, how can the latter be allowed to approach the altar of the Lord to intercede for others? If a layman is not worthy to hear Mass until he has endured such a lengthy period of penance, how is the priest to be thought deserving of celebrating the sacred mysteries? If the former, who has sinned less grievously, in that his life is spent on the broader paths of the world, is unworthy to receive the heavenly gift of the Eucharist in his mouth, how will the latter be judged qualified to take such a tremendous mystery into his polluted hands? But let us continue considering the Council of Ancyra and its second definition in regard to this crime.

*"Of Those Who Were Once Defiled with Animals
or with Men, or Who Still Succumb to This Vice"*

(36) "This holy synod has commanded that those who have committed acts of bestiality and have polluted others with the leprosy of unnatural vice, must pray among those possessed by an unclean spirit (demoniacs)."[55] Obviously, since the text does not say, "who have *corrupted* others with the leprosy of unnatural vice," but "who have *polluted* them," which also

---

55. Again Damian quotes the title as part of his citation. As his chief source, see *Collectio Dionysio-Hadriana* (PL 67.154D), *Regulae Ancyrani Concilii* 36; see also Ryan, *Sources* 31, no. 22.

concurs with the wording of the title that speaks of pollution and not corruption, it follows that a man, driven by lust, who is defiled in any manner with another man, is commanded to pray with those possessed by the devil and not with Catholic Christians. Hence, if sodomites of themselves are unable to discern their own identity, they may at least be enlightened by those with whom they are assigned to a common confinement for prayer.

(37) Certainly it is quite proper for those who, contrary to natural law and right reason, hand over their flesh to demons by such foul practices should share a common nook to pray with the diabolically possessed. Moreover, since human nature itself thoroughly rebels at these evil deeds, and since the problem of not being of different sex is repugnant, it becomes perfectly clear that they would never undertake such queer and repulsive deeds unless evil spirits had completely possessed them like "vessels of wrath made for destruction."[56] But once they begin their possession, they pour out the hellish infection of their malice into those they have seized, so that now they passionately desire, not what the natural emotions of the flesh might demand, but only that which the devil's urging suggests. For when a man assaults another man to practice sodomy, this is not a natural urging of the flesh but only an incitement of diabolical origin. The holy fathers, therefore, were careful to ordain that sodomites should pray in the company of demoniacs,[57] since there was never any doubt that they had become prey to the same satanic spirit. But how can a mediator, exercising the priestly office, stand between God and the people if he is excluded from associating with the congregation of the people and is never allowed to pray except with those possessed by the devil? However, since we have taken pains to use two texts from the same holy council, let us also quote what the great Basil thought about the vice we have been discussing, "that every word may be confirmed by the evidence of two or three witnesses."[58]

56. Rom 9.22.
57. For procedures against the demoniacs, see Burchard, *Decretum* 2.34. 632A.
58. Matt 18.16.

Of Clerics or Monks Who Are Seducers of Men

(38) For he says,[59] "Any cleric or monk who seduces young men or boys, or who is apprehended in kissing or in any shameful situation, shall be publicly flogged and shall lose his clerical tonsure. Thus shorn, he shall be disgraced by spitting into his face, bound in iron chains, wasted by six months of close confinement, and for three days each week put on barley bread given him toward evening. Following this period, he shall spend a further six months living in a small segregated courtyard in the custody of a spiritual elder, kept busy with manual labor and prayer, subjected to vigils and prayers,[60] forced to walk at all times in the company of two spiritual brothers, never again allowed to associate with young men for purposes of improper conversation or advice."

(39) Here the sodomite should seriously consider whether he is worthy to serve in any ecclesiastical office, since this sacred authority judges him to be deserving of such ignominious and degrading treatment. Nor, for all that, should he flatter himself for never having violated anyone by anal intercourse or by coitus between the thighs, since it is apparent from this document that anyone apprehended only in kissing or in some shameful situation will be rightly forced to suffer all these disconcerting disciplinary indignities. But if a kiss is punishable by such severe penalties, what does femoral intercourse deserve? For punishing such a crime or such a monstrous deed, would it suffice to prescribe public flogging, or losing one's tonsure, or shameful shaving of the head, or besmirching one with spittal, or lengthy confinement in prison, or loading one with iron chains? And last of all, he is to be put on a diet of barley bread, because he who "has become like a horse or a mule"[61] is quite properly deprived of human fare and fed on the fodder of animals.

(40) Moreover, if we neglect to weigh the gravity of this sin,

---

59. The source of this citation is Burchard, *Decretum* 17.35: *Ex dictis Basilii* (925D). See also Ryan, *Sources* 31, no. 23.

60. Both Burchard and his source, Regino, have "tears" where Damian uses "prayers."

61. Ps 32.9.

it will become perfectly obvious at least from the sentence by which penance is imposed. For whoever is compelled by canonical censure to undergo public penance, is surely adjudged by the Fathers to be clearly unworthy of ecclesiastical office. Thus, among other things blessed Pope Siricius wrote the following: "It was also proper for us to decide that just as it is not allowed for any cleric to undergo penance, so also is it forbidden that any layman obtain the dignity of the clergy after he had done penance and been reconciled. Although now cleansed of the stain of every sin, those who were once vessels of vice must not take in hand the instruments for administering the sacraments."[62] Therefore, since Basil commands that he who is guilty of this sin must undergo severe public penance, and Siricius forbids a penitent to enter the clerical state, it evidently follows that whoever is sullied with the ugly filth of homosexual vice is unworthy of service in ecclesiastical offices. They, moreover, who were once vessels of vice, as was said, are unfit to celebrate the divine mysteries.

A Fitting Denunciation of the Vice of Sodomy

(41) Unquestionably, this vice, since it surpasses the enormity of all others, is impossible to compare with any other vice. Without fail it brings death to the body and destruction to the soul. It pollutes the flesh, extinguishes the light of the mind, expels the Holy Spirit from the temple of the human heart, and gives entrance to the devil, the stimulator of lust. It leads to error, totally removes truth from the deluded mind, prepares a trap for the traveller and secures the pit and makes it impossible for the victim to escape. It opens up hell and closes the gates of paradise, changes a citizen of the heavenly Jerusalem into an heir of infernal Babylon, and turns a heavenly star into chaff for eternal fire; it cuts off a member of the Church and hurls him into the depths of the devouring flames of hell. This vice attempts to destroy the walls of our

62. See the *Collectio Dionysio-Hadriana* (PL 67.237A), *Epistola decretalis papae Siricii* 14; Burchard, *Decretum* 19.49, *Ex decretis Syricii papae* 14.994D; Ryan, *Sources* 31, no. 24. On the decretal of Pope Siricius (JK 255), see Fuhrmann, *Fälschungen* 68, 262.

heavenly fatherland and tries to rebuild the defenses of Sodom that were razed by fire. It is this vice that violates temperance, slays modesty, strangles chastity, and slaughters virginity with a knife dipped in the filthiest poison. It defiles all things, sullies all things, pollutes all things; and as for itself, it allows nothing to be pure, nothing to be spotless, nothing to be clean. "To the pure," as the Apostle says, "all things are pure, but to the corrupt and unbelieving nothing is pure."[63]

(42) This vice excludes a man from the assembled choir of the Church and forces him to pray with those possessed and obsessed by the devil; it separates the soul from God to associate it with demons. This utterly diseased queen of Sodom renders him who obeys the laws of her tyranny infamous to men and odious to God. She mobilizes him in the militia of the evil spirit and forces him to fight unspeakable wars against God. She detaches the unhappy soul from the company of the angels and, depriving it of its excellence, takes it captive under her domineering yoke. She strips her knights of the armor of virtue, exposing them to be pierced by the spears of every vice. She humiliates her slave in the church and condemns him in court; she defiles him in secret and dishonors him in public; she gnaws at his conscience like a worm and consumes his flesh like fire. He yearns to glut his appetite, but fears, on the other hand, to be seen in public, to draw attention, or to be known by people. Whom can such a man trust, since he is haunted by a dread suspicion of his own accomplice who shares their common fall? Of course, not even the one who is his companion in sin may become the judge of his crime in confession, where he may be free of hesitation in confessing not only the sin he has committed, but also revealing the person with whom he has fallen. Thus, just as one was unable to die in sin without causing the other's death, so also when he rises he may become the occasion of the other's resurrection. The flesh burns with the fury of lust, and the soul trembles under the icy chill of suspicion, and something like an infernal chaos starts to boil up in the breast of this

---

63. Titus 1.15.

unhappy man as every thought that pricks his conscience becomes, as it were, an excruciating punishment. Once this poisonous serpent has sunk its fangs into this unfortunate man, he is deprived of all moral sense, his memory fails, and the mind's vision is darkened. Unmindful of God, he also forgets his own identity. This disease erodes the foundations of faith, saps the vitality of hope, dissolves the bond of love. It makes way with justice, demolishes fortitude, removes temperance, and blunts the edge of prudence.

(43) Shall I say more? At times it expels the entire squadron of virtues from the court of the human heart and lets in the whole barbarian host of vices as if it had removed the bolts from the doors. The statement of Jeremiah, spoken in reference to the earthly Jerusalem, seems apt in this case: "The oppressor," he says, "has laid his hands on all she treasured; she has seen the pagans enter her sanctuary, men whom you had forbidden to enter into your assembly."[64] Surely, once this savage beast has seized a man in his cruel jaws, it restrains him with its chains from performing any good deed, and then lets him rush unchecked in wild descent into the worst depravity. Then once one has fallen into the depths of utter degradation, he becomes an outcast from his heavenly home, is severed from the Body of Christ, is rebuked by the authority of the whole Church, is condemned by the judgment of all the holy fathers, is despised among men on earth, and is rejected from the company of the citizens of heaven. For him it will be "a heaven of iron and an earth of bronze."[65] Burdened with the weight of his crime, he is unable to ascend to heaven, nor on earth can he any longer conceal his wickedness under the guise of ignorance. He cannot be happy while he lives, nor hope for heaven when he dies, for now he must bear the derision of men and afterwards the torments of eternal damnation. To such a soul the voice of the prophet in the *Lamentations* is well applied, when he says, "Behold O Lord, how great my anguish! My soul shudders; my heart is turned within me, for I am full of bitterness. Without, the sword slays at will, and within, it is like death."[66]

64. Lam 1.10.
65. Cf. Lev 26.19.
66. Lam 1.20.

LETTER 31

*A Tearful Lamentation for the Soul
Steeped in the Mire of Impurity*

(44) How I weep for you, unhappy soul,[67] and regret with all my heart the infernal fate that awaits you. I grieve for you, I say, O miserable soul, addicted to the filth of impurity, for whom a sea of tears should flow. Alas, "who will turn my head into a fountain, and my eyes into a spring of tears?"[68] It is more appropriate that this doleful cry should rise from my grief for you than that it came forth from the prophet himself. I do not lament the destruction of a fortified town with its towers of stone, nor the wasted walls of a temple made by hand, nor do I weep for the long lines of wretched men that were subjected to the yoke of the king of Babylon. Rather I mourn for the noble soul made in the image and likeness of God, purchased by the precious blood of Christ, more illustrious than many buildings and truly superior to all the mightiest structures of the earth. I deplore the fall of this illustrious soul and the ruin of this temple in which Christ had dwelled. May my eyes grow weak from weeping, may they shed torrents of tears, and in overwhelming sadness bathe my cheeks with constant grieving. With the prophet, "let my eyes run down with tears night and day, and let them not cease, since a crushing blow has fallen on the virgin daughter of my people, a terribly grievous injury."[69] Truly the daughter of my people has suffered a grievous injury, because a soul that had been the daughter of Holy Church has been cruelly wounded by the enemy of the human race with the shaft of impurity. She who had once been mildly and gently nourished on the milk of sacred wisdom at the court of the eternal king, is now viciously infected with the poison of lust and lies rigid and distended in the sulphurous ashes of Gomorrah. "Those who used to eat only the best, now lie dying in the streets; those who were reared in the purple, claw at the rubbish heaps."[70] And why? The prophet continues, Because "the wickedness

---

67. A similar lament is found in Burchard, *Decretum* 19.44.991ff., following the *Ad Theodorum lapsum* of John Chrysostom (PG 47.227–308). Damian's borrowing is slight.
68. Jer 9.1.   69. Jer 14.17.
70. Lam 4.5.

of the daughter of my people has outdone the sin of Sodom, which was overthrown in a moment."[71] The wickedness of a Christian soul surely outstrips the sin of Sodom, because now one falls more seriously in proportion to his failure to reverence the laws of grace contained in the gospel. And lest he find a remedy in subterfuge that might excuse him, his knowledge of the Law of God is his ready accuser.

(45) Poor unhappy soul, why do you not reflect on the exalted dignity from which you have been cast down, or on the beautiful splendor and glory of which you have been stripped? "Oh, how the Lord in his wrath has brought darkness on the daughter of Zion, has flung the glory of Israel from the heaven to the ground, and how all her beauty has departed from the daughter of Zion."[72] With compassion for you in this calamity and weeping bitterly over your disgrace, I say, "My eyes wasted away with weeping, my soul shudders, my heart is poured out to the ground because of the ruin of the daughter of my people."[73] And you, neglecting to ponder the evils that have befallen you, and taking courage from your crime, reply, "I am a queen on my throne and I am no widow."[74] Pitying your enslavement, I cry out, "Why was Jacob carried off as a slave, and why has Israel become prey?"[75] And you say, "I am rich, I have made a fortune, and have everything I want. But you do not realize that you are wretchedly and miserably poor, and blind and naked too."[76]

(46) Ponder, O miserable man, the darkness that oppresses your heart and the dense fog of blindness that surrounds you. Has wanton passion aroused desire in you for the male sex? Has the fury of lust excited you to be intimate with your own kind, that is, man to man? Does a buck, overcome by passion, ever leap upon another buck? Does a ram ever go mad with desire for coitus with another ram? A stallion can feed calmly and peacefully at the same trough with another stallion, but let it see a mare and at once it becomes crazy with lust. Never has a bull wantonly desired to mate with another bull, never

---

71. Lam 4.6.
73. Lam 2.11.
75. Cf. Jer 2.14.
72. Lam 2.1; 1.6.
74. Rev 18.7.
76. Rev 3.17.

has an ass brayed longingly for intercourse with another ass. But dissolute men have no fear of doing what dumb animals indeed abhor, and irrational animals pass a judgment of condemnation on that which human depravity dares to commit. Tell us, you unmanly and effeminate man, what do you seek in another male that you do not find in yourself? What difference in sex, what varied features of the body? What tenderness, what softness of sensual charm? What smooth and delightful face? Male virility, I say, should terrify you, and you should shudder at the sight of manly limbs. For it is the function of the natural appetite that each should seek outside himself what he cannot find within his own capacity. Therefore, if the touch of masculine flesh delights you, lay your hands upon yourself and be assured that whatever you do not find in yourself, you seek in vain in the body of another. Woe to you, unhappy soul, at whose death the angels weep and the enemy scoffingly applauds. You have become the prey of demons, the plunder of cruel men, and the spoils of the wicked. "All your enemies open their mouths in chorus against you; they whistle and grind their teeth and say, 'we have swallowed her up; this is the day we were waiting for; now we have it; we see it.'"[77]

That We Should Be Sorry for the Soul That Does Not Lament

(47) Therefore, miserable soul, I weep for you with unrelenting grief because I do not see you weeping. For this reason I lie prostrate on the ground for you because I see you wickedly standing erect after your grievous fall and even striving for the highest rank that the ecclesiastical order may offer. If, on the other hand, you had restrained yourself with humility, I should have rejoiced in the Lord with all my heart, assured of your reform. If compunction, which is the property of heartfelt contrition, had shaken your soul to its foundations, I would have rightly cheered and danced for joy. But as it is, you are truly to be wept over because you do not weep; and thus you need the grief of others because you do not

---

77. Lam 2.16. For the "swallowed her," see Sabatier 2.726.

grieve over your perilous calamity. And since you appear to be undisturbed by any personal sad feelings of regret, you need all the more the bitter tears and compassion of your brothers. Why do you merely neglect to gage the measure of your damnation? Why not stop heaping up vengeance for yourself on the day of wrath[78] by plummeting on occasion into the depths of sin and at other times soaring with conceit? I tell you, the curse that David hurled at Joab and at his house when he shed Abner's blood, falls upon you. This disease, called gonorrhea,[79] which brought vengeance to the house of Joab because of this savage assassination, now infests your body. When Abner was slain, David cried, "I and my kingdom are innocent forever of the blood of Abner son of Ner; may it fall on the head of Joab and on all his father's house! May the House of Joab never lack men suffering from gonorrhea," for which another version reads, "suffering from a discharge of semen, or from leprosy, or only fit to hold a distaff, or falling by the sword, or short of bread."[80] Truly, to be covered with leprosy is to be afflicted with the stain of serious sin. And to hold a distaff means abandoning the brave deeds of a manly life to indulge in the alluring softness of feminine behavior. One falls by the sword if he incurs the fury of divine wrath. One is short of bread if, as a punishment for his sin, he is compelled to abstain from receiving the Body of Christ, for "he is indeed the living bread which has come down from heaven."[81]

(48) Therefore, unworthy priest, if after the discharge of semen you became a leper and were forced by the Law to live outside the camp,[82] why are you still attempting to reach even

---

78. Cf. Rom 2.5.
79. The term *Gomorian*, found in the Latin text, seems to be a Latin corruption of γονορρυεῖς. See Jerome, *Ezechiel* 81f.: "... and whom in the Law Scripture calls γονορρυεῖς, i.e., those who are said to have a flow of semen and are called impure." Damian properly understood the term to mean 'gonorrhea,' the venereal disease, *spermatorrhoea*. Here, also, we see Damian at work amending and correcting the text of the Bible. See his Letter 18. See also G. Bareille, "Saint Pierre Damien," DTC 4 (1911), 40–54, esp. 50.
80. 2 Sam 3.28–29; cf. Lev 22.4.
81. Cf. John 6.51; 6.59.
82. Cf. Num 5.2.

the highest positions of honor within the camp? Did not king Uzziah though he proudly planned to offer sacrifice on the altar of incense, patiently allow the priests to drive him from the temple after recognizing that he had been divinely struck with leprosy, and even of his own accord did he not hurry to leave? This is what is written: "When Azariah the chief priest and all the other priests looked at him they saw the leprosy on his forehead and they quickly drove him out." And then shortly thereafter we read, "And he himself hurried to leave in fear because he was instantly aware that the Lord had struck him."[83]

(49) If a king afflicted with bodily leprosy does not bridle at being ejected from the temple by the priests, why do you, with leprosy on your soul, not allow yourself to be removed from the holy altar by the judgment of so many holy fathers? If the former, after relinquishing his royal dignity and command, was not ashamed to reside until death in a private home, why should you be disturbed at stepping down from the eminence of priestly rank to bury yourself in penance and eagerly to accept yourself as a dead man amidst the living? But to return to the allegorical history of Joab: If you yourself have fallen by the sword, how will you be able to lift up another by the grace of the priesthood? If you yourself, as you rightly deserve, are in need of bread, that is, if you are forbidden to receive the Body of Christ, how will you be able to provide others with food from the heavenly table? If you have been struck on the forehead with the leprosy of Uzziah, that is, if you bear the marks of infamy on your face, how will you be able to purge others from the accumulated deposit of crimes they have committed? Shame on your pretentious pride! Let it not seek vainly to rise above itself for the burden of its own guilt weighs it down far below itself. It should learn to assess its ills with careful scrutiny and humbly discover how it might compel itself to live within the bounds of its own limitations, not arrogantly seizing what it is in no position to attain. Indeed, it may lose forever that which true humility might hope to achieve.

83. 2 Chr 26.20.

That the Services of an Unworthy Priest Will Spell Ruin for the People

(50) For God's sake, why do you damnable sodomites pursue the heights of ecclesiastical dignity with such fiery ambition? To what purpose are you so eager to ensnare the people of God in the meshes of your own perdition? Is it not enough that you yourselves are plunging headlong into the depths of sin? Must you also expose others to the danger of your fall? If perhaps someone should come to me and ask that I intercede for him with a powerful man who was angry at him, but who was unknown to me, I should immediately reply: It is impossible for me to negotiate because I do not know him very well. Therefore, if one is embarrassed to act as intercessor with a man with whom he is not at all acquainted, how can one dare to act as an intercessor for the people before God if, in view of his life, he knows that he is not on friendly terms with the grace of God? Again, how can one ask him to pardon others if he does not know if God is well disposed towards him? In this matter one must doubly fear this further complication, that he who is thought competent to appease God's anger might himself deserve to feel its effects because of his own guilt. Certainly all of us are aware that when one who has caused displeasure is sent to negotiate, the disposition of the offended party is provoked to an even uglier response.

(51) Let him, therefore, who is still bound up in earthly desires, beware lest, reveling in his pride of position, he become the cause of destruction for his subjects for having more grievously inflamed the anger of a rigorous judge. Everyone, in fact, should discreetly judge himself and not dare to accept the office of the priesthood if accursed vice still has power over him. Nor should he who is the victim of his own depravity aspire to become an intercessor for the sins of others. Forbear, I beg you, and dread to inflame the inextinguishable fury of God against you, lest by your very prayers you more sharply provoke him whom your wicked life so obviously offends. If you are willing to accept your own destruction, beware of being responsible for the damnation of others. Remember

this: The more circumspect you are about your present lapses into sin, the more readily will you rise in the future when God in his mercy extends his hand, inviting you to penance.

That God Is Unwilling to Accept Sacrifices from Unclean Hands

(52) But if Almighty God himself refuses to accept sacrifice from your hands, whom do you think you are in presuming to thrust them upon him against his will? "The sacrifice of the unclean is abhorrent to the Lord."[84] But those of you who are furious with me and sneer at heeding my writing, should at least listen to the prophetic voice that speaks to you; give him a hearing, I tell you, as he preaches and proclaims, as he rejects your sacrifices, and openly cries out against your prayers. Here are the words of Isaiah, renowned among the prophets, or rather of the Holy Spirit speaking by the mouth of Isaiah: "Hear," he says, "the word of the Lord, you rulers of Sodom; listen to the command of our God, you people of Gomorrah. What are your endless sacrifices to me, says the Lord? I am sick of holocausts of rams and the fat of well-fed beasts, and the blood of bulls and sheep and of goats revolts me. When you come to present yourselves before me, who asked you to trample over my courts? Bring me your worthless offerings no more, the smoke of them fills me with disgust. New Moons, sabbaths, and other festivities I cannot endure; your assemblies are wicked. Your New Moons and your appointed feasts I hate with all my soul. They lie heavy on me, and I am tired of bearing them. When you stretch out your hands I will turn my eyes away from you; when you multiply your prayers, I shall not listen. Your hands are covered with blood."[85]

(53) You will notice, consequently, that even though the sentence of God's condemnation bears commonly on the evil inherent in all vice, it is principally leveled, however, at the leaders of Sodom and the people of Gomorrah. If, perhaps, the rash opinion of those who would contest this view is not prepared to believe human evidence pointing to the mortal

84. Prov 15.8.   85. Isa 1.10–15.

quality of this vice, it should at least agree with the testimony of God.

(54) If, moreover, someone should object that in the statement of the prophet, it says in conclusion: "Your hands are covered with blood;"[86] as if he preferred us to understand that this pronouncement of divine anger referred to murder rather than to carnal impurity, he should know that in Holy Scripture all sins are called blood, as David affirms when he says, "Deliver me from blood, O God."[87] In fact, if we also carefully study the nature of this vice and recall the statements of physical scientists, we find that the discharge of semen has its origin from blood.[88] For, as by the agitation of the winds sea-water is converted into foam, so also blood is turned into liquid semen by handling the genitals.

(55) Consequently, we may be quite confident that it is not contrary to sound reason to assert that the statement, "Your hands are covered with blood," seems to refer to the plague of uncleanness. And perhaps this was why the vengeance against Joab related only to the crime of shedding blood, namely, that he who had voluntarily spilled another's blood would be suitably punished if against his will he had to tolerate the discharge issuing from his own blood.

(56) But since we have reached a point in this long disputation where we have clearly shown that the Lord abhors the sacrifices of the unclean and categorically forbids them, why should we sinners be surprised if we are despised by them because of our admonition? If we see the command of God's voice belittled by gross hearted reprobates, why should we marvel that we who are of earth are not believed?

*That No Holy Oblation, Soiled
by Impurity, Is Acceptable to God*

(57) Now, therefore, he who despises the revered Councils of the holy fathers, who disdains the commands of the apostles and of apostolic men, who is not afraid to reject the pre-

---

86. Isa 1.15.   87. Ps 50.16.
88. See Isidore, *Etym.* 9.6.4, "For male semen is spume of the blood. . . ."

scripts of the canons, and makes light of the solemn command of God himself, should at least be advised to conjure up before him the day of his death; and should have no doubt that the more gravely he sins, the more severely he will be judged. As the angel says, speaking figuratively of Babylon, "As she exalted herself and played the wanton, so give her a like measure of torment and mourning."[89] He should be admonished to consider that so long as he continues to be afflicted with this vicious disease, he does not deserve a reward even if it is evident that he has done something good. Neither monastic observance, nor mortification, nor a life of perfection has any value in the eyes of the supreme judge if it is stained by the shameful filth of impurity.

(58) But that we may prove the truth of what we say, I would suggest turning to the evidence of the Venerable Bede: "Whoever," he says, "gives alms but does not abandon sin, does not benefit his soul which he allows to wallow in vice."[90] The truth of this statement a certain hermit proved in deed. After living a life of high virtue with a companion of his, this diabolically induced thought entered his mind: that whenever he should be excited by passion, that he should eject semen by handling his organ, just as if he were blowing his nose. Because of this, when he died, his companion saw him handed over to the devils. This companion, not knowing his guilt and remembering only his virtuous deeds, was almost in despair, and said, "If this man was damned, can anyone be saved?" But then an angel appeared to him, and said, "Do not be disturbed. Even though this man had achieved much, he defiled it all by the vice which the Apostle calls impurity."[91]

That All Four of the Methods Mentioned Above Are Sodomy

(59) Therefore one should not flatter himself because he has not sinned with another, if while alone he abandons himself to this debasing lust. For we know that the unhappy hermit, who was handed over to the devil just before he died, did

---

89. Rev 18.7. The *Vulgate* has "glorified" in place of "exalted."
90. Could not be identified; see Ryan, *Sources* 31, no. 25.
91. Cf. Rom 1.24.

not defile another but destroyed himself by his impurity. Just as various branches sprout from the same clump of vines, so also the four shoots that we have enumerated above emerge from one defiling sodomy as from a most poisonous root. No matter from which of them one should pick the baneful cluster of grapes, he will immediately die of poisonous infection. "Their stock springs from the vinestock of Sodom and their progeny from Gomorrah: their grapes are grapes of gall and their clusters are bitter."[92] The serpent we have sought to crush with the cudgel of our disputation is four-headed, and with whichever head it bites, it at once spews forth all its vicious poison.

(60) Therefore, if one defiles himself, or is convicted of sinning with another by touch, by femoral coitus, or by violating him from the rear, even though he does not indulge in these practices indiscriminately, he is, without a doubt, still guilty of the crime of sodomy. We do not read that the natives of Sodom practiced posterior intercourse only with strangers; more likely we can be sure that, given the urge of their unbridled lust, they indulged in various shameful methods on themselves as well as on others. Surely, if one were to show any leniency in dealing with this destructive vice, whom would we more likely pardon than the poor hermit who sinned through ignorance and fell through simple inexperience, thinking that this was allowed him as an ordinary natural function? Let these miserable souls learn to inhibit this detestable vice, manfully conquer the wantonness of enticing lust, repress the lascivious urging of the flesh, and fear in their bones the terrible judgment of divine anger. Let them always recall the threatening words of the Apostle when he says, "It is a dreadful thing to fall into the hands of the living God."[93] They should also remember the menacing tone of the prophet when he says, "In the fire of the anger of the Lord all the earth will be consumed,[94] and all flesh by his sword."[95]

(61) If carnal men are to be consumed by the sword of God,

---

92. Deut 32.32. For Damian's variant from the *Vulgate*, see Sabatier 1.390.
93. Heb 10.31. 94. Zeph 1.18.
95. Isa 66.16.

why do they now love their flesh to be damned for it? Why do they limply pamper the desires of the flesh? This is just the sword with which the Lord threatens sinners when he spoke through the words of Moses: "I will whet my sword like a bolt of lightning."[96] And again he says, "My sword shall feed on flesh,"[97] that is, my fury will swallow those who live on the delights of the flesh. Just as they who combat the monsters of vice are supported by the help of heavenly virtue, so on the other hand, those who have capitulated to carnal impurity are held for the special sentence of divine vengeance. To which point also Peter says, "The Lord knows how to rescue the good from ordeal, and to hold the wicked for their punishment until the day of Judgment, especially those who are governed by their corrupt bodily desires."[98] And elsewhere he rebukes them when he says, "They consider it among the delights of God to revel in the dissipation of pollution and disgrace, to carouse with you. They have eyes looking for adultery and endless sinning."[99]

(62) Nor should those who are in sacred orders pride themselves if their lives are detestable; for the higher they stand in their eminence, the deeper they will lie when they fall. Just as now they are required to surpass others in holiness of life, so afterwards they will be compelled to bear more frightful punishments, as Peter says: "When angels sinned, God did not spare them; he sent them down to the underworld and consigned them to the pits of hell, to be held for punishment until the day of Judgment . . . And he reduced the cities of Sodom and Gomorrah to ashes and destroyed them completely, as a warning to those who would act wickedly in the future."[100] Why is it, that after recalling the fall and damnation of the devils, the Blessed Apostle then turned his attention to the destruction of Sodom and Gomorrah, unless it was his pur-

---

96. Deut 32.41.
97. Deut 32.42. For the variants in these two texts, see Sabatier 1.391.
98. 2 Pet 2.9–10.
99. 2 Pet 2.13–14. The *Vulgate* here has "delights of the day"; cf *Beuron* 26.1 (1956–1969), 212.
100. 2 Pet 2.6.

pose to show that they who are now addicted to the vice of impurity will be condemned to eternal punishment together with the unclean spirits? He does this further to suggest that, along with the very author of all wickedness, the unquenchable flame will devour those who are tormented by the libidinous fires of sodomy. The apostle Jude also aptly concurs in this sentence, when he says, "The angels who had supreme authority and did not keep it and left their appointed sphere, God has kept down in the dark, in eternal chains, to be judged on the great day. Like Sodom and Gomorrah and the nearby towns in the same way fornicating and going after alien flesh, they have become a warning in paying for their crimes in eternal fire."[101] It is evident, therefore, that like the angels who did not keep their supreme authority and earned the punishment of hell's darkness, those who fall from the dignity of holy orders into the abyss of sodomy deserve to plummet into the depths of everlasting damnation.

(63) Now, to bring all this to a brief conclusion, whoever shall have soiled himself with the filth of shameful sodomy by any of the methods we have enunciated above, unless he has purged himself through effective penance, he can never obtain the grace of God, will never be worthy of the Body and Blood of Christ, will never cross the threshold of the heavenly fatherland. This is what John the Apostle clearly states in *Revelation*, when speaking of the glory of the kingdom of heaven: "No one unclean may come into it, no one who does what is loathsome."[102]

An Exhortation to Reform for One Addicted to Homosexuality

(64) Rouse yourself, I tell you, arise and be awake, you who were overcome by the sleep of pathetic pleasure; come alive at last, you who fell before the deadly sword of your enemies. The apostle Paul is here. Listen to him as he briskly demands a hearing, knocking at your door and calling to you in clearcut words: "Wake up from your sleep," he says, " and rise from the dead, and Christ will revive you."[103] If you hear Christ

101. Jude 6–7.   102. Rev 21.27.
103. Eph 5.14. The *Vulgate* has, "and Christ will enlighten you."

LETTER 31   45

who restores life, why do you feel uncertain of your restoration? Listen to his own words: "If any one believes in me," he says, "even though he dies he will live."[104] If life-endowing Life itself seeks to raise you up, why do you further tolerate lying dead? So, beware of drowning in the depths of despondency. Your heart should beat with confidence in God's love and not grow hard and impenitent in the face of your great crime. It is not sinners, but the wicked who should despair; it is not the magnitude of one's crime, but contempt of God that dashes one's hopes. If, indeed, the devil is so powerful that he is able to hurl you into the depths of this vice, how much more effective is the strength of Christ to restore you to the lofty position from which you have plummeted? "Shall he that has fallen never get up again?"[105] If the ass of your flesh has fallen amuck under its load,"[106] it is the goad of penance that urges it and the hand of the spirit that manfully draws it free. Because the mighty Samson wickedly revealed his secret to a flattering woman, he lost not only the seven locks of his hair by which his strength was nourished, but was also blinded after his capture by the Philistines.[107] Yet when his hair grew out again he humbly called for help to the Lord his God, destroyed the temple of Dagon, and killed a far greater number of his enemies than he had ever killed before.[108]

(65) Then, if your impure flesh has deceived you with homosexual persuasions, if it has stolen the seven gifts of the Holy Spirit, if it has extinguished not merely the light of your countenance but that of your spirit, do not be depressed and utterly despair. Once again collect your forces, bestir yourself like a man, dare to perform great deeds, and by so acting you will have the strength, through the mercy of God, to triumph over your enemies. The Philistines, indeed, had the power to shave Samson's locks but not to uproot them, which means

104. John 11.25.
105. Ps 40.9. The *Vulgate* has, "he who sleeps."
106. Cf. Exod 23.5; see also Burchard, *Decretum* 19.46.994A.
107. The term *Allophyli*, used in the Latin text, appears in the LXX version, and frequently throughout the Middle Ages. See Sulpicius Severus, *Chronica* 1.28, ed. C. Halm, CSEL 1 (1866), 31.
108. Cf. Judg 16.

that the evil spirits too, even though for a time they may deprive you of the charismatic gifts of the Holy Spirit, they will never succeed in totally denying you the remedy of God's forgiveness. How, I ask, can you despair of the bountiful mercy of the Lord, who even reprimanded the Pharaoh because after his sin he had not sought refuge in the remedy of penance? Listen carefully to what he says: "I have broken the arm of Pharaoh king of Egypt, and he has not begged that it be healed and made strong enough to wield the sword again."[109]

(66) What shall I say of Ahab, king of Israel? After he had built idols[110] and foully murdered Naboth of Jezreel,[111] he at last to some degree humbled himself and so was also in part shown mercy. As we ready in Scripture, after hearing the warnings of divine terror, he "tore his garments, put sackcloth next his skin and fasted, slept in the sackcloth and walked with head bowed down."[112] And what followed? "Then the word of the Lord came to Elijah the Tishbite, and said: Have you seen how Ahab has humbled himself before me? Since he has humbled himself on my account, I will not bring the disaster in his days."[113] Hence, if the repentance of this man was not despised, even though, as we know, he did not persevere, why do you doubt the generosity of God's mercy if you strive with all your strength to persevere? Begin an unremitting struggle against the flesh, always standing armed against the dangerous disease of passion. If the flames of unclean desire burn in your bones, extinguish them at once by calling to mind the everlasting fire; if the sly tempter puts before your eyes an enticing vision of the flesh, address your thoughts at once to the tombs of the dead and take careful note of what you find there that pleases the touch or delights the eye.

(67) Consider, moreover, that the poison now causing such an intolerable stench, that the corrupting matter that breeds and nourishes worms, that everything seen lying there in arid dust or ashes was once thriving flesh that in its prime sus-

---

109. Cf. Ezek 30.21. This paraphrase appears also in Burchard, *Decretum* 19.48.994BC.
110. Cf. 1 Kgs 16.32–33.   111. Cf. 1 Kgs 21.13–14.
112. 1 Kgs 21.27.   113. 1 Kgs 21.28–29.

tained passion like this. Notice finally the rigid sinews, the naked teeth, the disassembled array of joints and bones, the arrangement of all the members in horrible disarray. Thus, indeed, does the horror of this formless and confused vision dispel illusions from the heart of man. Think again of the peril of this exchange, that for a momentary pleasure experienced at the moment of ejaculation, a punishment will follow that will not end for thousands of years. Ponder how sad it is that because one member is not satisfied to the full, the whole body together with the soul is afterwards tortured forever in a dreadful holocaust. By using the impenetrable shield of thoughts like these, drive off the evils that threaten you and purge past sins through penance. Break the pride of your flesh by fasting; nourish your soul at the banquet of constant prayer. Thus, by disciplinary firmness the dominant spirit takes the lead in compelling its subject flesh and urges it daily to quicken its pace in striving for the heavenly Jerusalem.

That It Is Indeed Profitable to Consider the Rewards of Chastity as a Means of Subduing Passion

(68) It is also well worth the effort that you constantly keep in mind the promised rewards of chastity and that, stimulated by their sweetness, you may with unencumbered faith overcome any obstacle thrown in your path by the wiles of the crafty plotter. If you are seeking the happiness that is not attained except by death, the pangs of dying become light, just as the ditchdigger eases the tedium of his work by eagerly anticipating the wage that is his due. Ponder, therefore, what the prophet says of the knights of chastity: "The Lord says this to the eunuchs who observe my sabbaths and resolve to do what pleases me and cling to my covenant: I will give them a place in my house and within my walls, and a name better than sons and daughters."[114] They indeed are eunuchs who repress the excessive demands of the flesh and cut away from themselves the longing for wicked behavior. Many of those who are in bondage to the delights of carnal pleasure long to

---

114. Isa 56.4–5.

perpetuate their own memory through their posterity. This they pursue through every waking moment, since they are sure that they will not be wholly dead in this world if they continue their name in a fruitfully surviving progeny.

(69) But much more eminently and happily do celibates achieve this objective toward which those who bear children strive with such burning ambition; and that, because they are always remembered by him who because of the condition of eternity is not restrained by the laws of time. On the word of God, a name better than that of sons or daughters is promised to eunuchs, because without any threat of oblivion they deserve to have their name remembered forever, something that generations of children succeed in achieving only for a brief time: "The just man, indeed, will endure in eternal memory."[115] And again John says in *Revelation*: "Because they are fit, they will come with me, dressed in white, and I shall not blot their names out of the book of life."[116] Again in the same work it says, "These are the ones who have kept their virginity and not been defiled with women; they follow the Lamb wherever he goes;"[117] and they sing a hymn that can be sung only by the hundred and forty-four thousand.[118] Only those, moreover, who have kept their virginity sing this unique song to the Lamb, because they, more than all the faithful, rejoice with him forever, also because of the integrity of their flesh. Indeed, other just men cannot claim this, even though they are worthy to hear themselves ranked in the same blessed company; and this is true because, while through love they have joyously achieved their blessed state, they do not however attain the level of their reward.

(70) Wherefore, one must bear in mind and make every effort to reinforce the thought of the high dignity and great excellence of being ranked at the top, where being even in the last place is perfect joy; rising there to the highest privilege, where it is most fortunate to enjoy a status equal to that of others. Of course, just as Truth itself testified, not everyone

---

115. Ps 111.7.
116. Rev 3.4–5.
117. Rev 14.4.
118. Cf. Rev 14.3.

in this world can accept what I have said.¹¹⁹ So also, in the future not everyone achieves this glorious reward. Consider these points and many more like them, my dear brother, whoever you may be, ponder them in the secrecy of your heart, and with all your effort be quick to immunize your flesh from the attack of passion so that, as the Apostle teaches us, "you may know how to keep your body in a way that is holy and honorable, not giving way to selfish lust like the pagans who do not know God."¹²⁰ If you still stand firm, beware of falling; if you have fallen, reach out with confidence for the anchor of repentance that is always at hand. If, like Abraham, you are unable to live away from Sodom, you might, like Lot, move out when the heat of the fire nearby becomes intense. And if you should be unable to reach port with your ship unharmed, it is enough to have endured the storm and escaped shipwreck. If, moreover, it is not your fate to reach shore without harm, you may, as you lie out of danger on the beach, wish to sing with an eager voice that rhythmic chant of blessed Jonah: "All your waves and your billows washed over me. And I said, I am cast out from your sight, but I shall look again on your holy temple."¹²¹

Wherein the Writer Commendably Excuses Himself

(71) If, indeed, this small book should come into the hands of any one whose conscience rebels and who perhaps is displeased by what is contained above, and he accuses me of being an informer and a delator of my brother's crime, let him be aware that I seek with all my being the favor of the Judge of conscience. I have no fear, moreover, of the hatred of evil men nor of the tongues of detractors. I would surely prefer to be thrown innocent into the well like Joseph who informed his father of his brothers' foul crime,¹²² than to suffer the penalty of God's fury, like Eli, who saw the wickedness of his sons and remained silent.¹²³ For since the voice of God threat-

119. Cf. Matt 19.11. 120. 1 Thess 4.4–5.
121. Jonah 2.4–5; on which see D. J. Sheerin, "*Celeuma* in Christian Latin: Lexical and Literary Notes," *Traditio* 38 (1982), 45–73.
122. Cf. Gen 37. 123. Cf. 1 Sam 2.4.

ens in words of terror through the mouth of the prophet, "If you should notice your brother's wickedness and you do not warn him, I will hold you responsible for his death."[124] Who am I, when I see this pestilential practice flourishing in the priesthood to become the murderer of another's soul by daring to repress my criticism in expectation of the reckoning of God's judgment? I should become responsible for another's crime in which I was in no way involved. And since Scripture says, "Cursed be he who grudges blood to his sword,"[125] are you suggesting the sword of my tongue should fail, put away in a scabbard of silence and rusting away, while failing to be profitable for others because it does not thrust through the faults of those who live wicked lives? Surely, grudging blood to one's sword is tantamount to checking the blow of correction from striking one who lives by the flesh. Of this same sword it is also said: "Out of his mouth came a sharp two-edged sword."[126] How, indeed, am I to love my neighbor as myself if I negligently allow the wound, of which I am sure he will brutally die, to fester in his heart; if, moreover, I am aware of these wounds of the spirit and fail to cure them by the surgery of my words? This was not how I was taught by that famous preacher, who thought himself guiltless of the blood of his neighbor because he did not forbear to smite their vices, for he says: "And so here and now I swear that I am guiltless of the blood of all of you, for I have without faltering put before you the whole of God's purpose."[127] Nor did John instruct me to act in this way, for he was commanded by the voice of an angel: "Let everyone who listens answer, Come."[128] That is to say, he to whom the voice of conscience beckons, draws others to follow his inspiration by immediately crying out, lest he who was summoned should also find the doors closed in his face if he should arrive in the presence of his summoner with empty hands.

(72) Consequently, if you think it proper to reprimand me for reproving others, or to blame me for my presumptuous

---

124. Ezek 3.18.
126. Rev 1.16.
128. Rev 22.17.

125. Jer 48.10.
127. Acts 20.26–27.

subtlety in argument, why do you not correct Jerome who contended with all sort of heretical sects in highly corrosive language?[129] Why do you not rail at Ambrose who spoke publicly against the Arians?[130] Why not take Augustine to task for acting the stern prosecutor of Manichaeans and Donatists?[131] You say to me: It was proper for them because they opposed heretics and blasphemers; but you dare to lacerate Christians.

(73) Let me say a few words in reply: As it was their intention to bring back deserters and the errant to the fold, so it is my purpose to prevent the departure of members, regardless of their quality. Those mentioned above were saying, "They came out of our number, but they had never really belonged; if they had belonged, they would have stayed with us."[132] But I say: They really belong to our member, but are ill-suited. We should see to it therefore that, if possible, from now on they remain with us and are well-suited. I may also add, that if blasphemy is a terrible thing, I am not aware that sodomy is any better. The former indeed causes a man to err; the latter brings him to perdition. The one separates the soul from God; the other joins it to the devil. The former expels one from heaven; the latter buries him in hell. The one blinds the eyes of the soul; the other hurls one into the abyss of ruin. And if we are careful to investigate which of these crimes is the weightier in the scales of divine scrutiny, a search of Sacred Scripture will provide a satisfactory answer. There, indeed, we find that the children of Israel who blasphemed God and worshiped idols were taken into captivity; but we notice that so-

---

129. Damian could here have had in mind the spurious *Indiculus de haeresibus*, written about 400, and attributed to Jerome (PL 81.636C–646C). He may also be referring to several of Jerome's authentic works: the *Altercatio Luciferiani et orthodoxi* or *Dialogus contra Luciferianos* (PL 23.163–192), or the *Dialogus contra Pelagianos* (PL 23.517–618).

130. For the works of Ambrose against the Arians, see E. Dassmann, "Ambrosius von Mailand," *Theologische Realenzlopädie* 2 (1978), 362–386, esp. 364ff.

131. Augustine's *Contra Faustum Manichaeum libri XXXIII*, ed. J. Zycha, CSEL 25.1 (1891), 249–787, was formerly in the library of Fonte Avellana; Vitaletti, *La bibliotheca* 75; Pierucci, *Inventari* 170; today it is in the Vatican Library, *Codex Vat. lat.* 509.

132. 1 John 2.19.

domites were devoured in the sulphurous flames of a fire from heaven.[133] Nor do I mention these holy doctors for the purpose of presumptuously comparing a smoking torch to such bright stars, for I am scarcely worthy to quote such excellent gentlemen without offending them; but I say this because what they have done to repress and correct vicious living, they have also taught more recent men to do. If, moreover, in their day this disease had sprung up with such impudent license, I have no doubt that today we would possess many lengthy volumes which they wrote against it.

(74) So let no man condemn me as I argue against this deadly vice, for I seek not to dishonor, but rather to promote the advantage of my brother's well-being. Take care not to appear partial to the delinquent while you persecute him who sets him straight. If I may be pardoned in using Moses' words, "Whoever is for the Lord, let him stand with me."[134] That is to say, that everyone who calls himself a knight of God should earnestly arm himself to overcome this vice, not hesitating to fight with all his strength. He should strive to pierce and kill it with the sharp arrows of his words, wherever it is found. In so doing, while the enslaver is surrounded by the vast force opposing him, the captive is freed from the bonds to which he had been enslaved. As all together cry out unanimously against the tyrant, the victim being dragged away suddenly grows ashamed to become the prey of this fierce monster. Seeing, moreover, as so many are telling him, that he is being led to his death, he awakens to reality and without hesitation quickly returns to life.

In Which the Lord Pope Is Again Addressed

(75) And now, most holy Father, I return to you at the end of this work and address myself to you, so that he to whom the beginning of this piece was directed may rightly be the subject of its conclusion. I implore you, therefore, and humbly beg, if I may be so bold, that your grace scrutinize the decrees of the sacred canons, which, indeed, are well known to you;

---

133. Cf. 2 Kgs 17; Gen 19.24.   134. Ezek 32.26.

that you enlist the services of spiritual and prudent men to advise you in this urgent investigation; and that your answers to these questions be such as will remove every shred of doubt from my mind. Nor, certainly, do I presume to suggest this, unaware that, by the authority of God, your profound skill alone is sufficient in this matter; but that in using the evidence of God's word and in carrying through this matter with the consent and judgment of many others, the complaints which wicked men perhaps may brazenly mutter in opposition may be laid to rest. A case is not readily evident when settled by the decision of many. Frequently, however, a sentence that one man hands down from his reading of the Law, is judged by others to be prejudice.

(76) Therefore, after diligently investigating the four varieties of this vice enumerated above, may your holiness graciously deign to instruct me by solemn decree whether one who is guilty of these crimes is to be expelled irrevocably from holy orders; whether at the prelate's discretion, moreover, one might mercifully be allowed to function in office; to what extent, both in respect to the methods mentioned above and to the number of lapses, it is permissible to retain a man in the dignity of ecclesiastical office; also, if one is guilty, what degree and what frequency of guilt should compel him under the circumstances to retire. May the light of your authority dispel the darkness of our uncertainty so that your reply sent to me alone may instruct many others laboring under the same ignorance. And, to use a phrase, may the iron plow of the Apostolic See totally uproot the seed of all error from the soil of an indecisive conscience.

(77) Most reverend Father, may Almighty God be pleased during your pontificate to utterly destroy this monstrous vice, that a prostrate Church may everywhere rise to vigorous stature.

LETTER 32

Peter Damian to Bishop U⟨bertus⟩ of Sarsina. He thanks the bishop for having accepted a poor young man, named Henry, whom Damian had sent to him for tutelage. After begging for continued support of the young man, he exhorts the bishop to further his own eternal welfare by considering the possibility of sudden death, and by keeping in mind the reward of heaven.

(1049–1054)[1]

O THE MOST REVEREND bishop U⟨bertus⟩[2] of the church of Sarsina, Peter acknowledges the obligation of service in Christ.

(2) I thank you, dear father, as you deserve, because for the love of Christ and as a mark of charity to me you have gladly received this poor little man whom I sent to you, for truly as the pastor of the poor and the father of orphans you have given him every service dictated by humanity and compassion. Now, therefore, my dear friend, I humbly beg your reverence to complete what you have begun, to plant the shoot, cut off from the root of all human help, in the garden of your church, and which up to now, hidden under the protection of your mercy, you have not allowed to die. Be solicitous lest he whom the moisture of your concern has temporarily kept unharmed, be later scorched by the heat of excessive poverty. But why do I teach the master? Take good care of him, my dear friend, not because my stammering worthlessness has requested it, but as your sharply prudent mind might dictate.

---

1. On the probable date, see Lucchesi, *Vita* no. 35.
2. It is most likely that the addressee is Bishop Ubertus of Sarsina, who is mentioned in a charter of Conrad II, dated 20 May 1027. He later appears on 14 March 1052 as Bishop Humbertus Bobiensis (for the name Bobium in place of Sarsina, see *ItPont* 5.116); see also Schwartz, *Bistümer* 180.

(3) For the rest, my dear friend, observe what you are about and consider the end toward which your serenity is leading you. O, how unfortunate it is to enjoy temporarily the good things of this world, and to hasten toward everlasting fire as if one were daily carried about on a litter with eyes tightly closed. Who knows how near death might be, now unforeseen, as if it were lying in wait for us; or how little of life is left, which with false allurement provides us only with good times. But since in dealing with one who is wiser than most, I should perhaps rather pray than preach to him, I beg you, my dear father and lord, through Jesus, to arouse yourself and awaken, to be vigilant, to open your eyes and look up to heaven, and not to lose by sleep's momentary illusion the everlasting reward of true beatitude. Regarding our dear sweet brother Henry,[3] I also ask that you keep him with you as your dearest son. Show him the love of a tender father, since you will never regret the public praise he will always bestow on you wherever he may go.[4] Stay well, and I beg you to remember me, a sinner, in your sacred prayers.

3. Schwartz (*ibid.*) conjectures that in 1056 this Henry became the successor of Bishop Ubertus; Lucchesi, *Vita*, no. 25, proposes him as the first recluse in the hermitage of Ocri, established by Damian (*ItPont* 5.120f.).

4. On this optimistically prophetic remark of Damian, see Laqua, *Traditionen* 339f.

LETTER 33

Peter Damian to Pope Leo IX. He protests that the accusations brought against him are false. However, he gently accuses Leo for having accepted the word of his calumniators without proof, yet offers to accept punishment, even though he is innocent.

(1050–19 April 1054)[1]

TO THE LORD LEO, the most blessed pope, the monk Peter the sinner sends the homage of his most devoted service.

(2) This at least I will say to my accusers,[2] making my own the words that the people of Israel addressed to their spokesmen: "May the Lord see and judge, because you have befouled our reputation before Pharaoh and his servants."[3] For the ancient enemy, fearing that by my advice to you I might destroy what in these parts he has not ceased daily to build with new devices, has sharpened the tongues of the wicked against me, has caused his accomplices to fabricate lies, fashioning for himself some sort of organ through whose pipes he prattles, and has poured the poison of his malice into sacred ears. And who should wonder that the clever cunning of

---

1. For the dating, see Neukirch 95.
2. Damian's accusers in this case are not named, and consequently they and the issue of this letter are in dispute. The citation from Gen 18.20–21 might suggest that Damian is being harassed over the *Book of Gomorrah* (Letter 31), on which see Mittarelli-Costaduni, *Annales Camaldulenses* 2.109; A. Capecelatro, *Storia di S. Pier Damiano e del suo tempo* (1862), 163ff., and Lucchesi, *Vita*, no. 86, referring to "the outcry over Sodom and Gomorrah." But if the issue is his *Liber gratissimus* (Letter 40), then the nameless one might well be Cardinal Humbert of Silva Candida, whose work, *Against the Simonists*, ed. F. Thaner, MGH Ldl 1 (1891), 95–253, claimed that all who were tainted with simony, and indirectly this included Damian, had received orders invalidly, and must be reordained. See Dressler, *Petrus Damiani* 106, n. 121 and Ryan, *Sources* 155.
3. Exod 5.21.

men could deceive my lord, so overburdened with affairs, since David himself, filled with the prophetic spirit, while indiscreetly believing Ziba, immediately sentenced the innocent Mephibosheth to the forfeiture of all his property.[4] So convincing to him was this false accusation that he allowed the guilty servant to become a partner in the paternal inheritance and judged that he who was guilty of infidelity should be rewarded with his freedom.

(3) Indeed, if we carefully note the works of our Creator, we should not be so quick to believe evil of anyone. For he, "before whose eyes everything is uncovered and open,"[5] did not disdain to say, "How great an outcry there is over Sodom and Gomorrah! How grievous is their sin! I propose to go down and see whether or not they have done all that is alleged in the outcry against them that has come up to me. I am determined to know."[6]

(4) Surely this seems to have been said for no other purpose but to teach us that human ignorance should not believe what it hears without investigation, should not lightly judge things unknown, nor pass sentence before a doubtful case is approved by evidence.[7] While I am clearly aware that in other instances you have certainly taken this precaution, and since I was not on hand to observe, I do not accuse you, but consider it no more than I deserve. But in these matters I consult my conscience, I review the secrets of my soul in the certainty that I acted only out of love for Christ, whose poor servant I am, and that I seek the favor of no mortal man and fear the anger of no one.

(5) Wherefore, I call my conscience as my witness and humbly beg him, who, I dutifully believe, dwells in the sacred recesses of your heart, that, if he should judge it to be for my well-being, he at once command you by his authority to soften your attitude toward me and cause your serenity to be appeased on my behalf, so that he might unite me with you in

---

4. Cf. 2 Sam 16.1–4. 5. Heb 4.13.
6. Gen 18.20–21. For the variants from the *Vulgate*, see *Beuron* 2 (1951), 202–203.
7. Dressler, *Petrus Damiani* 106, sees this as an implied rebuke of the pope.

reconciliation, who, lest I remain inflexible, compelled me to seek favor from your clemency. Otherwise, if he should decide that I am to be beaten with the unbending scourge of your disfavor, I humbly expose my bruised shoulders, and seal my lips, and will no longer complain, but will raise my eyes in hope to him at whose just and secret decision I accept the things that have happened to me. Therefore, it is not you, but him I ask, without whose command, I believe, not a leaf falls from the tree,[8] that he deign to fill your heart, which he holds in his hand, with good will toward me, if that be to my profit.

8. Cf. Ps 1.3.

LETTER 34

Peter Damian to Robert, the bishop of Sinigaglia. This letter was occasioned by a small piece of land that Damian had received from Pope Leo IX in the Massa Sorbituli, an area in dispute between Bishop Benedict of Fossombrone and Bishop Robert of Sinigaglia. There Damian built a small church, consecrated by Benedict. He here excuses himself for having perhaps breached Robert's jurisdiction, stating that he did not wish to foster the dispute between the two bishops. In the meantime he has had a falling out with the bishop of Fossombrone. The letter is friendly, and begs Robert for his protection while promising devotion from himself and his brethren.

(ca. 1050)[1]

TO HIS LORD, sir Robert[2] the bishop, Peter, for what it is worth, his servant and son.

(2) Dear father, my conscience bears witness that I allowed this church to be consecrated by the bishop of Fossombrone,[3] not as an act derogatory of your position, but because I heard from the inhabitants there that it was his predecessor's customary right, even though a recent one. They reported that ever since the aforementioned bishop came to the Massa Sorbituli[4] he had consecrated churches in accordance with custom. And who am I to cause another to

---

1. For the date here ascribed, see Lucchesi, *Vita* 2.151.
2. The better MSS identify the recipient as R; only MS G1 gives the full name as Ropertus. Perhaps it was a good guess, because G1 is usually unreliable. Here, however, the sources agree: Mabillon (*Annales* 743) finds a bishop Rotbertus assigned to Sinigaglia on 14 March 1053. See also Schwartz, *Bistümer* 253; Lucchesi, *Vita* nos. 20 and 44.
3. This would seem to be Benedict, who occupied the see of Fossombrone since 1049 (Mansi 19.682; JL 4163). Consecrated by Gregory VI on the recommendation of Damian, Benedict later had poor relations with Damian. See Schwartz, *Bistümer* 243f. and Vernarecci, *Fossombrone* 191f.
4. This small piece of land was granted to Damian by Pope Leo IX; see *ItPont* 4.95, no. 4; Gibelli, *Monografia* 80.119f., and 348f. But see also Vernarecci, *Fossombrone* 193ff.

supersede one in possession, whether lawfully or unlawfully, and as a monk to cause dissension between two bishops.[5] I had no doubt, moreover, that scandals would necessarily come, but I feared what follows: "Woe betide the man through whom scandal comes."[6] And certainly, no matter who should find it unfavorable, this scandal, in that it was brought on for God's sake and in the name of justice, was quite necessary for me to occasion.

(3) From the day you came to this see with God's help—you may investigate whether this is correct—I have been unable to have good relations with the bishop of Fossombrone, and he who until then had been my devoted friend, not just secretly but quite openly became an enemy. It was my good fortune to have undergone such adversity. For the occasion of your anger with me has proven quite profitable to me who seeks to escape an enemy. Unbeknown to David, Saul was slain;[7] and the sinful monk[8] also, not through any effort of his own, but by the will of God alone, was freed from the snares of the bishop of Fossombrone.

(4) You are surely aware, dear father, that I love your diocese, and under God faithfully seek honor and well-being for you. In no way do I avoid rendering obedience to your see, but rather gladly hasten to do so. My dear friend, I therefore humbly beg you to restore the liturgical services, forbidden in our church, and with your authority defend not only this tiny piece of property, which without doubt belongs to your diocese, but whatever else we have, and in every respect consider it as yours. Thus may the brethren who with me are in God's service, rejoice to have you as their father and protector, and never cease begging God's mercy for you.

---

5. The controversy between Fossombrone and Sinigaglia was settled on 15 May 1070 by Pope Alexander II in favor of Fossombrone. See *ItPont* 4.216, no. 7; JL 4675; Vernarecci, *Fossombrone* 192f.
6. Matt 18.7.
7. Cf. 1 Sam 31.4–6; 1 Chr 10.4–6.
8. In the address of this letter Peter Damian simply refers to himself as Peter. In the text, however, he calls himself Peter the sinner, which later becomes his almost constant practice.

LETTER 35

Peter Damian, writing in the name of Pope Leo IX to the clergy and people of the diocese of Osimo. He warns them under threat of excommunication to abolish the custom of plundering a deceased bishop's house and property. He reminds them that even though the bishop be dead, Christ, the bishop of our souls, lives on and is offended by this custom.

(Easter Synod 1050)[1]

LEO THE BISHOP, servant of the servants of God, to the beloved in Christ, the clergy and people, sons of the diocese of Osimo,[2] greetings and apostolic blessings.[3]
(2) Since by the authority of God the special care of one church has been committed to us, in such a way that by reason of the dignity of the Apostolic See the general supervision of all other churches has also been delegated to our care, it seems to pertain to our office not only to correct whatever has up to now been rashly perpetrated against these churches, but also to provide against their presumptuous repetition in the future. From various reports we are aware of the perverse and wholly detestable practice of certain people, who at the death of the bishop break in like enemies and rob his house, like thieves make off with his belongings, set fire to the homes on his estate, and with fierce and savage barbarity cut down his grape vines and orchards.[4] If this practice is not corrected

---

1. For the dating, see Lucchesi, *Vita* no. 88. Following Neukirch 93f., JL 4210 places the letter in 1049/1050, amending the date 1049/1054 in the first edition (Jaffé 3274).
2. On Damian's relations with Osimo, see Lucchesi, *Vita* no. 40. That Leo should request Damian to write to Osimo in his name, reflects papal confidence in Damian's knowledge of the situation. It also seems to indicate that any mutual animosity, relating to Letter 33, was exaggerated.
3. Cf. JL 4210; *ItPont* 4.209, no. 3.
4. Such practices had been prohibited as early as 451 by the Council of Chalcedon (Mansi 7.399).

by the severity of ecclesiastical action, there is little doubt that the sword of sudden outbreaks of madness hangs threatening over these regions. If, indeed, the honoring of our parents is called the First Commandment with a promise,[5] that cursing our father or mother is to be punished by death,[6] what should the sentence of chastisement be for those who undertake to persecute not their natural parents, but like vipers attempt to destroy their mother, the Church, in which they were reborn by water and the Holy Spirit?[7] For even though a bishop die in the due course of human existence, Christ, who is the bishop of our souls, lives on forever by reason of his divinity.[8] As Paul says, "There used to be a great number of priests under the Law, because they were kept by death from continued existence; but Jesus, because he remains forever, has an everlasting priesthood."[9]

(3) He, therefore, is guilty of dishonoring God who, during a mortal bishop's lifetime, under pressure of earthly fear, refrains from injuries to the Church, but who, after he is dead, pours out the bile of his hatred and the virus of his ill will which up to then he had suppressed, and that, to the detriment of Christ who is the Church's immortal bridegroom. What if the bishop had injured someone during his lifetime? What sin has Christ committed, into whose care the Church has been entrusted? Therefore, if we are not to return evil for evil on him who has done harm, why do we not reverence the eternal high priest who repaid us with good things for the evil we have done? Surely, if the despoiler of the Church believed that the Son of God is truly the immortal bishop, if only he would bear in mind that he is everywhere present, knowing and controlling all things, he would not dare to commit such a wicked and sacrilegious crime before his very eyes. But truly in him is fulfilled what was said by the psalmist: "The fool says in his heart, 'There is no God.'"[10] Moreover,

---

5. See Eph 6.2; Exod 20.12.
6. Cf. Lev 20.9.
7. Cf. John 3.5.
8. Cf. 1 Pet 2.25.
9. Heb 7.23–24. For variants from the *Vulgate*, cf. Sabatier 3.918.
10. Ps 14.1.

if they who bestow their goods on the Church, by a happy exchange, obtain the remission of their sins, it follows that they who steal Church property with barbarian fury will fall into the abyss of eternal damnation. By a new and incomparable kind of crime they so surpass the perfidy of the Jews that they become more hateful still and exceed not only the wickedness of the gentiles, but also the depravity of heretics.[11] Surely, these men once again crucify Christ and cruelly wound his body, which is the Church. This unlawful venture must therefore be curbed and this wicked aberration, prompted by the devil, must be restrained. This daring rape of the Church's patrimony must be stopped, lest the sustenance of the poor be lost and the sacrifice already offered to God by the generosity of the faithful become the loot of brigands.

(4) But should anyone be guilty of violating our decree,[12] we ordain in the name of Almighty God and by the authority of the blessed apostles Peter and Paul that he be anathema, and with the sword of excommunication we cut him off from the body of the Church as a member that has truly become rotten. Unless he come to his senses, let him be cursed, Maranatha,[13] and let him know that all the maledictions of Mount Ebal have come down on his head.[14] But glory and honor and incorruptibility to those who observe our word and seek eternal life.[15]

---

11. On this widespread abuse, see E. Friedberg, "Spolienrecht," *Realencyklopädie für protestantische Theologie und Kirche* 18 (1906), 681–686; R. Elze, "Sic transit gloria mundi. Zum Tode des Papstes im MA," DA 34 (1978), 1–18, esp. 10.

12. From these words one should not infer that events had taken such a turn in Osimo itself, since this letter of Leo was written during the tenure of Bishop Gisler. On the latter, see Peter Damian, Letter 30 n. 2.

13. Cf. 1 Cor 16.22.   14. Cf. Deut 27.13.

15. Cf. Rom 2.7.

LETTER 36

Peter Damian to S., a religious priest; and to an archbishop A. Some time after first discussing the subject of the degrees of consanguinity as impediments to marriage,[1] he again takes up the matter. Further reading, especially in the Fathers and in Scripture, persuades him that his former conclusion might be subject to modification. He asks his correspondents for their opinion on the subject.

(ca. 1050)[2]

TO SIR S., a religious priest[3] the monk Peter the sinner in the unbreakable bond of charity.

(2) The wise man gives this advice: "Consult a religious man about holiness," he says, "and a just man about justice."[4] After that he also remarked: "But constantly have recourse to a devout man, whom you know to be one who lives in the fear of God."[5] Wherefore, venerable brother, knowing you, I judged it proper not to seek advice on worldly matters, but rather to discuss a spiritual and ecclesiastical subject. In my work where I commented on the degrees of relationship, I remember saying among other things, "In counting generations of relatives there must always be more than one person"; and as proof I added, "for a generation cannot consist of one person."[6] After applying several texts from Scripture, the discussion concluded that when genera-

---

1. See Damian, Letter 19.
2. The dating follows Neukirch 94.
3. This letter seems to have been sent to several addressees: once to a priest identified as S., in three MSS in Munich (M1, M2, M3) to an St., perhaps Stephanus; in *Urbinas* 1 (U1) and *Urbinas* 2 (U2) to an archbishop A., perhaps Alfanus of Salerno; and in Graz 1 (G1) arbitrarily, as usual, to a Guido. Cf. Reindel, *Korrespondenten* 209f. Letter 19, on which this letter depends, was sent to Bishop John of Cesena and to the Archdeacon Amelrich of Ravenna.
4. Sir 37.12. On the variants from the *Vulgate*, see *Biblia sacra* 12.307.
5. Sir 37.15.   6. Letter 19.

tions of relatives are to be counted it is found that there is always an additional person. For example: where there are five generations there must be six persons; where there are six degrees or generations, which is the same thing, there must undoubtedly be seven persons. And so in the rest, the number of persons exceeds the number of the degree.

(3) But as time passed, something came to my attention in reading the Scriptures that persuaded me that this method of computing relationship could be changed,[7] especially since several laymen argued that this conclusion had in it a cruel and inhuman rigidity, and declared that they could not agree with me unless I consented, at least to some small degree, to relax the rigor of this law. Every day I suffer this attack, this contradiction, with no truce.

(4) Therefore, it seems to me that, without fault, I can bow to the infirmities of the weak in deciding that the number of generations and of persons can be in agreement, so that one can say that there are as many persons as there are generations. But that this conclusion appear not to flow from my rashness but from the authority of the holy fathers, St. Jerome, while trying to solve the question posed by Genesis, where it says, "If anyone kills Cain, sevenfold vengeance shall be taken for him,"[8] stated that there are seven generations from Adam to Lamech, although we find only the same number of persons, namely seven. And I quote the very words of this learned doctor: "It is the opinion of our ancestors that they consider that Cain was killed by Lamech in the seventh generation." And then he adds, "Adam indeed was the father of Cain, Cain the father of Enoch, Enoch the father of Kenan, Kenan the father of Mahalalel, Mahalalel the father

---

7. In Letter 19 Damian based his argument on Burchard, *Decretum* 7.779–788, according to which parents and children comprise only one generation. This view he now corrects. Damian's opinion that a marriage was forbidden with a relative up to the seventh generation, was approved in 1063 by a Roman synod; see F. J. Schmale, "Synoden Papst Alexander II. (1061–1073) . . .," *Annuarium historiae conciliorum* 11 (1979), 307–338, esp. 317f.; Mansi 19.1037f.

8. Gen 4.15. For Damian's deviation from the *Vulgate*, see *Beuron* 2 (1951), 87.

of Methuselah, Methuselah became the father of Lamech, who is the seventh from Adam." And a little further on, "This then," he says, "is the opinion that Cain was killed in the seventh generation, and according to another version, suffered punishment for his crime, and I think that nothing obscure remains in it."[9] And so, in the words of this very learned man it is quite evident that while from Adam to Lamech there are only seven persons, they still added up to seven generations.

(5) Nor does the blessed Pope Gregory disagree with this generation count. In his *Exposition on Blessed Job,* he states that Enoch was the seventh generation, although only six persons who had been fathers are listed before him. These are the blessed man's words: "Among the elect Enoch was born in the seventh generation, because they seek the crowning of his happiness in the glory of the last judgment."[10] And certainly as the sacred history of Genesis relates, Adam was the father of Seth, Seth the father of Enoch, Enoch the father of Kenan, Kenan the father of Mahalalel, Mahalalel the father of Jared, and Jared was the father of Enoch.[11] Thus, as in Cain's line only seven persons are found succeeding from Adam to Lamech, so also in the series of the elect only seven persons are listed from Adam to Enoch. And as St. Jerome calls Lamech the seventh generation in the genealogy of Cain, so too St. Gregory lists Enoch, who is the seventh from Adam, as the seventh generation. Therefore, if I am not to disdain following the example of such men, it follows that one must say that there are as many generations as there are persons counted in each succeeding generation.

(6) Moreover, let me add something else that is of great importance and that enjoys the force of sacred authority. After Matthew the evangelist had drawn up the genealogy of Christ, he concluded by saying, 'The sum of generations is

---

9. Jerome, *Epistula* 36.4.271f. Damian's variants from the text of Jerome are based on the MSS of Damian's letters.

10. Gregory I, *Moralia in Iob* 16.10.15, ed. M. Adriaen, CC 143 (1979), 807.

11. Cf. Gen 5.1–18.

therefore fourteen from Abraham to David; fourteen from David to the Babylonian deportation; and fourteen from the Babylonian deportation to Christ."[12] However, in none of the three orders into which the tallies are arranged, does one find mention of more than fourteen parents or progenitors. What is more, if you observe carefully you will find that the third group, that is the last, contains only thirteen persons. On this subject some of the doctors differed among themselves and disputed with extended arguments to show that also is this group as in the others there were fourteen generations. St. Jerome stated that there were two Jechoniahs, father and son, with the father placed at the end of the second group, and the son at the head of the third.[13] But St. Augustine says that the one Jechoniah is counted twice.[14] But if this be credible, I do not see how the assertion of the sacred evangelist can be true, when he says that from the Babylonian deportation to Christ there are fourteen generations. For we know that whether you count one thing twice or more times it still remains one. Even though a thing be said many times, its essence is not increased, nor is its number multiplied just because we repeat it. I plainly fear to express myself on the opinion of both doctors, which seems doubtful to me, lest I appear, which God forbid, to be somewhat irritated by such illustrious teachers of the Church and heralds of truth. And so I do not dare dispute their revered statements, but merely explain my view in the matter.

(7) From the words, "After the deportation to Babylon Jechoniah was the father of Shealtiel,"[15] up to the statement, "Jacob was the father of Joseph the husband of Mary,"[16] there are thirteen generations. In Joseph we have the twelfth and in Mary the thirteenth generation. However, if Joseph and Mary as husband and wife had had sexual intercourse, we would correctly see in them only one generation. But since Mary did not have relations with Joseph, the line of genera-

12. Matt 1.17. 13. Cf. Jerome, *Jeremias* 196, 210.
14. Cf. Augustine, *De consensu evangelistarum* 2.10, ed. F. Weihrich, CSEL 43 (1904), 91.
15. Matt 1.12. 16. Matt 1.16.

tion down to Joseph, produced by a series of progenitors, suddenly shifts to Mary on the other side; and as the descent is deflected from its line and passes into the other, it produces something of an angle. For he who was born of her is, according to the Apostle "the corner stone";[17] and as the psalmist sings, "He proved to be the keystone."[18] Nor is it incongruous that Mary should constitute a generation, since she is the origin of that generation which is served by all preceding generations.

(8) Moreover, since Joseph on the one side comes from the direct line of related forbears, while Mary, on the other side, descends from the other line of relationship, this passage from line to line is a sacrament of mystical generation. For since Mary and Joseph were not carnally united, they are not together one generation, but Joseph counts as one, and Mary as another. Indeed, since it is not customary in the Scriptures to construct a line of relationship through women, Christ's genealogy comes down through men. But in his origin no virile seed is present, and therefore when we come to Joseph the line of succession no longer descends from the higher to the lower, but suddenly, and contrary to expectation, is derived from the collateral line of the Virgin. Thus, after generations in the flesh a spiritual generation took place, to be followed quickly by an event that was totally unheard of and unique. The spiritual generation was had from Joseph to Mary, the unique from Mary to Christ.

(9) But you say to me, whoever you are, how can one argue that there is a generation's difference between Joseph and Mary, since he is not her father? And now you must carefully answer my question in reply: Why does Matthew the evangelist, whose statement we are now discussing, say among other things, "Joram was the father of Uzziah,"[19] since Joram was certainly not the father of Uzziah, but rather of Ahaziah?[20] For whoever reads the history of the fourth Book of Kings is certainly aware that Joram was the father of Ahaziah,

17. Eph 2.20.
18. Ps 118.22.
19. Matt 1.8.
20. Cf. 2 Kgs 8.25.

Ahaziah the father of Joash, Joash the father of Amaziah, and Amaziah was the father of Uzziah, who is also called Azariah.[21] Why, therefore, is it said that Joram was not the father of Ahaziah, whom he begot, but rather of Uzziah, who is five persons removed from him? If therefore one can say that between Joram and Uzziah there is a generation, not that Uzziah was born of Joram, but that he descended from him by a long line of continual succession, what will hinder us from saying that by some sacramental force and mystery Mary and Joseph are a generation, since without doubt they are related by blood? And if it is not possible to understand how Christ was born of a virgin, why should we be surprised if some wondrous and amazing generation existed between his parents, when his origin is indeed unique, his conception new, and his birth unusual? All of this I will say with all deference to the authority of the holy doctors of whom I spoke above.

(10) But after this digression let me return to what I began to explain. In this begetting of the Lord, the rule that I stated elsewhere does not appear to have been observed, namely, that in counting generations we must expect to find one extra person. For if the rule were here applied, it would seem that we must add another person. But in this threefold collection accounting for the line of relationship, each group has only fourteen persons and as many generations. Nor does the number of persons seem to exceed the number of generations, for the generations there listed are nothing more than simply persons. So, as we consider this matter and carefully think it through, it becomes evident that the blessed evangelist not only does not observe the rule of counting generations that I set down, but carefully avoids it, diligently makes light of it, and prudently excludes it. For in deciding for some mysterious reason to arrange the genealogy of the Lord according to three groups of fourteen generations each, in order to show that each person was a generation, he rejected from his narrative the three kings I mentioned above, namely, Ahaziah, Joash, and Amaziah, and was content to introduce as

21. Cf. 2 Kgs 15.1.

many persons as he counted generations. Clearly, although a sufficient number of persons was on hand, he did not wish to have one more person than he had generations, but wanted the number of generations to equal the number of persons.

(11) Therefore, venerable brother, burn the midnight oil as you consider this question and be sure to confer with your wise friends, so that backed up by the advice of others you may be able to reply with something certain. In answering, therefore, tell me whether in calculating the degrees of relationship I should continue in the opinion I first described, or should rather follow the view that I lately came upon; so that as with your help, burdensome doubt in many things is removed for me, so through my effort many will give proper thanks to you.

LETTER 37

Peter Damian to the abbot Albizo. Noting that Albizo was without a horse, he offered him the opportunity of sending a monk to Fonte Avellana to choose for himself one of that convent's horses or mules. In conclusion, he begs Albizo to copy this letter in one of his books so that Damian's generosity might be remembered.

(1050–1057)[1]

TO HIS LORD ALBIZO,[2] the monk Peter the sinner, for whatever it is worth, his servant.

(2) My dear friend, it seems better to me to be without charity than to pretend it, and I think it more tolerable that someone be totally devoid of charity than to represent himself as possessing its fullness. For where there is no charity, by the grace of God it can be borne; but where it is feigned, where one lies about the truth by presenting it under false colors, it can never or only with great difficulty be corrected.

(3) Therefore, your charming holiness should know that I was truly sorry when I heard you complaining about your need of horses, that I did not at once dismount from mine and freely offer you both horses, and whether you wanted to or not, did not compel you to accept them. But among other things, this too comes to mind, and not without good reason, that while my heart overflows with such remorse because of this fault and deeply grieves with sighs and groans, I am disturbed in conscience as by a gnawing worm that I did not in charity fulfill my duty. After this life is over, what will one do

---

1. The dating follows Lucchesi, *Vita* 2.152f.
2. The recipient is designated in the two oldest MSS, Vl and Cl, as A. Samaritani, *Destinatari* 147, identifies him as Abbot Albizo of Pomposa (1056–1063). However, both Della Santa, *Idea monastica* 216 and Lucchesi, *Vita* 2.152f., correcting his earlier opinion in *Vita*, no. 56, agree that Albizo was the superior of an obviously poor monastery, which would hardly be true of Pomposa. See also Lucchesi, *Clavis* 41f.

who deplores the passage of time in which he could perform acts of charity, and yet is unable to make amends for his negligence because he failed to use the hour of favor and the day of deliverance.[3] For if it seems so grievous and bitter to have sinned in this life when it is still possible to correct one's faults, what will one do later when he is unable to make amends for his sin?

(4) But more of this at another time. Now, however, my dear friend, if you have acquired a horse, thanks be to God. Otherwise, if one is still lacking, send a monk to us with a note from you, so that he may carefully inspect all our horses and mules and take whichever he likes.[4] We also have an excellent piece of cloth which the same messenger will bring along for you; use it as a stake toward buying a second horse. For it is not proper that we who serve God in spirit should soil our souls by accepting gifts from evil men because we are in need of temporal things. But that you may not think that what I say is mere pretense, if you have no other source, and if you do not take any of the animals I freely offer, so that I too may have no doubt in trusting you, keep the stake I gave you. God forbid that earthly goods should separate me from him with whom I am united in spirit, and that I should deny him any external thing, for whom I would surely not hesitate dying, if that became necessary.

(5) I beg you not to let this short letter be destroyed, but copy it in one of your books, so that my affection for you may be remembered.[5]

3. Cf. 2 Cor 6.2.
4. See C. Pierucci, "San Pier Damiano e i beni temporali" in San Pier Damiano nel IX centenario della morte (1072–1972), 2 (1972), 291–305, esp. 299 n. 41; Lucchesi, *I viaggi* 85.
5. On his request that provides important evidence for the preservation of Damian's letters, see Reindel, *Handschriften* 97.

LETTER 38

Peter Damian to Gislerius, the bishop of Osimo. Aware that Pope Leo IX had addressed a letter to Gislerius in this matter, he now writes to the bishop, attacking the otherwise unknown Bishop Maurus. The latter had claimed that a monk, for various reasons, might abandon the religious life if he had not undergone a lengthy period of probation according to the *Rule*. Citing many canonical decrees and conciliar decisions, Damian shows how wrong the bishop's position is, and how dangerous to monastic institutions. He concludes with reasoned arguments filled with satire.

(April 1051)[1]

O SIR GISLERIUS, the bishop of Osimo,[2] Peter, the monks' least servant, promises the homage of his most fervent devotion.

(2) You have not forgotten, most reverend bishop, that as regards those wicked men who, after they had put aside the religious habit, returned to the world, we have often lamented together, and have often wept with common grief.[3] Recently, however, while you were ill[4] and I happened to be participating in the synod at Rome,[5] I thought it opportune to bring

---

1. For the date of this letter, see Neukirch 56, 94.
2. This is the only letter that Damian addressed and sent to Bishop Gislerius of Osimo, using the full name, and it is still not absolutely certain that he is the same person addressed in Letter 26 and Letter 30; on which, see Letter 30 n. 2.
3. These words make it most unlikely that the recipient of this letter is the same man addressed in Letter 26.
4. On the illness of Gislerius, see Lucchesi, *Vita* no. 40, where he takes it for granted that the recipient of this letter is the same as that of Letter 30.
5. It is not certain that the Roman synod here referred to is that of 1049, 1050, or 1051, since the Bishop Guido of Numana, present at this synod, died in 1051. Damian's name is not found among the participants at these synods. A letter from Pope Leo IX to Bishop Gislerius is usually dated for 1051. At first Lucchesi, *Clavis* 81, dated it for 1049, but in his *Vita*, no. 83,

up the matter with the lord pope.[6] Being a holy man and one whose heart is filled with genuine charity, he was deeply troubled over my account and at once sought to apply a proper remedy for this enormous wound. Consequently, because he could think of no more qualified person in this area to handle the situation, he decided to write to you,[7] so that you might prudently confront those evil doers with your eloquence, recalling those who were willing to obey their commitment, while punishing those who were rebellious with the sentence of perpetual anathema.

(3) At the same council I met sir Guido, the bishop of Numana,[8] and since he, as you know, was said to have abetted this vice—I confess my sin—I took it upon myself to let him know how angry I was with him. But being a man of great humility and patience, and learned not only in Sacred Scripture but also in the study of the liberal arts,[9] he patiently bore my incriminating remarks, and after denying, protesting, and calling God to witness, most fluently refused to accept any charge of guilt for the crime in question. Beyond that, after being falsely accused of fighting against me, he now unleashed a verbal attack that was all in my favor. But even though this venerable man has been found innocent, I did not curb the flight of the arrow already released, but, changing the name, I now brought up the other person with whom I was at odds, so that, of course, whoever it is who is looking for a fight in this matter may recognize that this name has been applied to him.[10] And although it is not clear who the author of this outrage is, still, while he tries to remain tem-

---

he corrected his statement to the later date. See also Palazzini, *S. Pier Damiani eremita* 82 n. 36, and Della Santa, *Idea monastica* 216, both agreeing with Lucchesi's later opinion and with Neukirch.

6. Pope Leo IX (1049–1054).

7. Leo's letter to Gislerius of Osimo has not survived.

8. On Guido (Wido) of Numana, see Bartoccetti, *Serie* 12, 109; Schwartz, *Bistümer* 254.

9. Here Damian admits his admiration of proficiency in the arts, a far cry from the charge of antiintellectualism often brought against him.

10. This statement also might well show that the recipient of this letter did not reach the same conclusion as that contained in the full presentation; see Reindel, *Korrespondenten* 214ff.

porarily hidden, he will not be able to enjoy the immunity of flight from his refuge. For the force armed against him in this dispute has blocked the opening to his dragon's pit, so that this man, just as he emerges, will immediately dash against a waiting sword.

(4) Wherefore, along with the letter from the highest authority,[11] please accept this little work too, and thus like a true son of Benjamin,[12] armed with a two-edged sword in both hands, attack the enemy arrayed against you, so that, like a strong plow blade, the letter might break up the ground, helping to uproot the poisonous plant from a heart sown with tares, and this work, like a common hoe that follows, may break up the clods, or rather, if I may use a more proper figure, like an orator may convict those of obvious crime, whom authority, like a presiding judge, restrains by the application of canon law. But now, with the assistance of God's grace, let me at once begin against him whom I am prepared to attack.

A Rhetorical Invective against a Bishop Who Invites Monks to Return to the World

(5) Forced by necessity, venerable Bishop Maurus,[13] I am compelled to write against you at some length. I am obliged, moreover, to go beyond my station as a priest, and employ nonsacerdotal language. On all sides I am urged and everywhere I feel the pressure telling me that it is a sin of pride to speak against a bishop, but that to be silent about such things is to give consent. Yet it is better that I appear to be arrogant alone than that the deadly vice that has now especially risen should begin to grow to the detriment of many. One should rather choose to be reproved for one's straightforward speech

---

11. See *supra*, n. 7.
12. Cf. Judg 3.15–20; 20.16. See also K. M. Woody, *Damiani and the Radicals* (1966), 93f. on Damian's use of ambidexterity.
13. Lucchesi, *Clavis* 203, thinks that this Bishop Maurus, introduced into the letter, is to be identified with Guido of Numana, but more likely that Damian here introduces a fictitious person. The rubric that immediately precedes this sentence, lends credence to the idea that Damian is engaging in a rhetorical device.

by a bench of bishops than to be condemned for silence in the court of the heavenly judge. Now, about two years ago while I was a recluse in my tiny cell, something evil and filled with sorrow was brought to my attention, namely, that certain wicked men, converted to following Satan, had the sacrilegious temerity to abandon the monastic garb and through despicable apostasy had finally gone back to secular life. These same people, moreover, who had fallen so deeply into crime, are said to have been incited to dare such action by your advice and to have been supported by your authority in stubbornly remaining where they were. You are reported to have said that if a person had not gone through a long protracted canonical period of probation, as the monastic rule prescribes, but otherwise, whether because of ill health, or for any other reason he had come to the monastic life, he was free to return to the world.[14]

(6) I remember that then I sent you a brief letter concerning this matter,[15] and with proper humility suggested that you abandon this dangerous doctrine. Recently, however, when I was in Osimo,[16] I learned from several people that you were still obstinately persevering in your purpose and that you have not given up teaching against the authority of God's Law and the norms of ecclesiastical custom. In all this I am greatly surprised at how a prudent man who is not at all a stranger to the study of letters, could propose such an inconsiderate, perverse, and harmful opinion that is truly contrary to mankind's common good and seems certainly to be propounded for no other purpose than to close the gate of the heavenly kingdom in the face of sinners. Tell me, I ask, who devised this opinion if not he who brought about the ejection of the first man from the pleasures of paradise? Who, I say, proclaimed this cruel and impious edict if it was not he who plunged the fratricide Cain into the depths of despair and

14. This seems to be a reference to the year of novitiate; *Benedicti regula* 58.9, 58.12, 58.13.147f. It may also relate to the possibility of returning after one has left the order; see *Benedicti regula* 29.93f.
15. No such letter has survived.
16. See Palazzini, *Chiesa Marchigiana* 173 n. 35, with references to Mittarelli-Costadoni, *Annales Camaldulenses* 2.120; Grillantini, *Osimo* 140f.

who, with the purpose of causing him to sink deeper and not to avoid the danger of damnation, taught him to say, "My wickedness is too great to deserve pardon"?[17]

(7) What insanity this is, what mad cruelty! Does man have free will to dispose of his property, only to be unable to offer himself to God? Does he have the right to give other men what belongs to him, but is not at liberty to surrender to God his soul? Is man allowed to drive off an animal from the mouth of an open pit into which it is about to fall, and not permitted through penance to free his soul that is on the point of falling into hell? If Almighty God himself, moreover, who was offended, is prepared to receive him, who is he that turns away from the very source of goodness those who would approach it? If the Creator is willing to overlook sins, who is he who would hold back a sinner from conversion? For what else does it mean to become a monk if not to be converted?[18] But he who claims that a man cannot undertake to become a monk when he is physically ill, surely states that he really cannot be converted. Once this is admitted, there is no doubt that penance, which is the hope of sinners and the one remedy for man's salvation, is destroyed.

(8) See, therefore, that the sinner's soul is lost, the gate to life is barred forever and all hope of man's restoration is snatched away. And yet the love of God cries out against this and says, "At whatever hour the sinner changes his ways, he shall live and shall not die."[19] And again, "I do not wish the death of the sinner, but that he changes his ways and live."[20] And when the man who has converted begins to lament, then he will be saved. And to quote a short statement that has canonical authority: "Whoever denies that even at life's last breath penance can take away sins, is a Novatian and not a Christian."[21]

17. Gen. 4.13.
18. See Micoli, *Théologie* 469.
19. Ezek 18.21, 28.
20. Ezek 33.11. For the variant from the *Vulgate*, cf. Sabatier 2.816.
21. See Burchard, *Decretum* 18.7. The text is actually from the "Liber sive definitio ecclesiasticorum dogmatum" 46, ed. C. H. Turner, *The Journal of Theological Studies* 7 (1906), 78–99, esp. 98. This work has been attributed to Gennadius. See also Ryan, *Sources* 31, no. 26.

(9) Since, therefore, becoming a monk is indeed a conversion, and since the remedy of conversion can occur at any hour and is not restricted to any proper time, it becomes quite obvious that, just as anyone who wishes to be converted when he is sick would not be hindered by any disabling authority, so also if one wishes to become a monk he may do so with no opposition from Law. And when James says, "Anyone who can bring back a sinner from the wrong way that he has taken will be saving his soul from death,"[22] of which murder, on the other hand, is he guilty who persuades a sinner against conversion? Unless I am mistaken, not of the murder of his body, which will eventually die, but of the slaughter of his soul which will live forever.

(10) But perhaps you will say that it is not forbidden for one who is ill to seek refuge in the harbor of the monastery, but that once he recovers, he is allowed to return to his former state of life. But Truth itself cries out, indeed it contradicts such obvious nonsense, when it says, "No one who places his hand on the plow and looks back is fit for the kingdom of God."[23] It is indeed right that just as a man who approaches God is fit for the kingdom of God, so a person who leaves God is not afterwards fit for his kingdom. For such people, as we know by experience,[24] do not stay at the same level of evil in which they had originally found themselves, but after "returning to their own vomit,"[25] they sink even more deeply into the whirlpool of wickedness. So it recently happened to him who at your advice, it is said, deserted the holy habit of the religious life: scarcely had a few days passed when he killed an innocent man with his own hands. Truly, in this unhappy person we see fulfilled what we heard spoken by Truth itself, namely, that the unclean spirit which had previously left him, later returned and brought with him seven other spirits more wicked than himself, and with all of these he sets up a still more pestilent household in his familiar ser-

---

22. Jas 5.20.
23. Luke 9.62.
24. Cf. *Benedicti regula* 59.6, 153.
25. Cf. 2 Pet 2.22; Prov 26.11.

vant, "so that the man ends up being worse than he was before."²⁶

(11) Surely, if it is not only secular laws that reject one who deserts from an earthly army, but the sacred canons too term him infamous,²⁷ so that his testimony is inadmissible in a court of law, by what opinion, what right, what effrontery can one who has sworn to bear arms for the divine emperor, who has put on the cloak of the heavenly army, strapped on the swordbelt of chastity, and has received from the leader of the army himself the bounty of the word of God, desert the camp to which he has sworn,²⁸ and delighting in his own vomit, return to the wantonness of the world that once he despised, renounced, and condemned? We make a temporal pact with mortals and we live up to it; we make a promise to God and do not fear to break our word. A man is held guilty if he violates his pledge to another man, and should one be judged innocent if he tries to break his word to the Creator of men? A deceitful debtor is put in jail by his creditor,²⁹ and should one be held immune who steals himself away from God? Is a slave worthy of pardon, if after breaking his word, he not only deserts his master, but more than that, goes into the service of his enemy? That God is at enmity with this world is clear from James, who says, "Anyone who chooses the world for his friend turns himself into God's enemy."³⁰

(12) But to return to the subject. Is not a fellow slave, who becomes the instigator of this flight, severely punished by the master and forced as an individual to bear the accumulated

26. Cf. Luke 11.24–26.
27. For this concept, derived from Roman law, see N. Tamassia, *Scritti di storia giuridica* 2 (1967), 649–670, esp. 664; Palazzini, *Note* 261; Burchard, *Decretum* 1.173.599D.
28. See Burchard, *Decretum* 1.173.599D, *Ex epistulis Stephani papae ad Hilarium*. This statement depends on Pseudo-Stephanus, *Epistola ad Hilarium episcopum* 1, in Mansi 1.887 (JK 130); cf. Fuhrmann, *Fälschungen* 139 n. 9 and 624; see also Ryan, *Sources* 32, no. 27, where he conjectures that here Damian is dependent on Burchard.
29. Here again we have echoes of Roman law, on which see Palazzini, *Note* 253, with reference to Damian, Letter 165.
30. Jas 4.4. For the variant from the *Vulgate*, see *Beuron* 26.1 (1956–1969), 46.

penalty that both deserved? Especially is this true if the slave charged with this deceit, acts in the place of the lord and is given charge of others, and instead of inviting outsiders to enter the service of his lord, forces his servants to leave; or, if I might put it so, he whose duty it was to guard his master's flock against the violent attack of wild beasts that infested it, prepares to offer his poor little sheep to the teeth of cruel wolves.

(13) What can I say to all this? How can I be consoled in my sorrow? I am forced to exclaim and pour out the bitterness of my heart by crying, What times and circumstances we live in![31] What an iron age is upon us![32] An iron age, I say, in which gold is turned into dross and a vein of lead tries to pass as silver;[33] in which "the stones of the sanctuary now lie scattered at the corner of every street,"[34] and as the people, so also the priest, as the servant, so also his master.[35] Now who can be found so lacking in eloquence that at the sight of all this he does not break forth in lamentations? Who is so ironbound, who so stoney, that his heart does not feel these wounds? "The sword has pierced right to the soul."[36] Now the world gives evidence that with ever increasing ruin it is crashing to its end,[37] and bishops, who should be eager to lead souls to God, see how they can cause men to leave God's service. The judge already approaches, and does the herald cry out so that the citizens scatter? The whole human race is being gathered before the tribunal of the heavenly judge, and does a bishop order men to disperse and take up with earthly affairs?

(14) How sad it is! Has the priestly order been reduced to this, that those who were ordained to bring light to the world by their holy preaching now attempt with all that is in them to blind men's souls with the darkness of their perverse doc-

---

31. Cicero, *In Catilinam* 1.1.
32. For this phrase, see Laqua, *Traditionen* 269 n. 15; I. S. Robinson, *Authority and Resistance in the Investiture Contest* (1978), 13 n. 27.
33. Cf. Isa 1.22; Ezek 22.18.   34. Lam 4.1.
35. Isa 24.2; cf. Hos 4.9.   36. Jer 4.10.
37. See Damian, Letter 12 n. 4.

trines? And should those who were charged to weed out all error from the fields of the Church not be ashamed to plant thorny briars of error and wickedness? Formerly when the world was young and was pleasing to the eyes of men, the shepherds' learned tongue led many to abandon it. But now when the world clearly appears to be despicable, the shepherd of the Church invites men to return to it.

(15) Every day we see men robbing others, eager to promote wars, oppressing the poor, and trying to hide the clever snares they set in the path of their brother. And if I may put all the world's evils within the compass of a few words, almost "all are more interested in themselves than in Jesus Christ."[38] But we are not inflamed against them with the fire of love, we do not confront them with reproach, nor do we resist them with any contradiction. And if on rare occasions someone from this mass of people is eventually converted to his Creator, either because he was struck by affliction or led by the grace of God's inspiration, we at once turn to compliments and persuasive flattery, we twist the flowers of sacred eloquence to conform to our distorted minds, and begin to teach that one who has been consecrated to the service of God can return to the mire of this world. And often the subtly examined meaning of a doctor overturns an error arising from a false understanding of the literal meaning of the words; and that, which in a phrase is thought to be correctly understood, is proven to be erroneous from a careful investigation of the context.

(16) And now let us examine the literature that speaks of the monks, so that my adversary may not complain that he was overcome only by wordy arguments. Dialectic cannot offer me the convolutions of its syllogisms, nor can rhetoric add the charming colors of its caressing persuasion, and worldly wisdom is unable to suggest to me the ornamental enticements of its urbanity. Let only the sole, unadorned authority of the Fathers step forward, in whose heart, as it were, Almighty God presides enthroned on his tribunal, from which

38. Phil 2.21.

he wishes to promulgate the decrees of his Law.[39] And so he that attempts to object must know that he was overcome, not by the fabricated words of sophists, but rather by the word of Truth itself. And that every escape through subterfuge may be eliminated, let him know that those who speak against him in advancing the prosecution are they whom the whole world accepts as judges.

(17) Therefore, let Leo the Great by his authority be the first to establish the argument, and indeed like an unconquerable leader let him carry the banner at the forefront of the battle. He says, among other things, these words: "The vow of a monk taken on his own initiative and of his own free will cannot be abandoned without sin. For what he has promised to God, he must render to him. Hence, one who has abandoned the profession of celibacy and entered the army or married must be purified by undergoing public penance. For although military service may be blameless and marriage honorable, it is a transgression to abandon a choice that is better."[40] It should be noted that this most learned man does not say, as our good bishop prates, the vow of a monk taken after long delay, but "the vow of a monk taken on his own initiative and of his own free will cannot be abandoned without sin." He, therefore, places no importance on the scrupulous observance of time, but attributes everything to the freedom of choice.

(18) If, therefore, one cannot retract a vow taken freely, it is necessary to state that it is a sin to abandon it. Similar to this is also the statement made by the same eloquent man when speaking of virgins: "Girls," he says, "who are not forced by the will of their parents, but have of their own choice taken the vow and the habit of virginity, if afterwards they choose to marry, they transgress, even if they have not yet received the grace of consecration, nor should they be

---

39. See Miccoli, *Théologie* 479.
40. Burchard, *Decretum* 8.8, *Ex decretis Leonis papae* 26.793D–794A; Burchard's source is Leo's letter to Bishop Rusticus of Narbonne (JK 544); the text is found also in the *Collectio Dionysio-Hadriana* (PL 67.290B), *Decreta Leonis papae* 26; on which see Fuhrmann, *Fälschungen* 289 n. 2; Ryan, *Sources* 32, no. 28.

deprived of this gift if they remain under vow."[41] Hear that, my good bishop, there is not a word about maturity in choosing conversion, nothing even about consecration, but the whole force of monastic perfection is made to depend on one's own free determination.

(19) The eminent Leo could, and truly should have been enough to refute the calumnies of my opponent if he could easily be brought to bend the stubborn neck of his heart to sacred authority. But since perhaps he has not yet bowed, let me also bring Blessed Pope Gelasius to the witness stand. He writes, among other things, these words: "Wherefore, once any one, whether man or woman, freely puts on or has put on the religious habit, or if he is a man, has been destined for a chapter of canons, or, if a woman, has been assigned to a monastery for girls, an apostate of either sex should be forced against his will to return to his promise so that the man be tonsured and the girl enter the monastery. If, however, they wish with the help of others to persist in their desertion, by episcopal decree they are to be considered as banished from the Christian community, so that no place is accessible to them."[42] Please look carefully at each word, so that by weighing them in the scale of your mind you may never wander from the norms of truth. Notice what is said: "Once anyone has freely put on the religious garb." So, according to the decree of Gelasius, if at any time, even if there has been no previous period of probation, one has once been clothed with the religious habit, he is absolutely forbidden to return to the world.

(20) Quite similar to this is the statement found in the Council of Chalcedon, where it says, "Those who have once been assigned to the clergy, or have chosen the monastic life, cannot, we ordain, enter the army or any other secular posi-

---

41. Burchard, *Decretum* 8.2, *Ex decretis Leonis papae* 17.792CD; also in the *Collectio Dionysio-Hadriana* (PL 67.290C); see Ryan, *Sources* 32, no. 29.
42. Burchard, *Decretum* 8.14, *Ex concilio Toletan.* 794D–795A and Regino, *De synodalibus causis, Appendix* 2.18.433f. depend on the same source. Damian mistakenly cited Gelasius as the source; on which, see Ryan, *Sources* 32, no. 20.

tion. But let those who attempt to do so and, not performing penance, do not return to that which for God's sake they have previously promised, be declared anathema."[43]

(21) The Council of Toledo also adds weight to the evidence we advance. It says, "A father's devotion or one's own free profession may make one a monk. Whichever of these is alleged will be binding, and thus we refuse these entrance into the world and forbid all return to secular life."[44] Again in the same council, but somewhat before this, we read among other things, the following: "And therefore, if one or both parents have decided that their children, of either sex, at any time in their minority, should receive the tonsure or the garb proper to religious life, even if it is certain that they had been received against their will or without their knowledge, and it did not appear that they were disinheriting their children, and if, in their presence or in the presence of the Church they had publicly permitted their children to have their share in the convent, it will be totally forbidden such children ever to return to secular life. But if after once being tonsured or invested with the habit it has been proven that they had done so, they must be recalled to the religious life and dress and by all means be forced to live by its observance."[45]

(22) Listen also, if you will, to what the Council of Trier has decided concerning monks who abandon their vow: "Whoever," it says, "among laymen accept the penitential life and are tonsured and later, going back on their word, re-enter the lay state, when taken by their bishop they are to be recalled to the way of penance that they had abandoned. But if some cannot be recalled to penance, and after being admonished do not return, they are to be sentenced with anathema as apostates in the eyes of the Church."[46] Notice that we are

---

43. Burchard, *Decretum* 8.4, *Ex concilio Chalced.* 7.793BC. This text is found also in the *Collectio Dionysio-Hadriana* (PL 67.173A); see Ryan, *Sources* 33, no. 31.
44. Burchard, *Decretum* 8.6, *Ex concilio Toletan.* 49.793CD; see Ryan, *Sources* 33, no. 32.
45. Burchard, *Decretum* 8.1, *Ex concilio Toletan.* 11.6.791CD; also in Regino, *De synodalibus causis*, Appendix 3.3.451; see Ryan, *Sources* 33, no. 33.
46. Burchard, *Decretum* 8.27, *Ex concilio Toletan.* 5.5.796D. His source is

here expressly taught that it is the duty of the bishops not to persuade monks to leave the monastery, but that they should compel those who have broken their vow to return. But what can we plead in the case of those people who are converted of their own free will, when it is not permitted those who have been tonsured against their will to return to the secular life that they had abandoned?

(23) To this point also this canon was published by the Council of Mainz: "Concerning clerics, however, we ordain that those who are still found to have been tonsured against their will, whether they be in the canonical or in the monastic order, if they are freeborn, let them remain."[47]

(24) But perhaps you will reply to me and still present a shield of futile defense against these many authentic statements of the holy fathers and the canons of the venerable councils. "I will grant you," you will say, "that those who were presented by their parents should remain where they are; that those who voluntarily converted should not return to worldly affairs; and that, according to good opinion, even those who were tonsured against their will should strive to persevere. For to dispute such clear statements of the holy fathers is only to have the stars shining brightly before us and to see nothing with our eyes wide open."

(25) "But tell me," I ask, "is it to be tolerated, and not, rather, attacked openly, when certain corrupt abbots of monasteries, who neither love God nor give evidence of seeking the welfare of souls, who can think of nothing but profit, so deceive simple souls with their charming persuasion that they attract them to the monastery after enticing them with empty promises? Would this be a valid conversion, in which burning avarice was more interested in the possessions a man had than in the man himself?"

Regino, *De synodalibus causis, Appendix* 2.31.444: *Ex concilio Toletan.* 4.55. See Ryan, *Sources* 33f., no. 34. In the MSS of Damian's letters at this point, there are references to a *Concilium Triburiense* and one to a *Concilium Treverense*, but both seem to be mistaken.

47. Burchard, *Decretum* 8.91, *Ex concilio Moguntin.* 23.810AB; the source is the *Concilium Moguntinense* (813) 23, ed. A. Werminghoff, MGH Conc. 2 (1906), 267; see Ryan, *Sources* 34, no. 35.

(26) To this I answer without hesitation and firmly assert that even these are not permitted to waver in the choice they have made. And that the proposition may not be lacking its own proofs, I again cite the Council of Mainz. After many other items it says the following: "This holy council ordains that bishops and abbots, who in their avarice are eager for profit and not for a harvest of souls, who tonsure men they have deceitfully enticed, and by such persuasion not only accept their goods but rather take them by force, shall be subject to canonical penance or to that established by the *Rule*, just as having engaged in business for filthy profit. But those who were deceived by empty promises or were persuaded by any sort of fraud, who acted irresponsibly, and not knowing that their property was their own, submitted to tonsure, are required to persevere in that which they have undertaken."[48]

(27) But since every device of a clever opponent is nicely overcome when one anticipates the arguments he is able to advance, and refutes them beforehand with a formidable battery of counter arguments, you will not, perhaps, blush to say that St. Gregory commanded that a man be taken from the monastery and returned to his wife, even though he had already been tonsured.[49] But I say to you, and not without cause, that an arrow shot at a rock sometimes ricochets and strikes the archer, and often a careless knight is himself mortally wounded by the very weapon with which he tries to strike his adversary. Now if you carefully examine the example given, it will be seen to stand in my favor and will give irrefutable evidence for the position I have taken. And that the point be made clearer by looking at it closely, it will not be out of place to quote a few words from Gregory's letter: "Agathora," he said, "the bearer of the letters before us, has complained that her husband became a monk against her will in the monastery of the abbot Urbicus. Since this accusation

---

48. Burchard, *Decretum* 8.93, *Ex concilio Moguntin.* 25.810C. Actually, the source is the *Concilium Cabillonense* (813) 7, ed. A. Werminghoff, MGH Conc. 2 (1906), 275; see Ryan, *Sources* 34, no. 36.

49. See John the Deacon, *Sancti Gregorii magni vita* 4.41.203C; cf. Ryan, *Sources* 34, no. 37.

undoubtedly implies the guilt of this abbot and puts him in a bad light, we command you, as a good administrator, to discover by diligent investigation whether perhaps he was converted with her permission, or whether she herself had promised to enter religion. And if this is found to be the case, he should be made to remain in the monastery and she, in accordance with her promise, should be compelled to change her way of life."[50] Note that nothing is said here of an extended conversion, nothing of a long period of probation. Only this is commanded, that if he is found to have entered the religious life with his wife's consent and with her promise, he should by all means be compelled to persevere in his purpose. And then the letter continues, "But if neither is warranted," that is, if he was converted against her will and without his wife's promise, "then let him return."[51]

(28) There is no doubt that this case greatly helps my position, for in enumerating the reasons why a man should be made to return to his wife, nothing was said about a long conversion. For if a long delay before conversion were of importance, and if the good investigator had thought it of any value, after examining other details, he would never have passed it over in silence. But since he said nothing, his silence teaches that it be passed over without further ado.

(29) Surely after seeing such a dense cloud of witnesses opposing your novel position, so that like a slippery snake held in the hand of strong reason, you find it impossible to go in any direction, perhaps you are still looking for some special argument to be raised about those who convert while they are sick. But if you will carefully note all that was said above, it is clear that you are debating in vain about this specific case since you were forced to agree to the entire genus. For if it is obvious that the monastic vows were valid for all,

---

50. John the Deacon, *Sancti Gregorii magni vita* 4.41.203D. The source is Gregory I, *Reg.* 11.30; 2.300 (JE 1820). Also in Regino, *De synodalibus causis,* Appendix 2.23.436 and in Burchard, *Decretum* 19.48.822D; see Ryan, *Sources* 34, no. 38.
51. *Ibid.*

not only for those who were voluntarily converted, but also for those who were forced, and for those who were deceived, how is it that the same conclusion is not reached in the case of the sick, who seek the same objective with the greatest ardor and beg for it with all their heart?

(30) Now even setting aside the men, whose salutary conversion is not prejudiced by considerations of age nor prevented by any season, even the virgins who are not permitted to be consecrated except on certain feast days and until they have reached their twenty-fifth year, have complete freedom if they are ill, both to be consecrated and to receive the veil. As I look about for evidence to back up this assertion, Blessed Gelasius comes first to mind. He says, "In the case of devout virgins, they are not to be given the holy veil except on Epiphany, in the octave of Easter, or on the feast days of the apostles, and not before they are twenty-five years of age, unless perhaps, as was said of baptism, they are gravely ill, in which case, if they request it, they are not to be denied lest they leave this world without this boon."[52] Do you not see, therefore, that this conversion too, which good health could call into question and render invalid, is strengthened by sickness and made acceptable by ill health? And, if I may put it so, when one who converts grows ill, conversion is also the occasion which restores him to good health.

(31) But if, perhaps, you should unjustly blame me for giving examples concerning women, since your concern is with men, I want you to know what was said by the Council of Verberie: "The same law," it says, "applies for men as well as for women."[53] And if you carefully investigate what has been said, you will not miss the point that I wrote not out of ne-

---

52. Burchard, *Decretum* 8.15, *Ex decretis Gelasii papae* 12.795C. The source is Gelasius, *Epistola* 14.12, ed. A. Thiel, *Epistolae Romanorum pontificum genuinae* 1 (1867–1868), 369, n. 72 (JK 636); cf. *Collectio Dionysio-Hadriana* (PL 67.306AB); Ryan, *Sources* 34, no. 39. The minimum age of twenty-five years is an addition of Burchard; cf. Palazzini, *Il diritto* 12.45.

53. Falsely ascribed to a council *apud Vermeriam* by Burchard, *Decretum* 9.27.819B. However, the council is fictitious. The source here is the *Decretum Compendiense* 8, ed. A. Boretius, MGH Capit. 1 (1883), 38; cf. Ryan, *Sources* 34f., no. 40.

cessity but purposely to further strengthen the force of the argument. It is clear that if I had attempted to quote all the evidence of ecclesiastical literature that one could find applying to my position, perhaps the day would end before my abundant supply of examples. And so, I have put off citing them here to avoid the distaste that accompanies long-windedness. Wherefore, if someone is so shameless as to seek still further evidence, I send him to what I have already collected: where the same rule applies both to the sick as well as to the healthy, and decrees that not only those who convert freely, but also forced conversions and those persuaded by deceptive means must persevere in their purpose.

(32) The holy fathers were of the opinion that the monastic habit is to be regarded with such veneration and guarded with such care, that no mater how one came to put it on, he should afterwards not be permitted to abandon it. And to back up what I say with evidence, is it not frequently forbidden in the sacred canons for a widow to be given the veil? And so, to omit the testimony of others, Gelasius says, "No bishop should attempt to give widows the veil."[54] But although even a bishop is forbidden to invest her, still if for any reason she herself should take the holy veil, she may not dare to change her mind and abandon it. And so we read it in the Council of Arles: "This synod decrees that widows who of their own will have taken the veil of holy conversion at the altar, must remain steadfast in this vow. We decree that it is not lawful, once they have consecrated themselves to the Lord by taking the veil, to allow them again to lie to the Holy Spirit."[55] And later on the same council says in another canon, "Supported by the authority of the Fathers, we decree in this

---

54. Burchard, *Decretum* 8.36, *Ex concilio Moguntin.* 6.798C, where the source is cited, *in decretis Gelasii* 13 (JK 636); also in the *Collectio Dionysio-Hadriana* (PL 67.306B), where the source is the same. But actually the source is the *Concilium Triburiense* (895) 25, ed. A. Boretius and V. Krause, MGH Capit. 2 (1890–1897); see also Ryan, *Sources* 35, no. 41.

55. Burchard, *Decretum* 8.35, *Ex concilio Aurelian.* 3.798BC. The source here is Regino, *De synodalibus causis* 2.178.283, ascribing the text to the *Concilium Triburiense*, which is correct. The false attribution is the fault of Burchard; see Ryan, *Sources* 35, no. 42.

holy council and freely judge that if a widow has of her own accord taken the veil, even though it has not been blessed, and in the church attends Mass with those who have been given the veil, whether she is willing or not, she must thereafter be clothed with the habit of nuns, even if she is prepared to confirm under oath that she took the veil only with the condition that she could again put it off."[56]

(33) It is apparent, therefore, that this conversion too, which did not proceed in a legal manner and should not have taken place, still once it had been accomplished, can no longer be violated out of reverence for religious profession. Hence, if the holy fathers give force to an accomplished conversion which they had forbidden to take place, what, I ask, should we think of that conversion to which they urge the candidates by exhortation, and whom after their conversion they charge to continue in persevering? So you also, if in any way a sudden conversion was displeasing to you, in order to show that you are not in disagreement with the norms set down by the holy fathers, you could, perhaps, tell the candidates something about a delay in entering the monastic life; but for those who have converted, God forbid that you tell them to retract what has irrevocably been undertaken. And since we have been speaking of women, why do we bring up the case of widows taking the veil when virgins, who have not yet been given the veil, if they have only pretended to remain in the state of virginity, are strictly forbidden to presume entering marriage? About these Pope Innocent says the following: "But those who have not been clothed with the veil, but who yet have represented themselves as permanently under the vow of chastity, even though they have not taken the veil, if they should nevertheless marry, they are to be recalled and must do penance, because they have been engaged to the Lord. For if the Apostle said that those who went back on their promise of widowhood 'would be condemned for mak-

---

56. Burchard, *Decretum* 8.36.798CD. See Ryan, *Sources* 35, no. 43, where Damian is shown to have misunderstood Burchard, and speaks of two Gelasian texts.

ing their original promise void,'⁵⁷ how much more they who have attempted to break their promise?"⁵⁸ And I too say, following the authoritative words of the venerable Innocent, that if the Apostle considered those worthy of condemnation who merely annulled their promise of widowhood, what should be said of those, or, indeed, what should they be called who desert the world, abandon their possessions, offer themselves voluntarily to their Creator, submit themselves to the authority of others, and, to appear completely dead to the world, put on the habit of mortification and holiness?

(34) Now, what we have been saying about women is not, I think, out of line with the purpose of this work. Remembering the statement made above, that the same law applies both to men and to women, my remarks extend also to the feminine sex, because the evil practice which we detect now growing among men may, I fear, eventually also spread to women. And since, as in the case of the former, I have tried to weed the garden with the hoe of invective, so also in the latter instance I hasten to block its germination so that it will not sprout, and that like an evil seed that sprouts prematurely, it be forced to die before it can grow, and wither away of itself before it springs up to full bloom.

(35) I should now like to turn my attention for a moment to what was said above and, putting aside the statements of the Fathers, argue with my adversary in my own words about the points I have already made, so that he who was thrown into disarray by the powerful authority of so many canonical arguments may also very likely be overcome by my reasoning. Thus may the circle of arguments everywhere seal his deceiving lips that he be forced forever to avoid such perverse teaching. In so doing, may it be rightly said of me that I did not give the sinner the advantage;⁵⁹ and of my opponent may we properly sing with the psalmist, "For the mouths of those speaking evil things are silenced."⁶⁰

---

57. Cf. 1 Tim 5.11–12.
58. Burchard, *Decretum* 8.12, *Ex decretis Innocentii papae* 20.794BC (JK 286). See Ryan, *Sources* 35f., no. 44.
59. Cf. 1 Macc 2.48.   60. Ps 63.11.

(36) Come now, what is it you say: "That unless a person has, following the *Rule*, gone through a long probation for the space of one year, even though he was converted as a result of sickness, he should be absolutely free to return to the world"?[61] Should such an opinion which refers to those who are healthy also hold for those who are sick? But anyone, even a man who is not in his right mind, can see that a sick man, or one at the point of death, is absolutely unable to fulfill this condition. If, therefore, St. Benedict included all alike in this statement, it is perfectly clear that he shut the door of conversion in the face of the weak and decrepit who cannot rise to bear this burden. But who could tolerate anything like that to be thought of this holy man, to whom not only this notion, but every other virulently wicked heresy as well was foreign, or, rather, filled with the Holy Spirit, was so obviously outstanding and confirmed by miracles? Who would allow it to be said that by accepting the heresy of the Novatians[62] he brought men to the brink of despair, when by the purity of his teaching he was daily seen leading countless souls to the hope of eternal life? We must therefore admit that the force of this precept touches only the healthy and in no way pertains to the sick.

(37) But if someone who is not ill has entered the monastic order without probation, will our good bishop say that he is never to go back on his word? Tell me, I ask, have you never read that a vow to lead the monastic life is a second baptism?[63] But since it is clear that this statement is found in the writings of the Fathers, one is not permitted to deny it. You are also not unaware that it is commanded by the decretal law of the

---

61. See *Benedicti regula* 58.9, 58.12, and 58.13.147f.
62. For reference to the Novatian heresy, see Isidore, *Etym.* 8.5.34.
63. This is a common statement in patristic literature. For an extended treatment of the subject, see Reindel, *Briefe* 1.295–296, n. 18. See Jerome, *Epistula* 130.7, ed. I. Hilberg, CSEL 56 (1918), 186; H. Hantsch, "Die 'Abrenuntiatio' im Taufritus und die Mönchsprofess, ihre Beziehungen zu einander und zu zeitgenössischen Rechtsanschauungen." *Österreichisches Archiv für Kirchenrecht* 11 (1960), 161–89, esp. 183f. Damian's reference to a second baptism in Letter 31 equates the sacrament with entrance into the clerical state. But in Letter 90 he repeats the statement found here in Letter 38.

ancients that one proceed to the grace of baptism over rather long intervals of time. And if I may briefly refer to the order of ecclesiastical practice, just as there are seven gifts of the Holy Spirit, so there are also seven gifts of baptism, namely, from the first food in the form of consecrated salt and the entrance into the Church down to the confirmation of the Holy Spirit through chrism; all of these, as is often the practice, should be arranged to extend over long periods of time.[64] But if someone did not observe the longer intervals and suddenly rushed ahead to receive the fullness of baptism, would you pronounce, I ask, this baptism invalid? Do you teach that this man should disdain the whole gift that he has received and, that he might be saved, must still approach the mystery of purification? Speak! Answer! Do you think that this man can rightly repeat the baptismal washing just because he dared to rush headlong into baptism without observing the proper procedure? Why are you silent? One who is so keen to speak his mind on all occasions should not be quiet if he has something sensible to say. But I have no doubt that you will firmly agree that this baptism is so certain and valid that it would surely be sacrilegious and totally wicked if someone so baptized should be recalled to the same sacrament of regeneration. It follows, therefore, that what you are forced to admit about the first baptism you must also inevitably agree to in regard to the second, namely, the monastic vows. And just as the first, once it has been received, may not be repeated, so also the second may not, by any construction of the law, be despised.

(38) But tell me, I ask, which of the saints, or which of the church fathers entered monastic life with this kind of probation of which you so insolently speak? Was it Anthony, or Paul, or Hilarion?[65] Do we read that St. Benedict himself, who, as you falsely state, seems to command these things, came to the monastic life after observing this type of proba-

---

64. Burchard, *Decretum* 17.44.928BD (JE 2003); see Ryan, *Sources* 36, no. 46; also Fuhrmann, *Fälschungen* 138 n. 6 and 263 n. 67.
65. On Damian's knowledge of the lives of these saints, see Dressler, *Petrus Damiani* 62f.; Della Santa, *Idea monastica* 174f.

tion? Scan all the sound histories of antiquity, I beg you, and since you will be unable to come up with even one who was tried by such a long period of probation, you will be forced to admit that you have been completely overcome and are deservedly subjected to the derision of the victor. Indeed, how can you pass over with arrogant disdain all the examples of the ancients, all the deeds of the Fathers, and with contempt for all of them so obstinately restrict yourself to one central opinion?[66] For if there is no doubt about their sanctity, we must consequently imitate them. And if they are not to be imitated, then it follows that they are not holy. Do you know, my worthy opponent, where your learned opinion is leading? You are being forced to admit that either our holy fathers were not holy after all, or those who now come to the monastic life are not in particular need of probation. Let your delirious tongue be ashamed, and since it is unable to be eloquent let it learn at least to be quiet. Since it does not know how to say anything useful let it learn at least to be harmlessly silent. This perverse speech of yours spreads like a cancer, and if one member does not cut it out with the sharp knife of reproof, it will doubtless spread like a disease to the healthy members of the Church.

(39) But perhaps you will answer to all of this, and say, "Why, therefore, is this probation commonly prescribed if it is generally not observed?" And I will ask you, "Tell me, who is it that requires that one come to the monastic life and forces him to undergo this probation, and yet is also of the opinion that if he came in some other way he might leave the monastic order? And since you are unable to indicate this, it is right that you agree that it was stated more as a wise precaution against wanderers and ambiguous characters than as an authoritative precept. And this can readily be detected if you will carefully read only the beginning of the sentence that speaks of the subject we are discussing. For it says, "When

---

66. It is uncertain whether Damian here refers to specific works on antiquity and the Fathers. The library catalog of Fonte Avellana, a document of the twelfth century, contains titles that would fit this reference. See Vitaletti, *La biblioteca* 76; Pierucci, *Inventari* 168, 171.

one first comes to conversion he should not be readily granted entrance, but as the Apostle says, 'test his spirit to see if it comes from God.' "[67] From which it is obvious that if one approaches conversion called by the Holy Spirit, he has no need of such a long period of probation. Surely, once you are certain that the spirit of deceit is not present, the probationary period should cease. If it is clear that the importuning spirit is he who says, "I stand at the door and knock,"[68] then certainly for him no delay is required, no probation should be set, and he who knocks should be allowed to enter at once. And finally, as we can gather from the Apostle's words cited above, "test his spirit to see if it comes from God," this testing is more necessary for him who receives the petitioner than for him who enters; that is, that the one receiving should be able to discern the kind of spirit that impels the aspirant. Nor is it useful to engage in probation when he who is to be proven is clearly known. For we light a lamp when there is something hidden that we do not see; but once the hidden thing is seen, we then put out the light. Just so, when we are in doubt about one's intention and about the purpose that leads him on, it is quite important that he be tested. But when his conscience stands fully revealed, probation becomes an empty exercise.

(40) Moreover, since on the testimony of the same book of the *Rule,* almost all these matters are left to the discretion and authority of the abbot,[69] when one comes to conversion in the manner commanded him by the abbot, how shameless, how inconsiderate and tasteless it would be to assert that this conversion should be judged invalid. Certainly again, the same *Rule* commands that there always be strangers and guests at the abbot's table.[70] But since at times the heads of cenobite houses do not follow this injunction to curb the excessive drinking and high spirits of some of the monks, would you say that they should be removed from office? They, indeed,

---

67. *Benedicti regula* 58.1–2.146; 1 John 4.1.
68. Rev. 3.20.
69. See *Benedicti regula* 58.19.149.
70. *Benedicti regula* 56.1.144.

who carefully look to the mind of the holy doctor, make light of following the superficial meaning of words. And while they think over the inner message of the life-giving spirit, they trample the chaff of the letter that kills.[71] But since in the case of Scripture, because of the refinement of meaning, you do not hesitate to accept the inner sense of the words, so consequently you should agree that it is also necessary to do the same regarding the conversion of a monk.

(41) Now that we have built an impregnable defense with the dressed stones of our arguments, it remains for us at the end of this little work to lock the gate, as it were, with the key of syllogism. It is clear, therefore, that all who have received the habit of monastic profession were converted either by their own decision, or by force, or after being deceived by clever persuasion. But those who were voluntarily converted, came to the monastery either after passing through probation or rushed ahead without encountering the period of trial. But it has already been established above by the authority of many canons that whoever were converted either voluntarily, or by force, or by deception, whether with probation or without it, excepting him who did not have the consent and promise of his wife,[72] in every case must all be made to persevere in the monastic profession which they have accepted. We must therefore conclude that all who received the habit of monastic profession, except for those converted without their wife's permission and promise, no matter how they may have come to this way of life, are wholly required to remain faithful to the vocation that they have undertaken.

(42) So there, I think, you find yourself so bound by the evidence of the Catholic fathers and surrounded by so much obvious and reasonable truth, and are so hedged in on all sides that you can find nothing more to say in opposition to all this and are completely unable ever again to take up the fight. Therefore surrender and confess that you did not know what you were saying, that you are completely disenchanted

---

71. Cf. 2 Cor 3.6.
72. John the Deacon, *Sancti Gregorii magni vita* 4.41.203CD.

with your own opinion, and that, in fact, you are prepared to use all diligence in retracting what you so inconsiderately proposed, so that with the help of God you may recall to right living those who on your account have fallen into error. Let your learning now change sides in this battle and strive earnestly to stand up for those whom once you so bitterly opposed that for the glory of God it may be said of you, as of Paul, "Is not this the man who organized the attack in Jerusalem against the people who were invoking this name?"[73]

(43) Please pardon what I have said, venerable bishop, whoever you may be, and if I have been sharp in my babbling against you, if I have been bitter in my agitation, do not take it for a kind of arrogance, but be pleased to forgive the zeal for justice I displayed. For if by my effort even one thorn of error can be removed from the pasture land of holy Church, I will not hesitate to provoke the odium of anyone who thinks ill of me. Nor should you be ashamed to correct your error at the reproof of a brother younger[74] than you, since you know that the least of the apostles opposed the prince of the apostles to his face.[75] And if, perhaps, you should reply that Paul, although he was the least, was still a fellow apostle, while I am not a fellow bishop, hear what God says to men: "Come now," he says, "and reprove me."[76] Therefore, if God invites men to reprove him, it is quite proper that a man corrected by another should calmly bear with a zeal born of fraternal charity.

---

73. Acts 9.21.
74. At the age of 44, Peter could still think of himself as a "younger brother."
75. Cf. Gal 2.11; 1 Cor 15.9.   76. Isa 1.18.

LETTER 39

Peter Damian to the canons of the cathedral of Fano. Having heard that a schism had occurred among them, some living in common, while the majority preferred to reside in their own lodgings, Damian exhorts them as a doctor of the spiritual life to return to community living. This letter is altogether exhortatory, differing radically in tone from the reforming piece (Letter 98) he would write twelve years later, in 1063.

(ca. 1051)[1]

O THE HOLY BRETHREN in Christ, the clerics of the church of Fano,[2] the monk Peter the sinner sends greetings.

(2) It is some time, my dear friends, since it became known in our area that dissension and strife had broken out among you over this problem, namely, that some of you undertook to live by the rule in a house of canons,[3] but that most of you did not agree to this, wishing only to reside individually in their own lodgings. I am not surprised, because this is hardly rare; but it pains me the more since it is improper.[4] Indeed, it seems quite absurd for one to pretend to be a cleric living

---

1. For the date see Miccoli, *Chiesa Gregoriana* 82.
2. Laqua, *Traditionen* 92, n. 188, discusses the effort of Bishop Arduin of Fano to enhance the common life of his clergy. One of the bishops of Fano, castigated by Damian as a thief in Letter 26, was deposed by Pope Gregory VI (JL 4247; *ItPont* 4.185, no. 4). On the canons of Fano, see V. Bartoccetti, "La lettera di S. Pier Damiani ai canonici di Fano," *Studia Picena* 15 (1940), 89–96; Prete, *S. Pier Damiani*, 119–128; Miccoli, *Chiesa Gregoriana* 75–100.
3. Whether Damian had a specific canonical rule in mind, is uncertain. On canonical rules in the eleventh century see C. Dareine, "Vie commune, règle de saint Augustin et chanoines réguliers au XIe siècle," RHE 41 (1946), 365–406, esp. 373, 389, 401. Damian himself in Letter 98, is more brisk than he is here in proposing remedies for canonical abuses.
4. On this state of affairs see F. Poggiaspalla, "La vita commune del clero dalle origini alla riforma Gregoriana," *Uomini e dottrine* 14 (1968), 138f.; on this letter of Damian see especially 152f.

a regular life, and to maintain a secular life style, and for one who by religious profession is separated from seculars it is a shame if his private life or the abominable possession of private property should prove that he is a layman.

(3) For what can satisfy his greed if the possession of God himself is not enough for him? Since a cleric, indeed, according to the etymology of that word, is God's very lot,[5] so Almighty God is thus shown also to be his fortune. To this point Jeremiah says, "My heart said: the Lord is all that I have; therefore I will wait for him patiently."[6] And elsewhere God said, "You are the work of my hands, Israel my possession."[7] Therefore, if a cleric is God's property and God is his, it would seem that he who is eager to accumulate earthly money over and above this exceptional endowment, grievously insults his Creator. In the book of Numbers God commanded Moses regarding the Levites: "You shall reserve the Levites for me in substitution for the eldest sons of the Israelites—I am the Lord—and in the same way the Levites' cattle for the firstborn cattle of the Israelites."[8] And again, "Take the Levites as a substitute for all the eldest sons in Israel and the cattle of the Levites as a substitute for their cattle. The Levites shall be mine. I am the Lord, let them observe my commandments,"[9] as if he were quite evidently saying, As I claim them in a special way as my very own, so I decree that they are to be in my service without ever subjecting themselves to any worldly way of life, nor will I allow them like servants to be basely under the yoke of secular affairs, since they are dedicated to my service and are endowed with the noble title of freeborn.

(4) We should further note that the Lord claimed as his own not only the Levites but also their cattle, that he might clearly teach us that those who are bound to ecclesiastical ser-

---

5. Jerome, *Epistula* 52.5.421; Isidore, *Etym.* 7.12.2; Papias, *Vocabularium latinum* 67; R. Klinck, "Die lateinische Etymologie des MA." *Medium Aevum. Philologische Studien* 17 (1970), 82f.
6. Lam 3.24.
7. Isa 19.25; for variants from the *Vulgate*, see *Biblia sacra* 13.93.
8. Num 3.41; cf. *Biblia sacra* 3.89.
9. Num 3.45; cf. *Biblia sacra* 3.90.

vice owe God not only their earnest devotion and labor, but also the ownership of whatever property they might possess, and that they must recognize that they and all they have are not theirs, but belong to God. For to the clerics of our day it seems—I am speaking of some of them—to be a minor matter if by their carnal living they withhold from God what is theirs, so long as they do not also retire from the Church's official prayers and the administration of the sacraments by living in the midst of the narrow streets and marketplaces. Indeed, they think it more delightful to smell of the innkeeper's tavern than to daily frequent God's sanctuary, more pleasing to watch the women at their weaving than to busy themselves with the pages of Sacred Scripture. After he was weaned, the boy Samuel never returned home with his parents, but constantly remained in the service of the temple.[10] To retain his purity and innocence, John at a tender age hurried away to the solitude of a dry wasteland and there received the grace of prophetic preaching, which while living in crowded areas he could not have obtained.[11] But now, on the contrary, those who are vowed to carrying on divine service, despise remote churches and desire to live amid the bustle of the noisy marketplace.

(5) But let us hear what God's authority prescribed about the encampment of the Levites, and thus we can learn where clerics should especially live. "You shall not," he said, "record the total number of the tribe of Levi or make a detailed list of them among the Israelites, but you shall put them in charge of the Tabernacle of the Tokens, with all its vessels and whatever belongs to divine service. They shall carry the tabernacle and all its equipment; they shall be its attendants and shall pitch their tents around it."[12] And a little further on after he had stated, "The sons of Israel shall pitch their tents, each one according to his troop and squadron and army."[13] Then he continued, "But the Levites shall encamp

---

10. Cf. 1 Sam 1.1.
11. Cf. Matt 3.1; Mark 1.4; Luke 3.2.
12. Num 1.49–50.   13. Num 1.52.

around the tabernacle."[14] Therefore, if the Levites at God's command were to encamp near the tabernacle and were not allowed to withdraw from the tabernacle or live among the multitude, why do clerics now abhor living near their church, as God's Law requires, so that they may more freely and undisturbedly spend their time meditating on the word of God? At least they should give to the Church, made illustrious by the splendor of grace that flows from the Gospels, the service which the Levites rendered the tabernacle, shrouded in the darkness of ignorance by figures and mysteries. Surely it would be highly preposterous if we were now to deny the same reverence to the truth which formerly was given to a foreshadowing image. For the Lord testified that the tabernacle was not the truth, but was only a copy of the truth, when he commanded Moses, "See that you work to the design which you were shown on the mountain."[15] Hence, what Moses saw on the mountain was the truth that is ours; what the Israelites made as their tabernacle was only the figure of the truth. In those days the ministers of the tabernacle ate manna and were surely to die; but in the Church of Christ we receive the sacraments and will live for all eternity. And Paul says of the Church, that "it is the real sanctuary, the tent pitched by God and not by man."[16] Concerning the temple of Solomon, moreover, of which we read that it was constantly and elaborately served by its ministers since you are hardly unaware of this, I think it superfluous to write about it. Who will not have clearly noted the account, especially in the book of Chronicles, that Solomon, "following the practice of his father David, drew up the roster of service for the priests and that for the Levites for leading the praise and for waiting upon the priests, as each day required, and that for the doorkeepers at each gate"?[17]

(6) Therefore, if those who by the prescription of the Law

---

14. Num 1.53.
15. Cf. Exod 25.40; Heb 8.5. Damian seems to have conflated these two texts in his citation.
16. Heb 8.2; for Damian's variants from the *Vulgate*, see Sabatier 3.919.
17. 2 Chr 8.14.

were bound by marriage ties, showed such diligence in the service of their holy places, what should now be done by clerics who, indeed, endowed with the purity of chastity, are freed from the bonds of all carnal intercourse? Clearly, how can one deserve to be called a canon unless he lives by his rule? How can he be called a monk unless, in keeping with his name, he is also solitary? These wish to have the name of canon, that is, of a regular, but not to live regularly. These seek to share in the Church's common property, but reject the idea of living in community near their church. Certainly, this is not the pattern of the Early church,[18] and it deviates greatly from the discipline of apostolic origin by which all were united in heart and soul, sold their land and laid the money at the feet of the apostles, and distributed it to each according to his need. Not a man of them claimed any of his possessions as his own, but everything was held in common.[19] The prodigal son, on the contrary, said to his father, "Give me the share that is coming to me,"[20] and then wasted all his money on prostitutes. Here, indeed, we see the line drawn between the chosen and the damned, since the former are happy to have what is theirs in common with others. But the latter in breaking the bonds of charity, certainly deprive their brothers of the things they have in common. For when property is divided, there is certainly no unity in spirit. Clearly, charity produces community, while avarice leads to disunity. Hence also Luke says, "A man from the crowd said to Jesus"—he was not one of the great, but from the crowd, for he was befouled with the stinking filth of avarice: "Master," he said, "tell my brother to divide the family property with me." When Jesus answered, "My good man, who set me over you to judge or arbitrate," he promptly said to those who were standing by, "Beware! Be on your guard against greed of every kind, because when a man has more than enough, his wealth does not give him life."[21] By these words Truth clearly shows that some men long to divide common property

---

18. For this concept, see Miccoli, *Chiesa Gregoriana* 225–299.
19. Cf. Acts 4.32–35.   20. Luke 15.12.
21. Luke 12.13–15.

because they burn with the fire of cupidity and greed. Ananias and Sapphira were struck down bodily by the sentence of death, not because they divided up common property, but because by retaining something that was theirs they did not share it with others.[22] Because Judas was not content to have money in common with the others, he fell into the depths of betrayal and lost his position in the community of the apostles.[23] By breaking company with Abraham and dividing their possessions, Lot was compelled to endure the harsh servitude of the barbarians.[24] Esau with his attachment to hunting, by running about through the woodlands lost his birthright. Jacob by simply living among the tents received the fullness of his father's blessing.[25]

(7) In the monastic life, those whom we observe living by the rule in the cloisters under the authority of an abbot, we indeed call monks. But those whom we see having their own property, indiscriminately running about here and there, lawlessly living in a dissolute way according to their whims, we judge worthy of being called vagabonds, or better, unruly vagrants, rather than monks.[26] Therefore, as there are vagrant monks, so also are there vagrant clerics. But the Lord says, "He who is not with me is against me, and he who does not gather with me scatters."[27] Now those who do not gather with God by practicing brotherly love, and thus rend the pouch of men's souls by spreading discord, lose the fruits of their virtues, if there be any at all, which as it were they spill out through the breach. And so Solomon says of the foolish man, that "he gathered wealth and put it into a purse with a hole in it."[28]

(8) Moreover, we not only call schismatics those who break up the unity of the faith, but those too who by the vice of

22. Cf. Acts 5.1–10.
23. Cf. Matt 26.14–25; Mark 14.10–20; Luke 22.1–21; John 13.18–26.
24. Cf. Gen 13.5–12; 14.10–12.
25. Cf. Gen 27.
26. See *Benedicti regula* 1.19.
27. Luke 11.23; cf. Matt 12.30.
28. Hag 1.6. Here Damian mistakenly attributes this citation from Haggai to Solomon.

pride or avarice remove themselves from fraternal love. Nor is faith a greater virtue than love. For since God is love, and he who dwells in love is dwelling in God,[29] he who fails in charity is to be no less censured than he who wanders from the faith. If one were to observe all the commandments, but should fail in one, that is in charity, he is guilty of all, and is thus shown to be liable also for heresy. Surely, if according to the words of Peter "the devil, like a roaring lion, prowls around looking for someone to devour,"[30] he who deserts the sheepfold of fraternal community willingly subjects himself to the teeth of the cruel beast. When a heifer grazes with the herd, it does not fear the attack of the wolf; but when it takes off on its own to wander through the woodlands, it will certainly satisfy some wild beast's hunger. When geese fly in formation they pay little heed to the falcon; but should one of them ever lag behind, it will be pierced through by the falcon's beak and will not escape its claws. When bees are in their hives they produce honey, and so long as they stay together, the sweet product of the honeycomb, which is their work, can be placed before kings; but if they go off alone and fly about like rogues without their leader, they will surely suffer from hunger.[31] If one is surrounded by the enemy and leaves the tightly drawn battle line, he exposes himself to the enemy and becomes a target for his arrows. The Church of Christ, as prophetic evidence attests,[32] provides strongholds of God which enemy attack will not invade, so long as the knights of Christ, armed with the weapons of virtue, rally together in love and unity of spirit. But whoever becomes an unfortunate imitator of Achan and is separated from these knights by coveting silver or a bar of gold, will be stoned in keeping with the sentence of the true Joshua and all the people.[33]

(9) Wherefore, my dear friends, I implore you in your ho-

---

29. Cf. 1 John 4.8 and 4.16.   30. 1 Pet 5.8.
31. Here Damian appears to follow the notion of antiquity and the earlier Middle Ages that bees were led by kings. See Verg. *Georg* 4.168; Isidore, *Etym.* 12.83.
32. Cf. Gen 32.2.   33. Cf. Josh 7.24–25.

liness to throw away the leaven of the Pharisees.[34] With the patriarch Abraham, leave the home of your birth,[35] and gather together with the apostles in the upper room near the church.[36] With those true renouncers of wealth, Barnabas and Stephen,[37] put all that you have to common use that the Holy Spirit may justly deign to visit you, living in brotherly unity. "You are the salt of the earth," but as Truth itself says, "If salt becomes tasteless, how is its saltiness to be restored?"[38] With just a little salt much is sweetened, and by a small number of clerics the multitude of the entire Christian people is instructed and informed. Just as the bishops are known to have obtained the primacy of the twelve apostles, so too priests in the Church represent the order of the seventy disciples.[39] This very thing is figuratively indicated by the encampment of the Israelites at Elim.[40] For twelve apostolic springs of water were flowing there, which would water the parched hearts of men with the flood of God's word. Seventy palm trees flourished there, just the number of the disciples, who would bring the palms of Christ's victory to a world oppressed by the slavery of the devil's tyranny. The springs, to be sure, watered the palm trees, since the holy bishops overflow with the words on which the rest of the priests in the Church thrive without interruption in the hope of heavenly reward. Now those who in number are ten times seven, seem to indicate that the decalog is fulfilled by the sevenfold grace of the Holy Spirit.[41] And so when the Lord sent these seventy

34. Cf. Matt 16.6.
35. Cf. Gen 12.4.
36. Cf. Acts 2.1.
37. This observation clearly alludes to Barnabas' divestment of property (Acts 4.36–37), and to Stephen's change of lifestyle to engage in missionary work (Acts 6) that led to his martyrdom (Acts 7.59).
38. Matt 5.13.
39. On the symbolic use of these numbers, see P. Mandonnet, *Saint Dominique. L'idée, l'homme et l'oeuvre*, ed. and rev. M. H. Vicaire and R. Ladner 2 (1937), 170. See also Miccoli, *Chiesa Gregoriana* 84. Mandonnet 171, n. 11 refers to a similar eleventh-century use of this number symbolism in *Capitula incerti auctoris ad ecclesiae regimen congesta* 1 (Mansi 19.704).
40. Cf. Num 33.9.
41. See the *Decretum Gelasianum* 1, ed. E. von Dobschütz, *Des Decretum Gelasianum in libris recipiendis et non recipiendis* JU 38.4 (1912), 21.239f.

disciples two by two to go before him, and after admonishing them that they who were to teach others should themselves live blamelessly, he stated at the outset of their mission as a most necessary principle, that they should despise money, avoid the filth of avarice, and not possess personal property. "Carry no purse or pack," he said, "and travel barefoot."[42] In Mark he also forbade them to take bread, to have money in their belts, or to have a second coat, but with sandals on their feet they should go on their journey carrying only a stick.[43] Why was this done? Was it only for their benefit? But come now, if it was done just for them, why was it recorded in writing unless it was also for us? "For whatever was written, was written for our own instruction."[44]

(10) So why do we read these words in our churches if it is not that the things that we read we should also carry out in deeds? It was necessary especially for those who, throughout the changing times of succeeding centuries, should take their place in office to live in accord with their example. Hence God forbids his preachers to possess any earthly thing, so that those who are appointed to extinguish the flames of greed in the hearts of their audience should themselves take care not to loosen the reins on their own ambition and avarice and thus cause disaster to others. To this we may add that often on his trips the minister of the altar meets up with a beautiful woman and experiences a rising passion. For when leaving for the church or while returning home, suddenly the evil spirit lays a snare by conjuring up the vision of living with a woman, or deceptively presents a seductive face for him to look at. But how dare one in conscience approach God's altar if he is incited by greed or passion? And so it was that the sons of Aaron were destroyed by fire that came from God because they dared to offer the Lord an illicit fire. For it is written: "Now Nadab and Abihu, sons of Aaron, took their censers, put fire in them, threw incense on the fire, and presented before the Lord fire which he had not commanded.

42. Luke 10.4.
43. Cf. Mark 6.8–9.
44. Rom 15.4.

Fire came out from before the Lord and destroyed them; and so they died in the presence of the Lord."⁴⁵ The Lord's altars will not accept illicit fire, but only that of the love of God. And he himself spoke of this: "I have come to set fire to the earth, and how I wish it were already kindled!"⁴⁶ And so whoever burns with the fire of worldly or carnal passion in the censer of his heart, and does not fear to take part in the sacred mysteries, will, as a result, doubtless be consumed by the fire of divine vengeance, of which Scripture says, "And now fire will consume his enemies."⁴⁷ It is quite impossible, my brothers, for one who is burdened with fiscal responsibilities, who by living among and conversing with throngs of people is daily involved in their affairs, to take part in the sacred mysteries with heart unsullied. It is in these awesome sacraments, to be sure, that heaven opens and the angelic powers associate with men. What purity, therefore, must clerics possess, how spotless they must be, and finally, how removed from every stain of secular affairs, since as companions and members of the same household they consort with angels and share God's work as distributors of his heavenly sacraments.

(11) I am speaking here, not only of priests, but of all clerics who from whatever grade of the ministry derive their rights to serve the altar. For even though he himself be pure, he is often contaminated by associating with evil men. Surely, if this did not occur in some cases, the prophet would never have complained: "Woe is me," he said, "for I am a man of unclean lips and I dwell among a people of unclean lips."⁴⁸ Obviously he stated that he was of unclean lips because he lived among those who had unclean lips. Moses is known to have endured this very thing in the land of Midian, when he subtly inquired why the Lord wished to kill him. For it is written: "During the journey, while Moses was encamped for

---

45. Lev 10.1–2.
46. Luke 12.49; for the variant, see Sabatier 3.324.
47. Heb 10.27.
48. Isa 6.5. Damian omits "because I have held my peace," that follows "me" in the *Vulgate*.

the night, the Lord met him, meaning to kill him."[49] It is most astonishing to read that the Lord suddenly wished to kill him, when he had already made him his close confidant and associate, revealing to him the secrets of his plans and purposes, which now he directed to be carried out in obedience to him. But without a doubt we are led to believe that from his extended stay among the Midianites he had contracted some stain of sin, and was therefore to be cleansed by terror and by a correction of his neglect since for the correction of others he was to become the bearer of heavenly commands. His wife Zipporah wisely understood this, and Scripture at once goes on to say of her, "Then Zipporah picked up a sharp flint and cut off her son's foreskin."[50] It would surely have been absurd if Moses had appeared to be a gentile in the person of his son, since he himself was an Israelite. Therefore, he who is to instruct others in the way of holiness must be most careful lest, which God forbid, he appear to take the false path in anything. And thus it happened that the Israelites burned with zeal for justice in avenging the crime of Benjamin, and still that same people fell before the swords of Benjamin.[51] Who is not surprised that when twice the Lord was asked, he twice approved their attack against Benjamin, and still twenty-two thousand Israelites fell in the first engagement, and eighteen thousand in the second.[52]

(12) What should we understand about these happenings, what should we think but that they who seek to attack the malady of another's wickedness must first be cured of the swelling of their own wound, so that they who are quick to purge the evil in others, should themselves be cleansed by taking vengeance on themselves? As it says in the Gospels, "That one of you who is faultless should throw the first stone at her."[53] And so it was right that when consulting with the Lord, they should say, "Who of our army shall lead the attack against the sons of Benjamin," and he should answer, "Judah

---

49. Exod 4.24.
50. Exod 4.25.
52. Cf. Judg 20.18–25.
51. Cf. Judg 20.8–11.
53. John 8.7.

shall attack first;"⁵⁴ for since Judah is interpreted to mean confession,⁵⁵ it was proper that Judah should lead this battle, so that they who would help others to confess their sins should first seek to correct their own faults through confession.

(13) Wherefore, my friends, if you would stand before the people of God as possessing the words of life, a people for whom you were appointed to give good example and among whom you should shine as lights in this world; if you should wish, I repeat, to gather a harvest of souls among them and call back the errant to the right path of religious practice, you should first straighten what is awry in your own lives, if that be necessary, and gathering in the school of Christ, you should remain together in a common way of life and in unanimity of spirit. There should be among you no separate housing, no division of purpose, no distinction in property. Always remember that the Lord disapproved of an altar built of hewn stones: "For if you use a chisel on it, you will profane it."⁵⁶ They indeed are hewn stones who refuse to live together in fraternity, who are unwilling to live with their brothers and act together in unity. Christ does not incorporate such as these into his own body, because he considers them cut off from unity with his members. Rather the altar should be built of stones such as those to which the apostle Peter referred: "Come, and let yourselves be built, as living stones, into a spiritual temple."⁵⁷ For such a temple the Lord is surely the foundation, and besides him no other can be laid;⁵⁸ he is the summit who has become the chief cornerstone.⁵⁹ In addition, was it only idly that the Lord commanded, "Do not store up for yourselves treasure on earth, where it grows rusty and moth-eaten, and thieves break in to steal it"?⁶⁰ Who, I ask, will accept this command if the cleric does not observe it? Will it be married people with children to feed, and who by God's

---

54. Judg 20.18.
55. Cf. Jerome, *Nom. hebr.* 61.27 (CC 72.136).
56. Exod 20.25. 57. 1 Pet 2.5.
58. Cf. 1 Cor 3.11. 59. Cf. Ps 118.22.
60. Matt 6.19.

command pay their tithes? He who offers gifts, as Paul says, "must have something to offer."[61] Then how can one who is required to chant in choir concentrate on his prayers if he is concerned with purses and wallets which some daring hand might snatch; if he worries whether his storerooms and barns are served by thieves, or whether the bars on the doors are strong enough to resist entry, and if he fears that thieves will always be breaking in? I may perhaps be lying, but can Truth lie when it says, "For where your treasure is, there will your heart be also"?[62] Or perhaps might it be thought better if they were to recite the divine office in their rooms, and not laboring so far away could seek God in the same place they keep their property, so that when it is said to them, "Where your treasure is, there will your heart be also," one could add, not inappropriately, "There will your God be also"?

(14) But since this is no laughing matter, but rather something to be deplored, I beg you, my dear brothers and lords, do not make light of my observations, but come together in the school of Christ under the teaching of the Holy Spirit, so that, as he promised, he might be with you now and until the end of time,[63] and may afterwards lead you to a happy reward in the glory of his Father. I might perhaps displease some of you, in that while striving to compel others to live within the bounds of the regular life, I myself exceed the limits of epistolary brevity. But the reader is well rewarded, even if he criticizes the ineptitude of the writer, so long as he in the meantime wisely profits from his advice.

61. Heb 8.3.
62. Matt 6.21; cf. Luke 12.34.
63. Cf. Matt 28.20.

LETTER 40

Peter Damian to Henry, the archbishop of Ravenna. Since 1047 the question of the validity of simoniacal ordinations had been exercising the Roman curia. Two schools of thought on this matter were found among the advisers of Pope Leo IX: one, that clerics who had been ordained by simonists must be reordained, the opinion of those agreeing with Cardinal Humbert of Silva Candida;[1] the other, opposing reordination, held by those represented by Peter Damian. In the Roman synod of 1051 Leo had asked all the bishops for their opinion, and in this letter Damian responds to the pope's request. His investigation, based on canon law and historical precedent, led him to the conclusion that ordinations by simonists were valid. Perhaps his most celebrated work, this letter is called the *Liber gratissimus*, "because it was written about those who had been ordained gratis by simonists."[2]

(Summer 1052, *addendum* 1061)[3]

1. Humbert's work, *Libri tres adversus simoniacos*, ed. F. Thaner, MGH Ldl 1 (1891), 95–253; ed. also E. G. Robison, *Humberti cardinalis libri tres adversus simoniacos*, Ph.D. Diss. (Princeton, 1971), is the counterpiece to Damian's *Liber gratissimus*. Whether Damian was the unnamed adversary of the first book of Humbert's work, is highly disputed; see Reindel, *Briefe* 1.432f., n. 82. But there can be little doubt that Damian's ideas were the target of Humbert's wrath. On the other hand, Damian does not name Humbert as his opponent. In his other works Damian is ambivalent regarding Humbert. In his Letter 72 he says of him, perhaps ironically, "These things were told me by Archbishop Humbert, whose words seem to be grounded in apostolic truth." Perhaps also the couplet, composed by Damian (Lokrantz, *L'opera poetica* 70, no. XCI), in which Humbert is placed, with the sheep, at the pope's right hand, while Damian is assigned to the left with the goats, is indicative of the stress that existed between them.

2. The title, *Liber gratissimus*, 'The Most Gratuitous Book,' was given to this work by Peter Damian himself. See his Letter 146: "And what I wrote in the little work I entitled *Liber gratissimus*." The meaning of this title is here described in a rubric from MS Paris BN Lat. 2470 (P1).

3. Lucchesi, *Vita* nos. 91–94, 2.157, assigned the dates accepted here. L. von Heinemann, *Liber gratissimus*, MGH Ldl 1 (1891), 15–75, dated the work for the summer of 1052. But because the MS base from which he worked was too limited, he supposed that the letter had appeared in three different editions. Reindel, however (*Briefe* 385–388, n. 3) has demonstrated that Letter 40, originally addressed to Henry, the archbishop of Ravenna, contained

Verses on Simonists

Simon the forger's anvil God destroys, his coinèd hoard,
He overturns his pestilential stalls.
The thief creeps through the postern gate defiled,
The shepherd freely comes by wideflung door.
Yet where the monger's criminous deals are not,
Nor purse swells heavy with its venal gold,
The vendor is no bar, for trade is clean.
Where money fails, what harm can wealth inflict,
Or damage to the trees a foulèd hand?
An ailing healer oft whole rice prescribes,
Lamed[4] sires boxers; blind, sighted brood beget,
Titans from bedfast, comely from gnarled have sprung.
Nor must the child with forebear's crime be charged.
Each bears his burden, free from another's stain.

The Work, Entitled "The Most Gratuitous Book," of the Lowly Monk, Peter Damian

TO SIR HENRY,[5] the venerable bishop of the see of Ravenna, Peter, the humblest servant of Christ's life-giving cross, sends greeting in that same mystery.

---

41 chapters, and that only the *Addendum*, explaining that he was now submitting it to the Holy See, was appended in 1061 after the Easter synod held in April of that year.

4. The Latin word used here is *mancipites*, a variant of *mancipedis* (?) meaning 'lame' or 'bearing guilt.' See Lokrantz 74 C, line 11, and n. to line 11.

5. Henry was chosen archbishop of Ravenna during Lent of 1052; see Hermann of Reichenau, *Chron.* 131. Lent of that year extended from 4 March to 19 April. His consecration did not occur till 14 March 1053 in Rimini; see Mabillon, *Annales* 538.743; Schwartz, *Bistümer* 157f. Lucchesi, *Vita* no. 91, is in error in stating that he was the vice chancellor of Emperor Henry III. Nothing is known of his background, though he was certainly German. J. Fleckenstein, *Die Hofkapelle der deutschen Könige* 2 (Schriften der MGH 16, 1966), 291, conjectures that Henry belonged to the staff of the royal chapel. On his reaction to Damian's dedication of this letter to him, see the *Addendum* at the end of Letter 40; see also Dressler, *Petrus Damiani* 108 n. 126, who thought that this letter might first have circulated anonymously; on which see Laqua, *Traditionen* 320f.

(2) Since by the gift of God you were recently consecrated bishop, I thought that no more appropriate literary offering could be presented to you than one written about bishops. I am sure that it has not escaped your holiness that for three years now a great discussion has occurred in three Roman synods[6] concerning those who were consecrated gratis by simonists,[7] and that grave doubt and confusion is expressed daily even in this region, especially since, in the growing atmosphere of uncertainty, it has come to the point that some bishops have reordained clerics who had been promoted by them. Wherefore, some of my brothers, urged on presumably by charity, demand and, if I can use the expression, compel me with the violence of their request to overcome my reluctance at this moment of necessity to be of some help, and at least to write some short treatise explaining my point of view in this matter. But for some time now I have declined, hoping first to receive permission from the most blessed bishop of the Apostolic See. It was delivered recently as he was about to journey this way.[8] For it was my view that I would be free to discuss any ecclesiastical subject if the authority to do so should come to me from the head of the Church himself. But since I remembered that in the last synod[9] the venerable pope had already asked all the bishops in the name of God, together to implore God's mercy, that he reveal to them in their doubt the decision that should be reached in this subtle matter, I

---

6. This reference is usually understood to include the three Roman synods held by Leo IX in 1049, 1050, and 1051. In these synods the attitude of the Holy See stiffened over the issue of the validity of simoniacal orders, and in this letter Damian himself states that Leo IX at first considered such orders invalid. But when the participants in the synod pointed out that administration of the sacraments would cease, far and wide, this position was altered. For full bibliographical coverage of this matter, see Reindel, *Briefe* 1.390–392, n. 9.

7. Damian here limits the discussion only to those who had received ordination from simonist bishops without paying for this service, and whether their orders were valid.

8. See Steindorff, *Heinrich III* 2.181, n. 8; Neukirch 95 maintains that this statement could refer only to Leo's trip from Benevento to Padua in July 1052. Lucchesi, *Vita* no. 91, citing JL 542f., states that Leo IX was in Padua in July/August 1052.

9. The synod of April 1051.

judged that it would be totally in compliance with his command if by word or in writing I should, with the help of God's grace, be able to solve such a knotty problem concerning the Church.[10] Wherefore, firmly hoping in him "Who opens the book and breaks its seals,"[11] I am setting forth to answer this question, and since I am not eloquent, with zeal for the charge delegated to me, I will at least attempt to communicate with gestures and nods where I do not know how to speak.

That Even Though Christ Bestows His Gifts Through Many, the Fullness of All Grace Still Remains in Him

(3) It is clear that from the very beginning of man's redemption Christ Jesus, the mediator between God and man, organized his Church in such fashion that, on the one hand, he distributed his spiritual gifts through ministers of his word, and still as their source retained within himself the fullness of all graces.[12] For the very apostle who says, "We have this treasure in earthen vessels,"[13] also acknowledged that "in the heart of Jesus are hid all the treasures of wisdom and knowledge."[14] If, however, all treasures without exception are found in the heart of Jesus, what then remains to be stored up in the earthen vessels of men? Yet what he possesses wholly by nature, they have through grace by partaking of him according to their capacity. For it has been said of them that "this is the work of one and the same Spirit, who distrib-

---

10. Even though he was not yet a bishop, Damian felt himself obliged to follow the pope's request. This might explain why he did not send his work directly to the pope, but to Archbishop Henry of Ravenna instead. Laqua, *Traditionen* 321f., referring to the salutation and to title XL, thinks that, besides requesting theological review of his work, Damian also clearly recognized Ravenna as a center of reform.
11. Rev 5.5.
12. See Augustine, *In Iohannis evangelium tractatus CXXIV*, ed. R. Willems, CC 36 (1954), 5.9,45; F. Seekel, *Geistige Grundlagen Petrus Damianis untersucht am Liber Gratissimus*, Ph.D. Diss. (Berlin, 1933), 36.
13. 2 Cor 4.7.
14. Col 2.3. For the variant "in the heart of Jesus," see *Beuron* 24.2 (1966–1971), 393, where the only other source is Bede, *Homeliarum evangelii libri duo* 1.9, ed. D. Hurst, CC 122 (1955), 61.

utes different gifts to different people just as he chooses."[15] But John the Baptist says of the only-begotten Son, "It is not by measure that God gives the Spirit":[16] and again, "Of his fullness we have all received."[17]

(4) Since, therefore, all the just draw their vital energy from this one source, it is always necessary for them to go back to him with gratitude. They are convinced that they cannot receive the gifts of divine grace from any other, unless he from whom they certainly derive bestows them. They, indeed, who deem themselves indebted to man and not to God for divine favor, must necessarily wither away in their weakness just as if they had been deprived of moisture from its source. Nor are they able to produce moisture of themselves so long as they forget to draw from the prime fullness of the source for the abundance of their growth. Hence Solomon aptly says, "Into the sea all rivers go, and yet the sea is never filled, and still to their source the rivers return that they may flow again."[18] Luke the evangelist mystically describes this ebb and flow of spiritual streams when he says that "after Jesus had called the twelve apostles together, he gave them power and authority over all devils and to cure diseases, and he sent them out to proclaim the kingdom of God."[19] Notice here the flow of the rivers. And afterwards he added, "On their return the apostles gave him an account of all they had done."[20] Here we have the ebb. Hence, "to their source the rivers return," because each of the elect is certain that he is indebted to him from whom he has drawn everything from which his spirituality flows. Hence Paul also says, "There is a variety of gifts but always the same Spirit; there are all sorts of services, but always the same Lord; and there are varieties of working, but it is the same God who inspires them all in everyone."[21] Clearly, by speaking first of the Spirit, and then adding Lord, and finally including the word God, he is demonstrating that

15. 1 Cor 12.11.
16. John 3.34.
17. John 1.16.
18. Eccl 1.7.
19. Luke 9.1–2.
20. Luke 9.10.
21. 1 Cor 12.4–6.

the Holy Trinity, truly one God, is beyond doubt the author of all graces. He it is who distributes his gifts and by a hidden providence determines in each his merits and the variety of his functions.

That a Bishop Is the External Minister, but That God Consecrates Unseen

(5) Wherefore, one must believe in the fullness of faith that Christ delegates to his ministers the office of ecclesiastical ordination in such a way, that he primarily retains within himself the sacrament of all orders, and grants his servants the ministry of promoting co-servants in such a way, that he transfers to no one the right itself or the power of ordination.[22] For even though bishops seem to ordain by reason of the office of ordaining enjoined upon them, it is he really that ordains who invisibly confers the Holy Spirit. There is one, indeed, who prays but another who hears the prayer; the one who asks, differs from him who approves the petitions. What man dares to compare himself to Peter and John? And yet it is said of them that when they were sent to Samaria to impose hands on those who had been baptized, they prayed for them and they received the Holy Spirit.[23] Therefore, it was not from their bounty but because of their ministry, and in effect, not as a result of their gift but of their prayer that the Holy Spirit entered into those who believed. For there is one high priest, one supreme pontiff who entered only once, not just any holy of holies, but into heaven itself to appear before the face of God on our behalf.[24] It is from him, clearly, as from its summit, that all priesthood is poured out upon the members of the Church, and from him that all that is sacred ineffably has its growth. Hence, when he sent out his disciples to baptize he did not hand over to them the power of the sacrament but commanded their obedience; he did not cause

---

22. See Augustine, *In Ioh.* CC 36.6.6, 56 and 7.3, 68; Seekel, *Grundlagen* 37.
23. Cf. Acts 8.14–17; Augustine, *In Ioh.* CC 36.6.18, 62f.; Seekel, *Grundlagen* 38.
24. Cf. Heb 9.24–25.

them to become the authors of baptism but its ministers. For when he says, "Go into the whole world, baptize all nations in the name of the Father and of the Son and of the Holy Spirit,"[25] he clearly shows that it was not they but he undoubtedly who was the author of baptism, in whose name they baptized. Hence also John the Baptist states, "He who sent me to baptize with water had said to me, 'The man on whom you see the Spirit come down and rest is the one who baptizes.'"[26] And still John the evangelist says, "Even though it was not Jesus who had baptized but his disciples."[27] Note that the Lord did not baptize, and still it is said of him, "He is the one who baptizes,"[28] because no matter who may exercise the ministry of baptism, it is still he who produces the sacrament with its profound effect.

That as There Is Only One Who Baptizes, so It Is One and the Same Who Preeminently Ordains

(6) But if someone perhaps should object at this point that baptism for human rebirth is one thing and ordination to ecclesiastical dignity is quite another, I will say that whatever I believe in this context about baptism, I also subscribe to completely in the matter of ordination. For, since baptism is the origin and the first beginning of all that is a sacrament in the Church, as baptism is from God and not from man, so too all ecclesiastical ordination pertains especially to him from whom the fullness of all blessings flows. It is, of course, in this connection that the Apostle says, "Who has blessed us with all the spiritual blessings of heaven."[29] Nor, indeed, would even baptism or any other consecration at all be considered something important, except in regard to the Holy Spirit who is imparted through their instrumentality. "For," as it is said, "what is water, but water? Yet, a word is added to the element, and at the descent of the Spirit it becomes a sacrament."[30]

25. Matt 28.19; for variants from the *Vulgate*, see Sabatier 3.180f.
26. John 1.33.   27. John 4.2.
28. John 1.33.   29. Eph 1.3.
30. Augustine, *In Ioh.* CC 36.80.3, 529; Seekel, *Grundlagen* 39. On the problem of the sacraments of baptism and orders, see N. M. Haring, "The

Since, therefore, in both kinds of sanctification the sum total and the grandeur consist in this that the Holy Spirit is received, either by those who are baptized or by those who are ordained. Just as baptism is not attributed to human capacity or power but to God as its author, so also in every circumstance must each ordination in the Church be ascribed to him, for God's manifold grace is at work in both, so that the former might obtain absolution of sins, and the latter might be promoted to the ranks of spiritual dignity. The former, after putting off the old man with his false deeds, to be clothed with the new, the latter, that as priests of God they may be vested with justice;[31] the former, that like newborn babes, they might hunger for pure spiritual milk, the latter, that they might arrive at maturity in the fullness of Christ.[32] Grace is active in the former, making them adopted sons, but in the latter that they might become servants and stewards of the mysteries of God.[33] In the first instance, indeed, they are reborn by the Spirit; but in the latter, by order of the same Spirit, they are now chosen to beget sons of God.

That Along with Baptism the Lord Also Received Priestly Rights

(7) It is therefore a statement of pure and perfect faith, that like baptism, priestly ordination is in no way contaminated by the defect of sordid ministers, nor damaged by another's crime. No matter how scandalous or involved in countless crimes the consecrator might be, the one ordained suffers no loss to his sacred office on this account, nor is he deprived of any heavenly grace. For it is not because of the quality of the bishop, but by reason of the office in which he functions that the mystery of ordination is transmitted to another,[34] nor is it

---

Augustinian Axiom 'Nulli Sacramento injuria facienda est,'" *Mediaeval Studies* 16 (1954), 87–117, esp. 90; R. Carletti, "La nozione di sacramento in San Pier Damiani," in *Fonte Avellana nella societa dei secoli XI e XII*. Atti del II convegno del centro di studi avellantini (1978), 395–404, esp. 402.

31. Eph 4.24; cf. Ps 131.9.
32. Cf. 1 Pet 2.3; Eph 4.13.
33. Cf. Eph 1.5; 1 Cor 4.1.
34. Cf. Augustine, *In Ioh.* CC 36.5.19, 52; Pascasius Radbertus, *De corpore et sanguine Domini*, ed. B. Paulus, CCCM 16 (1969), 12.80; Seekel, *Grundlagen* 40.

necessary to inquire into the consecrator's manner of life but only into the ministry that he received. For just as there are many who exercise the office of baptizing, and yet there is but one who baptizes; so also, even though there are many bishops, there is only one who specifically ordains by his own right. It was, indeed, in that very dove which hovered over the Lord after his baptism[35] that he received the rights of the true priesthood along with the sacrament of baptism, when the oil of jubilation, of which the psalmist sings, flowed over him: "God, your God," he says, "has anointed you with the oil of gladness, above all your fellows."[36]

(8) The proof that our Redeemer, along with baptism, received also the sacrament of the priesthood is evident from this that after his baptism he at once began to preach, to choose disciples, and to glow with new miracles. This we do not find him doing up to this time, even from a careful reading of the gospel text. Hence it is that Holy Church has derived from its very head this normative practice and preserves it faithfully, that following the example of the Lord himself no one may become a bishop who is not yet thirty years of age. For unless it had been a certain belief that, together with baptism, the Lord had received the priesthood also, why would canonical authority so strongly have forbidden anyone to aspire to the mitre before reaching the age at which Christ had been baptized?[37]

(9) Why, moreover, should the case of the Lord's age be used in the matter of receiving episcopal honors if it was not believed that at that time the Lord had received baptism along with the priesthood? Just as in his human nature he received both baptism and the priesthood for our salvation, insofar as he is God, he is both the author and minister of both sacraments. Of this the Apostle says, "Where he has en-

---

35. Cf. Matt 3.16; Mark 1.10; John 1.32.
36. Ps 44.8.
37. The canonical source for his contention that a candidate for episcopal consecration must be 30 years of age is the *Concilium Neocaesariense* 11, ed. C. H. Turner, *Ecclesiae occidentalis monumenta iuris antiquissima*. Canonum et conciliorum graecorum interpretationes latinae 2.1 (1907), 132f.; cf. Burchard, *Decretum* 2.9–10.627 AB; Ryan, *Sources* 37, no. 47.

tered before us on our behalf, to become a high priest for ever after the order of Melchizedek."[38] The holy apostles themselves are not reported to have been ordained by the Lord in any other context but the reception of baptism. Nor do we actually read that they were immersed in the waters of baptism, but rather that they carried out the command to baptize, by which they were ordered to baptize those who believe in the name of the Father, and of the Son, and of the Holy Spirit. Moreover, since the Lord said to them, "John baptized with water but you, not many days from now, will be baptized with the Holy Spirit,"[39] it is clear that they received the sacrament of complete baptism, together with an all pervading ordination, at the time when the Holy Spirit descended upon them in a variety of tongues. Since, therefore, we see both the Lord and the apostles receiving both sacraments together at the very beginning of man's redemption, it is evident that baptism is the foundation and principle of ecclesiastical ordination, in the sense that he who is recognized as exercising primacy over baptism is also believed without the slightest doubt to be the author of ordination.

That Since One Would Not Venture Being Rebaptized, There Is No Reason Why He Should Be Reordained

(10) With this in mind, since one who is baptized even by a heretic is not to be rebaptized, I see no reason why one who is promoted by a so-called simonist should be either deposed or reordained. For if baptism administered by a murderer or by an adulterer or even by a heretic must be considered valid, and that, by reason of the gospel statement, "The man on whom you see the Spirit come down and rest is the one who baptizes,"[40] there is no reason at all why also in ordinations[41] we should not refer to the identical author of both sacraments, and with equal force be able to say he is the one who ordains. Did the dove indeed descend with the power of bap-

---

38. Heb 6.20.   39. Acts 1.5.
40. John 1.33.
41. Cf. *Collectio Dionysio-Hadriana* (PL 67.314A), *Decretum Anastasii* 7; JK 744. See also Ryan, *Sources* 37, no. 48.

tizing upon the mediator between God and men and not descend with the power of ordination? For what does the baptized person receive if not the Holy Spirit? And similarly, what but the Holy Spirit comes to him who is ordained? If, therefore, one baptized by some infamous person is not rebaptized because we believe him to have received the Holy Spirit, it is not because of his worth but by reason of his office; and that this derives not from him but from Christ, of whom alone it is specifically said, "He it is who baptizes";[42] and also, since he who is ordained receives none other than the same Holy Spirit, and that from the very same Christ, there appears to be absolutely no reason to distinguish between a baptized and an ordained person in this regard. Therefore, of things having the same cause one must have the same opinion, unless perhaps one is to conclude that there is one Holy Spirit who is given at ordination and another at baptism. But who would rashly presume such a sacrilegious thing in view of the Apostle's clear statement, "There is one God, one faith, one baptism";[43] and again, "If some one comes and preaches another Christ than the one we preached, or received a different Christ from the one you received, or a different gospel from the one you accepted, you might submit to it readily enough."[44] To this we might add, as witnessed by canonical authority, that rebaptism is forbidden, so that the name of the Blessed Trinity in which baptism is administered does not appear to be voided.[45] But if this is the reason why one should not be rebaptized, to whom does this more obviously apply than to someone ordained by a simonist, who not only ordains in the name of the Blessed Trinity, but also totally observes every prescription of Catholic ordination? Yet, a simonist, even though he has become a heretic through his shady trafficking,[46] is still

---

42. John 1.33.
43. Eph 4.5.
44. 2 Cor 11.4.
45. See Ryan, *Sources* 37, no. 49 where he cites Burchard, *Decretum* 4.39.734BC.
46. On the evaluation of simony as a heresy, see Gilchrist, *Simoniaca haeresis* 217, and the literature there cited.

by faith a Catholic, and his condemnation apparently derives rather from ambition than from disbelief. Although, if we carefully examine Peter's judgment hurled at Simon, not even Simon's faith is found to be innocent: "You and your money," he said, "may you come to a bad end, for thinking God's gift is for sale!"[47] For by saying, "for thinking God's gift is for sale," he clearly indicated that Simon then believed that if he should pay the price, he would in justice receive the Holy Spirit and in the bargain the power to perform miracles.

That Ordination, If It Is Catholic, Is Also Valid

(11) Simonists in our own day, however, since they have little hope of being famous for their miracles, do not desire the Holy Spirit nor his gifts, but inflamed by their ambition of procuring a bishropric, strive only for a place in the sun. Therefore, with respect to the faith they are sound; but in relation to the mechanics of moneymaking they are caught in the damnable meshes of simony. We hear of two originators of this heresy, one emerging like a plague in the writings of the prophets, the other surfacing in apostolic times: Gehazi, who appears as the teacher of the sellers, and Simon, the original of the buyers.[48] And so, their followers, inasmuch as they are no different in their fault, are not distinguishable in their condemnation. Yet, if their ordination is properly Catholic, even though they approach unworthily, they fully receive the holy office of the priesthood. For the power of the Holy Spirit is the same, both when his grace is sold and when it is given freely. Nor does the power of God lose its proper effectiveness because of transactions that flow from human perverseness. Obviously, our Savior himself, just as he was sold and that pestiferous sum of money was already bulging the purse of the traitor, restored the ear of the servant Malchus even as he fell into the hands of his persecutors.[49] And so he clearly demonstrated how much more powerful he was than those who now held him captive. That he did not work mir-

---

47. Acts 8.20; for variants from the *Vulgate*, cf. Sabatier 3.527.
48. Cf. 2 Kgs 5; Acts 5.
49. Cf. John 18.10; Luke 22.51.

acles when Herod importuned him, resulted not from a lack of power but because he wished it so. For he who made the request was unworthy, while effective power was not wanting to him from whom results were expected. Moreover, when he hung on the cross, after breathing his last, as the earth trembled and the sun was darkened, the temple veil was also rent, the rocks were split, and the dead arose[50]—all of these events clearly attest that he was no less powerful during his death agony, than now that he is lifted up to sit at the right hand of his father's glory.

(12) In the same way also we are compelled to believe of the Holy Spirit, that he possesses the same power, both when it appears, as it were, that he is the victim of venality and when he is bestowed through the gratuitous imposition of hands. And thus, just as our Redeemer, when he was sold and when he suffered, could not be weakened in his majesty, so also the Holy Spirit, even though the sad specter of venality creeps in, in no way suffers a loss of the power that is his. Even though to all appearances the priest seems to be functioning, it is Christ himself, the true priest and supreme pontiff, who grants his gifts to those who approach him with varying results. For some, indeed, his gifts lead to salvation, for others to damnation.[51] To be sure, the gift is altogether good, even though he who accepts it is unworthy.[52] A good physician, surely, would not give his patient poison to drink.[53] Was not the morsel which the Lord handed to Judas, good for him?[54] But that which was the cause of salvation, for him became a means of damnation because he was not at peace when he accepted the instrument of peace.[55] All of us surely know that the mystery of the Eucharist, which we receive from the sacred altar, is indeed good, whether we be just or sinners. Neither does the good man receive something better,

---

50. Cf. Matt 27.51–52.
51. Cf. Augustine, *In Ioh.* CC 36.6.14–15, 61; Seekel, *Grundlagen* 44f.
52. Cf. Pascasius, *De corpore* 12.80; Seekel, *Grundlagen* 45.
53. Cf. Augustine, *In Ioh.* CC 36.6.15, 61; Seekel, *Grundlagen* 42.
54. Cf. John 13.27; Augustine, *In Ioh.* CC 36.6.15, 61.
55. Cf. Augustine, *ibid.*

nor the bad man something worse.⁵⁶ And still the Apostle says that "the unworthy recipient eats and drinks his own condemnation without recognizing the Body of the Lord."⁵⁷

(13) If, therefore, it is the Body of Christ that the unworthy person receives, obviously for the evil man a good thing turns into a disaster, while for the good it is meant to provide salvation. Nor can we call a thing evil just because it proves harmful, nor, in consequence, does it cease being a sacrament because the one who receives it is accursed. We should rather assert that one and the same thing became the occasion of death for the unworthy, while for the good it provided a means of salvation.⁵⁸ Therefore, we must believe without a doubt that if ordination to any rank is granted within the Catholic Church, namely, within the unity of orthodox belief, and where both possess the true faith, whatever is given by a good minister to a good recipient is also effectively tendered by an evil minister to an evil recipient, because this sacrament does not depend upon the merits of the minister or the recipient, but upon the rite ordained within the Church and on the invocation of the name of God.⁵⁹ And since, just as there is one who baptizes, and without doubt it is one and the same who ordains, that which is granted through the abundant generosity of Christ is not deserved by the recipient. While "he makes his sun rise on the good and bad alike, and sends the rain on the honest and the dishonest,"⁶⁰ why should we marvel that he pours forth a shower of his grace on a barren strand? Why is it novel if he also strikes the eyes of the blind with his radiant splendor so that they might rightly sing in the words of the unhappy Balaam, "The oracle of the man," he says, "whose eye was closed; the oracle of him who hears

---

56. Cf. Pascasius, *De corpore* 12.76; Augustine, *In Ioh.* CC 36.6.8, 57.
57. 1 Cor 11.29; cf. Augustine, *In Ioh.* CC 36.6.15, 61; Seekel, *Grundlagen* 42.
58. Cf. Augustine, *In Ioh.* CC 36.6.15, 61; Seekel, *Grundlagen* 43.
59. Cf. Pascasius, *De corpore* 12.76; Seekel, *Grundlagen* 45; Gilchrist, *Simoniaca Haeresis* 220.
60. Matt 5.45.

the words of God, who knows the teaching of the Most High, and sees the vision of the Almighty, falling down, but having his eyes uncovered."[61]

That Balaam Was a Simonist and Still Did Not Lose the Spirit of Prophecy

(14) Now, whence did this offspring of avarice have the power to see such mighty deeds and to announce with such clarity and exactness the redemption of the world that would occur in the distant future, if he were not endowed with the presence of the Holy Spirit? For, as the celebrated doctor says, "Who knows what a man is but the man's own spirit within him? In the same way, only the Spirit of God knows what God is;"[62] especially since the same Scriptures also say that "the Spirit of God came upon him, and he took up his discourse, and said"[63] just what we previously quoted. Do we say that the gift of the Holy Spirt is not granted by a simonist? Are we not aware that the heresy of simony was already thriving in the time of this very Balaam? Did he not attempt to sell the grace of the Holy Spirit when, as he was promised his price, he produced his divination? For so the Scriptures state that the elders of Moab asked him, "with the fees for divination in their hand."[64] And yet again he sent other messengers to him saying, "Thus says Balak, son of Zippor, 'Do not delay coming to me; I am prepared to do you honor, and whatever you wish I will give you.'"[65] He was certainly afire with a love of money, but still through him the Holy Spirit announced profound mysteries.

(15) So there we have Balaam and Balak, both obviously at cross suits with God, both proven to be hostile to God's people, yet one is eager to buy the gift of divine grace and the other is ready to sell. And still, the former, beyond his deserts, made known secrets of prophetic revelation, while the latter,

---

61. Num 24.3–4. Damian's "teaching of the Most High" is not in the *Vulgate*; for variants used here, see *Biblia sacra* 3.213.
62. 1 Cor 2.11.
63. Num 24.2–3.
64. Num 22.7.
65. Num 22.16–17.

indeed, heard them unworthily. And that we might wonder the more at the generosity of God's goodness, when Balaam tried to curse, contrary to his intention he pronounced a blessing: "I received a command to bless," he said, "and I cannot refuse the blessing."[66] By the power of God a muzzle had been fastened about his mouth and he was unable to use his tongue in any other way but in the manner the directing Holy Spirit wished it to turn. His tongue fought with his will, and he was unable to cause the turbulent brackishness, which his precondemned mind had conceived, to flow from his mouth. Wherefore, since he could not hurl curses at the people of God as he had been requested, he had recourse to deception and placed the Midianite stumbling block in their path.[67] If he, therefore, who wished to curse was never able to produce his curses, are we not compelled to reach the same conclusion about simonists, in whom the mind and the tongue are certainly at one in blessing? But he, who had irreverently abused the office of prophet, how did he with this privileged grace that had been given him end his career? After relating the victory of the people of Israel, the Scriptures then went on to say, "They also put Balaam son of Beor to the sword."[68]

(16) In the same way, too, simonists and other criminals may devote themselves to receiving ministries in the Church, and from the kindness of the giver they acquire the gift of heavenly grace; and still they do not escape the just reward of their excesses. For that which was intended for the salvation of those who are worthy is turned for them into their destruction. And from this they fall into the danger of eternal death while others, from the same source, are striving more vigorously to grasp the rewards of life. Anyone, certainly, who scans with a sharp eye the pages of Scripture which tell of the aforementioned Balaam, does not at all doubt that this unhappy man was truly a complete simonist—except that Simon, from whom this detestable title takes its name, had not yet existed—and had put his grace of prophecy up for sale;

---

66. Num 23.20.
68. Num 31.8.

67. Cf. Num 31.16.

and that despite it all the Holy Spirit had clearly spoken through him; and, what is no less marvelous, while his heart was already aflame with the fires of concupiscence, God day and night nevertheless spoke to him like a friend. And lest, perhaps, he be thought to lack the Holy Spirit, since Moses calls him a soothsayer, you should carefully read the words of this same account and you will find Moses stating that "when he saw Israel encamped in their tents,"[69] the spirit of God suddenly came on him and at once inspired him as a real prophet to discourse in prophecy. And therefore, while being a prophet, he is called a soothsayer, because he whom divine favor had raised to prophetic dignity was, by his own depravity, disfigured with the obscene name of soothsayer. Here we must consider the depth and subtlety of God's judgment, and what is more, how much God is to be feared for his deeds among mankind,[70] since in fact this miserable man, on account of his wicked crime, did not lose the grace that he had once acquired, and still because of the very grace that he had abused, was unable because of his unworthiness to avoid the sentence of God's vengeance. Why should we marvel that almighty God, who is always what he is and does not experience change,[71] should nevertheless still preserve the ancient rights of his judgment and retain the same norms by which he customarily acted; that what he did in the case of Balaam he should do no differently today with those who behave in similar ways; and that, while exercising his bounteous goodness in granting his gifts to the unworthy, he at the same time decrees in his justice to inflict on them the punishment that they deserve?

That the Prophetic Spirit Took Possession of the Reprobate, Saul, and His Men-at-Arms

(17) This too is not unknown, that when Saul directed his agents to seize David, and when they, according to the actual account, "saw the company of prophets prophesying, and

69. Num 24.2.
71. Cf. Mal 3.6.
70. Cf. Ps 65.5.

Samuel there as their leader, the spirit of the Lord also came upon Saul's agents, and they began to prophesy."[72] And when Saul sent still other agents a second and a third time,[73] and they too fell into an ecstasy, Saul at last became angry, as Scripture relates, and he himself went to Ramah. Before he arrived, however, the spirit of God came upon him too, and all that day, stripped of his clothes, he prophesied with the rest in the presence of Samuel. Therefore, why should we marvel that evil men, as the full measure of their damnation, should receive the gifts of God of which they are unworthy, when it was granted to Saul himself, whom God had rejected, whom even now the devil had grown accustomed to tormenting quite frequently, not only to receive for an hour the spirit of God, but along with his agents was permitted to prophesy at length? Aroused by the poison of violent anger and burning with the fire of malice and hate, and, without dwelling on the point immoderately, emptied of God, he was irrevocably enslaved to the spirit of evil. And still, after he had come to the place where the company of prophets was prophesying, the spirit of God suddenly seized him and took possession of him like a fire that leaps to consume an object in its path. It should not, therefore, appear incredible that in the Holy Church which undoubtedly is the throne of God, the sanctuary of the Holy Spirit, and the repository of all heavenly gifts, an unworthy person should receive sacramental grace with which he fails to conform by intent or by a worthy life.[74] This is true precisely because it is not deserved by the grantor or the recipient but is a gift of the supreme Benefactor. One does not read that the spirit breathes where he is deserved, but rather it is said, "He breathes wherever he wishes,"[75] so that actually spiritual grace, which flows from the liturgical practices of the Church, derives from the will of God rather than from the deserts of men.

(18) For the Holy Spirit does not always come in response to one's merit, but he always remains in each one according

---

72. 1 Sam 19.20–21.   73. Cf. 1 Sam 19.21–22.
74. Cf. Pascasius, *De corpore* 12.80; Seekel, *Grundlagen* 46.
75. John 3.8.

to his deserts, that is, to procure his salvation. This is why Truth says, "If anyone loves me, he will keep my word, and my Father will love him, and we shall come to him and make our home with him."[76] If one promises to come to his lover, and also states immediately that he will make his home there, it becomes perfectly clear that God abides in some and is only a guest in others. In the same vein he also says, "On him who is humble and calm and who trembles at my word, upon him will my spirit rest,"[77] as if to say plainly, Yes, he will come to others, but he will rest upon this one precisely because he is worthy. For just as before our time it was said that the Holy Spirit, when favorably disposed and appeased, grants peace to those who are gentle and humble of heart,[78] and when in opposition and hostile, he produces restlessness in those who are hard and proud. Such restlessness was symbolized by the tiny mosquitoes over which Pharaoh's magicians failed, saying, "This is the finger of God,"[79] admitting that the Holy Spirit residing in Moses was their opponent. It is indeed proper that the Holy Spirit, who is the third person of the Blessed Trinity, should be presented in opposition to restless men, symbolized by the plague of mosquitoes which was the third plague. Such unrest was experienced by Jehu who, when inspired by divine fervor, became violently angry and took vengeance on God's enemies, especially the devotees of Baal, but who himself did not abandon the golden idols which Jeroboam had worshiped.[80]

What the Doctors Think About Baptism and the Eucharist of the Lord's Body

(19) As we know, three principal sacraments are commonly received in the Holy Church, namely, baptism, the saving mystery of the Body and Blood of the Lord, and the ordination of clerics. On baptism, St. Augustine in the *Explanation*

---

76. John 14.23.
77. Isa 66.2. For this variant from the *Vulgate*, see Sabatier 2.634, who cites Gregory I, *Moralia in Iob* 5.45.78 (CC 143.276).
78. Cf. Matt 11.29, but not referring directly to the Holy Spirit.
79. Exod 8.19.   80. Cf. 2 Kgs 10.

of John the Evangelist[81] and Pascasius in his book *On the Eucharist of the Body of the Lord*[82] are in such agreement in their discussions that they state that these sacraments do not become better when effected by good priests, nor worse by bad priests. Thus, whether these sacraments are confected by thieves, or adulterers, or even by murderers, they differ in no way from the sacraments which holy priests produce. For anyone who has diligently read these works, this fact is clearly beyond debate. On the ordination of clerics, however, there has not been much discussion, because after the two prior sacraments were explained in clear terms, no doubt or hesitation remained about the third. Now, however, by acting immoderately, human curiosity propounds a new question before the world, and by closer scrutiny that results in lesser vision, tries to impose darkness onto the clear light. How, they ask, is the grace of the Holy Spirit given through evil men or received by them? They are not aware that it is by the grace of the Holy Spirit that orders of ecclesiastical dignity themselves are received, which, indeed, the Holy Spirit who disposes the rights of his Church, renders valid, whether an unworthy person bestows or receives them. For as the blessed Jerome says, "Bishop, priest, and deacon are not titles of merit, but of office."[83] Similarly, in the case of a tribune, who is himself a poor specimen, or of some one baseborn promoted by him to military status, the general would still confirm everything that was done to preserve discipline in his army. Nor does he overthrow the tribune's established command if he has not yet degraded the tribune from his proper rank. Yet, on the other hand, someone will say, "Note what the gospel states: 'The man who does not enter by the door, but climbs in some other way, is nothing but a thief or a robber.'"[84] So be it, that one who steals in secret is regularly

---

81. Augustine, *In Iohannis evangelium tractatus CXXIV*, ed. R. Willems, CC 36 (1954), 1.6.8, 57.

82. Pascasius Radbertus, *De corpore et sanguine Domini*, ed. B. Paulus, CC CM 16 (1969), 12.

83. Jerome, *Adversus Iovinianum* 1.34 (PL 23.270A); cf. Seekel, *Grundlagen* 70, no. 1.

84. John 10.1.

accused of theft or robbery; for me, however, who came in through the door, his action in no way makes me an accomplice in his crime. Let him, therefore, suffer the punishment for his crime so long as the disadvantage of someone else's guilt does not involve me, nor render me culpable of another's sin, since my own purity and innocence free me from any charge.

(20) Moreover, as to the statement that an unworthy man is unable to receive the grace of the Holy Spirit, there is, doubtless, complete agreement that the Body of the Lord, offered on the sacred altar through the instrumentality of a holy priest, is made living and hallowed by the power born of the Holy Spirit that it might bring us life and make us holy, just as one says in the silent prayers of the Mass which we revere: "Through whom, O Lord, you always create all these good gifts, you sanctify them, and give them life, and make them holy."[85] We are of the opinion, moreover, that in no other way can we be made to live except by the Holy Spirit, since, as Truth itself testifies, it is the Spirit who gives life.[86] I ask, therefore, when a holy priest by chance administers to some wicked man this heavenly gift, brought to life and sanctified by the power of the Holy Spirit, and, as I can confidently assert, truly filled with the grace of that same divine Spirit, does the Holy Spirit on that account abandon the Body of the Lord and withdraw in disgust as he would from a vessel defiled by filth? But if that is so, how can it be true, as the Apostle says, that an unworthy recipient "eats and drinks judgment on himself if he does not discern the Body of the Lord"?[87] Consequently, if after the Spirit's departure it is no longer the Body of the Lord but simply common bread, he who receives no sacrament is not subject to judgment. But since it is obviously absurd and impious to separate the Holy Spirit from the Body of Christ because of those who receive unworthily, it should not appear severe to say that evil men can also receive the Holy Spirit with the final outcome that they deserve.

85. *Canon of the Mass.*
86. Cf. John 6.63.
87. 1 Cor 11.29.

(21) That is why the blessed Augustine says in his *Explanation of the Letter of St. John the Apostle*,[88] "Even an evil man can have baptism, even an evil man can have prophecy. We find that King Saul had the gift of prophecy; that he who had persecuted holy David was filled with the spirit of prophecy and began to prophesy.[89] An evil man, too, can receive the sacrament of the Body and Blood of the Lord. For of such it is said, 'One who eats and drinks unworthily, eats and drinks judgment on himself.'[90] An evil man can also have the name of Christ, that is, an evil man can also be called a Christian. Of such it is said, 'They have profaned the name of their God.'[91] Therefore, also an evil man can possess all the sacraments, but to have charity and also be evil is not within his power."

(22) Therefore, if according to the statement of the great doctor an evil man possesses all the sacraments, how can man's ridiculous folly impudently bleat forth the opinion that a simonist does not possess the sacraments? Listen to what the same eminent doctor says in another work on the same subject, so that the opinion he held on the question we are discussing may become clearer the more often he explains it. In speaking of the blessing that Isaac gave his son, he added,[92] "The will of the just man," he said, "insofar as it relates to conscience, is good; but relative to foreknowledge, it is free of unfortunate consequences, for it is God alone who judges the future. On this account, the just man Isaac, in keeping with his time-bound human condition, thought that his elder son was more worthy of receiving his blessing. But God, who has knowledge of hidden things,[93] made clear that the younger son deserved the blessing, demonstrating that in a blessing the favor is not from man but from God, because God's blessing is attached to the dignity of the office and not to the value of the man. And so in the book of Numbers

---

88. Augustine, *In epistolam Joannis ad Parthos* 7.6 (PL 35.2032); Seekel, *Grundlagen* 70, no. 2.
89. Cf. 1 Sam 19.23.
90. 1 Cor 11.29.
91. Cf. Ezek 36.22; 43.8.
92. Cf. Gen 27.23, 27–29.
93. Cf. Dan 13.42.

God's word went forth to the priests, Moses and Aaron: 'Call down my name on the sons of Israel, I the Lord will bless them,'[94] so that the conferral through the ministry of the ordained person might transfer grace to men; and that the will of the priest can neither hinder nor benefit, but only the worthiness of the one who requests a blessing. We may here note the high dignity of the priestly office. Among other things it was said of the wicked Caiaphas, the murderer of the Savior: 'He did not say this of his own accord, but as the High Priest in office that year, he was prophesying.'[95] From which it is obvious that in granting grace, the Spirit does not follow the person or the dignity, but ordination, so that even though a person is highly deserving, he cannot bless unless he was ordained to provide the office of ministering. For it is God who causes a blessing to become effective."[96]

(23) The words of this blessed man are, therefore, so plain and clear that anyone, after once he sees them, and in his stubbornness is still ready to oppose them, is guilty of defying not Peter,[97] who counts for nothing, but instead the great Augustine. For what is clearer than the statement that "in a priestly blessing the favor is not from man but from God"; or, "it is the dignity of the office and not the value of the man to which the blessing of God is attached"; or lastly, "that in granting grace the Spirit does not follow the person, or the dignity, but ordination"? And, indeed, why should it be my concern to determine the worthiness of him who ordains me, so long as he freely grants me that which he perhaps has bought, and even though he has secretly stolen into office, he admits me by the door, he the exile, I the citizen, he the stranger, I the member of the household, he the hireling, I the heir? What is really important to me is not by whom, but to what I am promoted. It is obvious, therefore, that like the two sacraments of which we spoke above, namely of baptism

---

94. Num 6.27.   95. John 11.51.
96. Pseudo-Augustine, *Quaestiones veteris et novi testamenti* 127, ed. A. Souter, CSEL 50 (1963), 11.1, 35f.; cf. Seekel, *Grundlagen* 70, no. 3. See also I. S. Robinson, *Studi Gregoriani* 11 (1978), 299–395, esp. 321.
97. Here Damian refers to himself as Peter.

and of the saving Eucharist, neither better results are produced by the good nor less worthy outcomes from the evil, so too it is with the ordination of clerics.

That the Holy Spirit Is Given, not Because of the Worthiness of Priests, but by Reason of the Ministry

(24) Need we ask finally whether Caiaphas, through whom the Holy Spirit spoke concerning the mystery of the life-giving death of Christ, was himself a worthy man? For when he said, "It is more to your interest that one man should die for the people, than that the whole nation should be destroyed," the evangelist at once added, "He did not say this of his own accord, but as the high priest in office that year, he was prophesying."[98] Quite certainly, for the moment he received the prophetic spirit not for the purpose of acknowledging what he had foretold, but rather that he be all the more eager to incite his co-conspirators to greater effort in hastening the death of the Lord. It was, in fact, for our benefit and not for his that he saw and revealed the hidden treasure of wisdom which he did not recognize. Clearly, too, Caiaphas can hardly be considered different from simonists if we look closely at the record of ancient history. For as Eusebius of Caesarea relates in his *Ecclesiastical History*, to use his own words here: "Since the regulations of the law at that time had lapsed through force and ambition, no one in fact was given the high priestly honor by reason of his life or hereditary descent, so that they were changed after a year in office." Then, according to the testimony of Josephus, he tells that in one four-year period four high priests succeeded one another in office annually. "Valerius Gratus," he said, "put an end to the priesthood of Annas and appointed Ishmael, the son of Phabi, high priest, and after a short time he removed this one, and named as high priest Eliezer, the son of Annas, the high priest. And after a year had passed he removed this one also and passed over the high priesthood to a certain Simon, the son of Kamithus. But no more than a year passed with him in office

---

98. John 11.50–51.

when Josephus, known also as Caiaphas, became his successor."⁹⁹ Notice that Caiaphas is known to have received the priesthood neither freely nor legally, in that after the removal and violent expulsion of others, he usurped the dignity of others, and still, though unworthy, received the spirit of prophecy. About which St. Jerome, in his *Commentary on Matthew the Evangelist*, says, "At the command of God Moses ordered that high priests succeed their fathers and that a geneology for priests be established.¹⁰⁰

(25) Josephus relates that this Caiaphas purchased the high priesthood from Herod and held it for only one year."¹⁰¹ As I might put it, the light was handed to a blind man, not that he might see, but that he might be at the service of others. He did not deserve to receive the prophetic spirit, but had it because of the service that he rendered. As we know, the crown and the priesthood were both instituted by God,¹⁰² and hence, even though the person of the administrator is deemed to be unworthy, still the office which is clearly good, was at one time invested with suitable grace. This is why only Nebuchadnezzar, even though many others were present, after throwing the three young men into the fiery furnace, could see the fourth man, whose appearance was like the Son of God.¹⁰³ Surely we must believe that it was the Holy Spirit who opened the eyes of his mind so that only he could see what was hidden from others, and that what he saw he might, of his own accord, also acknowledge. So too it happened that Pharaoh had a dream by which he obviated the coming unproductive years and saved Egypt, weakened by hunger, from ruin.¹⁰⁴ We note also the case of Abimelech who obtained a message from God and heard that he should return Sarah to

---

99. Rufinus, *Hist. eccl.* 1.10.75. The translator here follows the readings of E. Schwartz (see *Bibliography*, s.v. "Rufinus"): *Phabi* for *Baffi*; *Eliezer* for *Eleazar*, *Annas* for *Ananias*, *Kamithus* for *Canifus*, and *Caiaphas* for *Cayphas*.
100. Cf. Exod 29.28–44.
101. Jerome, *Commentariorum in Matheum libri quattuor*, ed. D. Hurst and M. Adriaen, CC 77 (1969), 259.
102. See Marc Bloch, *Les rois thaumaturges* (1961), 30, n. 2 and 195; see also Fornasari, *Prospettive* 501f.
103. Cf. Dan 3.   104. Cf. Gen 41.

her husband lest he suddenly die.[105] Kings and priests, indeed, even though some of them were worthy of condemnation because of their notorious lives, are still found to be called gods and anointed ones by reason of the sacramental ministry they received.[106] Thus it was that a Hebrew slave was commanded in the Law to be taken to the gods, that is, presented to the priests.[107] So too it is stated elsewhere: "You shall not revile the gods;[108] that is, you shall not disparage the priests; so also Saul, even after he was deposed from the heights of his royal office by the command of God, was nevertheless still called the anointed of the Lord right up to his death.[109] In the Law it was also commanded that every firstborn son should be consecrated to the Lord.[110] But if the worthiness of everyone is closely investigated, would Esau, the firstborn, be rightly called holy? For of him God said, "I had hatred for Esau."[111] Was Amnon a holy man, when in burning passion he raped his sister, and was drenched in his own blood by the sword of his brother Absalom, the avenger of his crime of incest?[112] Can Manasses, or Ochozias rightly be called holy men, when, as Scripture attests, the first "worshipped the whole array of heaven,"[113] and the other, after consulting Beelzebub, the god of Accaron, on the extent of his life, died miserably in despair because of his perfidy?[114] Obviously, it is one thing to be holy as a result of one's worthy life, but quite another to be called holy because of one's public office.

One Need Not Wonder That Unworthy Men Receive the Holy Spirit, Since the Son of God Himself Also Fell into the Hands of the Wicked

(26) While the quality of holiness cannot be conveyed to another, the ministry of orders, however, is handed on to many others as the regimen of the Church requires. Here it

105. Cf. Gen 20.6–7.
106. See Laqua, *Traditionen* 305.
107. Cf. Exod 21.6.
108. Exod 22.28.
109. Cf. 1 Sam 24.7; 26.9.
110. Cf. Exod 13.2.
111. Mal 1.3.
112. Cf. 2 Sam 13.
113. 2 Kgs 21.3.
114. Cf. 2 Kgs 1.

is not a question of the person who exercises the office of consecration, but of what he possesses.[115] For the external sign of grace is something quite different from grace itself. Almighty God, to be sure, dispenses the sacrament of grace even by means of wicked men, but gives grace itself only through himself.[116] It often happens, as was said before, that from the fullness of his mercy God grants his Spirit even to those whom he does not acknowledge because of their evil lives. Is there any doubt that they too had the Spirit of God, who at their appearance before the judge's tribunal, shout, "Lord, did we not prophesy in your name," and all the rest that follows?[117] And to these he immediately responds, "Out of my sight, you and your wicked ways, I never knew you!"[118] While claiming to have the spirit of prophecy and at the same time submitting to the sentence of their own rejection, they obviously demonstrate that in some the Holy Spirit is not driven out because of the wickedness of their lives, and yet their accursed lives are not excused, on account of the Holy Spirit, whom they treated disrespectfully. Since, as the Lord states, "You do not know where the Spirit comes from, or where it is going,"[119] so too you cannot know why at times he comes also to men who are worthy of damnation and expresses his will through them. Now, inasmuch as the Apostle says that "a man gifted with the Spirit can judge the worth of everything, but is not himself subject to judgment,"[120] who would pass judgment on the Holy Spirit himself, if, due to some secret discernment which he himself knows, he does not recoil from descending even upon evil men, when he was unwilling to free even the Son of God, co-equal to him in essence and eternity, from the grasp of the wicked? Thus it was that Solomon said, "The spirit of wisdom is a kindly spirit, yet he did not acquit the accursed one of his words."[121] We properly call the Holy Spirit "kindly," because he grants good

115. Cf. Pascasius, *De corpore* 12.81; Seekel, *Grundlagen* 47.
116. Cf. Pascasius, *De corpore* 12.83; Seekel, *Grundlagen* 48.
117. Matt 7.22.
118. Matt 7.23; for variants, see Sabatier 3.42.
119. John 3.8. 120. 1 Cor 2.15.
121. Wis 1.6.

things to those who deserve evil, and to them who merit punishment he imparts the gift of his grace.

(27) In this passage, who but the Savior can be meant by the word "accursed," since it was he who was willing to submit to curses that he might free us from the bonds of malediction? And so Paul says, "Christ bought us freedom from the curse of the Law by becoming for our sake an accursed thing; for Scripture says, 'Cursed is everyone who is hanged on a tree.' And the purpose of it all was that the blessing of Abraham should in Jesus Christ be extended to the gentiles, so that we might receive the promised Spirit through faith."[122] The kindliness of the Holy Spirit, consequently, did not acquit the accursed one of his words because all the sufferings of the Lord's passion and death, which previously he had predicted of Christ by the mouth of the prophets, he effectually fulfilled in deed when the time was right. Then, indeed, to some degree would he have acquitted him of his words if what he had spoken of him through the prophets had not been carried out in the course of events. Here we should note how profoundly and mystically these statements of the two doctors agree with one another. For what the one said, namely, "that the spirit did not acquit the accursed one of his words," is exactly what was stated by the other, that is, "that we might receive the promised Spirit through faith." Indicating, moreover, about just which accursed one he was speaking, the wise man added the following to his previous statement: "Since God sees into the innermost parts of him, truly observes his heart, and listens to his tongue."[123] Since the unity of the Father and the Son is inseparable and of the same essence, it is rightly said that the Father sees into the Son's innermost parts and truly observes his heart, for the Son is in his power and wisdom, in no way unequal to the Father, and is evidently believed to be separated from him by no disassociation. As he has stated, the Father also listens to his voice: "Father," he says, "I thank you that you have heard me. I knew already that you always hear me."[124] It is obvious,

---

122. Gal 3.13–14. 123. Wis 1.6.
124. John 11.41–42.

therefore, that the Spirit did not acquit the accursed one of his words because God witnesses and observes his heart and hears his words, just as if he were to say: The Son of God underwent the sufferings of the passion because it was the Son, possessed of the same will and providence as the Father and the Holy Spirit, who ordained it to happen for the salvation of the human race. In reference to which the Apostle said, "Who loved me and surrendered himself for me."[125] But now returning to the matter in hand, why should we marvel that the Holy Spirit at times comes to scoundrels, since the Son who partakes with him of the same nature and power surrendered himself into the hands of the wicked, and did not consider it below his dignity not only to be struck by their blows but to suffer a cruel death?

That the Gift of God Is Not Defiled by Unclean Ministers

(28) If, in fact, the brightness of the visible sun is not affected by the gloom and dankness of the grave, if it is not defiled by filth from the sewers, is there any wonder that the most high and infinite Spirit should touch ever so lightly with his splendor the dark and squalid hearts of certain men,[126] only to remain clean and unsullied in his own purity? Anyone who ordains, therefore, and is guilty of any crime—whether he is proud, or lustful, whether he is a murderer, or even a simonist—he is, indeed, tainted and undoubtedly steeped in deadly leprosy, but the gift of God that is passed on through him is defiled by no one's corruption, nor infected by anyone's disease. That which flows through the minister is pure, and passes to a fertile soil, clean and limpid. Holy Church, to be sure, is a garden of delights, a spiritual paradise, watered by a river of heaven's choicest gifts. Let us assume, therefore, that wicked priests are like channels made of stone; in channels of stone water makes nothing grow until after flowing through them it pours out on fertile, cultivated fields.[127] Even

125. Gal 2.20.
126. Cf. *Collectio Dionysio-Hadriana* (PL 67.314A); Ryan, *Sources* 38, no. 50. Seekel, *Grundlagen* 48 cites Pseudo-Isidore 656 and Augustine, *In Ioh.* CC 36.5.15, 50 as sources.
127. Augustine, *In Ioh.* CC 36.5.15, 50; Seekel, *Grundlagen* 49.

though the passing years should successively produce many unworthy priests, so that both they that ordain and they that are ordained are found equally corrupt, this living fountain is, nevertheless, not restrained from flowing thought he glade of the Church to the end of time, and from this fountain not only the ranks of the priesthood but also all who are reborn in Christ raise to their lips the cup of salvation.[128] Through priests, to be sure, baptism and holy oil come to us, as well as every dispensing of the sacraments of the Church. If, therefore, the wickedness of priests were able to inhibit God's gifts by their fall from duty, it would necessarily follow that the whole human race would withdraw from receiving God's bounty.

(29) On the other hand, if from faithful ministers men should receive these heavenly gifts, but from fallen ones they obtained nothing, they would necessarily reckon not God but priests to be the cause and the moving force of their own salvation. God forbid that an evil servant should be able to injure me when, without doubt, the master is good; or a malicious crier, where the judge is benevolent! The Dove should not be horrified, nor disgusted at the ministry of certain foul individuals, provided that he alone upon whom he descends in his fullness [i.e., Christ] possesses the supremacy of consecration. The unity of the Church is established on this principle, that Christ retained as his own the power of ordaining and did not transfer his title to any of the ministers of ordination. For if ordination were to proceed from the worthiness or the power of the bishop, it would obviously not belong to Christ at all.[129] Even though the bishop imposes hands and by the ministry committed to him recites the words of the blessing, it is certainly Christ who ordains and consecrates by the hidden power of his majesty. So it was that God commanded Moses: "Say this to Aaron and his sons: 'This is how you are to bless the sons of Israel. You shall say to them: May

---

128. J. Cavigioli, "De sententia s. Petri Damiani circa absolutionem complicis in peccato turpi," *Apollinaris* 12 (1939), 35–39.
129. Cf. Augustine, *In Ioh.* CC 36.5.11, 46 and 6.6, 56; Pascasius, *De corpore* 12.77; Seekel, *Grundlagen* 50.

the Lord bless you and keep you. May the Lord show his face to you and be gracious to you. May the Lord turn his face to you and bring you peace.'"[130] And immediately he added, "They are to call down my name on the sons of Israel, and I will bless them."[131] It is, therefore, the function of the bishop to invoke God's name on those who are to be ordained, but it is proper only to God to bless them inwardly. The external rites of ordination are obviously granted to the minister, but the efficacy of ordination itself is reserved solely to the Lord. For this reason the Lord said in Exodus, "It is I, the Lord, who sanctify you."[132] Therefore, if it is the Lord who sanctifies, why should we fear that the guilt of some minister who deserves punishment might stand in the way?

Whether a Minister of the Word or of the Sacrament,
He Cannot Block the Gifts of God

(30) The Apostle complained that certain false brethren, because of jealousy and competition, were not preaching Christ with the right intention.[133] But what is the point? Did he decide to stop them? Then listen to what follows: "What does it matter," he said, "so long as, one way or another, either from pretence or from love, Christ is proclaimed, and for that I rejoice, and shall continue to rejoice."[134] Christ, moreover, has ministers of the word and ministers also of the sacrament; in both ministries, surely, some are good and faithful, while others are false and wicked, but one receives neither something better from the good, nor something worse from the wicked. The ministers in fact are quite different, but that which is given is obviously one and the same. For the originator of the gifts is certainly good and that which he gives is in no way marred by the service of the ministers.[135] The flow of the stream is pure, and so it is superfluous to pay attention to the leprous hands of him who gives you a drink,

---

130. Num 6.23–26.
131. Num 6.27.
132. Exod 31.13.
133. Cf. Phil 1.15.
134. Phil 1.18. For the variant, "love," cf. *Beuron* 24.2, 68; see also Augustine, *In Ioh.* CC 36.5.19, 52; Seekel, *Grundlagen* 51.
135. Cf. Augustine, *In Ioh.* CC 36.6.8, 57.

so long as what one drinks is clear and sparkling. Why should we be much concerned whether the minister is good or bad, so long as he who is the principal author of word or of sacrament is always one and the same?[136] For in working signs and miracles, or in the pronouncements of the prophets, or even in possessing the virtues of true religion, the grace granted by the Holy Spirit either ebbs or flows. So it was that Elisha begged his master in these words, "Let me inherit a double share of your spirit."[137] It was obvious that this petition was granted as is clear from Elisha's miracles, in which we detect greater power than in Elijah's wonders, and twice their number. This fact will not escape anyone who carefully studies their record. But this difference does not occur in the degrees of ministry, for no one is more a priest or deacon or any other officer than another. In the former case, surely, we look to the faith and devotion of the one making the request, but in this case one merely carries out the order instituted by the Church.

(31) Listen to what the Lord says of evil preachers: "The scribes and the pharisees sit in the chair of Moses. Therefore, pay attention and do everything that they tell you, but do not be guided by what they do."[138] If, then, the wickedness of any priest does not prejudice the words spoken by him to an audience, how can it stand in the way of a sacrament that is given, not by man, but by the authority of God? For both he who preaches and he who ordains is the minister and not the grantor. And so, it happens at times that a teacher's language is quite the same, but his words do not bear fruit in the same way in the minds of his hearers. For while the heart of one grows numb and is as cold as ice, the mind of the other, upon hearing his words, quickly becomes warm with the fire of divine love. How does it happen, therefore, that words which flow from one and the same mouth and uniformly strike the ears of many, do not penetrate the depths of the heart in the same way, except that the one who outwardly serves by reason

---

136. Cf. Pascasius, *De corpore* 12.80 and 83.
137. 2 Kgs 2.9.   138. Matt 23.2–3.

of the office of preaching is quite different from him who, by his own power, produces profound effects through the words of the preacher?[139] Hence, whether he dispenses doctrine by his words, or confers the orders of the Church, the priest in no way uses his own resources but merely carries out the office and the ministerial functions with which he was endowed. Otherwise, if these effects were to flow from the worthiness of the priest, they would indeed nullify all faith in God's grace.

That It Was not Moses, but God Who Granted Something of Moses' Spirit to the Seventy Men

(32) Man does not give what is divine, but it is God alone who uses evil man for good purposes, and he alone who dispenses his gifts either by the hands of good men or even by the wicked. And so the gift of divine grace is neither diminished by the administration of the wicked nor increased at all by the performance of the good. This fact is clearly recognized when we call to mind the following passage from sacred history. There the Lord said to Moses, "Gather seventy of the elders of Israel, men you know to be the people's elders and masters. Bring them to the door of the tent of the covenant and let them stand beside you there, that I may come down to speak with you; and I will take some of the spirit that is on you and put it on them."[140] Here we should note that he did not say, you will take some of the spirit that is on you and put it on them, but rather, I will take and I will put, to show clearly that man does not hand over the Holy Spirit to another man, but that it is he alone who distributes the gifts of his grace just as he wishes. And thus a few lines later it is said, "The Lord came down in the cloud. He spoke with him, and took some of the spirit that was on Moses and put it on the seventy men."[141] The Lord is said to have given some of Moses' spirit to these men, to teach us plainly that both those who ordain and those in orders should have the same spirit,

---

139. Cf. Granata, *Contributio* 737.
140. Num 11.16–17.
141. Num 11.25.

so that those who are in charge of the Church should never hold opinions that are at odds with one another, from which, may God forbid, schism and heresy rise like the plague, but that all should teach the same thing in harmony, and with one mind live in the unity of the Spirit.

(33) Moreover, just as the seventy men whom the Lord ordained after choosing the apostles[142] (virtually the same number as those he wished to associate with Moses in bearing the people's burden) revealed the figure of priests, so too we observe first Moses and later the apostles receiving the dignity of bishops. And just as the former were unable to receive the Holy Spirit from the apostles and the latter from Moses, so also undoubtedly must we judge of bishops and of other orders of dignity in the Church, that is, since there is only one omnipotent God who arranged these men in various ranks of sacred orders by the grant[143] of his governance, so it was he alone, according to his own knowledge, who dispensed the grace of his Spirit to each of them. Nor could Moses assume for himself any other prerogative in the grant of his spirit except that which the voice of God commanded him, namely, that he choose the men, bring them to the door of the tent, and stand with them. This is the substance of what Moses was to do. What, therefore, could Moses recognize of his own power in this gift of God when, in addition, as Scripture relates, two of those who were on the list stayed back in the camp, did not go to the tent, and still, without his knowledge, received the spirit along with the rest?[144] In this situation, therefore, where it is stated that some of Moses' spirit was taken and given to others, we must not admit that Moses suffered any loss of his own spirit, just as when an object borrows light from a burning lamp, the lamp on that account does not suffer any loss of light.

142. Cf. Luke 10.1.
143. Cf. Granata, *Contributo* 738.
144. Cf. Num 11.26.

That They Who Come Forward for Ordination May Already Have the Holy Spirit

(34) It is clear that just as there are seven gifts of the Holy Spirit, so there are seven degrees of rank in the Church.[145] While in all these grades some are considered to be of greater dignity, such as patriarchs, archbishops, and bishops, these do not receive a new order, but rather, within the same priesthood these ranks are considered to be of higher honor. Now, since a priest (*sacerdos*) is so called because he gives something holy (*sacrum dat*), that is, because he offers sacrifice to God,[146] what can be found in the Church to be of greater dignity, what more eminent than the priesthood through which, as all agree, the mystery of the Body and Blood of the Lord is offered? Consequently, even though prelates are specially endowed with certain privileges that are compatible with the ministry that each performs, nevertheless since in common with all other priests they possess that which is greater than all else, along with them they too deserve to be called priests. Thus, when ministers of the Church are advanced to these ranks they should not be thought of as receiving the Holy Spirit anew or suddenly, as if this heavenly guest were only visiting for the first time those who till then were void of the Spirit, but rather in this fashion, that by an increase of grace he brings those in whom he already dwells to the advancement of higher office. At any rate, how could one who succeeds to such honors receive him for the first time, since by law these ranks are conferred after extended periods of time, and since baptism, to which the first fruits of the Spirit are attributed, was obviously received long before? In the case of the apostles as well, the same distinction was clearly observed, namely, that they again received the Holy Spirit whom they had already possessed, and that they desired to rise from

---

145. The seven gifts of the Holy Spirit have their source in Isa 11.1–3. But the comparison of these seven gifts with the seven ranks of ecclesiastical orders is unique in medieval symbolism. See Hopper, *Medieval Number Symbolism*, 84.

146. Cf. Isidore, *Etym.* 7.12.17.

grace to grace as they progressed with his endowment. Keeping in mind, obviously, the mystery by which divine providence, as we know, was at an early stage secretly at work in their hearts, we read that twice they publicly received the gift of the Holy Spirit, first of all when the Lord breathed on them and said, "Receive the Holy Spirit";[147] and the second time when fire appeared above them in the form of tongues.[148]

(35) And even before this clear evidence of his gift, they were obviously inspired by God at the very beginning of their new vocation. For how could they cast aside all that they had physically beheld and, at the command of a single voice, quickly run after things unseen, unless the grace of the Holy Spirit had already enlightened them with internal vision? And so Paul says, "He who does not possess the Spirit of Christ does not belong to him."[149] Even though this statement of the Apostle had not yet been written, it was undoubtedly already true. They would never have committed themselves to Christ's apprenticeship and, therefore, belonged to Christ if they had not already possessed the first fruits of his Spirit. Consequently, what the hand of God's bounty had already given to his faithful, he granted again and again, that by repeating his gift he might make their cold and arid hearts glow more fervently and be flooded with his riches. And so, human nature which had been wasted by the age-old squalor of sin was to be restored by certain processions of growth to a new and flourishing life. If, therefore, in keeping with what was included above, one could not be appointed to some lower rank of orders, nor even be baptized without the Holy Spirit, whoever is promoted to the priestly office does not receive the Holy Spirit anew, but is afforded an increase of him whom he already possesses. Just as the single soul is spread through all the members of the body, so is the Holy and Universal Church animated by the one Spirit of God. Thus Paul says to the Corinthians, "Just as a human body, though it is made up of many parts, is a single unit because all these

147. John 20.22. 148. Cf. Acts 2.3.
149. Rom 8.9.

parts, though many, make one body, so it is with Christ. For indeed, in the one Spirit we were all brought into one body by baptism."¹⁵⁰

(36) But while the soul is one and truly gives life to all the members, it does not furnish one and the same power to all the parts; to certain ones, indeed, by some sort of privilege it grants that which it does not bestow on the others. While other parts have life in common through it, the eye specifically receives from it the power not only to live but also to see, the ear to hear, the heart to feel, the nose to smell, and the tongue to speak. And even though the soul is in no way diversified, it still imposes various duties on the individual parts. So also the Holy Spirit, while dispensing faith to all who are reborn in Christ, infuses life, as it were, into all the members of the Church, as God's word declares: "By faith my righteous one shall find life."¹⁵¹ But when he promotes some to the ministry of ecclesiastical dignity, he grants special gifts to certain apparently superior members. Moreover, whether the eyes are crossed, the ears crooked, or the noses snubbed, the soul pays little heed. But whether the members be distinguished or ugly, to each it dispenses an office in its own right, so that in a way it seems to make little difference what these members are like, but it notes only the positions to which they are naturally consigned. So too the Holy Spirit does not concern himself with the worthiness of the individual in conferring the sacrament of spiritual grace, but with the office of the grade assigned to him; thus it is of hardly any importance whether members of the Church be deformed or comely but is concerned rather with where they are placed. So we too should consider not the worthiness but rather the position, especially since the Apostle says, "God appointed each limb and organ to its own place in the body, as he chose."¹⁵²

(37) But it often happens that the very organs to which more important sensate duties are assigned, suffer from malformation, while others are conspicuous for their beauty. The latter, indeed, participate in the other's functions that serve

150. 1 Cor 12.12–13.
151. Heb 10.38. 152. 1 Cor 12.18.

the utility of all, without, however, bearing any of their blemish or deformity in themselves. With this the Apostle agrees when he says, "Those parts of the body which we regard as less honorable are treated with special honor."[153] Thus it follows that what clerics have specifically as a class they owe not so much to themselves but rather to the common utility of the whole Church. And so it happens that if they are unworthy, they owe to others even the honor for which they are esteemed, and they do not escape judgment for the guilt that overwhelms them. For if they had received the priestly ministry only for their own benefit, it would not be unreasonable for people to discuss their worthiness. But since this grace is granted for the common welfare, one need not consider the quality of those to whom it is given but only the question of for whom it is given. Truth, moreover, says, "I am the vine, and you are the branches."[154] From this vine various branches grow, some destined for timely pruning, while others are to be left intact for bearing fruit. But as for those to be pruned, so long as the sickle of the gospel or of canon law is not applied,[155] their fruit is not to be distinguished from that of the good branches, but is to be regarded without distinction.

Of Wicked Bishops, Whose Ordination, However, Was Valid

(38) And so it was[156] that all the ordinations performed by Liberius, who was both a heretic and a turbulent man, were considered valid and immutable. Liberius, moreover, who was deceived by error and disbelief, is known to have subscribed to the Arian heresy, and because of his transgression many horrible crimes were committed. Many priests and clerics were killed because of his wickedness, and the remaining Catholics were forbidden to use not only the churches but also the baths. Subsequently, Liberius apostatized and lived on for six more

153. 1 Cor 12.23.
154. John 15.5.
155. See Pascasius, *De corpore* 12.81; Seekel, *Grundlagen* 55.
156. The source of what follows is Auxilius, *De ordinationibus a Formoso papa factis* (PL 129.1059–1074). Cf. W. K. Firminger, *Journal of Theological Studies* 26 (1925), 80; Ryan, *Sources* 38, nos. 51–54; S. P. Lindemans, "Auxilius of Naples," NCE 1 (1967), 1122; Reindel, *Briefe* 1.431f., n. 82.

years. Yet whatever he did regarding ordinations remained valid and firmly established in all its vigor.[157]

(39) And what shall I say of Pope Vigilius?[158] Even though he was an impious and criminal man, none of the popes dared to quash any of his ordinations. You are aware that this man was the same Vigilius, who had earlier conspired against Pope Boniface, so that while the latter was still alive sacrilegiously he might usurp the Apostolic See; but because the senate resisted, he was unable to carry out his illicit and abominable undertakings. Afterwards, however, he used his customary dirty tricks to attack Pope Silverius and deprive him of his apostolic office. But the latter quickly discerned his purpose. He gathered a council at which, by the authority of the Holy Spirit and by apostolic prerogative, he anathematized him as a simonist and a usurper of the Church. Following the sacrilegious plans he had conceived, however, Vigilius employed imperial forces and bribes, and with the help of false evidence viciously condemned the aforesaid Pope Silverius, clothed him in a monk's habit, and deported him to the Pontine Islands, "feeding him with the bread of affliction and the water of distress."[159] There this blessed pope became a witness of the faith, died, and was buried, and at his tomb many sick people were restored to health.[160] Vigilius, on the other hand, snared in the net of the anathema he deserved, and also guilty of murder, with criminal boldness made himself pope. But with what incalculable love the goodness of God operates! Given up for lost because of his sins, Vigilius was spared to do penance when he refused to enthrone the heretical patriarch Anthimus,[161] whom he had promised reconciliation. For which he was forced into lengthy exile, suffered harsh conditions, and received just recompense for his deeds, and at length died far from his native city, finding rest in the Lord.[162] And still,

---

157. Auxilius depends on the *Vita Liberii* (*Liber pontificalis* 37.1, 208).
158. The source for Auxilius is the *Vita Bonifatii II* (*Liber pontificalis* 57.1.281).
159. Cf. 1 Kgs 22.27.
160. See the *Vita Silverii* (*Liber pontificalis* 60.1.292f.).
161. Anthimus I, patriarch of Constantinople (535–536).
162. See the *Vita Vigilii* (*Liber pontificalis* 61.1.296–299).

as was stated, his ordinations remained perpetually firm. These events which I have reported about Silverius and Vigilius can be read in part in the synodal decree of the aforesaid Silverius, in part in the accounts of the *Liber pontificalis*.[163]

(40) If, therefore, the decisions of such infamous popes are not declared null, how can the acts of a simonist stand in the way of an innocent man when his own conscience does not condemn him? How can another man's iniquity deprive one of God's grace when his own way of life recommends him before God? The Holy Spirit is indeed given through him who certainly does not possess him. But that my listeners may believe what my feeble mind proposes, let the blessed Augustine step forward to provide me proper support. He reproaches the Donatist Parmenianus in these words: "What we read," he says, "in the Book of Wisdom: 'The Holy Spirit of discipline flees deceit and withdraws from senseless counsels.'[164] should be so understood, that he does not assist in his salvation, but does not abandon the ministry that, through him, accomplishes their salvation. Wherefore the Apostle says, 'If I do it of my own choice, I am earning my own pay; but if I do it apart from my own choice, I am simply discharging a trust.'[165] As if he were saying, It benefits those to whom I discharge this grant, but not me who dispenses."[166] The same celebrated doctor in his *Explanation of John the Evangelist* also says, "'You have already been cleansed by the word that I spoke to you.'[167] Why does he not say: You have been cleansed by baptism, by which you were washed, but 'by the word that I spoke to you,' unless it is that the word that cleanses is also in the water? Take away the word, and the water is neither more nor less than water. The word is added to the element, and it becomes a sacrament, itself becoming a kind of visible word. He had also spoken to the same effect when washing the disciples' feet: 'A

---

163. The spurious bulla of Silverius (JK 899), the so-called *Damnatio Vigilii*, is in Pseudo-Isidore 628f.; cf. Fuhrmann, *Fälschungen* 187f., n. 110–111.
164. Wis 1.5.   165. 1 Cor 9.17.
166. Augustine, *Contra epistulam Parmeniani libri tres* 2.11.24, CSEL 51 (1908), 74; cf. Seekel, *Grundlagen* 70, no. 6; Ryan, *Sources* 38, no. 53.
167. John 15.3.

man who is bathed, needs only to wash [his feet]; he is altogether clean.'[168] Whence does water have such efficacy that in touching the body it cleanses the soul, except by the operation of the word, and that, not because it is spoken, but because it is believed? For even in the word itself the passing sound is one thing, the abiding efficacy another. 'This is the word of faith which we proclaim,' says the Apostle, 'for if on your lips is the confession, "Jesus is Lord," and in your heart the faith that God raised him from the dead, then you will find salvation. For the faith that leads to justification is in the heart, and the confession that leads to salvation is upon the lips.' "[169]

(41) "Accordingly we read in the *Acts of the Apostles*, 'Purifying their hearts by faith.'[170] And in his epistle the Blessed Peter says, 'So also with you, baptism is what saves you, not the washing away of bodily pollution, but the appeal made to God by a good conscience.'[171] 'This is the word of faith which we proclaim,'[172] by which, doubtless, baptism is also made sacred that it might possess the power to cleanse. For Christ who is with us as the vine, together with his Father, the gardener,[173] 'loved the Church and gave himself up for it.'[174] And then reads the Apostle, and see what he adds: 'To consecrate it, cleansing it by washing with water and word.'[175] The cleansing, therefore, would on no account be attributed to the flowing and unstable element, were it not for that which is added, 'by the word.' This word of faith possesses such virtue in the Church of God that through its beliefs, offerings, blessings, and baptism, he cleanses even the smallest infant, even though with its heart it is as yet unable to believe unto justification, and to confess with its own lips unto salvation. All this is done by means of the word, of which the Lord says, 'You have already been cleansed by the word that I spoke to you.' "[176] Therefore, according to the teaching of this blessed man, or

168. John 13.10.
169. Rom 10.8–10.
170. Acts 15.9.
171. 1 Pet 2.21.
172. Rom 10.8.
173. Cf. John 15.1.
174. Eph 5.25.
175. Eph 5.26.
176. John 15.3; Augustine, *In Ioh.* CC 36.80.3, 529; cf. Seekel, *Grundlagen* 70, no. 7.

rather, in keeping with the saving doctrine of our Savior himself, the mystery of any sacrament does not depend on the worthiness of the consecrator but on the word of consecration, so that it is not of great importance to examine what may lie hidden in the consecrator through his own deserts, but what, through the words, comes down upon him who is to be consecrated. He also says the same in his *Exposition* on Psalm 10: "'But what has the just man done?'[177] If Caecilianus offends you, what has Christ done to you? It was he who sent his betrayer along with the other disciples to preach the kingdom of heaven,[178] a man whom he called a devil,[179] who before betraying the Lord could not be trusted even with the Lord's purse;[180] that he might show that the gifts of God come to those who receive them with faith, even though he through whom they are received be such as Judas was."[181]

On Anatolius and Polychronius, Who, After Their Early Years in Crime, Were Properly Converted and Demonstrated That They Were Worthy of Their Rank

(42) Why, therefore, do human pride and foolhardiness boast that the sins of others can defile the purity of an innocent man, and that the crime of vendors should overwhelm those who are completely ignorant of the deal, while often those who began badly, finish well, and by the compensation of a perfect life bring their perverse beginnings to a happy conclusion? But that I might confirm by an example what I have been talking about, it is not unknown that while Flavian, the bishop of Constantinople, was still living in exile because of the Catholic faith, Anatolius was consecrated by heretics to take his place. To him the holy Pope Leo addressed these words: "When Flavian, your predecessor of blessed memory, was deposed for his defense of Catholic truth, it was believed, and not unjustly, that your ordainers, acting contrary to the provisions of the holy canons, seemed to have consecrated one like themselves. But God's mercy was present in this, directing

---

177. Cf. Ps 10.4.
178. Cf. Matt 10.5–7.
179. Cf. John 6.70.
180. Cf. John 12.6.
181. Augustine, *Enarrationes in Psalmos* 10.6.79.

and confirming you, that you might turn bad beginnings to advantage and show that you were promoted not by men's judgment, but by God's loving kindness. And this may be accepted as true, on condition that you lose not the grace of this divine gift by another sin."[182]

(43) Moreover, what should I say about Polychronius,[183] the bishop of Jerusalem? As we read in the *Deeds of the Bishops*, while proudly declaring himself to be the occupant of the primatial see of Jerusalem and insolently asserting that he was the supreme pontiff, he was engulfed by the simonist heresy, so that he would not promote clerics without payment, nor in a vicious deal accept less than ten pounds in gold for dedicating a basilica. What more is there to say? At length bishop Sixtus[184] of the Roman See called a council, and together with seventy-six other bishops condemned him to be removed from his see, and stipulated that he was to have a usufructuary right to only three properties belonging to the Church. He commanded that his see be kept intact, suspended him from office, and left a certain bishop, Theodolus by name, to be vicar in his diocese. After nine months, however, as Jerusalem was being oppressed by scarcity and famine, Polychronius sold the lands he had received for his use, and, in a lawful exemption from the law, disbursed the money so acquired to the poor. When Bishop Sixtus learned of this from the accusation of Priscus the deacon, who charged him with this pious crime— the latter stating that he was not allowed to alienate Church property that had been received only temporarily for his use—the holy pope was overjoyed, and immediately informed the Emperor Valentinian of this benign felony. The Roman pontiff then called a synod at which Valentinian also presided,

182. Auxilius, *De ordinationibus* 24 (PL 129.1068 AB); Firminger, *St. Peter Damian* 79, points out that Damian had taken the letter of Leo I, *Epistola* 106 (PL 54.1001BC; JK 483) from Auxilius. Cf. Ryan, *Sources* 38, no. 54; Seekel, *Grundlagen* 70, no. 9.

183. For the complex problem of Damian's use of the *Gesta Polychronii*, belonging to the group of Symmachian forgeries, see J. Chapin, "Symmachus, Pope, St.," NCE 13 (1967), 876–877; Reindel, *Briefe* 1.438f., n. 94.

184. Pope Sixtus III (432–440); cf. G. Schwaiger, LThK 9 (1964), 809–810.

and they began to discuss Polychronius' fate, in that from the poverty of his deprivation he had given away everything he owned, laudably imitating the widow in the gospel who had been praised by the Savior.[185] A suitable decision was reached, directing that he who had imitated the widow in giving away the necessities of life should not be deprived of his see. And so, Polychronius who, because of his prior pride and avarice, had properly lost his rank, in view of his generosity and humility afterwards regained the dignity of his former office.[186] If, therefore, a holy life could excuse Anatolius, who, as was said above, after expelling a bishop who was still alive, was then consecrated by heretics; if one grant of alms could restore the obviously simonist Polychronius to his former honors, how can one maintain that a person promoted by a simonist in no way enjoys the fruit of the honor he accepts?

That Miracles Are Often Performed Even by Unworthy Priests

(44) Why should we marvel, moreover, that Almighty God permits the priestly office to be preserved in his Church by evil ministers, when through them he frequently produces miracles, obviously not because of their worthy religious life, but by reason of the sacrament of priestly ministry they have received? To touch briefly on a few examples chosen from among many, there was Raimbaldus,[187] the bishop of Fiesole, who most patently was twice a simonist in that he had not only purchased his high office of bishop, but scarcely ever ordained clerics or consecrated churches free of charge. In addition, besides other women he had one who was publicly and almost always with him like a wife to whom he was legally married, many of whose sons and daughters are still alive, allied by marriage, with an ever growing accumulation of children. And yet we hear that many miracles have been produced through such a man. Here it will be enough to report one of these, so that from a single example we may infer what in all

---

185. Cf. Mark 12.41–44; Luke 21.1–4.
186. Cf. Seekel, *Grundlagen* 55f.; Ryan, *Sources* 39f., no. 55.
187. On Raimbaldus, bishop of Fiesole since 1017, see Schwartz, *Bistümer* 205; Capitani, *Immunità* 125, n. 9.

probability we may believe of others for which he became famous. This account was reported to me by Rozo,[188] master of the choir, a priest of the church of Florence, who was a man superbly trained in letters. He told this story at a great gathering of his clerics at which his bishop, the most reverend sir Gerard,[189] was present. "Once," he said, "a woman possessed by the devil was brought to our episcopal church, just as we were celebrating the feast of the Finding of the Cross of our Lord.[190] When we reached the offertory, where the verse, 'A most distinguished man came up to Constantine,'[191] is recited, suddenly—I know not why—the clerics forgot the melody they were singing. All at once this woman jumped up as if she were coming to the aid of the singers who had broken down, and sang out in such excellent voice, and with such zeal held to the tune of that sweet song, that all were in admiration of her performance. When the demon was charged to leave the woman, he replied that only Romulus could compel him to go. Hearing this, the poor woman's associates left quickly for the church in Fiesole and waited there before the altar of Blessed Romulus for God's mercy.[192] There, under questioning, the devil replied that he would never depart unless Bishop Raimbaldus appeared on the scene. And when the aforesaid bishop arrived with great pomp, the devil used the occasion to say: 'Woe, woe! Now the bishop is mounting his horse; now he is at such and such a place; and now he is passing this or that house.' And they, noting the names of the places, verified that all these things were true, just as the lying spirit had stated. Finally, the bishop arrived and after invoking the name of Christ, at once expelled the evil spirit from the body of the possessed woman and sent her home, safe and sound."

(45) Also at that time when the pestilence of simony was

188. On Rozo, the choir master, see Davidsohn, *Geschichte* 822.
189. Later Pope Nicholas II (Dec. 1058–July 1061). He had been bishop of Florence since 1045; cf. Schwartz, *Bistümer* 209f.
190. On this feast, celebrated on 3 May, see L. Duchesne, *Origines du culte chrétien* (1925), 290f.
191. Cf. Davidsohn, *Geschichte* 154 n. 3.
192. See Davidsohn, *Geschichte* 158f.

spreading with deadly effect through the whole body of the Church, growing freely in all ranks of ecclesiastical orders, there was a certain priest named Marinus, the father of the most reverend and honorable man, Eleuchadius, who is now the abbot of the monastery of the Blessed Mother of God, the Ever-Virgin Mary, located near the walls of the city of Faenza.[193] The former was not ashamed to live publicly with this Eleuchadius' mother as his legitimate wife. It was obvious that divine providence had conferred such grace on this priest that if one sprinkled the crops of the field with water blessed by him, there was no further damage from the plague of worms, or caterpillars, or locusts, so that after the sprinkling with holy water they all at once swarmed and disappeared. On one occasion, however, the lord of the priest Marinus, a man named Jeremiah, was filled with overwhelming hatred and jealousy for a certain rival of his, a near relative by marriage, a man thoroughly hostile to him. Among other damage that he might suffer from the latter's enmity, he feared that his enemy by some cunning trick might bewitch the keenness of his hunting dogs, and so he begged the aforementioned priest to bring him a bucket of holy water to be used in an exorcism, because he was convinced that it was needed for his purposes. When the priest in all simplicity had done what he had been ordered to do, Jeremiah, who was indeed aware that what he did was evil, but totally ignorant of the power of the sacrament, did not fear feeding pearls to swine.[194] Foolishly he mixed the holy water with the bran and fed it to his dogs so that they could not be put under an evil spell. But divine providence thought otherwise, and his idea turned out differently. For the evil which he maliciously wanted to avoid befell him, and while inconsiderately trying to benefit his animals, he instead brought harm to himself. When the dogs were let in to be fed and had scarcely opened their hungry mouths for the first bite, and before even touching the deadly food, of which they had just got a whiff, they all suddenly fell over dead. Doubly disturbed

---

193. The monastery in which Peter Damian was later buried; see Lucchesi, *Vita* no. 50; A. Savioli, "La chiesa di S. Maria 'foris portam' a Faenza e la tomba di S. Pier Damiani," *Studi Gregoriani* 10 (1975), 111–130.
194. Cf. Matt 7.6.

in that he had sinned and was punished by the loss of his property, Jeremiah notified Marinus of the whole course of events just as it had happened, and in tears begged for a penance for having committed a sacrilege so presumptuously. Marinus, however, refused to accept authority over such a crime, and in the face of requests from all sides, declared that he was not prepared to prescribe any other remedy in the case except the necessity of consulting the Apostolic See if he truly sought forgiveness. Compelled by circumstances, Jeremiah finally obeyed and accepted from the Roman Church the penitential decision that he had requested.

(46) On another occasion a wolf seized a little girl that the same priest, Marinus, had baptized, and carried her off into the depths of the forest and into secret ravines, with many folk following in pursuit. Her mother, half dead with fear, was also in the search party. Suddenly she came upon the priest Marinus and amid her tears cried out to him, sobbing and weeping, "O my God, father," she said, "little did I think that my poor unhappy daughter whom you held in your arms at the baptismal font would fall prey to cruel beasts and become food to satisfy the wild appetite of wolves." The priest said to her, "My good woman, don't be afraid, for if it is true that she is the child I baptized, the beast will never be able to devour her." Then boldly but thoughtlessly he added, "If it is I," he said, "that cleansed her in the waters of holy baptism, and the beast tears her to pieces, I will never again believe that God reigns in heaven!" Then a wonderful thing happened. After about four hours the child was found safe and unharmed among the bushes about eight miles deep in the woods. And near her stood the innocent wolf. Just as the lion was not allowed to violate the body of the prophet returning from Samaria,[195] so too this wolf did not dare to harm the girl. But as far as we can learn, it was also seen willingly guarding her. The little girl was found completely unharmed, except that her legs and arms were bleeding from the pricks of thorn and briar bushes.

(47) Recently there was also another priest in this area, the

---

195. Cf. 1 Kgs 13.28.

brother of the most reverend Bishop Gerard, who is now the abbot of the monastery of St. Donatus in the suburb of the town of Imola.[196] This priest lived almost like an ordinary person of the world, but he acquired such grace from God that if he was told that someone had been bitten by a serpent, he immediately gave the informant a drink of water he had blessed. After he had drunk, the efficacy of God's power was suddenly so apparent, that he spit out every bit of poison acquired by the wounded man, just as if the snake had actually bitten him. But as for the man who had been struck, totally free of the poison, his bowels thoroughly purged of noxious humors, he continued on, undisturbed and healthy.

(48) There was still another priest, a man of hardly any importance, who was without the slightest talent in worldly affairs, scarcely able to stammer out his words in syllables in a boorish manner. It happened that one evening a hawk snatched his hen, and this loss caused him to become so bitterly angry that he threatened the saint to whom the church he administered was dedicated, that unless he returned to him the fat bird he had lost, he would never again officiate at divine services in the church. And acting as though the madness of his words did not suffice, he dared to surpass his words by his deeds and aggressively beat on the altar with a club. To make a long story short, the next morning the hen returned, plucked of all its feathers, except for those on its head and wings, but evidencing not the slightest damage to its body, clearly demonstrating that God's benevolence never turns its back on the prayers of a priest, even a mad one, in that the hawk was not permitted by him to devour that fat African hen.

(49) And why should we marvel that divine providence works miracles through priests of whatever kind, so long as they are orthodox, since he often demonstrates his power also through heretics?[197] For, in passing over the rest in silence, it does not appear beside the point simply to quote in its very

---

196. On the monastery of St. Donatus near Imola, see *ItPont* 5.170; on St. Romulus, see A. Amore, LThK 9 (1964), 37.
197. Cf. Granata, *Contributo* 738.

words what we read in the *Tripartite History*: "In the meantime," it says, "a fire broke out in the city of Constantinople and gradually reached the baths of Achilles, then to the place named Pelargus, so that the church of the Novatians was being attacked. It was reported that their bishop Paul remained behind in the flaming church, begging God not to allow the church to be burned with all the rest. The place was spared and to this day stands unharmed, and there on 17 August the Novatians gather for divine worship. From that time Christians as well as pagans venerate this site."[198]

(50) Now these wondrous signs which divine providence works, either through heretics or through unworthy priests of the true faith, since they are granted not because of the worthiness of any of them but by reason of their office, will in no way free them from the punishment they deserve, or excuse them of the crimes they have committed when they come before the bench of the severe judge. For in that from which they seek glory they fall into ignominious confusion, and the more they are praised by the applause of flatterers, the more liable they are to plunge into the depths of eternal damnation. And often such men, as they are struck down by a terrible death, clearly show how truly worthy they were of damnation, who to all appearances seemed so admirable.

(51) As an example, the bishop of Fiesole,[199] of whom we spoke before, lived such a wicked life that his brother, a layman of upright behavior, would have nothing to do with him. And still he so radiated miraculous powers as was consistently stated by those who witnessed the event, that during the dedications of just one church he cured five men possessed by the devil in the presence of all the people. But when he came to die the avenging chastisement of his body, set aflame before it went to hell, indicated that in life he was distinguished not by his own achievements but by those that belonged to another. For when an infected swelling appeared on his foot,

---

198. Cassiodorus, *Historia ecclesiastica tripartita* 12.10.1–3, ed. R. Hanslik, CSEL 71 (1952), 678f. The last two sentences seem to be an addition from an unknown source.

199. See *supra*, n. 187.

causing a dreadfully burning itch, it so took hold of the entire sole of his foot, of his leg and hip together with the groin and genitals, that it gradually reached his vital parts, consuming his internal organs as if they were dry firewood. He burned with a hidden radiance so that it seemed that here and now some primordial fire had engulfed him whom the flames that never die would afterwards devour. Oppressed by the intensity of this intolerable and overwhelming pain, he neither recognized that he was receiving payment for his sins, nor was he willing to put away the women who were living with him, whose service, even then, he was not ashamed to use. Moreover, since our Savior says "that by the finger of God he drove out devils,"[200] and the finger of God is doubtless understood to be the Holy Spirit, it is clearly recognized that devils are never expelled from the bodies of men except by the power of the Holy Spirit. Consequently, it is obvious that this bishop, even though he was unworthy, even though he was a simonist and was stained by the filth of seductive lust, would never have been able to put devils to flight unless he had within himself the power of the Holy Spirit. With Samson also, who frequented harlots from a foreign land contrary to the command of God's Law, how would he have been unable to break such powerful bonds, and alone and unarmed kill thousands of men unless the strength of the Holy Spirit had fortified him?[201]

(52) That false prophet, moreover, did not lack the prophetic gift of the Holy Spirit when, as a master of deceit, with deliberate lies he persuaded the man of God in Bethel to return and eat contrary to God's command, saying, "An angel told me this by the Lord's command: 'Bring him back with you to your house to eat your bread and drink your water.'"[202] And then the Scriptures continue: "He deceived him," they say, "and brought him back with him."[203] And they immediately add this: "And as they sat at table, the word of the Lord came to the prophet who had brought him back and he cried

---

200. Cf. Luke 11.20.
202. 1 Kgs 13.18.

201. Cf. Judg 16.
203. 1 Kgs 13.19.

out,"[204] that is, announcing the course of events in which he would be killed because he had disobeyed the voice of the Lord. It should be noted here that he whom Scripture in the first place obviously charges with deceiving his brother, is then unquestionably declared to have received the word of God and to have prophesied things that were true. And certainly, if one gives careful thought to the circumstances of this event, it becomes clear that this deceiver undoubtedly murdered an innocent man; and yet the Holy Spirit did not hesitate to come to such a person and, in the very act of sophisticated deception while preparing to mislead by lying, he was compelled to prophesy by the oracle of truth itself. Who, moreover, is not aware that Eli was a priest rejected by the Lord, and that both for his laxity and for the unbridled license of his sons as well was condemned by the decree of divine chastisement? And yet, because of his blessing Hannah, for whom he had prayed that she might bear many children, was not sterile. To this point Scripture says, "Eli blessed Elkanah and his wife and said: 'May the Lord give you children by this woman for the loan which she lent to the Lord,'"[205] and then adds, "And the Lord visited Hannah and she conceived and bore three sons and two daughters."[206] It was not the merit of the man that rendered this blessing efficacious but rather the priestly office, and what was lacking in the minister was reinforced by reason of the ministry.

That Often Evil Beginnings Lead to Happy Results

(53) What harm, then, does the simonist inflict, if he imposes hands on those to be ordained, since he is unable to remove that which is present, or block what God increases? For the gift of heavenly grace is not handed out from the purse of the external paymaster, but is granted from the treasury of him who invisibly presides over this ordination. Even though he who sows be a thief, it is still the earth, under God's influence, that gives strength to the growing crops. Even

---

204. 1 Kgs 13.20.
206. 1 Sam 2.21.

205. 1 Sam 2.20.

though the hand that plants be unclean or leprous, the fruit that is gathered is certainly untainted when it reaches maturity. Often a beautiful child is born of an adulterous union, and from the indecent lust of parents an admirable line of offspring comes into being. Jacob, indeed, begot some of his children from legitimate wives, while others he sired from concubines of lowly status.[207] But when both came to take over their inheritance, the property was equally divided among them. Phares was born of her who played the harlot and sat at the crossroads, but he was not considered a lesser prince among his Israelite kindred.[208] Solomon is known to have been born of a woman who was the wife of Uriah, and still was without equal when he came to wield the royal scepter.[209] Obed certainly was begotten of Ruth the Moabitess, and yet he was deserving enough to have as his nephew the great and illustrious King David.[210] Rahab the harlot, moreover, gave birth to Boaz, and still he was found worthy to be included in the Lord's royal genealogy.[211]

(54) And why should I recall others, seeing that the mediator between God and men himself sprang from sinners and received the unleavened bread of sincerity from the leavened dough without the slightest infection from the old leaven;[212] but rather, to speak more clearly, from the very flesh of the Virgin, who was conceived of sin,[213] his flesh came forth without sin, which for its part destroyed the sins of the flesh. Why should we wonder, then, that the mighty hand of the Lord, so effective in performing whatever he wishes, should do this thing in the spirit which gives life, when it is certain that he so acts in the flesh which counts for nothing?[214] For how can we believe that he who causes adverse beginnings to have a

---

207. Cf. Gen 30.
208. Cf. Gen 38.
209. Cf. Matt 1.6.
210. Cf. Ruth 4.17.
211. Cf. Matt 1.5; Josh 2.1.
212. Cf. 1 Cor 5.8.
213. Even though the doctrine of the Immaculate Conception of Mary had not yet been defined, Damian comes close to denying it. See E. D. O'Connor, "Immaculate Conception," NCE 7 (1967), 378–382; S. Baldassari, "La mariologia in S. Pier Damiano," *La Scuola Cattolica* 61 (1933), 304–312, esp. 307f.
214. Cf. John 6.64.

favorable outcome, and that in affairs that are clearly of this world, will not be more favorably disposed to do the same in respect to the sacraments of the spirit? Thus we may ask why he who ordains that fruit from the trees be untouched by the grime of a filthy planter, should not also be permitted to decree that those who are ordained be entirely protected from the guilt of a criminous consecrator? He admitted bastards and the offspring of slaves to the company of legitimates and heirs in the division of inheritance, and in no way discriminated between the former and the latter in matters of equality; so why should we wonder if he should also endow those who were promoted by wicked bishops with dignity in the ranks of the priesthood equal to those who were ordained by worthy men? This, clearly, is never brought about by the good quality of the consecrator, but rather by the word of the living and eternal God. Finally, in the words of God the Father it was said, "Let the earth put forth vegetation: seed bearing plants, and fruit trees bearing fruit, each according to its kind."[215]

(55) And notice that this word remains unimpaired even today, so that crops in no way follow the diversity of farmers, but each according to its kind produces its own seed or its own fruit.[216] And, indeed, this seed is once again put into the earth and later the harvest is no different, but follows its own species. If, therefore, by the power of God's word the earth produces exactly what it has received, why should one marvel that the priestly blessing, which like seed is sown in the soul of the ordained, should invisibly produce the priesthood through the inspiration of the Holy Spirit? And so, is it not now improper to look to the fruit for the likeness of him who sows in the field, but only, so to speak, to see that the likeness of the seed comes forth? For God said to the animals, "Increase and multiply."[217] Now, by the efficacy of his word, up to now all living things were created, not principally as new beings, but produced by descent from the same original

---

215. Gen 1.11.
216. Cf. Pascasius, *De corpore* 12.78; Seekel, *Grundlagen* 57.
217. Gen 1.22.

seed.²¹⁸ Since, therefore, these words which were spoken only once, are of such unalterable force, what should be thought of the words of sacerdotal blessing which are totally sacred and divine and are always externally repeated in ordinations to produce an internal mystery? But since it is claimed that the words of magicians possess such power, that when they are cast like stones a serpent struck by them is broken into pieces, why should we marvel that the priestly blessing contains within itself the sacrament of God's power, by which he who is promoted becomes a priest? Are we to believe that magical words are of greater power than the efficacy that is at once mystical and made sacred by calling on the name of God?

It Is Unreasonable to Admit That What a Simonist Can Do in Granting the Holy Spirit by Baptizing, He Cannot Do by Ordaining

(56) We must surely marvel at those who, with such absurd stupidity, shamelessly state that simonists can effectively baptize but are absolutely unable to ordain. And although this topic was briefly discussed above, it does not appear beside the point to treat the matter still more plainly. Let us, therefore, focus our attention on a simonist who baptizes, and on the same person who also ordains, and let us decide, if we can, why baptism administered by him is valid, why ordination becomes invalid and, as is said, loses the power of a true sacrament.²¹⁹ Notice that after teaching the catechumen the first rudiments of the faith, he who baptizes then recites over him the prayers prescribed by the practice of the Church. These, indeed, were composed for this occasion by priestly authority, and thus by the grace of exorcism he expels the wicked enemy who had previously held tyrannical authority over him, and by pious and prayerful invocation caused the comforting Spirit to take up residence within him. But then, what more does the consecrator do than by also reciting canonical prayers call down the same Holy Spirit upon him who is being or-

218. Cf. Pascasius, *De corpore* 12.77; Seekel, *Grundlagen* 57.
219. Cf. Gilchrist, *Simoniaca haeresis* 224.

dained, and beg that he deign to descend upon him, except that the action of the baptizer is greater than that displayed by the services of the consecrator? For it is of greater importance for the Holy Spirit, as an initial favor, to come down upon one in whom he had not yet resided than to advance a man in whom he was already present by faith to a higher order. Indeed, by the office of instructing for baptism or of baptizing, the unclean spirit is expelled and living quarters for God's arrival are prepared in the new man, as we note in the words of exorcism themselves, in which the evil spirit is addressed by imperious command: "Now depart, O devil, for the judgment of God is at hand!"[220] In ordinations, however, we do not expel evil which, as we believe, is already destroyed and absent, but by the addition of more and more grace we increase the good that was granted. Are we, then, to believe that one and same man is able to do that which is greater, but cannot accomplish a thing of lesser importance?

(57) But perhaps in rebuttal one might say that some things obviously apply to the first beginnings of the faith which are never used in the rites of ordination, such as the salt that is placed in the mouth of the neophyte, the water into which the person to be baptized is immersed, or also the chrism with which he is anointed. But these, indeed, considered per se, are mere elements and are recognized as having no hidden or mystic value; at the prayer of the priest, however, and at the invocation of God's name they give birth to the sacrament's interior power. The sacraments of baptism and of orders, therefore, do not depend on material or earthly things but on the prayers of priests and the invocation of God, even though holy oil is certainly used also in the ordination of priests. And since one and the same simonist in both recites the canonically prescribed prayers, and in both, conformably to the rules of ecclesiastical discipline, calls upon the name of God, it does not penetrate our rational perception nor does human insight understand how the Holy Spirit can be granted by him in baptism and how he is not granted in promoting to priestly orders.

---

220. Exorcism in the Order for Baptism of Adults.

(58) But in countering this position it is said that the simonist cannot give what he does not have. Very well! What is the significance of the priest blowing on the face of the catechumen, saying, "Depart from him, unclean Satan, pay homage to the living and true God, give honor to the Holy Spirit"?[221] Surely, at these words one can see that by this act of blowing on a person the evil spirit is expelled and the Holy Spirit deigns to enter through the hidden and mysterious agency of God's power. Since all this comes about just as well through the breathing action of this simonist as by the services of a good priest, why is it that what we grant as possible in one sacrament we consequently deny as possible in the other? For in baptism—which God forbid—if, notwithstanding the vehement prohibition of the sacred canons, it is administered for gain, one may in no way believe that the sacrament lacks the mystery of complete and perfect regeneration. And therefore, one who receives baptism on condition of a payment of money is neither properly required to be rebaptized nor is he thought to be devoid of God's gift.[222] But if one should rush into a position of such insane stubbornness as to state that even simonist baptism is invalid, not only would my vehemence in reply at this point not be worn thin, but the overall discipline of the Catholic faith would oppose and the universal Church would arm against him who attempted to destroy all the provisions of the holy fathers.

That We Must Consider What Is Received and Not From Whom a Thing Is Taken

(59) But perhaps one might object by noting what the Blessed Pope Gregory observed about the condemnation of simonists, when he said, "For him a blessing is changed into a curse because he was ordained for the purpose of becoming a heretic."[223] I, indeed, approve of this statement and admit

---

221. Exorcism and Anointing from the Order for Baptism of Adults.
222. The source is Gelasius, *Epistola* 14.5, ed. A. Thiel, *Epistolae Romanorum pontificum genuinae* 1 (1867–1868), 364; JK 636; cf. Ryan, *Sources* 40, no. 56.
223. See Gregory I, *Reg.* 9.218 (MGH Epist. 2.206); John the Deacon, *Sancti Gregorii magni vita* 3.2 (PL 75.129C); Ryan, *Sources* 40f., no. 57.

that it is improper to dissent from it. He certainly is accursed, and is a heretic, who in an evil manner received what was good. That which was received, however, was in itself good, but for the recipient it became something evil. The morsel that was offered to Judas[224] was not changed from something good into an evil thing, but for him it became something evil in that he received something good in a wicked, unworthy manner.[225] And so, if Judas had handed the same morsel to another, it would not necessarily have followed that the sacred gift would have been essentially contaminated by the sin of the donor, nor that any pollution would have redounded to the recipient. Today, too, if anyone should unworthily receive the Body of the Lord from the sacred altar and give it to another, that which is received is undoubtedly pure, nor is the gift of divine grace defiled by the stain of the befouled minister. And although a perverse person eats and drinks judgment on himself,[226] still that which is eaten and drunk is the grace of God. For it is by God's grace that that which is Christ's human nature tasted death.[227] To all who are pure, everything is pure, but to those who have been corrupted and to the unclean, nothing is pure.[228] If, therefore, that which is pure is itself impure to those who have been corrupted, it must be acknowledged that the priesthood, which for a good man is truly the spiritual cause of his dignity, for a simonist becomes the grounds for damnation, so that the source by which the former, who is certainly Catholic, becomes a priest, is also that by which the latter may be truly declared a heretic.

(60) Nor is it any wonder that this should happen in spiritual things, since in bodily matters one can easily find the same diversity. For it often happens that food which invigorates one person, oppresses another, and that from the same medical remedy one person dies while the other recovers. It is, more-

224. Cf. John 13.26.
225. Cf. Augustine, *In Ioh.* CC 36.6.15, 61; Seekel, *Grundlagen* 42; Capitani, *Episcopato* 345 m/ 68, refers also to Augustine, *De baptismo libri septem* 5.8, CSEL 51 (1908), 270.
226. Cf. 1 Cor 11.29.   227. Cf. Heb 2.9.
228. Cf. Titus 1.15.

over, the same fire by which wax turns to liquid and the earth becomes dry; the same candle which is consumed by fire, but is used to illumine those who come near it. The light, which to the candle causes destruction, becomes for us the instrument for seeing in the dark. Of what concern is it to me that the candle is reduced to ashes, so long as the light that I borrow from it unfailingly burns on for me? Let the simonist burn and burn, the one from whom the Catholic is enlightened; and by the same light by which he is of service to others may he proceed to the darkness of his own eclipse, so that what burns may die and what is illumined may live. To those who seek the light, the priesthood is surely the light; but to those who burn with the fire of ambition, it is a consuming flame. Therefore, what one possesses that is conducive to his own death and destruction, the other receives to further his assurance of salvation. Samson, remember, extracted a honeycomb from the mouth of a dead lion and slaked his thirst at the water that flowed from the dry jawbone of an ass.[229] But in the water he failed to taste the slothfulness of the donkey and in the honey he did not detect the ferocity of the wild beast. For in both cases his mouth tasted what he had taken according to its peculiar properties; he paid little attention to determining whence it had come. So why should we wonder that what we see happening in the water of baptism we judge to be little different from what is done by simonists? For through it we are born anew in Christ, although after the function is complete, the same water is considered waste and is poured into the sewer.

*That the Novatians Were not to Be Deposed,
nor the Arians to Be Rebaptized*

(61) But now let us look through the sacred canons, as briefly as time permits, and although we do not often find an obvious opinion on the proposed question, we may establish what should be held from a few comparisons of the matters

---

229. Cf. Judg 14.8; 15.17–18.

contained.²³⁰ For we know that the Council of Nicaea decreed that the Cathari²³¹ who returned to the Catholic church were to be received according to their rank of ordination, with the sole proviso that they submit to the imposition of hands. And why was this, except that this type of heretic had remained faithful to the integrity of the Catholic faith, even though they had erred in certain other non-accredited beliefs. It is known, for example, that Novatus, whose errors these people followed, had taught that it was improper to associate with those who had remarried, or with those who had apostatized during the persecutions, even after they had done penance.²³² If, therefore, even those who were ordained by such heretics were not to be deprived of their honor because their consecrators had not faltered in the faith, what should be thought of ordinations by simonists who observe almost all the laws of ecclesiastical institution? But perhaps one may object that simonists are certainly not perfect in the faith, in that they sin against the Holy Spirit who, they think, can be bought with money. To that I can easily reply that if one uses this device of strict judgment, one also finds the Novatians to some extent guilty of heresy against the Holy Spirit.²³³ For since forgiveness is granted to repentant sinners through the Holy Spirit, who is the remission of sins, it is clear beyond a doubt that one opposes the Holy Spirit if he does not associate with apostates after their repentance. But it is one thing to sin against the faith and quite another to fall away from the faith.²³⁴ A soldier, for example, who loses his nerve and flees from battle should be charged quite differently from one who deserves punishment for having broken his military oath by going over to the enemy camp and surrendering. We do not impose the

---

230. This paragraph provides a brief insight into Damian's canonical methodology. See Ryan, *Sources* 41, no. 58.
231. Known also as Novatians, the Pure, etc.
232. *Collectio Dionysio-Hadriana* (PL 67.149AB), *Concilium Nicaeen.* 8; see Ryan, *Sources* 41, no. 59.
233. On Novatian and his followers, see P. H. Weyer, "Novatian and Novatianism," NCE 10 (1967), 534–535.
234. See Gilchrist, *Simoniaca haeresis* 216.

same punishment on a serf who fails against the orders of his lord in household matters, and on another who casts off the bonds of service and chooses the authority of an alien overlordship. Even though the Novatians to some extent seem to offend against the norms of faith, it is not so serious that they should be accused of denying the Holy Spirit with heretical perverseness. And therefore when they return, hands are to be imposed on them because they have sinned; but because they denied nothing at all, they are not to be deprived of the office of priestly orders.[235] Arians, on the contrary, who are in open and totally impious conflict against the divinity of the Holy Spirit,[236] when returning to the Catholic faith cannot continue in the dignity of the orders which they sinfully received. For they believe, as is clear from their sacrilegious declaration, that the Father is the Creator, the Son a creature, and culpably assert that the Holy Spirit is the creature of a creature. Therefore, since they do not have the power of the Holy Spirit in their faith, by which every rank of ecclesiastical dignity is accomplished, ordination performed by them is declared invalid by decree of the canons.

(62) And so I think it will not be out of place if I should quote something from the very words which Pope Innocent in his decrees left us on this subject: "In the case of the Arians," he said, "and other pests of this kind, while we admit their laymen who convert to the Lord by the imposition of hands as a sacramental sign of penance and by the sanctification of the Holy Spirit, it does not appear that their clerics receive any ministerial dignity when ordained to the priesthood. While we allow that they have only baptism, which indeed is conferred in the name of the Father, and of the Son, and of the Holy Spirit, we are of the opinion that they do not have the Holy Spirit resulting from this baptism and from these rites. For since their founders abandoned the Catholic faith, they lost the perfection of the Spirit which they had received, nor can they grant his fullness which is especially

---

235. See Gilchrist, *Simoniaca haeresis* 229.
236. See V. C. De Clercq, "Arianism," NCE 1 (1967), 791–794.

operative in ordinations, which they lost, because of what I should call their impious heresy rather than faith. How is it possible for us to judge their sacrilegious priests worthy of the honors of Christ while admitting their defective laymen, as I said, with the sacramental sign of penance, to receive the grace of the Holy Spirit?"[237]

(63) Now in the words of this decretal we are clearly given to understand that in the promotion of clerics we quite properly look into the faith of the person who ordains, on which depends the judgment whether the ordination be valid or invalid. For what the ordaining prelate holds in faith, the one ordained receives with the order conferred upon him. Now if the orthodox faith were present in the Arians, ordination conferred by them would not lose its value, even though some depraved error should taint them. And here we must note how greatly one should reverence the invocation of God's name, since those baptized by them whom a perfidious faith, as I might put it, condemns, should under no circumstance venture to be rebaptized. For since their founders, as was said, did not possess the orthodox faith, hands are imposed on them for the purpose of receiving the grace of the Spirit; but because they were immersed in water with the invocation of the Blessed Trinity, they are not to be baptized anew. Since, then, the mere words spoken without faith in the context of the Arian heresy should not recklessly be judged invalid, why should simonist ordination be without effect, where also the other rites prescribed by law are in keeping with the faith?

That the Effect of Ordination Rests upon the Foundation of Faith

(64) Concerning the Donatists,[238] moreover, we are aware that at the Council of Carthage it was granted that when any of them were disposed to return to unity with the Catholic church, if this appeared to be in the interest of Christian peace, they were received at their rank in the Church.[239] As

---
237. See *Collectio Dionysio-Hadriana* (PL 67.255D–256A), *Innocent I, Epistola* 24.3; JL 305; Ryan, *Sources* 41, no. 60.
238. See D. Faul, "Donatism," NCE 4 (1967), 1001–1003.
239. This Council of Carthage was held on 13 September 401; see *Registri*

we learn, however, from the general catalog of heresies,[240] Donatists are not completely committed to errors of faith, but rather, because a certain Cecilian was installed in the see of Carthage against their wishes, in their anger they went into schism and were cut off from communion with the Church. And although it is certain that no one can receive the Holy Spirit except within the Catholic church, still anyone ordained by them, if this be in the interest of peace, is not to be deprived of his dignity because he has persevered in the faith. Therefore, since a Donatist, who without doubt is schismatic and is certainly without the gift of the Holy Spirit, may at times be permitted to remain at the rank of the dignity he has received, it becomes perfectly clear that ordination is not a boon for the one ordained or for the one who ordains, but rather that the sacrament totally relates to the faith of both. Otherwise, whether a Donatist promotes a Donatist to clerical orders, or a Novatian promotes a Novatian, what meritorious dignity is to be found in either that would allow the former to grant or the latter to receive the mystery of divine grace? But between evil and evil, that is, between him who grants and him who receives, the good stands undecided and cannot be prevented by the wickedness of either from acting magnanimously. A leper, for example, may give gold to a leper, and it indeed glitters, in no way affected by the scabrous hands that hold it. If a blind man hands a lamp to another blind man, the light, unaware of blindness, does not give place to darkness at the hands of the bearers. Wherefore, if true faith is present, namely, if one rightly believes in the Father, the Son, and the Holy Spirit, the ordination of even an unworthy priest takes place without discrimination. Nor is the gift of divine grace diminished in its perfection because of the quality of an unworthy minister. And so Pope Innocent, of whom we spoke above, when discussing in the same breath the two heresies,

---

ecclesiae Carthaginiensis excerpta 68, ed. C. Munier, CC 149 (1974), 200. Damian's source was the *Collectio Dionysio-Hadriana* (PL 67.204A–C); cf. Ryan, *Sources* 41f., no. 61.

240. See Augustine, *De haeresibus ad Quodvultdeum* 69, ed. R. van der Plaetse and C. Beukers, CC 46 (1969), 331.

namely, that of the Paulianists[241] and that of the Novatians, explained why he had decreed that converts from Paulianism were to be baptized while totally forbidding the same to Novatian converts, explaining his position in these words: "Because the Paulianists," he said, "do not baptize in the name of the Father, and of the Son, and of the Holy Spirit, and because the latter, namely, the Novatians, never raised the question of the unity of the Father, and of the Son, and of the Holy Spirit. And therefore among all those who were separated from us, this group alone was selected, to which we must grant their belief in this doctrine, because in no way did they sin against the mystery of the Father, and of the Son, and of the Holy Spirit."[242]

(65) Now these words of the venerable Innocent are so final and so clear that they remove every doubt from our minds and unquestionably resolve every difficulty in the problem here proposed. For if the sacrament cannot be administered by the Paulianists because they do not believe in the Blessed Trinity, but can be given by the Novatians, however, because, while being heretics in other matters, they still retain the fullness of the orthodox faith, it follows without question that if faith is present, ordination takes effect, and that which rests on the foundation of faith is not shaken by defect in the function.

That Bishops Who Are Illicitly Consecrated Possess the Grace of Ordination for Others but Not for Themselves

(66) That being so, let me concede or rather assert that a simonist is a heretic, just as a Novatian and a Donatist are likewise heretics.[243] But a simonist sins against the Holy Spirit because he purchases God's gift, and a Novatian certainly sins against the same Holy Spirit because he despairs of those who

---

241. A sect that seems to have derived from Paul of Samosata, not to be confused with the Paulicians; see G. Joussard, "Paulos von Samosata," LThK 8 (1963), 213; P. Lebreau, NCE 11 (1967), 26.
242. Innocent I, *Epistola* 17.5 (PL 20.533); JK 303; *Collectio Dionysio-Hadriana* 55 (PL 67.260–261). Damian's citation does not include the complete text. Cf. Ryan, *Sources* 42, no. 62.
243. See Gilchrist, *Simoniaca haeresis* 215 n. 27.

deserted from the faith, and of their forgiveness even after they have done penance. The Donatist likewise sins against the Holy Spirit in separating himself from the Church, outside of which certainly the Holy Spirit cannot be found. Why, therefore, when the heretics' ordination is determined to be valid, should simonists' ordination be judged worthless, especially since we are not trying to retain the simonists in the office which they improperly purchased, but are rather seeking to forestall the loss of position for those who were freely consecrated by them? We should here note how greatly those under consideration differ from one another, in that Donatists are promoting Donatists to higher orders in the Church, Novatians are ordaining Novatians, that is, persons caught up in the same error, while simonists are not ordaining simonists, but men who are innocent and Catholic. In the former case, moreover, we may object that not only were they ordained by heretics, but that all involved were indiscriminately heretics. The latter, however, were in no way guilty of simoniacal heresy, even though they were normally promoted by simonists, free from every taint of venality, and were endowed with administrative offices in the same churches in which they had received the sacrament of holy baptism. Whether such men should justly be excluded from their offices can be easily determined on the authority of Blessed Leo, if it is not too much trouble to note his decretal pronouncement, given here in his own words. For he says, "No consideration allows entry into the episcopate for those who were not elected by the clerics, nor requested by the people, nor consecrated by the provincial bishops with the consent of the metropolitan. Hence, since questions may often arise about one who came to his office irregularly, who would doubt that it should never be granted by those upon whom, we know, it had never been conferred. If, however, there are clerics ordained by these pseudo-bishops in those churches which belonged to their proper bishops, and if their consecration was performed with the consent and decision of those in office, the action may be considered valid, so that they may remain in their churches."[244]

244. Leo I, *Epistola* 167 (PL 54.1203 AB); JK 544; Burchard, *Decretum* 1.11, 552f.; Ryan, *Sources* 42, no. 63.

(67) Here, then, by the authentic judgment of Pope Leo, those whom the consenting clergy and people have not chosen, nor whom the assenting bishops of the province with the consent of the metropolitan have consecrated, are not to be considered bishops. And yet, those who were ordained by them in their own churches by the decision of those in office, are not to be deprived of the honor of the office conferred. In other words, that he who rushed into the office of bishop by such usurpation that the votes of almost everyone concur against him, and that what he received was in no way of benefit to him since he was not considered to be on the list of bishops, but that it be of advantage to others who, even though they were promoted by him, were not to be deprived of their honor. But who would deny that venality might intervene in this case, where one had stolen into office at the highest rank with such obstinate and distressing ambition? Thus, such a person possesses for the benefit of others something that he does not have for himself, in that he is permitted to consecrate others, while he himself is not considered to be a bishop. Often, indeed, a fruitful branch is grafted into a sterile trunk and, in germinating, maintains its own natural function and not that of the trunk.

That Often Those Who Are Ordained by Infamous Heretics Are Not to Be Removed from Their Offices

(68) What should I say when ecclesiastical authority seems to aid those who were ordained by the most outrageous heretics, and when, in publishing its decrees in this dispute, it considers not the long standing infidelity of the consecrators, but the new faith and change of heart of those who are promoted? But whoever takes the trouble to look carefully at the decrees of the popes, will not fail to notice that the same Pope Innocent, of whom we spoke a moment ago, gave permission for all who had been ordained by the heretic Bonosus before he was condemned, to remain in office if, after abandoning and denouncing his error, they were disposed to continue in union with the Church.[245] This same Bonosus, as we discover

---

245. Bonosus, bishop of Naissus in Dacia, was condemned in 391 for de-

in the aforementioned decrees, was known to have been a Photinian. Now the Photinians deny that Christ was God, existing before all ages, born of the substance of the Father. These same people, since together with the Jews they do not hesitate to disavow the Son of God, share with them the same condemnation.[246] Since, therefore, these men who not only allegedly were consecrated by such a pernicious heretic, but were also involved in his errors, were permitted to remain in the orders they had received, it is easy to decide how we should judge those who were promoted by simonists, but without the taint of simony.

(69) Hardly different from this case is the decision of Pope Anastasius regarding the heretic Acacius.[247] His decretal statements are so clearly expressed and so conform in all points with my position that, even though everything I had said at greater length were wanting, they would fully suffice to prove my contention in this dispute. Hence I do not hesitate to quote at some length from his writings so that it will be obvious that my remarks are not of my own invention but are excerpted from the decrees of the Fathers. Among other things, he said to the emperor Anastasius, "According to the customs of the Catholic church," he wrote, "as your Serenity's most profound understanding will acknowledge, none of those whom Acacius had baptized or had ordained priests or deacons according to the canons was touched by any portion of the damage attaching to the name of Acacius, by which, perhaps, the grace of the sacrament might appear less powerful. For baptism, which in the last instance is administered by the Church, whether it be performed by an adulterer or by a thief, reaches the recipient as an unsullied gift because the voice which spoke through the dove excluded every stain of human contamination. This follows from the statement which says, 'He it is who

---

nying the virginity of Mary; see H. Rahner, LThK 2 (1963), 602–603; *Collectio Dionysio-Hadriana* 50 (PL 67.256D–257C), Innocent I, *Epistola* 16 (PL 20.519ff.); JK 299; Ryan, *Sources* 43, no. 64.

246. On Photinus, see Hefele-Leclercq, *Histoire* 1.841–862. Damian's source is Innocent I, *Epistola* 41 (PL 20.607f.); JK 318; see also Ryan, *Sources* 43, no. 65.

247. On Acacius, see H. Chirat, "Acacian Schism," NCE 1 (1967), 61–62.

baptizes with the Holy Spirit and with fire.'[248] For if the rays of the visible sun are not defiled by contact with pollution when passing through the foulest places, so much more unsullied by the unworthiness of a minister is the power of him who made the sun visible. Indeed, whatever Judas did as an apostle by reason of the dignity granted him, even though he was a thief and committed sacrilege, the favors given by this unworthy man in no way suffer damage thereby, as the Lord most clearly stated: 'The doctors of the Law and the pharisees,' he said, 'sit in the chair of Moses; therefore do what they tell you. But do not follow their practice, for they say one thing and do another.'[249] Therefore, whatever any minister of the Church appears to do for the advancement of his fellow men as a function of his office, is totally the result of God's action, as Paul, Christ's spokesman, asserts: 'I planted the seed, and Apollos watered it; but God made it grow.'[250] And further on the same Anastasius said, 'And so he too, whose name, I say, should not be mentioned, by ministering good things in an unworthy manner harms only himself. For the inviolable sacrament administered by him produced for others the completeness of its own power.'"[251]

(70) Here, then, we have this apostolic man coming to my aid, as it were, and obviously defending my position, so that in this matter there is hardly anything left for me to say. So let the new critics go their way, wickedly resisting such an authority, not accepting as adequate what seemed proper to the ancient fathers, that while acting indiscreetly they should also be wanting in reverence. Some men, indeed, wishing to appear more holy than they are, go to such pains to excise corruption that they proceed to mutilate what is authentic; and that they might seem in public opinion to be staunch defenders of justice, are not ashamed to deviate harshly from the path of human compassion.

---

248. Matt 3.11.   249. Matt 23.2–3.
250. 1 Cor 3.6. See Anastasius papa II, *Epistola* 1.7, ed. A. Thiel, *Epist. Rom. Pont.* 1, 620ff.; JK 744; *Collectio Dionysio-Hadriana* (PL 67.313f.), *Decretum Anast.* 7; Ryan, *Sources* 43, no. 66.
251. See *Collectio Dionysio-Hadriana* (PL 67.622f.), *Decretum Anast.* 8.

That Those Also Whom Acacius Consecrated After He Was Condemned, Were Not Deprived of Their Honors[252]

(71) What would they say if they had heard what the same pope decided also about the men Acacius consecrated after his condemnation? For it seems to me that these critics have not read his opinion, in that it is clear that they rashly disagree with his judgment. So let them hear of the Apostolic See's compassion and soften the severity of their own position. After stating what we have already quoted, he added the following: "But if the scrupulous suspicion of some," he said, "goes so far as to imagine that the decree of Pope Felix later had no effect on the sacraments which Acacius administered unlawfully, and that we should therefore be concerned about those who received the sacred mysteries granted in consecration or in baptism, and feared that the divine favors were invalid, let them call to mind that in this matter also a higher consideration likewise prevails, since the accused performed his function not without usurping the priesthood, by which, in granting his power to those who received these mysteries, he in no way harmed others in that he himself was guilty. Surely, the note played on David's instrument was pertinent in this case: 'The Lord will smash the heads of his enemies, the hairy skull of those who parade their guilt.'[253] Pride, you know, brings ruin on itself and not on others. So it is stated by the universal authority of the heavenly Scriptures, just as the Holy Spirit spoke through the prophet: 'He who acts proudly shall find no room in my house.'[254] Thus, when this condemned man appropriated the title of bishop, swelling pride struck at his own head, for it was not the people thirsting for the benefit of his ministry who were denied, but his own soul which had sinned was duly subject to the judgment of God, as the word of Scripture informs us at every turn."[255]

(72) And now what can be said in response? What tricks

---

252. See *Collectio Dionysio-Hadriana* (PL 67.313D), *Decretum Anast.* 7, *titulus*.
253. Ps 67.22.   254. Ps 100.7.
255. Again see *Collectio Dionysio-Hadriana* (PL 67.314C–315), *Decretum Anast.* 8; Ryan, *Sources* 44, no. 69.

can ingenuity devise against these pronouncements? What arguments are available for those who oppose the truth? Notice that we are dealing here with one person in particular, but a case that is defined in general terms can be universally applied. I do not, as if I were defending heretics, write out these points to destroy the other more severe statements of the holy fathers, which are levelled at them and their ministry; but only that, while heeding the moderate discretion of these holy men of old, our contemporaries might in no way through intemperate justice exceed the limits of correct judgment; lest the saying of the Apostle also seem to apply to them as it did to certain men of the same ilk: 'They have zeal for God, but it is ill-formed.'[256] Those, therefore, who were promoted by a heretic, by one condemned by the authority of the Apostolic See, are not to be deprived of the administration of their office, and those consecrated by simonists without payment will be forced to live with a threat to the honor they have received hanging over them. This is certainly a cruel decision and a totally inhuman sentence based on an unwise investigation, that punishment should convict as guilty those whose conscience renders them innocent, and that judicial severity should reach out to those whom the foolhardiness of presumed sin does not accuse. For where crime is not committed, why should expiatory punishment be inflicted? Where there is no guilt, why should an innocent person be exposed as guilty? Why should that which is thought prejudicial in secular courts be considered correct in the councils of holy priests? Certainly devout bishops usually groan from the depths of their being at the degradation of each and every priest, weep bitter tears, and all present are constrained to expressions of holy compassion. Note that now almost the entire Church of Christ is robbed of its priests at one condemning stroke, and does that appear tolerable? A vast number of priests is deposed to a man, and do we consider this a laughing matter? Why at least do we not call to mind what God's voice announced through Ezekiel, when he said, "The soul which has

256. Rom 10.2.

sinned is the one who must die; a father is not to suffer for the sins of his son, nor a son for the sins of his father. To the upright man his integrity will be credited, and to the wicked his wickedness."[257] Those who are eager to see harm come to their brothers strive at all costs to bring death to the soul of him who has not sinned and to have the innocent party pay the penalty for the crime of another. They pant to have sons charged with the guilt of their fathers, to have the virtuous proscribed for the crimes of the wicked, and to speak more clearly, they sentence those who are not simonists to the penalties of simonists and condemn them for the latter's trafficking even when they are totally ignorant of the offence involved in this cursed business.

That the Heresy of Simony Has Prevailed to the Present Day

(73) Who could be unaware that up to the reign of the most benign King Henry[258] and to the pontificate of Pope Clement[259] of venerable memory, and also of the most blessed and apostolic Leo,[260] under whose leadership Holy Church now rejoices in its governance, the poison of simonist heresy spread its deadly influence through the kingdoms of the west, so that what was everywhere accepted as licit was never judged to be subject to condign punishment, and what was thought proper virtually by all, was held to be the rule, as if it were decreed by law? Therefore what guilt did he incur, what sin did he commit in simply going to his mother, the Church, in which indeed he was reborn of water and the Holy Spirit, and also received the grace of consecration where he had been baptized? It was certainly not for him to argue about the person about to consecrate him. Wherefore, he judged that the man who was bishop of his church for that reason was adequate for promoting him to orders. What was he to do, since it was urgent for him to register for entrance into the militia of Christ, and not permissible to travel to a bishop in another

257. Ezek 18.20.
258. The Emperor Henry III, here called king.
259. Clement II (25 Dec. 1046–9 Oct. 1047).
260. Leo IX (12 Feb. 1048–19 April 1054).

diocese? Why are the ancient acts and decrees of the holy Fathers not more carefully investigated so that, the same moderate approach might also be adopted in arriving at their judicial decision?[261] For it was the same eminent Leo, referred to above, who ordered that all clerics converting from heresy were to be accepted in the orders to which they had been ordained, but forbade them to be promoted to higher orders. I am satisfied here to cite in brief only the title of his decree, but suggest that they who would read through his statements on this subject at greater length, should go to the text. He says, "That every cleric of whatever rank, who abandons the Catholic community and joins one that is heretical, if he should return to the Church, may remain in the grade he previously held, without promotion."[262] I conclude, therefore, that simonists differ in no way from other heretics, and like them break communion with the Church by entering a schismatical sect, but that they who were promoted by them to the priesthood or to other orders should be allowed to remain according to the Leonine opinion.

Here It Is Clearly Proved That the Holy Spirit Is Received Through Simonists

(74) But it is said by the opposing position, Note that the Blessed Pope Gregory states: "If any one by virtue of his office has not flared into action to correct the crime of simonist heresy or of the neophytes, he should not doubt that he has thrown in his lot with him who originated this sinful villainy."[263] We concede, I say, and think no differently, God forbid, from this holy man; namely, that all the faithful should

---

261. See Capitani, *Immunità* 126 n. 11, where he derives Damian's statements from Burchard, *Decretum* 1.166f., 1.71, and 2.39–42.

262. Cited here is the title to Leo I, *Epistola* 18 (JK 416) in the *Collectio Dionysio-Hadriana* (PL 67.285D–286A).

263. See John the Deacon, *Sancti Gregorii magni vita* 3.4 (PL 75.131D–132); *Reg.* 12.9 (MGH Epist. 2.357); JE 1859; Ryan, *Sources* 45, no. 71. The interpolation of the heresy of simony and of the Neophytes occurs in John the Deacon. It is not in Gregory's letters. Gregory (*Reg.* 2.208.10) defines *neophytus* as one who, after recent conversion, encroaches on the dignity of higher clerical orders.

make every effort to correct the shameful practice associated with both diseases, and should be eager, after proper investigation, to see that simonists and neophytes are both deposed. And so, I do not side with simonists whom the full authority of Sacred Scripture condemns. Yet, as I conclude from various decrees of the holy fathers, I frankly declare that those freely ordained by simonists are by law to remain in orders. Therefore, they who cite Gregory as evidence for their case, should not hesitate to reciprocate also in admitting his testimony, and not just some indifferent statement, but one that touches this subject to the quick, as we say, and for the future calls a halt to litigation by those who like to talk. And so, while discussing simonists in one of his homilies, he added, "Who are they who today sell doves in God's house, if not the people who receive payment for the laying on of hands, by which imposition, to be sure, the Holy Spirit is divinely bestowed?"[264]

(75) Consequently, if one decides to give credence to the authority of this holy man, there is no reason to further protract this discussion. What could be more clear and obvious than the statement: by the imposition of hands which is sold, the Holy Spirit is divinely bestowed? And, to be more explicit and to instruct the slow-witted more fully in the meaning of his words, he did not hesitate to repeat what he had previously stated so plainly: "Hence the dove is sold, in that the laying on of hands, by which the Holy Spirit is received, is put up for sale."[265] If, therefore, the Holy Spirit is received through this laying on of hands, which is offered for a price, to what extent is less of the sacrament to be found in simonists than in priests who were freely promoted, except that they themselves were steeped in damnation at the source which brings salvation to others, and like vipers meet their death while giving birth to their offspring?[266] Is there any wonder, then, that in the ministry of the spirit good ministers should rise from wicked ordaining prelates, since something similar happens

---

264. Gregory I, *Homil. in Evangel.* 1.17 (PL 76.1145B); Seekel, *Grundlagen* 71, no. 19.
265. *Ibid.*
266. Isidore, *Etym.* 12.4.10.

even in human generation? For it is certain that sighted children are often born of blind parents and that tall offspring who are sound of limb may come from hunchbacks and cripples. Quite clearly neither the virtue of the ordaining prelate will benefit those who have no fear of following a devious path, nor again does their wickedness stand in the way of those who walk the line of an upright life. Who is known to be prejudicial to Samuel just because he was a disciple of Eli?[267] Or what good did it do Nicholas that by apostolic election he had been raised to the order of Levitical service?[268] The latter, to be sure, received along with Stephan imposition of hands from the apostles, and perished; the former lived surrounded by the wickedness of Hophni and Phinehas, yet because he was a prophet faithful to the Lord he became known to all. Hence it would be proper that they who are eager to depose all by group action should observe the moderate solution proposed by Innocent, of whom we spoke above. For in discussing those who were ordained by heretics, after many remarks he added these words: "As often," he said, "as a sin is committed by whole peoples or by a large group, since it cannot be avenged on all because of their great number, one usually lets it go unpunished."[269]

How Great the Absurdity That Follows from Uninformed Discussion

(76) In such matters, when was discretion ever more important and necessary than now, when we scarcely find a single church that is not acquainted with these people? Should we judge it more salutary to do without the divine sacraments than to use the ministry of an invalid priest? But a world grown old[270] cannot accept new dogma, and it thinks it base to absent itself from the Church's services for a long time, contrary to contemporary custom. There also exists among us

267. Cf. 1 Sam 3.1. 268. Cf. Acts 6.5–6.
269. Innocent I, *Epistola* 17.6 (PL 20.535); JK 303; Ryan, *Sources* 45, no. 72.
270. On "a world grown old," see Letter 12, n. 4.

an intolerable confusion about persons, which for the insecure might produce no little obscurity, and for the excessively careful might dull the sharpness of their mind. For example, when one says that should a person receive a lower rank from a simonist, whatever should later be ascribed as coming from a good bishop would rightly be considered totally null and void. For, they say, he who does not possess lower orders cannot aspire to higher rank. But he could not be promoted by a simonist even to a lower order, and therefore he did not come to higher rank. And thus from such fictions and subtleties spiteful dissension is born and the purity of the Church is disturbed. We often find one good man between two simonists; or again, one good bishop is found conferring various orders on one person between two simonists. In these and other ways, therefore, which would take us too far afield, such perplexing confusion plagues us today at every turn, that if divine mercy had not come to our aid through Blessed Pope Leo, now reigning, pernicious error, to our great harm, will become settled in the Church of Christ.

(77) To this we may add that, if it is once admitted that a sacrament administered by such men be judged invalid, all basilicas dedicated up till now would have to be destroyed along with their altars. Finally, which is still more impious, the faithful departed are deprived of hope, so that we are forced to believe that past ages utterly perished without any remedy applicable to man's redemption. Otherwise, how can we believe that they are now reigning with Christ if they had not been able, as is said, to receive the sacraments of the Christian religion, especially since truth itself says, "Unless you eat the flesh of the Son of Man and drink his blood, you will have no life in you."[271] For if those men were not priests and therefore were unable to consecrate or administer the sacraments of the Body of the Lord, how could we believe that their followers, as dead men, crossed over to life which they did not have when they were among the living? But if we admit this, we must also believe that all who were burdened with grave sins passed

271. John 6.53.

in without the sacrament of penance. For since of old lepers were commanded to show themselves to the priests, and now it is required that penitents submit to canonical sanctions at the hands of the bishop, how could one be bound or absolved by priestly ministry when priests themselves were nowhere to be found? But why do we complain that they were without the remedy of penance, when beyond that they were neither Christians nor baptized according to this perverse line of argument? For according to the sacred canons, baptism is considered valid even if it is administered by a believing layman. But how could simonists, or those ordained by them, administer baptism if they, as our opponents calumniously assert, did not possess the Holy Spirit? For they would not even be considered Christians if they did not have the Spirit of Christ. Indeed, according to Paul's statement, "if anyone does not have the Spirit of Christ, he does not belong to Christ."[272] And if they were not Christians, they could not bestow Christianity. This is the reason then, as was said above,[273] why those baptized by Paulianists had to be baptized, because since it was evident that they do not possess the Holy Spirit, they were utterly unable to baptize. Therefore, according to the dangerous inventions of those holding this kind of opinion, any of our predecessors who appeared to be Catholics, are to be forever condemned like Arians and all other heretics. This, to be sure, proves to be so absurd and so contrary in its cruelty to orthodox belief, that it would destroy not only the sacraments of ages past, but would completely destroy the foundations of the present and future Church.

(78) This we can easily gather from the following. For since the Roman See, which surely is the mother of all churches, was under the power of venality, as from an infected root the poison of this simoniacal plague spread also through the branches of the other churches. Then, following the example of this see, in other churches everywhere forged money began to be struck. Yet, whether these were good or bad, it was necessary that they transmit the sacrament of orders to others,

272. Rom 8.9.   273. See *supra*, n. 64.

so that it would flow down to us through changing succession. But it is said that formerly the ordaining prelates had nothing to transmit, nor could the ordained receive anything from those who had nothing. And so it is that in modern times, in place of the grace of consecration nothing is granted; but what does it matter, since we ourselves are promoted by those who were ordained, however long ago, either by simonists or by their successors. And coming now to my own case, after Leo, the supreme pontiff, had learned that I was unaware of this trafficking involving my consecrating archbishop,[274] even though a money changer at that time presided over the Apostolic See,[275] he still granted me in my unworthiness the priestly office with which I was endowed.[276] But how does this ungodly dispute exclude me from the empty-handed, since I have proven that the wave of ordination grew dry at its original source, the first see itself?

(79) Note, therefore, that this opinion is not only in conflict with the statutes of all the ancient fathers, but also cruelly attacks the decision of this blessed pope.[277] For however far removed from a simonist he may be who attempts to ordain, what difference does it make, since what did not proceed from him, who indeed was not in possession, was not passed along to any other? If, however, there should be other dioceses, which were in no way contaminated by this kind of disease, in this regard what is conferred on the sons of other dioceses, since by canonical prohibition it is forbidden to ordain anyone from another diocese? Hence, according to this line of argument, within certain dioceses the river of divine grace became so dry during the first age of simonists, that it could neither flow into them, nor through them later pass on to others. Now, you teachers of accursed doctrine, do you see where your

274. Archbishop Gebhard of Ravenna.
275. John XIX would then have consecrated Gebhard in 1027. See Laqua, *Traditionen* 341 nn. 229, 230. See also *supra*, n. 100, where some doubt is expressed about Gebhard's innocence. But see also T. Schmidt, *Alexander II* 184, n. 244.
276. We can therefore place Damian's ordination before 1 May 1045. See Wilmart, *Une lettre* 131f.; Spinelli, *La data, passim*.
277. On Leo IX's position, see *supra*, n. 6.

gloomy prudence leads us? Have you carefully considered what your sophistical arguments might beget? By your wrangling has it come so far that you presume to place limits on Christ's mercy and take from his Church the fellowship of hope? But I acknowledge him faithfully, "because he is good, and because his mercy endures forever."[278]

That Those Who Had Been Promoted by Simonists are Renowned for Miracles

(80) This fact, moreover, which frequently I hear repeated on all sides, should not, I think, be passed over in silence. How is it that many highly regarded men who, as we know, were certainly promoted to the priesthood by simonists, and who continually celebrated Mass until their death, are now recognized as famous for their outstanding miracles? In our own day, such blessed men as Romuald of Camerino,[279] Amicus of Rambona,[280] Guido of Pomposa,[281] Firmanus of Fermo,[282] and many others were outstanding for their pursuit of holiness. By authority of an episcopal synod consecrated altars were erected over their venerable bodies, where, when miracles happened during the offering of the sacred mysteries, it became evident how acceptable their sacrifice was in the sight of God. Through them the divine economy shines forth as clear as day, for the darkness of another's wickedness obscures no one illumined by the brightness of his own good service of God, nor does the guilt of promoting prelates eclipse the proven purity and innocence of those promoted.

(81) I now recall that, while once discussing such matters with certain worthy bishops, Hubert of Rimini,[283] a most revered and upright bishop, asserted, "It was the same," he said,

278. Ps 105.1.
279. Cf. F. Ughelli, *Italia sacra* 1 (1717), 551; L. Jadin, DHGE 11 (1949), 594–600.
280. Cf. C. Carletti, "Amico," *Bibliotheca sanctorum* 1 (1961), 1007f.
281. Cf. D. Balboni, "Guido," *Bibliotheca sanctorum* 7 (1966), 510ff.; on Damian's relationship to Guido, see Laqua, *Traditionen* 45f.
282. Cf. G. D. Gordini, "Fermano," *Bibliotheca sanctorum* 5 (1969), 633f.
283. See Ughelli, *Italia sacra* 2.419, there called Humbertus, who became bishop in 1052.

"with my predecessor Bishop Hubert,[284] who in the process of acquiring his sacred see, as the whole district knows, paid nine hundred pounds in the coin of Pavia. And yet later he ordained blessed Arduin[285] to the priesthood, by whom today Almighty God works so many astonishing miracles." Forthwith, when I inquired whether the holy man had in his condition discontinued saying Mass, he replied that he had diligently continued offering the Holy Sacrifice right up to the moment of his last illness. Since, therefore, all these men whom we have noted above, asserted that they were ordained by simonists, and still persevered in their office to the end of their lives, and were so pleasing in the sight of God that because of their amazing qualities they worked wondrous signs as evidence: it is certainly obvious that the promoter's purchase of office is not prejudicial when the one promoted is unaware of the graft involved, nor does the guilt of the trafficker pass on to him who is not himself guilty of the crime of venality.

(82) And, indeed, perhaps it would somehow seem tolerable were these false assertions only to disturb affairs today, and had not in the previous century also destroyed all hope and the source of Christian piety. For they say that what then seemed to be a Church, was simply a house; what one thought was the altar, was merely a stone; priests and those seen functioning in other orders were only laymen, strangers to all the powers that flowed from a spiritual sacrament; that as far as the Body and Blood of the Lord was concerned, it was simply bread and wine, only an earthly substance, in no way filled with the power of the Holy Spirit.[286] All of these things, therefore, would be considered as false and frivolous and having nothing to do with the truths of Christian redemption, whence

---

284. See Schwartz, *Bistümer* 251. It is of interest to note the going price of 900 pounds in the coin of Pavia for one see; cf. P. Grierson, *Münzen des MA* (1976), 111.

285. See Schwartz, *Bistümer* 251; P. Burchi, "Arduino de Rimini," *Bibliotheca sanctorum* 2 (1962), 387–393.

286. For such ideas in the heresies of the eleventh century see the condemnation of the Italian Gandulf at the synod of Arras (*Synodus Attrebatensis*, c. 3, Mansi 19.436f.; c. 17.459f.).

it follows that our fathers, whether they knew that these things were false, or judged truth to have been a lie, all indiscriminately perished by inevitable necessity.[287] For to what avail do we recognize danger, if we are unable to avoid it? Or how can one arrive at the source of truth, if he chooses to wander, even without knowing it, through devious and winding ways? Was it therefore only Simon who had the power to restrain the flow of divine grace and, like an obstacle standing between God and man, was able to detach the human race from the company of the Creator? May the day never dawn when a false human being should tear to pieces what the true Godman had joined together. God forbid that one should be able to overwhelm all men and that human perversity should destroy the bounty of God.

(83) But what, I ask, should I say of those, who after a despicable commercial deal, are seen occupying their pontifical thrones for almost forty or fifty years, down to the present day? But let us pass over their predecessors, near or remote, of whom this same man at another time or place made thieves. All who were ordained when these men crept in, have either now departed this life, or burdened with old age, have been retired from their official functions. Hence it is necessary that we consider the sacraments performed in their own dioceses only by those clerics who received orders from such simonists who are still alive. But what should we think of them, what should we say? Must it not be said that under them thousands of men are perishing in that they are deluded in receiving sacramental grace under false sacramental appearance from those who had no such power? Must we not tell the people either to engage priests from other dioceses, or to go abroad to receive the sacraments from those who had not been ordained by simonists? But note that the sacred canons stand in the way and refuse communion to those crossing the boundaries of dioceses without a letter of recommendation from the bishop. To these, therefore, when we are consulted, what counsel shall we give? According to the folly of this hope-

---

287. See Miccoli, *Chiesa Gregoriana* 258, n. 81.

less assertion, then, are natives unable to bestow upon them the sacred mysteries, or is it not allowed for them by canonical authority to go to strangers?[288] And so, to the injury of the bountiful goodness of God an inevitable necessity of perishing is imposed on these people, for whom, indeed, cut off on all sides, no remedy of divine refuge is available. Even so, I put off pursuing these ideas any farther, so that I might leave to the judgment of a rational mind the things which when heard should at least be feared, understood rather than read, and with these few words the prudent reader should recognize how much error and impossibility entangle the authors of this doctrine.

How That Which Is Often Used as an Objection Should Be Understood

(84) Now then, it has become necessary for me to set down what my opponents often throw up to me from the authority of the canons, so that while their objection appears idle to clear reason, all argument over these issues may rightly be silenced once and for all. As often as we speak in favor of those who were ordained by simonists, they come up with *Ventum est*, they have recourse to *Ventum est*, they force me to look at *Ventum est*. And now let me also take up *Ventum est*, but in such a way that when one has come to the words I may not depart from a sound understanding of them. Note, therefore, that the same Pope Innocent who was already cited, inserted this statement among the several chapters of his decree, saying, "We now come (*Ventum est*)," he said, "to the third question, which because of its difficulty, demands a longer explanation. Since we say that those ordained by heretics are wounded in the head by that imposition of hands, medication must be applied at the point where the wound was inflicted so that it can be healed. This healing, following upon the wound, cannot take place without a scar, and where the remedy of penance is necessary, there is no place for the dignity

---

288. See Burchard, *Decretum* 2.136 (648C); *Canon apostolorum* 13.13; cf. Ryan, *Sources* 45f., no. 73.

of ordination. For if, as we read, 'whatever the unclean person touches will become unclean,'[289] how may that be granted to him which is customarily received as cleanliness and purity? But on the contrary it is asserted that he who has lost his dignity cannot grant dignity, and that he has received nothing, because there was nothing in the donor for him to receive. We agree, and this is a fact; certainly he could not grant what he did not have. But damnation, which he did possess, he granted through the wicked imposition of hands, but we cannot understand how he, who was partner to one condemned, could receive his dignity. But it is said that the true and honest blessing of a legitimate bishop removes every blemish that was caused by a corrupt one. Therefore, if that be so, those who have committed sacrilege, adulterers, and those guilty of all crimes should be presented for ordination because crimes or vices are reputedly removed by the blessing of ordination. There would be no need for penance, since ordination can bestow what a long period of satisfaction usually bestows. But it is the law of our Church for those coming from heresy, who, however, are then baptized, that only lay association is granted by the imposition of hands, and that not even the least clerical right is afforded by this action. Yet those, however, who passed from the Catholic church to heresy, who should otherwise not be received except by way of penance, with you not only do they not do penance, but they are also loaded with honors,'[290] and similar statements which follow.

(85) I have, indeed, quoted at length from this decree, and still have omitted many items which seemed necessary, so that I might throw light on the line of argument from which error derived, and yet, so that the tempered prolixity of the full statement might not bore the reader. My opponents imagine that these words should be understood in such a way that, as they assert, the heretics in this text should be called simonists, and that those ordained by them have received a capital

289. Num 19.22.
290. Innocent I, *Epistola* 17.3–4 (530f.); JK 303; see Ryan, *Sources* 46, no. 74, citing *Collectio Dionysio-Hadriana* (PL 67.259–269A). On the canonical tradition of *Ventum est*, see Gilchrist, *Simoniaca haeresis* 210f. n. 3.

wound, that is, by the very imposition of hands, so that the dignity of ordination can no longer be lodged in them. Their understanding of these words is confused by an obscuring of the truth, because they did not properly examine the text of the entire decree. In no way, certainly, does the purpose of the author here include simonists, but strikes rather at those heretical sects which are known to have neither the faith nor the grace of the Holy Spirit. Let them read the whole document, I say, so that at one insight they may grasp everything that is said. And let them more deeply consider the Paulianists and Novatians so distinct from one another because of the difference of sect, that those returning to the Catholic faith from Novatianism may be received in their orders, while from the Paulianists they must even be rebaptized. And they may gather why this is so from the fact that they were not baptized by the Paulianists in the name of the Blessed Trinity, while among the Novatians there is no question of faith in the same Blessed Trinity because it is complete.[291]

(86) They should also consider that it is accepted that Peter and John confirmed those who were properly baptized by Philip, the preacher of the gospel, solely by the imposition of hands.[292] But when the Apostle Paul found some people washed by the baptism of John, he asked whether they had received the Holy Spirit; when they admitted that they had not even heard his name, he ordered them to be baptized.[293] Since, therefore, after speaking of heretics in general, when coming to specifics he did not have the simonists in mind but rather cited the Paulianists and Novatians, it is doubtless clear that the decree is not leveled at those of whom there is no mention.

(87) We must, therefore, properly examine the meaning of this decree in this way. The Macedonians deliberated whether it was permitted to reconsecrate those returning from these heretics, by whom they had been promoted and were not allowed to remain in their orders. And in the meantime, after

---

291. Damian here paraphrases Innocent I, *Epistola* 17.5 (531–535).
292. Cf. Acts 8.   293. Cf. Acts 19.2–6.

considering the consequences of the arguments, they concluded that it could lawfully be done because heretical ordination, since it was not valid, would also be worthless, in that he who had lost his competence could not grant competence, for indeed there was nothing in the donor which the donee could receive, and therefore it seemed to them that such persons should in some way come to orders anew. Moreover, to add strength to the force of their arguments in favor of their position, they also added this, that the true and honest blessing of a legitimate bishop would wholesomely extract whatever vice had damnably entered through the heretic, so that the sacred hand would somehow wash away whatever filth the sacrilegious hand had spattered. By this line of argument they asserted that those ordained by heretics should reasonably be again promoted by Catholic bishops. But this Innocent completely forbade and decreed that they could absolutely not be reordained. This, indeed, is easily discerned if one carefully notes the whole tenor of his decree. My opponents, therefore, should be admonished to read through these documents attentively and let them clearly understand that they are concerned, not with simonists, but with heretics belonging to these impious sects.

That Rebaptism and Reordination Are Equally a Crime

(88) Since, therefore, it is now the proper time to speak of reordination, and since this alone remains for our composition, I should find it no trouble to discuss this theme also, if only briefly. Certainly, the regular student of Sacred Scripture has learned that rebaptism and reordination are weighed in the same balance. Just as one who was rebaptized is guilty of having put off Christ with whom he had been clothed, so too, one who is reordained is clearly shown to have lost the Holy Spirit whom he received. And since the godhead of the supreme Word and of the Paraclete is one, and since we certainly believe them to be of the same essence, he who loses one will not possess the other. And so, as it is an impious thing if, in repeating baptism, one should presume to banish Christ, so also it is despicable for one to have no fear of renouncing the

Holy Spirit through reordination. And if we take the trouble to cite a brief passage from the decree of Pope Felix, where he speaks of the rebaptized, we can there clearly conclude what also we should think of reordination. "It is plain," he said among other things, "that those who were bishops or deacons, and who have clearly either by choice or by force thrown overboard this unique and life-giving baptism, these have also divested themselves of Christ whom they put on, not only by the gift of regeneration, but also by the grace of the dignity they have received, since it is evident that no one can come to baptism a second time unless he should openly deny that he is a Christian and profess himself to be a pagan. While this is a detestable thing for all in general, it is all the more horrible when heard or said of bishops, priests, and deacons. But because the same Lord and Savior is most loving and wishes no one to perish, it will be proper for them, if they repent, to remain in the state of penance until the day of their death. Nor are they to be present in any way at the prayers, not only of the faithful, but not even of catechumens, with whom lay union is to be restored at death."[294]

(89) In these words we should carefully note, that if a rebaptized person for this reason must be said to have denied Christ, because after receiving baptism he denied that he was a Christian, he also who comes forward to be reordained is therefore guilty of having denied the Holy Spirit, because he then admits that after ordination he did not receive the Holy Spirit. A reordained person, therefore, is not to be distinguished by some other condemnation from one who has been rebaptized, since he is clearly associated with him through the same impious offense, unless perhaps one should claim that he sins more grievously because of what Truth says, that whoever sins against the Father and the Son will be forgiven; but whoever sins against the Holy Spirit will not be forgiven either now or in the future.[295]

---

294. See *Collectio Dionysio-Hadriana* (PL 67.323D–324A), *Decretum Felicis II*; JK 609; Burchard, *Decretum* 4.99 (647B). Damian inadvertently omitted "priests," in the first sentence, following "bishops."

295. Cf. Matt 12.32.

(90) And indeed, if with more thoughtful subtlety we examine the decrees of the Catholic pontiffs, we find at times that permission was given to rebaptize, which certainly was totally denied for reordination. For if we have not allowed what was said above to escape our memory, we note that it was quite in order for those baptized by the Paulianists and by other heretics who did not have the Holy Spirit, to be baptized.[296] In which case, however, baptism is not said to be repeated, because the prior impure washing does not appear to be a baptism. But it is totally disallowed for them to be reordained, no matter what kind of heretics they may be, because this the holy canons completely reject. Wherefore I am quite amazed that some of them are so mad in their enormous blindness that they would conclude that persons ordained by simonists should be once more ordained. Indeed, they publish a decree on simoniacal ordination that proves to be inapplicable even for those heretics who appear to have not even the slightest vestige of orthodox faith.

(91) Some heretics, for example, possess the correct faith and should be received in their orders; others are lacking in the proper faith and are not allowed to continue in their honors. And since I am unable to protect simonists from the stigma of heresy, by which they would rightly appear to be classified as heretics, let me sharply distinguish. Now either like the Novatians they must be considered to have the correct faith, or like Paulianists or Arians they are beguiled by perfidious errors. But if together with Novatians they possess the correct faith, just as those coming from the Novatians must be received in their honors, so also those ordained by simonists need not be removed from functions in the office committed to them. But if, together with Arians or Paulianists, they are caught up in the error of infidelity, just as those who have left the latter are in no way permitted reordination—a thing which a moment ago we observed Pope Innocent totally forbidding[297]—so also those promoted by simonists cannot be

---

296. Cf. Ryan, *Sources* 47, no. 78.
297. Cf. *Collectio Dionysio-Hadriana* (PL 67.255f.), *Decretum Innocent. I* 47; JK 305; Ryan, *Sources* 47, no. 79.

reordained under any circumstances. It follows, therefore, that whether they possess the proper faith or believe falsely, they are by no means to be ordained again.

(92) And so, in consequence of what has just been said, it is necessary that those ordained by simonists be considered as belonging to the Catholic faith and must be allowed to remain in their office; or, they are truly guilty of abject infidelity and thus lose what was received, so that they cannot receive further ordination. Indeed, who is unaware that these men not only remained firm in the orthodox faith, but that most of them as true Catholics are distinguished in all things as men attempting to lead holy lives and uprightly practicing all virtues? It follows, therefore, that they should remain in the orders they received, in which their holy life agrees with the purity of their faith. Let us, then, put away this blasphemous indiscretion and suppress this unlawful daring, and let those who demonstrate that the rebaptized have put off Christ also detest the reordained as having with equal impiety denied the Holy Spirit.

That as One Cannot Be Rebaptized, so Too It Is Impossible to Be Reordained

(93) Well then, let them who argue as they please, that those once ordained can receive a second imposition of hands, not content with their own devices, go ahead and attempt to prove their point with evidence from canonical authorities. Let them then say, who take these statements of the holy fathers for granted, who at least are the authors of these imagined works? And since authentic writings of these ancients that would give evidence of approbation are wanting, let them admit that they alone must be considered the authors of a new doctrine. And indeed that which we can nowhere find commanded by the authority of the doctors, turns up beyond expectations to have been even forbidden. For Blessed Pope Gregory, writing to John the bishop of the church of Ravenna, stated that just as no one could be rebaptized, so too it is impossible to be reordained to the same rank, using these words, "What, moreover, you assert," he said, "that he who was ordained may be or-

dained again, is too ridiculous for words and should be beyond consideration for a man of your intelligence, unless perhaps you were using this as an example, showing that anyone said to have done such a thing was condemned. Far be it from you, my brother, to stand for such a thing. Just as one who is baptized must not be baptized again, so one who was once ordained cannot be again ordained to the same orders."[298]

(94) By these words, therefore, it is clearly shown that as in rebaptism Christ is cast off, so also in reordination, he who was wickedly promoted is deprived of the grace of the Holy Spirit. For what is this sacrilegious ordination if not a twofold degradation, by which, indeed, while one is accursedly ordained, both are rightly deposed? Hence with good cause we read in the *Canons of the Apostles* that "If any bishop, priest, or deacon should receive a second imposition of hands from anyone, let him and the one who attempted to ordain him be deposed. For it is impossible for those who were baptized or ordained by such a person to be either members of the faithful or clerics."[299] But if anyone should object that Formosus, the bishop of the see of Rome, had been restored to office after his deposition, he should know that many bishops have indeed been reconciled, but we never read that they were again ordained to the same office. It is one thing for someone to be restored by synodal action to the rights of orders he has lost, quite another to obtain the grace of the Holy Spirit by the sacrament of ordination, which cannot be repeated;[300] especially since in him who is deposed, even though he may lose the privilege of publicly using his dignity, the sacrament of orders, once received, nevertheless remains in force; in the same way also, since the sacrament of baptism persists, someone guilty of crime is excommunicated but is not deprived of that sacrament, even though he is never reconciled with God.

298. See Auxilius, *De ordinationibus* 17 (PL 129.1066BC); JE 1198; Ryan, *Sources* 47f., no. 80.
299. See Auxilius, *De ordinationibus* 18 (PL 129, 1066C); Ryan, *Sources* 48, no. 81; *Constitutiones apostolorum* 8.47.68, 585. On this Canon 68, see also Reindel, *Briefe* 1.489f., n. 184.
300. See Auxilius, *De ordinationibus* 27 (PL 129.1069CD); Ryan, *Sources* 48, no. 82.

That It Is False to Say That Anyone Ordained ⟨by a Simonist⟩ Is No Different from a Layman

(95) But even though I have had much to say about the wickedness of reordination, lest the subject still remain in doubt, in the absence of authority from public records let me produce an example from ecclesiastical history so that the consecration of any priests may be seen to be, as one says, not insignificant. And we cite here the exact text: "At the time that bishop Alexander was celebrating the feast of the martyr Peter in Alexandria, while waiting for his clerics to convene for the banquet that followed the ceremonies, he saw at some distance, at a place near the sea, a group of boys playing on the seashore, imitating, as was usually done, a bishop and the rites customarily performed in church. But after watching the boys for a while, he saw them doing things that were especially secret and mystical. Disturbed at this, he at once ordered his clerics to be called to him and pointed out to them what he had been observing. He then directed them to go and collect the boys and bring them to him. When they had arrived, he inquired about their game, what they were doing, and how it was played. The boys, as is usual at their age, scared out of their wits, at first said they did not know, but then explained the affair in sequence and admitted that certain catechumens had been baptized by them, led by Athanasius, who was playing the boy bishop in their game. Then diligently inquiring of them what those presumably baptized had been asked, and what they had answered, and likewise by him who had been the interrogator, seeing that everything had been done in accord with the rite of our religion, after conferring with his clerical council, he is reported to have ordered that for those on whom water had been poured after their sound questions and answers, baptism was not to be repeated, but that the ceremonies customarily administered by priests should be supplied. But Athanasius and those whom the game considered priests or subordinate ministers, after alerting their parents and calling God to witness, he committed to the Church for their education," and the rest of the story, in which it is re-

ported that Athanasius actually became a bishop just as he had played the part as a boy.[301]

(96) I have taken pains to use this example from antiquity against those who assert that ordination by simonists is nothing at all, and who contend that those ordained by them are no different from laymen. For if this game in which boys played the role of priests and ministers was of such importance that the bishop, with God as his witness, committed them to their parents to be educated for the Church, and did not judge it proper that they, who by a kind of foreshadowing imitation had pretended to be clerics, should remain in the secular state, then why should they be considered no different from laymen, when it is obvious that they had received the sacrament of orders according to ecclesiastical custom? If pretension alone separates the boys from laymen, how is it possible that the false vanity of men should claim that those who indeed had received everything according to law were in no way distinct from laymen? "For everything that was written," as the Apostle says, "was written for our instruction."[302] And in his *Moralia*,[303] if I remember correctly, we find Gregory saying that a simonist stands between two dangers, namely, whether he deserts the flock committed to him or remains in the dignity he wickedly accepted, he does not escape the snares of sin. Nor does he expressly define either point, but only states that where the situation appears easier, one should as quickly as possible swim to safety. If a simonist is, therefore, as you say, a layman, in what, I ask, does he fail if he gives up the office of sacerdotal dignity? If, however, he does not have the sacrament of the priesthood in some degree, why is he guilty if separated from the pastoral ministry, to which he is not bound by sacramental obligation?

(97) But tell me brothers—with your permission I speak—if simonists or those ordained by them differ in no way from

---

301. Rufinus, *Historia ecclesiastica* 10.15.980f.; cf. Seekel, *Grundlagen* 72, no. 26.
302. Rom 15.4. For Damian's emphasis on the importance of this text, see Laqua, *Traditionen* 121.
303. Not found in the *Moralia*, nor in any of Gregory's other writings.

laymen, as you assert, how is it that the sacred canons decree that simonists are to be deposed in a synodal gathering? If a layman is convicted of usurping the rights of the priesthood, does the case need synodal action for him to be solemnly deposed?[304] Will it not be enough for him to be corrected by some private distraint, so that even with simple words he is thwarted in his rash presumption? After deposition, can a simonist freely participate in public penance by the imposition of hands, bear secular arms, get married, or engage in commercial pursuits? For even though they lose its exercise, they still cannot lose the sacrament of orders.[305] Therefore, since you must judge that none of these items can square with simonists, though you cannot deny they are appropriate to any layman, we must admit that both differ from one another in kind, in that you clearly see different qualities belonging to both.

What Innocent Thought of Reordination

(98) Let us also take a look at what the above cited Pope Innocent pointed out, even though in passing, about his thoughts on reordination. In the decree, written to the bishop of Naissus, he says, "Some time ago, if I recall correctly, I remember having sent similar letters about the clerics of Naissus both to you, my dear friend, and to our brothers and fellow bishops, Rufus and the others, concerning those who asserted that before Bonosus was condemned, they had been ordained priests and deacons by him, to the effect that if after deserting and condemning his error, they wished to be united to the Church, they would be gladly received, lest perhaps as men worthy of regaining salvation they should perish in the same error.

(99) "But now while I am living in Ravenna because of the many needs of the Roman people, Germanius, who asserts that he is a priest, and Lupentius, who calls himself a deacon,

---

304. See *Collectio Dionysio-Hadriana* (PL 67.144D), *Canon apostolorum* 30; Burchard, *Decretum* 1.112 (583A); Ryan, *Sources* 48, no. 83.

305. See Ryan, *Sources* 49, no. 84, where he cites several possible sources for Damian's position.

after receiving what seemed to be a legation of many such men, undertook prayerfully to express to me their own distress, stating that they indeed had churches located in your beloved's jurisdiction, but that they have been unable to obtain union with you, for the reason that a certain man named Rusticus had received the priesthood by repeated ordination and is no little hindrance, either in that they are grieved that such a man remains in the Church, or in that he thinks there must be sin in the case of others, just as he recognizes that there is sin in his case."[306]

(100) Here, then, it is clearly seen what opinion Innocent had of reordination, since he sought to reunite with their episcopal jurisdiction those who, out of zeal for justice, grieved that a reordained man was retained in the Church. He reports that this man judged that the bishop had to sin against others to the extent that he had sinned, in his case by ordaining him anew. With the usual diligence of evil men he attempted to ensnare others in the toils of the same condemnation in which he himself had not feared to be the first to be caught. Hence not without reason they deemed that such a man should be condemned, and as a heretic be totally excluded from the Church, since he had no respect for himself and provided danger for others.

(101) Lest someone, however, accuse me of writing obscurely as they complain that perhaps I introduce too many citations from the canons, let them know that without doubt the reason is this: namely, that by frequent persuasion and advice I cannot bring those with whom I am dealing to examine the sacred canons. And for this reason I think that the opinions of the holy fathers should be set down here, so that I might place before their delicate and tender eyes at least excerpted passages, to the end that while they consider my point of view in the sections I have produced, they may also yield to the authority on which I depend.

(102) And to be sure that they get everything confused, in

---

306. Cf. *Collectio Dionysio-Hadriana* (PL 67.256D–257B), *Decretum Innocent. I* 50; JK 299; Ryan, *Sources* 49, no. 85.

this too they act against the canons when in reordination they receive all orders simultaneously.[307] And so, when I was informed of a certain individual known to me, who was recently reordained, I admit that I was appalled at the crime. What more should I say? At length I approached the man and said, "Had you already been in any of these orders which you recently received from the bishop?" "None at all," he replied, "why should I receive something that I obviously already had?" And I added, "Therefore you were no different from a layman, indeed, you were nothing but a layman." "Yes," he answered, "I was just a layman in that I had nothing that could be called clerical." "But if a layman," I said, "should on the same day on which he was a layman break into the ranks of the priesthood, by your own judgment he became a neophyte, and for that, surely, he should at once be deposed." At that he blushed in confusion, and because he could not shake these arguments, by his silence confirmed the necessary conclusions.

(103) This too appears to be no small part of their madness, that those who reordain in our time do not observe the fasts prescribed by the canons, they do not reserve Saturdays for the conferring of holy orders, but use any month or day for granting this dissordinate ordination, as if the first ordination warranted this second ordination, so that while confusing the orders by administering them simultaneously, one should also confuse the statutes regarding times, and that a thing should be licit in reordination which even they would consider totally absurd in ordination.[308]

---

307. See Ryan, *Sources* 50, no. 86; *Collectio Dionysio-Hadriana* (PL 67.180BC), *Canones synodi Sardicensis* 13; see also Burchard, *Decretum* 1.17 (PL 140.554AB).

308. See *Collectio Dionysio-Hadriana* (PL 67.306A), *Decretum Gelasii*, c. 11; JK 636; Ryan, *Sources* 50, no. 87.

LETTER 40

He Addresses the Bishops, That They Advise
Caution to the Apostolic See

(104) Therefore, I beg you, good bishops,[309] in the divine spirit of holy zeal unite against this impious teaching and be unanimous in resisting the new heresy that is emerging in our time. Let the mouth of those who speak evil be stopped, so that the hand of sinners may not shake the foundations of apostolic faith.[310] May the doctrine of the Church be preserved in its purity, and may the seditious sagacity of this world not be permitted to disturb it. The enemy rises while it is dark to sow weeds throughout the field of Christ,[311] but you who walk by day, root out the evil crop with the hoe of sound doctrine. At night the Philistines fill the wells with rubble, by day let Isaac hasten to reopen them.[312] In the dead of night the thief tries to break into the treasury of Christ, so let his dogs be roused to bark their warning. But should one of your number emerge, arrogantly presuming to teach such wicked nonsense, you must remonstrate with him with a vigor equal to that by which he, who should be the guardian of the Church, attempts to attack her.

(105) Therefore, suggest to our blessed lord, the pope, that he apply the rigor of ecclesiastical severity to the guilty in such a way, that he not involve also the innocent in his judgment, as undiscerning men might wish. For it seems a wanton judgment that has sentenced children to death for the crime of the father, and let it go ahead, envigorated with divine force, and destroy simonists as it has begun to do, but not to the extent that it allows their ordination to depend on the intemperate judgment of a few. Surely he who in Peter's place possesses the keys of the Church,[313] he especially should rise up against this new dogma and pierce these innovators of evil

---

309. On the bishops addressed here, see Dressler, *Petrus Damiani* 104 n. 103; Laqua, *Traditionen* 300 n. 107.
310. Cf. Ps 62.12.   311. Cf. Matt 13.25–29.
312. Cf. Gen 26.15–18.
313. On the meaning of this statement, see M. Maccarrone, "La teologia del primato romano del secolo XI," *Miscellanea del centro di studi mediovali* 7 (1974), 74 n. 190.

with the lance of condign punishment; and he who stands at the helm of the boat that was entrusted to fishermen,[314] should be zealous to separate the bad fish from the good, but taking care not to condemn the good along with the bad. He should consequently say to unthinking men what we read of the householder speaking to his slaves: "No," he replied, "pull up the weeds and you might take the wheat along with them,"[315] so that later the weeds might be bundled up to burn, while the wheat is gathered in the barn. When sentencing Ananias and Saphira to their just punishment, did the Blessed Apostle decree that their children and relations should also be punished?[316] The sentence hurled against Simon himself did not reach down to those who perhaps might have elicited something of the truth from him. For with the words, "May you and your money go straight to hell,"[317] both the money and the trafficker are struck down. But where money is wanting, one need not fear the blow.

(106) Therefore, venerable fathers, together with the blessed supreme pontiff so dispose everything under equity and discreet examination, that in your decisions you too may be seen observing the rule handed down by this great teacher; that in the great body of the Church, whatever is corrupt may feel the cautery, the sound parts remaining in their own good health; let excesses deserving punishment be penalized so that while legal severity is displayed against the guilty, immunity for the innocent be preserved; let the rotten tree be subject to the ax, so that cuttings transplanted from it may take root and grow by virtue of its greenness.

What Pope Leo Eventually Decided in the Case of Those Who Were Promoted Gratis by Simonists

(107) And yet, I do not consider it a waste of time to explain what the venerable Pope Leo decreed in the matter. When by authority of an activist synod he rendered all simoniacal ordinations null and void, immediately the Roman bishops broke

---

314. See Woody, *Sagena piscatoris*.
315. Matt 13.29.
316. Cf. Acts 5.1–11.
317. Acts 8.20.

forth in a great seditious uproar,³¹⁸ so that it was claimed, not only by them, but by many other bishops that nearly all major churches would be without episcopal services, and especially that all celebration of Mass would have to be stopped, leading to the overthrow of the Christian religion and to the despair of all the faithful everywhere. Should I say more? After long and voluminous discussion on all sides, it was finally pointed out that Clement,³¹⁹ the bishop of this same see, whose memory we esteem, had decreed that whoever had been consecrated by a simonist, not unaware at the time of his consecration that it was a simonist to whom he had presented himself for promotion, must now perform forty days of penance, and could then function in the office of orders he had received. Immediately the venerable Leo agreed that this decision should remain valid, and ordered that for the future all should continue in the orders to which they had been advanced, subject to the aforesaid penance.³²⁰

(108) And yet, even today you notice that there are some, who while being ordained to various orders by such men, were elevated to the heights of the episcopate by this same pontiff. Nor was this irregular, because while canonical authority decrees that "whoever had obtained his sacred office by payment of money, both he and his ordaining prelate should be deposed,"³²¹ it is clear beyond a doubt that in condemning the simoniacally ordained and the ordaining prelate, he at once fixed the limits of justice, and did not extend the sentence agreed upon also to him who might have been promoted by such men. For if the author of this canon had decided that anyone promoted by a simonist should be deposed,³²² brand-

318. This report seems to relate to the Roman Synod of 1049, whose acts have not survived. But there is confusion here, with the Acts of Pope Leo I falsely ascribed to Pope Leo IX; see Hefele-Leclercq, *Histoire* 4, 1007; Ryan, *Sources* 50, no. 88; JL, p. 530.

319. *Concilium Romanum*, 1047 January; MGH Const. 1 (1893), 95; Cf. JL 526f.; Hefele-Leclercq, *Histoire* 4, 991.

320. The reference is to the Roman Synod of April 1049.

321. Cf. *Collectio Dionysio-Hadriana* (PL 67.144), *Canon apost.* 30; see Ryan, *Sources* 51, no. 90. As usual, this was Damian's preferred source.

322. On Damian's use at this point of Fulbert of Chartre's *Epistola* 13 (PL 141.207) to Leutericus of Sens, see Ryan, *Sources* 70, no. 120.

ing both him and his ordaining prelate, he would not, in consequence, have remained silent about those who might be promoted by him, so that truly he would have said, "let him and his ordaining prelate be deposed," and at once would have added, "and whoever will have been ordained by him." And indeed, since he did not say this, he indicated that we too should not so judge.

In Which the Emperor Henry Is Honored with Due Praise

(109) Moreover, as I recall the deeds of the venerable pope, it follows that there is good reason to turn my attention also to the glorious renown of the great king Henry. After God, certainly, it was he who rescued us from the mouth of the insatiable dragon; it was he who used the sword of divine power to cut off all the heads of the multicephalous hydra of simoniacal heresy.[323] He it is who, to the glory of Christ, can say, and with good reason, "All who came before me were thieves and marauders."[324] For up to the time of his reign the counterfeiting priesthood, as I might put it, offered unappeasing provisions to the Babylonian Bel. But, by God's authority, after taking over the government from his father, he at once threw balls of pitch into the dragon's mouth, and like another Daniel killed this wild beast.[325] Indeed, the love of money can readily be compared to pitch which burns and binds. It so burns in the furnace of an avaricious heart that it restrains one from generosity in showing mercy and loving compassion. What does it mean to throw balls of pitch into the dragon's mouth if it is not to say plainly, as Peter did, "May you and your money go straight to hell"?[326] And that, indeed, our leader himself truly asserted when he overthrew the stalls of those selling doves,[327] expelled the money changers, and forbade commercial activity in the temple of God. Nor does there appear to be a difference in meaning when Daniel is described mixing fat and hair with the pitch. What

---

323. See Lacqua, *Traditionen* 88f. for the literary source of Damian's "insatiable dragon."
324. John 10.8.
325. Cf. Dan 14.26.
326. Acts 8.20.
327. Cf. Matt 21.12.

do we understand by fat, but carnal pleasure? And what is meant by hair, which is external to the bodies of animals, but some exterior substance? And so the king mixed fat and hair with the pitch, and thus caused the dragon to burst asunder, because in total hatred of the simonist poison he not only did not yield to avarice, but also sought no carnal pleasure or profit from outside gain in appointments to ecclesiastical office.

(110) And so, after the dragon, who had previously battled with Michael, was slain,[328] cast from heaven, carrying with him a third of the stars, and bound in chains in the abyss, let us deride him joyfully with Isaiah: "O Lucifer, who rose in the dawn, how have you fallen from the heavens! How are you cast down to the ground, you who afflicted the nations!"[329]

(111) Until the time of this emperor all the canonical decrees, which were published by the Fathers regarding this plague, had long ago been forgotten by most. But he, like the famous Josiah of old, on finding the book of the Law from the Lord, tore his garments because of his grief, destroyed the altars, overthrew the detestable idols, and abolished all the superstitious and sacrilegious practices of former kings.[330] And since he did not wish to observe the norms of the princes before him, so as to obey the precepts of the eternal king, a not ungrateful divine economy granted him this favor, which up to that time it had not conferred on any of his predecessors, namely, that at his pleasure the Holy Roman Church should now be provided with leadership, and that aside from his authority no one at all may choose the bishop of the Apostolic See.[331] Clearly, if David after defeating Goliath, the Philistine, deserved to be espoused to the daughter of the king,[332] why should we marvel that this emperor also, as victor, should receive the Holy Church, which indeed is the daughter of the highest King, for having overcome Simon, the leader

---

328. Cf. Rev 12.4–7.   329. Isa 14.12.
330. Cf. 2 Kgs 23.
331. Cf. the *Concilium Romanum*, December 1046; JL 525; Hefele-Leclercq, *Histoire* 4, 989f.; Ryan, *Sources* 51–52, no. 91.
332. Cf. 1 Sam 17.26.

of the heretics, who had truly heaped reproach on the forces of the living God?

(112) And in some measure to rightly compare him with David, the latter had a craving for water from the cistern of Bethlehem that lay behind enemy lines. But when it was given him by the warriors who had carried out his wishes, he refused to drink it and poured it out.[333] And then the writer added, "He poured it out as a libation to the Lord."[334] Therefore, if water that is despised becomes a sacrifice to God, how precious in the sight of God must we deem the gift of money that is refused. David, to be sure, poured out water; but the emperor offered an equally pleasing sacrifice to God when out of love for him he treated gold rather than water with contempt. And since there was no lack of those endowed with royal dignity, who doubted they could administer their governments if they did not augment their treasury by the sale of churches, see how the omnipotent God, in whose power resides victory for those who triumph, authority for those who rule, and the disposition of all honors, without revenues from this unseemly profit subjected most frontier nations to his servant, tamed the wild tyranny of those who opposed his rule, caused the proud necks of his enemies to bend to him, allowed him to prevail over the barbarian nations around him, and forced the rebels among his pagan subjects to submit to his yoke. And all of this to show that victory comes from above, that it does not depend upon grants of money, but comes down to us from the generosity of divine grace.

(113) It would appear, therefore, that this emperor has won a victory over the enemies of the Catholic church not unequal to that of the Emperor Constantine. The latter crushed the doctrine of the Arian sect with the weapons of the orthodox faith;[335] Henry, by treading avarice underfoot, wiped out the plague of simonist heresy. Constantine, the defender of the faith, stood his ground so that Arius would not disrupt unity; Henry went forth as the conqueror of concupiscence so that Simon would not acquire pestiferous authority in the Church.

---

333. Cf. 2 Sam 23.15–16.   334. *Ibid.*
335. See V. C. De Clercq, "Arianism," NCE 1 (1967), 791–794.

(114) Let others attempt to construct triumphs for kings with the stylus of history, with pronouncements of choice praise extol their distinguished honors in battle and their mighty deeds. To me it seems that this victory, which we recalled above, is much nobler and incomparably more glorious, in which human blood is not shed, a vast array of knights is not diminished, but the whole Catholic church spread everywhere throughout the confines of the Roman Empire, is freed from the bonds of ancient condemnation as from the horrors of an infernal prison, so that rescued by divine providence at the hands of the emperor, it might sing to God with unimpeded voice: "You have loosened my bonds, O Lord," it sings, "to you will I offer sacrifice of praise."[336]

The Author Attacks the Simonists

(115) I lodge complaint against you simonists, who have caused me this grave inconvenience of burning the midnight oil. Indeed, I have defended your interests, but only that I might forever condemn you. Thus I admit the things that were done by you and show my judgment of how abominable you are and how worthy of the supreme punishment that befits the incorrigible. Judas, to be sure, believing the Lord to be a mere man, sold him; but at once he threw away the blood money as he prepared to pay the penalty that was his due.[337] But you, with no doubt of the divinity of the Holy Spirit, ascribe to him the venal transaction and hold on to the benefits of this sacrilegious deed, and you, who should have been subjected to punishment, profit by the crime that you commit. To whom should I rightly compare you, who hold the gifts of God not for yourselves, but for others? That which amasses salvation for them is turned for you into judgment and eternal damnation. In my view, you are plainly like the Jews, who while at heart were unaware of Divine Law, everywhere in the world became bureaucrats to the Christian people. You almost seem to have the appearance of bees, which carry hard earned

336. Ps 115.16–17.
337. Cf. Matt 27.3–6. Damian's comment on the theological belief of Judas is not based on this text.

honey to sweeten the lips of men, but which grow weak from hunger and are soon destined to die. Therefore, you unfortunate and miserable men, consider to what utter depths of perdition you have fallen, where not only evil things are evil, but where for you also good becomes evil; in which blessing is turned into malediction, divine gifts into heresy, sacraments into sacrilege, honor into shame, and preferment into ruin. To this we may add that you are also responsible for as many souls as there are faithful subject to your prelacy. Enjoy your affluence now, in your pride gather your crowds of clients; soon you will see all the army of angels furiously enraged against you, the apostles, martyrs, and the hosts of all the saints in terrifying force against you, with one mind and with equal judgment concurring in the sentence of your damnation.

(116) Him, indeed, have you offended and consequently made hostile, the wronging of whom is forgiven neither here nor hereafter. By the frightfulness of your cruel and most detestable crime you are worse than adulterers, you exceed murderers, you surpass plunderers, the sacrilegious and incestuous, parricides, and the infamy of nearly all criminals. And still this is too little! For if the thing be seen as it is, the very perfidy of the Jews and all heretical depravity are in no wise equal to your excesses. For you, night has fallen at midday, the storm has come amid the calm;[338] the sky above has turned for you into iron, and the soil into bronze,[339] for you do not rise because of the weight of evil resting upon you, and do not hide from men that which, in conscience, you have committed.

(117) Certainly, if even now, as patristic evidence asserts, blessings are turned for you into curses when you are observed being blessed by the word of the bishop,[340] what will happen to you then, when the very voice of God calls you accursed and rejects you, when the fury of the judge dismisses

---

338. Cf. Isa 16.3.   339. Cf. Lev 26.19.
340. See John the Deacon, *Sancti Gregorii magni vita* 3.2 (PL 75.129C); Ryan, *Sources* 52, no. 92.

you from his presence and hands you over to the torturers? Then truly will you learn how much the bitter purchase of your negotiated honor was worth, when at that moment the infinitely wide jaws of hell will be forced to swallow you, the cruel caldrons of gehenna to receive you. Then will the crackling, hissing flames feed on your bones, dripping their fatty marrow, then will the ravenous fire, like that belching from a furnace, never cease discharging steam through your mouth, your eyes, your ears, your nose. Then, indeed, will it be your lot to share the fate of your leader, Simon, the prince of heretics; and to those for whom paradise, freely promised by Christ, did not suffice, let hell, bought with money by the devil, be given as their reward.

(118) And yet, I will acknowledge that you, and not unjustly, are more worthy of damnation than the author of your error, presiding on the pestilential throne, so that you rightly excel him in punishment because you have vilely exceeded him in guilt. For he wished only to buy a heavenly office, but was unable to satisfy the thundering concupiscence that possessed him. You, however, both willed and accomplished it, you both approached and entered by stealth. The workshop was constructed, and the coins poured forth. And finally, he who plays at being God ends up being a dog; as he is lifted up, he is struck down; as he seems to ascend into heaven, he falls into hell. Consequently, also you, as you seek the heights, are brought low; not content at appearing equal to other men, despised in both divine and human opinion, you suddenly become like unclean dogs. Truly I waste my time on trifles if I should attempt to bring dry bones to life by rebuke, as if I were prophesying.[341] We can only pray that with honors set aside, they may again put on flesh and nerves, and thus again come alive through the breath of the Holy Spirit. But now having crossed the sea, securing the rudder I lower the sail, because with Christ as the skipper and with land in sight, I approach the harbor.

341. Cf. Ezek 37.4.

In Which a Summary of the Completed Work Is Addressed to the Archbisop of Ravenna

(119) Finally, Henry, venerable father, I come back to you, returning now at the close of this work to where I began. Here, I trust, you will not look for refined style or elaborated diction, nor seek for the bite of my studied wit, but for my rough simplicity and sorry language that can barely express what I mean to say. For I have proposed to set various grim and necessary things before the hearts of my brothers, and by serving utility rather than brilliance, purpose not to charm the ear with the allurements of inane words. You are not unaware that a studied style deprives thought of its vigor, and that elaborated brilliance saps the force of statements. They, indeed, may employ grand and erudite words, who with a certain pleasing adornment of captivating speech strive to capture the applause of men. But I, who am required to walk with unshod feet,[342] must not write shod with the buskin. And for those living under the command of silence, the superfluous verbosity of excessive eloquence does not seem to be in order.

(120) Wherefore, my dear friend, I offer you this piece, composed in inelegant and unskilled style like fruit of low account, and ask that you not despise my gift, for rustic ways have produced no better. Since, indeed, if I may put it so, you have risen to the highest position in the place where I was born,[343] I have sought you out especially as the recipient of my little gift, that this slender little sheep might offer his shepherd the offspring, not of the womb but of the mind. I know, in short, that your church, like the senate of the apostles, excels not only in number but also in the revered and mystic array of its holy bishops.[344] By their zeal, your church so pre-

---

342. See Letter 18, n. 29, and Letter 50.
343. Damian was born in Ravenna in 1007. Laqua, *Traditionen* 324–325, sees in this Latin sentence a hexameter, taken from John the Deacon's *Versus de Gregorio Magno*, MGH Poetae 4 (1923), 1069.
344. On the comparison of the bishops of Ravenna to the senate of the apostles, see Laqua, *Traditionen* 328–331.

serves the correct line of apostolic tradition, so immovably perseveres in the purity of genuine faith, that with the removal of every heretical irregularity, it may today imitate that new church which existed at the time of the apostles, or even appear to duplicate the very Nicene foundation of faith.

(121) Let your holiness, therefore, united with those whom you see fit, carefully investigate and prudently examine whether it agrees with the Catholic faith and with sound doctrine. But if this book be found even slightly blameworthy, prudently correct it and then show it to the most blessed pope, should he pass your way, as rumor has it,[345] so that what is belittled because of the artless composition of its author, might be commended by the service of so great a bearer. But if, which I hardly believe, it should appear to be everywhere so in need of alteration that it cannot be corrected, before it is presented for publication, let it be burned. Here we may aptly apply this passage: "Aaron and Hur are staying with you. If anyone has a complaint, refer the matter to them."[346] It is not to my shame to have my writings wiped out, so long as I do not blush in freely confessing what I believe, just so he who censures a speechless man may find it possible to reward him for his fidelity.

An Addendum to the Above Work

(122) In my clumsy and unskilled way I have written this little book with some hesitation and uncertainty, due to caution, and, as is seen at its conclusion, I have referred it to the definitive judgment of apostolic authority. But in the time of the venerable Pope Nicholas,[347] this question was raised again and subjected to lengthy discussion. Finally, after many disturbing encounters, after tangled and tortuous changing in these doubtful questions, the matter was at last settled by the

345. Pope Leo IX was in Padua in the summer of 1052.
346. Exod 24.14.
347. Nicholas II (24 Jan. 1059–27 July 1061), at the *Concilium Lateranense posterius* 549ff. On which, see Miccoli, *Il problema delle ordianzioni* 73ff., who concludes that this *addendum* (Chapter XLI) must be dated 1061, and not 1060; see also Laqua, *Traditionen* 322 n. 179.

judicial conclusion, that those who were hitherto ordained freely by simonists should remain in the dignity of the office they had received, but that those not yet promoted by them would not in the future be permitted advancement;[348] but with this proviso, that as a result of the severity of the sentence neither the entire ecclesiastical order should be destroyed, nor that in view of its leniency the plague of simony should acquire, by some lawful provision, the power of conferring the grades of ordination, all with a view that what in past ordinations had been valid, should for future ones be totally forbidden. For my part, I do not stubbornly affirm my own assertions, but humbly bowing to synodal decrees, follow the decision of the Apostolic See, either that which has already been published, or I profess obedience to that which in the future will be more precisely and more profitably decreed, so that just as we received the rudiments of a nascent faith from the blessed apostles through the brilliance of the gospel, so, after them, we may hold to every rule of living and thinking handed down by the popes.

(123) Furthermore, the bishop of Ravenna,[349] to whom this book was first sent, because he had been recently promoted and was therefore unknown to me, was thought to be proficient in scriptural theology. But since I was unable to elicit from him even the slightest spark of a solution in this matter, I decided to be satisfied with the authority of the Apostolic See, so that whatever should be prescribed by its synodal judgment would for me be certainly authentic, and would clearly appear to be supported by the vigorous authority of the canons.

348. The decision of the *Concilium Lateranense posterius* 550 of April 1061 (JL 562f.), regarded by most scholars as a victory for Damian's ideas, must have been a severe blow for Cardinal Humbert. Within a month he died on 5 May 1061.

349. Archbishop Henry.

LETTER 41

Peter Damian to Henry, the archbishop of Ravenna. This fragment was preserved in the *Liber testimoniorum veteris et novi testamenti* (Collectanea) of John of Lodi, and was first edited by Cardinal Mai in 1832. Damian here contends that it makes little difference whether at Mass wine or unfermented grape juice is offered, and similarly, whether leavened or unleavened bread is used.

(About the close of 1052)[1]

... Just as it makes little difference whether at Mass we offer wine or unfermented grape juice,[2] so, it seems to me, it is all the same whether we offer leavened or unleavened bread. For that "living bread that came down from heaven,"[3] just as he wished to manifest himself under the appearance of wheat, he did so also under the form of the vine. "Unless," he said, "a grain of wheat falls into the ground and dies, it remains a solitary grain."[4] And again, "I am the real vine."[5] Therefore, it suffices for me to offer either whatever is made from grain or whatever is produced by the vine. Nor am I too careful to inquire whether the bread was preserved in an immature dough until it could ferment, or also whether the grape juice was kept in a vat until it could turn into what one calls wine. But since it is not my purpose here to discuss these matters, I leave them to be handled by others....

1. This fragment was probably written at the end of Letter 40, immediately before its new conclusion. Neukirch 96f. dated Letter 41 between the end of 1052 and 1058. Archbishop Henry of Ravenna held his office from Lent 1052 until his excommunication in 1065. He died under the bann in early 1072.
2. Recent liturgical legislation would certainly consider grape juice or unfermented must to be gravely illicit. For the use of unleavened or leavened bread, see F. Cabrol, "*Fractio panis*," DACL 5.2 (1923), 2103–2216; *idem*, "Azymes," DACL 1.2 (1924), 3254–3260. Damian's reference in this letter to the essential substances in the sacrament of the Eucharist seems to have escaped all historians of the liturgy.
3. John 6.51.
4. John 12.24–25.
5. John 15.1.

LETTER 42

Peter Damian to Bishop O⟨dalricus of Imola⟩. The bishop had asked Damian to adjudicate a case in which a certain donor and his sister had willed their property to another man, with the proviso that the donor retain possession until his death. The recipient, in the meantime, violently took over the property and almost fatally wounded the donor. Damian's decision: The recipient, by using violence, had forfeited all rights to come into possession of the grant. Whoever opposes this decision, is liable to excommunication.

(1053–1067)[1]

TO THE MOST REVEREND lord, Bishop O⟨dalricus⟩,[2] the monk Peter the sinner sends greetings in the Lord.

(2) Regarding the matter about which you inquire,[3] venerable father, it seems to me to be a case whether the man who was wounded had injured the man who had wounded him, for which he suffered this evil, or whether with single purpose he had performed a good deed in his regard, and in return was wrongly treated. And especially, whether, as it is said, together with his sister he had willed his property under the condition that so long as he lived he would possess the property as its owner, but that the other man not only dispossessed him of his property, but also wounded him so severely that he almost died. God forbid that the latter, whether he is in possession of a deed or not, should ever own the property, or that it should ever come to him by inheritance,

---

1. On the dating, see A. Campana, "Due lettere, nuove di S. Pier Damiani," *Revista di Storie della chiesa in Italia* 1 (1947), 85ff.

2. There is a lack of consensus on accepting Odalricus of Imola as the recipient of this letter. See Reindel, *Briefe* 2.2–3, n. 2.

3. On the legal problem here involved, see Palazzini, *Note* 255f., with references to Justinian, *Institutiones* 117.2.15 and to the *Codex Iustinianus* 8.55.10.367.

lest what the prophet Elijah said to Ahab concerning Naboth should happen to him: "Have you killed your man, and taken his land?"[4] Therefore, he who did the injury should lose his right, and he who is proven to have unjustly wounded his benefactor, shall not enjoy the possession of the grant, but for his offense should lose what he would have received as the donee. Whoever violates an agreement, must pay the penalty for having violated it.

(3) But should anyone unjustly act contrary to what I say, he should fear being compelled to undergo the punishment of canonical excommunication.

4. 1 Kgs 21.19. Damian omits "as well" (*insuper*), the last word of this citation; see Sabatier 1.519.

LETTER 43

Peter Damian to the Emperor, Henry III. He petitions the emperor for the release of Gisler, otherwise unknown. He reminds the emperor of his promise on the occasion of their previous meeting at the monastery of St. Apollinaris in Classe, that he would eventually free his friend, and begs him to fulfill his promise.

(1055–1056)[1]

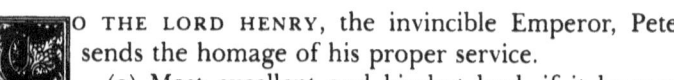

TO THE LORD HENRY, the invincible Emperor, Peter sends the homage of his proper service.

(2) Most excellent and kindest lord, if it be your pleasure, now would seem to be the proper moment to show mercy to Gisler[2] in his misery, to grant him freedom from the chains he has borne in extended captivity, and to allow him to return to his home after his long exile. I trust that my lord emperor has not forgotten what King David did when he fled from the threat of Absalom; that while Shimei threw stones at him and uttered curses more grievous still against the king, saying, "Be off, be off, man of blood and scoundrel,"[3] as he went on surrounded by his bravest fighting men, not only did he refuse to kill him, but even harshly rebuked Abishai who wished to kill him, saying, "What business is it of mine and yours, sons of Zeruiah? Let him go on cursing me. The Lord commanded him to curse David, and what right has anyone

---

1. Lucchesi, *Vita* nos. 78, 100. On the dating for 1047 by Neukirch 92f., Steindorff, *Heinrich III* 1.332, Dressler, *Petrus Damiani* 91f., Woody, *Damiani* 187, and Laqua, *Traditionen* 294, see K. Reindel, DA 35 (1979), 637.

2. This Gisler is hardly the bishop of Osimo, to whom Damian addressed Letters 30 and 38, but rather a Gisler, arrested in Ancona by Henry on his first progress into Italy in the spring of 1047. See Reindel, *Briefe* 2.4, n. 1, citing the evidence of Benzo, a contemporary to these events.

3. 2 Sam 16.7. On this parallel treatment of Henry III and David, see Letter 20, n. 6–7; on David's *misericordia*, see Isidore of Seville, *Sententiae* 1.11–12 (PL 83.613A).

to say, 'Why has he done this?'"[4] Nor are you unaware that, at Abigail's intercession, David spared the fool Nabal who spoke these words against him: "There are many servants nowadays who run away from their masters."[5] You also know that he did not dare lay a hand on Saul who was fiercely tracking him, even when he could have killed him.[6] Give thought to these and similar examples of holy kings, my lord, and after imposing a punishment, grant mercy to the sinners. "Indeed, everything that was written was meant to teach us something."[7]

(3) And since, as all the world knows,[8] your expansive generosity informs all the kingdoms of the earth which are subject to your rule, how is it that only Gisler should be barred from your mercy, so that neither layman nor cleric can help him in winning your forgiveness? May the natural excellence of the Roman empire now be enhanced,[9] so that divine goodness may indeed be happily victorious over him to whom God, by his own design, has subjected all his enemies. For perfect victory consists in this that he, who through Christ's generosity enjoys victory, should be overcome only by the goodness of Christ.

(4) Most gentle lord, with tears I implore your mercy. Prostrate at your feet I beg you for the love of Christ now to free this miserable man, and permit me, your servant, to rest quietly as I pray for your holy empire.[10] If this be your pleasure, promise me by letter that beyond all doubt you will pardon him, and command me to come to you with all speed as soon as possible.[11] My lord king will remember that at the monas-

---

4. 2 Sam 16.10. For "me" as the object of "cursing," see Sabatier 1.542.
5. 1 Sam 25.10.
6. Cf. 1 Sam 24.7; 1 Sam 26.9.
7. Rom 15.4.
8. In reference to this statement, see R. W. and A. J. Carlyle, *A History of Mediaeval Political Theory in the West*, 4th ed., 3 (1962), 172f.
9. See C. Koch, "Pietas," RE 39 (1941), 1221–1232.
10. For this rarely noted concept, "the holy empire," used here by Damian, see Hauck, *Kirchengeschichte* 3.575; and G. Koch, *Auf dem Wege zum Sacrum Imperium* (Forschungen zur ma. Geschichte 20 [1972], 266).
11. No letter of Henry III on this matter is known. If Damian visited the Emperor, he very likely did not travel to Germany; see Lucchesi, *Vita* no. 78.

tery in Classe,¹² when I was about to leave your majesty, you said to me, "Without a doubt you should know that I will eventually pardon him for whom you petition me, and that whatever in my mercy I do for him, I will certainly do from motives of the love of Christ and your kindness."

(5) So now, most illustrious lord, show compassion to this unhappy man and fulfill in deed the solemn promise you made to your servant, since, as the prophet says, "God loves mercy and truth; may the Lord give you grace and glory."¹³

12. Because of Damian's reference (*supra*, n. 2) to Gisler's "extended captivity" and his "long exile," this meeting at Classe must have taken place on Henry III's second progress into Italy in 1053, and the Emperor must still have been in Italy when he received this letter. See Lucchesi, *Vita* no. 78.

13. Ps 83.12.

LETTER 44

Peter Damian to the hermit, Teuzo. Formerly a monk of the monastery of St. Mary in Florence, after a severe dispute with his abbot, Teuzo left that house to take up residence as a hermit in the city. Acting as peacemaker at the abbot's request, Damian visited Teuzo and was rewarded by being almost bodily thrown out of his cell. He argues against this type of urban eremitic life, and tries by examples from the lives of holy monks to bring Teuzo to a reconciliation with his abbot.

(1055–1057)[1]

TO SIR TEUZO, the hermit,[2] the monk Peter the sinner sends a needle for mending charity.

(2) One is shown to love his neighbor less if he so disguises his dispute with the person who causes him injury, that he forces himself to be completely silent about the matter. For while excusing himself as if he were acting under the guise of patience, he makes light of extending his hand in salutary discussion to his unfortunate brother; and while excessively serving the cause of patience, he hardly escapes the charge that his charity is feeble indeed. For the Lord did not say, "If someone sins against you, bear it and keep silence," but "if your brother commits a sin against you, go and rebuke him,"[3] so that reprimanded over his fault, he might come to his senses; and while correcting his sin, he may again reach the heights of charity from which he had fallen. There are two individuals here: the one who has failed and the one who was injured. And thus charity which has to decide between them, must so weigh them in the scales of justice, must so

---

1. Probably between 1055, associated with the synod of Florence, and 1057; on which see Lucchesi, *Clavis* 89.
2. On references in the sources to the hermit Teuzo, see Reindel, *Briefe* 2.8–9, n. 1.
3. Matt 18.15.

respect their mutual rights by the evenhanded exercise of equity, that it is no less careful to keep the injured man, which God forbid, from sinning through impatience, than to help the fallen man to rise again by the exchange of proper satisfaction.

How Difficult it Was for Albizo and Peter to Gain Admission

(3) I looked for you in far-off places in regions unknown, along mountain precipices, and throughout the rocky and rugged mountains of the Alps,[4] and finally arriving at your door after much pleading on our part, and questions and abuse of all kinds on yours, tired to the point of exhaustion we were at last admitted—sir Albizo[5] was then my companion—as if we were men of unfit character. Intent and, in fact, most eager to receive a lesson in edification, at the very beginning of our conversation we were suddenly compelled to submit to various quarrelsome contentions, and we who were prepared to discuss subtle and hidden topics concerning spiritual combat, were hardly able to ward off the perplexing and useless questions, the tasteless and impertinent arguments you so arrogantly put forth. We who came to see Elias or Paul humbly hidden away in the desert, beyond all expectation found Xenocrates,[6] as it were, holding forth grandiloquently in his academy. Even more, we who thought we would meet a mild lamb whom we might imitate, instead ran into a ferocious bull menacingly brandishing its horns. But in the midst of this heavy hailstorm of question and controversy, as far as it was possible, I was reminded of that humble preacher who had said, "Have nothing to do with foolish and ignorant speculations. You know they breed quarrels, and the servant of the Lord must not be quarrelsome, but kindly toward all."[7]

---

4. The reference here is to the Apennines; see Isidore, *Etym.* 14.8.13.
5. Perhaps the hermit to whom he later wrote Letter 165; see also Mittarelli-Costadoni, *Annales Camaldulenses* 2.154.
6. See Diogenes Laertius, *De clarorum philosophorum vitis, dogmatibus et apophthegmatibus* 4.6.
7. 2 Tim 2.23–24.

And again, "Stop disputing about mere words; it does no good, and is the ruin of those who listen."⁸ And this too should not be completely overlooked: "Avoid empty and worldly chatter; it leads further and further into godless courses."⁹ While quietly mulling over these and similar ideas, my conscience, with something like a shattering silence, replied with the same Apostle: "If you insist on arguing," I said, "let me tell you, there is no such custom among us."¹⁰

(4) What more shall I say? When at last in the very thick of things I was overwhelmed by the perplexity of your many objections, when all sorts of reasoning proved to be in vain, I then took refuge in narrative accounts of the saints, so that you might at least trust those whose authority was unhesitatingly accepted as a proof in any matter. But at one point in the discussion when St. Romuald¹¹ was used as a witness, you at once inquired whether this Romuald was in his day considered to be a saint, or whether he was now in heaven. And although airing these questions about this holy man was contrary to the belief of the whole Church in our area, to strengthen my position, I put forward in evidence only those saints whose celebrated and long-standing reputation could not be shaken even among ordinary inexperienced people. I cited Leo, for example, and Gregory,¹² former outstanding bishops of the Roman See, one for publishing authentic decrees of the sacred canons, the other for refreshing the Church at the clear, deep streams of his heavenly eloquence. But after bringing up these names it was the same old story. For about these, too, the question was raised: How can we be sure that these men were such that one could believe them without fear of contradiction, or that they were even worthy to be listed in the catalog of the saints.

---

8. 2 Tim 2.14.   9. 2 Tim 2.16.
10. 1 Cor 11.16.
11. On Romuald's career and sanctity, see B. Hamilton, "Romuald, St.," NCE 12 (1967), 661, which cites Damian's own biography of Romuald as the primary source.
12. Leo I (440–461) and Gregory I (590–604) are frequently cited by Damian throughout his letters.

Again, with What Lack of Manners They Were Put Out
(5) After these and many other subjects had shamelessly emerged in the course of our conversation, which not only had not borne fruit in edification, as I had wished, but instead had generated a useless fog of interminable questions, remembering at length the saying, "The Lord will make his words short,"[13] after apparently escaping from the stormy winds of a wave-swept sea, I tried to land in the shelter of a safe harbor as I approached the subject of charity, in which there seemed to be no problem. Now there was between you and the abbot of your monastery intolerable enmity and long-standing dissension.[14] And as he was a mild man of simple disposition, he went beyond all the duties of proper satisfaction and humility in his agreements with you, and brought me in to arbitrate the contract between you and him. And so, as I inadvisedly tried to promote friendship among others, I brought down implacable hatred on my own head, so that as I tried to avoid shipwreck in the watery depths at the foot of Scylla, I instead fell into the roaring whirlpool of the Charybdis.[15] Then after you had somewhat irrationally given a few reasons, followed by heated and impatient quarrels hardly calculated to uproot this beamlike hatred but to cause it to be more strenuously implanted, at length you seized me by the belt and violently put me out and slammed the door, not allowing me further intimate conversation. Properly punished for having committed the crime of recommending charity, I was judged worthy of perpetual hatred, which even for murderers is considered a stiff punishment. But as not to appear lighthearted in laughing over these matters, which by conscientious persons should be deplored with brotherly compassion, let this tale of indecent confusion that I have told, suffice.

---

13. Rom 9.28.
14. For Teuzo's career in the monastery of St. Mary in Florence, see Reindel, *Briefe* 2.11–12, n. 15.
15. On Scylla and Charybdis, see Isidore, *Etym.* 13.18.4–5.

That Pride Overtakes Monks Who Live in the Town

(6) Now as to the source of this fatal disease that so suddenly seized you, I will not take pains to explain, so long as it is impossible for you to listen patiently. Never having been subjected, as it is said, to any monastic discipline, never having been brought to live under the restraint of superiors, and remaining stiffnecked and rigid even while you were still being formed in this new way of life, you went your own way, teaching before you had learned, first giving orders before you had observed the Law yourself.[16] And so it happened that you decided to live an eremitical life, not in the wilderness, but within the walls of a densely populated city, where anything that is said by a man of such great reputation is seized upon as if it were some oracular prophecy proceeding from a Sibylline source. But, I ask, if you are a monk, what business do you have in cities? If you are a hermit, what are you doing among the crowds in town? What do noisy marketplaces or towered fortresses contribute to a cell?

(7) Now of those who act as if there were a shortage of forests and seek solitude in the cities, what else are we to think but that they are not looking for the perfection of solitary life, but rather for applause and glory? There, surrounded by the plaudits of the crowd, whatever might come to mind, even if unforeseen, should in your judgment be taken for the Law, and whatever should suddenly emerge from your lips, ought to be considered as something of great significance. Nor do you judge yourself by the testimony of your own conscience, but rather according to the opinion of a flattering mob, with whom slave-like pallor on the face and just hearing the word fasting cause them to go out of their mind. For to be unacquainted with wine[17] in the city would be a miracle, but to drink it in the hermitage is quite unbecoming. In the hermitage olive oil is a delicacy; among the

---

16. See Capitani, *L'istituto eremitico* 155f.; I. M. Resnick, *Repentance, Forgiveness, and God's Power over the Past, A Study of St. Peter Damian's "De divina omnipotentia."* Th. Diss., University of Virginia (1983), 40.
17. On the use of wine by hermits, see Damian, Letter 18, n. 21.

people, however, to those who do not at least use lard, we give a prize for abstinence. In a hermitage, a hairshirt is a garment, in town it is something to be wondered at. In the hermitage it is indeed the rule to go barelegged and barefooted, but in the marketplace this penance is viewed as an indiscretion. In the hermitage a soft bed covering is made of rushes or papyrus, but among the burghers they approve if someone is satisfied with a flimsy quilt. In the town infrequent conversation is something extraordinary, here our fraternal living takes it for granted; and what there is praised to the skies, hardly deserves a mention here.

On the Abstinence of Certain Brothers

(8) Would that you would visit us and could judge by your own observation what is being done in these woods by unknown and despised men! But that it might make an impression on you, even though perhaps there is a bit of bragging involved, you will not be offended by hearing something of their way of life. Not to mention their continuous temperance in eating, the seediness and poor condition of their clothes, their rigorous silence, and the constant perseverance in living alone, there are some here who, among other methods of penance, are so careful to restrict themselves in the use of wine that for almost ten years, not even at Easter, have they drunk this beverage. Of these, some are still in the flower of their youth, others are verging on the maturity of venerable old age. There are even some who deprive themselves of grapes and sour wine, and many abstain from fat, eggs, and cheese, just as they avoid meat.[18]

On Martin Storacus[19]

(9) We have here in one of our cells a certain uneducated peasant who can hardly stutter through fifty psalms in one way or another, but who repeats them six times a day, always followed by litanies. For almost fifteen years now he has not

---

18. See Blum, *St. Peter Damian* 109, n. 14.
19. On Martin Storacus, see Leclercq, *S. Pierre Damien* 48; Palazzini, *S. Pier Damiani eremita* 103.

left this place, has not cut his hair or shaved. Evidence for this is his hair, which is now so long that it almost reaches down to his heels. Nevertheless, I do not approve of this kind of penance.[20] His constant way of living is such that three days a week he eats nothing; on three other days he takes a certain portion of bread and water. On Sundays and on the principal feasts he does not even prepare a stew or any kind of soup, but has only some fried dish for his meal. If one were to see it, but not touch it, he would say that it was almost worth eating, but to have tasted it or even smelled it, would, I think, be a part of the penance.

(10) It is said, moreover, that there are two snakes which for many years now crawl about in his cell in a friendly fashion. When he is alone, lying prostrate and reciting his litanies, these snakes, as he admitted, move around his head as if at play, and with no notion of using their poisonous bite, dutifully follow him about the cell as if he were the head of the family. Please note that even poisonous animals agree in being devoted to the monks, while monks themselves, sad to say, recoil from one another with serpent-like fierceness. It is a wonder that he can bear the awful stench of his place without complaining; for days he keeps in a large jar the dirty drinking water that looks like bilge water; and he never washes his underclothes and never changes his garments except when he is going to receive the Eucharist. Afterwards he promptly takes them off and puts them away to keep them clean for this function.[21] He never has anything to eat before sundown, but out of reverence for Sundays, he partakes of one of the small breads that are offered for the Mass, and that about noon, and thus in accordance with the *Rule*, he breaks his fast.[22]

(11) What shall I say of his unusual vigils? Once he himself told me, "During the day," he said, "at no time do I take any rest, but in the evening after chanting and praying, I then

---

20. For Damian's attitude toward excessive penance, see Blum, *St. Peter Damian* 123, and Della Santa, *Idea monastica* 86f., n. 96.
21. On these practices, see Peter Damian, *Vita Romualdi* c. 27.58f.
22. See *Benedicti regula* c. 41.112.

finally rest my weary bones when I know that the time for divine office is approaching, so that as soon as sleep has fully overtaken my body, suddenly, as it were, the ringing of the bell[23] sounds its daring and violent invasion." Often when I am asked to undertake some matter of ecclesiastical importance, or some arbitration case, and know that it will be difficult for me, even though others are at hand, I take advice from this brother with every confidence that God's grace will deign to inspire him to tell me what I should do. And at once, in a few words his holy simplicity gives an answer to what I had proposed. "What benefit comes to a candle," he will say, "if it gives light to others when at the same time the hungry flame devours it?"[24] I tell you, I gladly accepted this response, and only making sure that I would not offend against charity or obedience, decided to observe it as if it were given me by God.

On Leo of Sitria and Three Other Hermits

(12) But while I have taken too much time in telling of the virtues of one man, and delayed by the long interlude that hindered me from even briefly discussing others, I will now come to my lord Leo,[25] truly a lion, who with continuous rivalry provoked the ancient dragon, the chief and author of all evil, to do battle, and who from the very beginning of his monastic life, when he was still a very young man, until advanced old age, tirelessly fought against him in hand to hand combat. Truly, I say, he is a lion who sleeps with one eye on the world,[26] and while taking his rest gives his attention to divine contemplation. What further can I say of this man but to observe that he is dead to the world and with Christ is nailed to the cross? He is surely the norm for perfect morti-

---

23. On this imagery, see Reindel, *Briefe* 2.16, n. 33.
24. See H. Walther, *Proverbia sententiaeque latinitatis medii aevi* (Carmina medii aevi posterioris latina 2.1 [1963], no. 2278).
25. For Leo of Sitria, the companion of Damian on this occasion, see Reindel, *Briefe* 2.17, n. 36, with literature there cited.
26. See Isidore, *Etym.* 12.2.5, and various references to the *Physiologus*. On which, in general, see Damian, Letter 86, where he makes extensive use of this source.

fication, the rule for solitary living, and has the discipline worthy of imitation by those who would strive to reach the heights of perfection. Almost everything that was said above about penance and self-restraint you are sure to find in this man, and can find admirable in him, especially his charity, humility, and gentleness. And finally, his speech is as sweet as honey, consoling the sorrowful, teaching the ignorant, pacifying the angry.

(13) For who has ever decided not to be reconciled when deterred by his sharp correction? And what is more, who was ever depressed by the darkness of any attacking temptation and did not go away consoled? To those who live properly he is indeed pleasant, but is severe with those who have done wrong, but in such a way that his charming manner is stern and his very severity is relaxed. For while his firmness arouses a pleasant disposition when acting with authority, that same pleasant meekness in turn curbs severity. His abstinence is so rigorous that one sees in his face only a ghost and not the actual flesh of a living being. When I asked him one day how I might get relief when it seemed to me that during the fast the measure of bread was so small, he at once gave me this advice: "On normal days in the fast take only half the allowed ration of bread; but on the day you wish to relax a bit from the restrictions of the rule, you can indulge yourself by eating the total amount prescribed, and if what now is generally given us seems so little, it will then, if rarely allowed by you, be sufficient. This remedy, given at a time of necessity, was somehow acceptable because of the worthiness of my counsellor, but, I must admit, the eager drive of my gluttony did not listen to the advice that had been given me.

(14) Recently, moreover, as we were engaged in familiar conversation, he remarked, "My brother," he said, "let others perform great deeds as God's grace has ordained for them, but I am not ashamed if my weakness is able daily to complete only two years of penance." At times when he was prudently instructing me how to deal with temptations, he told me about his problems as if they had happened to others. "I know a brother," he said, "who was worn out by a fantasy to commit

fornication, and as he was all the while praying like mad, at length one night an angel of God stood immediately at his bedside, and taking a knife cut off his testicles. But when he was sure he was awake, but subdued by divine authority, not daring to inquire what had happened, he experienced such pains in his genitals as if a real scalpel had cut off a part of his body. From that time on this brother not only did not experience this kind of passion, but felt no further incentive to impurity as if he were already dead." When I inquired who this brother was, he told me it was none of my business. A long time later when forgetfulness allowed him to be taken by surprise, among other things I said to him, "Did you not once say, father, that such a thing had happened to you?" Not prepared for such a question, he then thought he could not deny that he had once said such a thing.

(15) But why do I dwell on individuals when I recall the great number of illustrious men around me? I will therefore not mention my lord Lupus, a truly meek lamb indeed. Even before he had perpetually cloistered himself in this prison in exchange for eternal freedom, he never drank wine for almost three continuous years, and never indulged in eating soup. I will pass over Peter who never permitted anything like a bed in his cell, but summer and winter always lay naked on the ground. I will also not speak of Leo[27] who always wore an iron chain next to his flesh lest he eat too much and exceed the bounds of sobriety.

On Leo of the Hermitage of Preggio

(16) But now another Leo[28] comes to mind, a man who is now almost forgotten because of his advanced years, and for having lived so long, endures the feebleness of old age. Although he is a knight who is worn out in service, he guards the camp of God's army, I might say, with the fervor of a raw recruit. Among other virtuous gifts that he possesses, he is so

---

27. On Damian's reference to various persons named Leo, see Palazzini, *S. Pier Damiani eremita* 103.

28. For literature bearing on Leo of Preggio, see Reindel, *Briefe* 2.20, n. 43. Damian refers to him again at some length in Letter 153.

outstanding in spending the night in prayer, that there is no night, even the shortest during the entire year, before the brothers have assembled for the night office, that he has not scrupulously completed the chanting the psalter with its litanies and, according to the custom of the hermitage, has not then recited a psalter for the dead. Now, moreover, as many think, he is more than one hundred and forty years old. After he became a permanent recluse here, he subjected himself to the rule that he would daily scourge himself, and besides, on no day except the greater feasts did he ever eat before sundown. During his whole life he never underwent phlebotomy, never took any medicine. This too must not be overlooked, that God's grace had so anointed him with the oil of gladness,[29] that advanced old age was unable to compress his lips with sadness, nor could a life of solitude bring to his face any appearance of rigidity or harshness, but he was always happy, always gay, and ever joyful, endowed with a certain courteous serenity.

On Dominicus Loricatus

(17) But when recalling holy men, why do I go about looking in various odd places, since right here at home I have someone at hand whom I cannot even begin to praise sufficiently? He and I are separated from one another by the church that stands between us,[30] with our cells on either side, and if I were to stay up nights recounting his virtues, days would pass, I think, before I ran short of material to write about. I am speaking of Dominic,[31] my lord and teacher, whose language, to be sure, is the vernacular, but whose life is truly accomplished and elegant. His life is a better tool for edification when he preaches in living deeds, than some sterile language that foolishly weighs each word in the neat balance of classical usage.

---

29. Cf. Ps 44.8.
30. The building plan at Fonte Avellana is discussed in Della Santa, *Idea monastica* 64, and in Pierucci, *Struttura* 134.
31. For the literature on Dominic, see Reindel, *Briefe* 2.21, n. 48. Damian addressed Letter 76 to him, and wrote his vita in Letter 109.

(18) For many years he wore an iron corselet next to his flesh, and engaged in implacable combat with the evil spirits. This eager fighter was always ready for battle, armed not only in spirit, but also bodily went forth against the enemy lines. He was so accustomed to this way of life that hardly a day passed without chanting two psalters, beating his body with both hands armed with scourges, and that, even at times when we relaxed from our penance.[32] In the Lenten season or when he had a penance to perform—often he took to doing a hundred years of penance—he then punished himself daily with blows of the scourge, meditatively reciting at least three psalters. Now a hundred years of penance, as I learned from Dominic himself, is performed in this way. While three thousand blows regularly count as one year of penance here, chanting ten psalms accounts for a thousand blows, as we have often proven. Since we know that the psalter contains one hundred and fifty psalms, five years of penance, if we count correctly, are contained in disciplining oneself throughout one psalter. Now if you multiply five by twenty or twenty by five, you arrive at a hundred. And so, when one has chanted twenty psalters while taking the discipline, one is sure that he has performed a hundred years of penance.

(19) Yet also in this matter our Dominic surpasses many others, for while some use one hand in administering the discipline, he, like a true son of Benjamin,[33] untiringly fights against the rebellious desires of the flesh with both hands. As he himself admitted to me, as is his custom, he easily completes a hundred years of penance in six days. I also recall that at the beginning of one of the Lents that was approaching, he asked me to allow him to take on a thousand years of penance, and completed nearly all of them before the season of fast was over.

---

32. On flagellation see Damian, Letter 45, n. 4.
33. Cf. Judg 3.15. On the ambidexterity of Benjamin see Woody, *Damiani* 93f., n. 2.

The Purpose for Using the Discipline

(20) If this kind of penitential discipline should appear to some people to be harsh and even, perhaps, superfluous, and if they neglect to do what he does and are even totally unwilling to do so, let me explain in a few words what I, a sinner, think about this opinion. When the faithful, in reverent devotion recall their sins and punish themselves with strokes of the discipline, they believe that they are partaking in the passion of our Redeemer. For, on the testimony of the Gospels, our Savior himself was scourged;[34] the apostles too were beaten before the council,[35] and five times Paul received forty blows of the whip, less one.[36] Whoever will read their lives, can hardly be unaware that numberless martyrs also had to undergo severe scourging. Therefore we rejoice in also receiving from them this type of penance, just as from them we have learned of all the tools for living the spiritual life. Moreover, if we accept fasts, nighttime prayer, nakedness, hairshirts, genuflections, and other similar things as penitential practices for repressing the allurements of vice, and substitute, on the other hand, bitter experiences for the delights of the flesh, which of these can more aptly be called penance than scourging, in which a sinner presents himself naked before his judge, and like a thief caught in the act, chastises his offending flesh by scourging? To this we may add, that we read of some saints, who after their sin were carried away in a dream to the tribunal and underwent this punishment.[37] Therefore, can we believe that God will refuse to accept this kind of penance freely offered by those devoted to him, when he required it of those who were unwilling? I have spoken excessively in recommending the discipline that I might forestall soft and delicate monks from daring to hold back.

(21) Now let me return to Dominic about whom I had begun to speak. Even now when he is bent down by old age and

---

34. Cf. Mark 15.15; John 19.1.
35. Cf. Acts 5.40.   36. Cf. 2 Cor 11.24.
37. See Jerome, *Epist.* 22.30, CSEL 54 (1910), 190.

frequently weakened, moreover, by sickness, one must wonder at how fervent and eager he is in not letting down, always remaining tireless in his spiritual exercises. For, as I know from his own words, he often continuously recites two psalters while standing and taking the discipline, never once sitting down nor resting for a moment from flogging himself in an unbelievably fervent mood. When once I asked him whether he was able to perform any genuflections, what with the weight of his iron garment, he answered me in this rather obscure way: "When my health allows me to do what I wish, I am sometimes accustomed to perform a hundred genuflections for each fifteen psalms of the whole psalter." At that time I did not pay much attention to what he had said, but later when thinking it over, I marvelled that such a weakened man could perform a thousand genuflections[38] in the course of one psalter.

(22) One day after vespers he entered my cell. "Master," he said—his humility urged him to address me with this title that I did not deserve—"today I did something I do not remember doing up to now: I completed eight psalters in the usual way during the course of a day and a night." His whole appearance seemed to be so beaten with scourges and so covered with livid welts, as if he had been bruised like barley in a mortar. Chanting the psalms has indeed become so easy for him because, as he asserted, he does not recite them verbatim, but vigorously runs through their meaning mentally.

(23) At one time he lived somewhat removed from my cell. When he came over and I asked him what norms he was now living by, he replied that he was now living sensually, and that always on Thursdays and Sundays he relaxed from his normal rigorous abstinence. When asked whether he ate some dish made with eggs or cheese, he said no. "What about fish or fruit," I asked? "If we have any fish or fruit," he said, "I give them to the sick, of whom, sad to say, there are quite a number in our area." When in determined fashion I backed

38. For the translation of *metanea* as genuflection, see Blum, *St. Peter Damian* 115 and 157, n. 79.

him into a corner, saying, "How can you say that on those days you relax a bit from your penance, when you eat nothing that needs cooking or is to be found on trees?" he answered, "I enjoy eating fennel with my bread." So now I was an expert in knowing how sensually a man could live who considered fennel a delicacy. He clearly has a copious gift of tears,[39] but only from time to time. When he is all alone, living in the strictest silence, he breaks into tears just as often as he wishes. But if he takes part in conversation, he complains that he has lost the gift of tears. I would often reproach him over the lack of tears caused by my dryness, saying, "Alas, my father, these tears of yours do not bear fruit, since they cannot beget tears in others when they ask. For I would surely wish that since you are a father to me, your tears should also beget my tears."

A Necessary Admonition to Practice Discretion

(24) I could still write many other things to you, some indeed not less noble, about brothers with whom I am acquainted, if I were not trying to avoid tiring you with my great rush of words. I am also afraid that this letter might fall into the hands of those about whom I spoke and might offend them, since laudably they despise being honored in this life. But I held up these models for you, so that perhaps while thinking over the greater achievements of others, you might come to a decision about your own, and abandoning your eccentric pride, you might not fail to run the race along with many others in God's army. As soon as those things were said that were beyond his own powers, Job at once sought to protect himself by doing penance, so that he put his finger to his lips, saying, "I have spoken inconsiderately."[40] Indeed, after Elijah had heard that seven thousand men had not bent the knee to Baal,[41] he was aware that he should no longer be proud that he was alone, since he had company in observing God's Law. And those whom I mentioned above are not, in

---

39. On the gift of tears, see P. Adnès, "Larmes," *Dictionnaire de spirtualité* 9 (1976), 287–303. It is a commonplace in Damian's letters.
40. Job 39.34.   41. Cf. 1 Kgs 19.18.

popular opinion, celebrated, famous, or outstanding men, but judge themselves to be despicable and ragged creatures, so inferior to all good people, that in no respect do they consider their lives superior to mine or to others like mine. Eating what I eat, they do not refuse to take part in the common table,[42] and as equals, moreover, show me every sign of affection like members of the family.

(25) You too, if you wish to walk straightly, discreetly, and profitably on the road of true religious life, should be so severe and stern with yourself that to others you appear happy and relaxed. Within yourself attempt to excel in the life of virtue, so that you might know how to show mercy also to weaker brothers. So arrange the strictures of justice before the tribunal of your own mind, that you do not obdurately deny pardon to those who have sinned. There should be sorrow in your heart, but gladness on your face. When a brother comes to you, you should feel refreshed and should not worry over not completing what you are normally doing. When a brother knocks on your cell, all signs of sadness should disappear, your rigid lips should relax, and your face should appear untroubled, glowing with a festive air.[43] For yourself, consider sin to be mortally dangerous, but in others see it as a sign of their weakness. Decide that where someone else deserves to be beaten with a switch, you ought to be lashed with a bullwhip. Do not be holier than the holy, and as you yourself fear committing sin, do not hesitate to show pardon to sinners.

(26) That form of justice is improper that drags others down into the pit of despair. A medicine is hardly acceptable if, while it retards the infected part, at the same time it causes damage to the tissue that is healthy. A fire is harmful if it is used to burn brush, so that its fury also spreads to cause houses to go up in flames. It is only too true that he who customarily takes pleasure in reviling the failings of others will not avoid sinning himself, since even if he is zealous in

---

42. For this reference to the brothers eating together in the refectory, see Della Santa, *Idea monastica* 86f., and Peter Damian, Letter 50.
43. To further understand this passage, see Blum, *St. Peter Damian* 120.

practicing justice, at some time he will have to fall into the snares of slander. Obviously, if our lives did not seem to us so splendid, another's way of life would not appear to our way of thinking so displeasing. If we were strict with ourselves, as we should be, another's sin would not find us such severe faultfinders; that is, our vigorous discipline would not encompass others, while at the same time we apply only the rules of love and mildness to our own excesses.

(27) But where does all this lead? You are said to render such a severe and haughty verdict on your brothers, that only once during a whole year did you receive the sacraments, and that not from priests of your own monastery, but from those you sought out elsewhere. I will tell you what you said: "Who ordained this priest?" And someone answered, "This bishop." "And this bishop," you said, "who promoted him to the episcopal office, and in what manner?" "It was the pope who did so." But as to how fit they were, you then added, "Granted that the pope consecrated him a bishop gratis, did the pope himself come gratis to the apostolic throne?"[44]

(28) Therefore, so far as you were able, you confound the whole world with the pernicious darkness of your endless questions, and like the sea that begets its storms from you, you never rest and will not let others live in peace. From this and similar silly indecision heresies and schisms often emerge, cutting off people who are uncertain from Catholic unity. But to address you in words the Apostle used, "Who are you to pass judgment on someone else's servant? Whether he stands or falls is his own master's business; and stand he will, because God has power to enable him to stand."[45] In the palace of justice, all do not share the highest power in handing down decisions, nor does everyone in the Church receive the keys of the Church. When someone is proudly determined to judge others, he is found to be less keen in considering his own situation. For the order of social life is then properly arranged when each one is satisfied within the bounds of his

---

44. Woody, *Damiani* 47 sees this remark as a reference to Bishop Gerard of Florence rather than to his predecessor, Bishop Atto (1032–1044).
45. Rom 14.4.

own rights. But where one oversteps the boundaries of another, then indeed every norm for right living is necessarily confused. It should suffice for us to be occupied with our own problems, lest by excessive concern for the affairs of others we lose the fruit of our own work and its just reward. "For if a man keeps the whole Law except for one single point, he is guilty of breaking all of it."[46] And as Paul says, "A little leaven, leavens all the dough."[47]

Of a Monk Who Died in the River

(29) I once saw a monk living the eremitical life quite strictly and correctly, a man of pallid complexion who appeared to have severely tortured his body, dead to the world, with downcast eyes, who had not tasted wine for almost eleven years. But how terrible is the judgment of God, how deep the abyss of hell with its extreme punishment! Sad to say, one day this man went mad and with the savage fury of a wild beast, got away from those who were trying to restrain him, and suddenly breaking the bonds with which he was tied, jumped into the seething waters of a river, just where it was the wildest, and drowned. But although no one can lose the reward of his life, whatever the time or manner of his death, I have narrated these events so that we never stubbornly trust in any of our good words, but always fearing what God's judgment will be in our regard, we should not rashly presume to judge those with whom we live. Even though at the present we see where we are going, still we never know how our life will end. The path we tread may be clear, but where it leads is hidden from us.

Of a Monk Who Sought the Support of the Devil

(30) And since I have the opportunity, I should not like to overlook the terrible case of another monk, even though it seems to me that it has little to do with this essay. In the monastery at Perugia, dedicated to our blessed Savior, where I was recently superior,[48] there was a certain monk a bit be-

---

46. Jas 2.10. 47. Gal 5.9.
48. For an extensive bibliography on this monastery, see Reindel, *Briefe* 2.28, n. 61.

fore my time, a man named Guinizo,⁴⁹ a very astute and clever person, quite interested in secular learning and litigation at law.⁵⁰ While he never rested until they had changed abbots and the brothers had been disturbed, it at length came to this that he sought the help of the devil in putting down his rivals, and even bound himself bodily to the devil's authority. At his demand the deceitful spirit promised him beforehand that he would tell him of his death three days before he died. The unhappy monk believed this, and during the many years of his life enjoyed this deceptive security.

(31) At length he fell sick and the iniquitous bondsman appeared, and as he had promised, told him he would die on the day after tomorrow. Suddenly he called the brothers and told them in detail about everything he had contracted with the evil one. As they urged him on by saying, "Hurry and go to confession, do penance," he suddenly went to sleep, and they were unable to wake him either by shaking him or by shouting at him. But if they remained silent, or said nothing about penance, he at once woke up and spoke to them. But if he again heard the word penance, he suddenly became stiff and fell asleep, unaware of his surroundings, until arriving at his horrible death, he unhappily fell into the hands of him to whom he had surrendered. Afterwards, moreover, for several nights a pack of black dogs was always present at his grave as if guarding their charge, so that observers were filled with horror. O, what a ruinous thing is a stubborn and argumentative spirit in a monk! For since he refused to live at peace with his brothers in this life, he lost the happiness of everlasting peace by being buried in hell. But even though this story does not quite belong in the present work, I have taken care to have it written down in these pages so that such a memorable thing should not be forgotten, as if I were fastening it with string to a peg, so that here every restless person might learn where a violent dispute may lead.

49. See Cantin, *Sciences séculières* 195f.
50. Cf. Peter Damian, *Vita Romualdi* c. 1.14, n. 2.

On the Patience of the Blinded Monk

(32) And so of all the things that are commanded us by God's Law, there is nothing for which a monk should more earnestly strive than that in all circumstances he have patience,[51] by which he might calmly bear the offense given by another's wickedness. This virtue brings a monk to the heights of perfection and makes the soul, struggling with the enemy, terrible to behold. It provides victory over all vices, and renders the human soul unconquerable against the headlong attack of a maddening world. And what more should I say? Remember that whatever was previously said or could be said of the rigors of abstinence or of every kind of bodily penance, is almost of no avail if patience, this nurse of virtues, is lacking, as the Apostle observed when he said, "The training of the body does bring limited benefit, but the benefits of patience are without limit."[52]

(33) When I was a young man attending grammar school[53] in Faenza, I happened to hear what I now relate. There was an argument between two men of this town, and one of them put out the other's eyes. After the blind man became aware that he was of no further use in the world,[54] he entered a monastery. But later when the perpetrator of this injury became ill and eagerly sought to be received to the religious habit, he judged it unbecoming to go to the same monastery because of the presence there of the man he had handled so cruelly. When the monks were speaking in a low voice about this secret matter, news of the affair reached the ears of the blind monk, whose hearing had become sharper. Learning more fully what was in the wind, he began to beg with all his might and urgently implore with every prayer he knew that the brothers accept this man in all charity, and that they see to it that he himself be appointed his guide and be allowed to care for him as his servant. At length because of his per-

---

51. On the advice to practice patience, see *Benedicti regula* c. 58.148.
52. 1 Tim 4.8. In this citation the *Vulgate* has *pietas* and not *patientia*.
53. Lucchesi, *Vita* no. 7, dates these events for 1022–1025.
54. On the notion that blindness rendered one "useless in the world," see Bultot, *Pierre Damien* 46.

sistent pleading he succeeded, and with the sharp eye of charity he served the man he could not see with his natural sight. When he lay ill, the diligent servant was at his side, warmed him with blankets, brought everything he needed, and even coaxed him to eat his food. It was even said that he often gladly led the sick man to and from the toilet. And so he who had lost the use of both eyes, was able to see, as it were, through charity and patience, the two eyes in the countenance of the soul.

In Which the Author Begs Pardon for What He Has Said Above

(34) I have told you the above stories, father Teuzo, so that you might stop taking pride in your solitary living, and that, if they should occur, you might even learn to bear the offenses of younger brothers with patience. But what I considered most necessary for your behavior, to be discussed in narrative form, I have kept to last. So now refrain from your excessively tough and lusty hostility, and adjust yourself to your brothers with patience and gentle charity. For he who cannot live peaceably with his companions because of his furious spirit, will be forced to live alone like a wild animal. He who refuses to live as a disciple of his Redeemer should learn to show his neighbor that he is meek and humble. "Learn of me, for I am gentle and humblehearted."[55] And finally, he who wishes to be the temple of the Holy Spirit, if I may go back to him, must not abandon humility and quiet gentleness. For he says, "On whom will my Spirit rest, if not on the humble and gentle man."[56] You should not, therefore, disturb the minds of peaceful men with your loquacious questions, nor brandish your horns at them like a fierce-necked bull, lest when others flee from you, this saying be thrown up to you, as was said in ancient times of an ox that gores with its horns,[57] "This is a dangerous fellow."[58]

55. Matt 11.29.
56. Damian's citation echoes those of Isa 11.2 and Isa 66.2, as found in the *Vetus Latina*, but not exactly; see Sabatier 2.634. For the exact citation of the text as used by Damian, see Reindel, *Briefe* 2.32, n. 68.
57. Cf. Cantin, *Sciences séculières* 411.
58. Horace, *Sat.* 1.4.34.

(35) Therefore, to all who observe you, put on a peaceful and quiet air, and especially submit with all obedience and humility to those who are on God's side, so that those who seek Christ in you may consequently find Christ, and in the meekness that they outwardly behold they may see the author of meekness himself presiding on his high throne within you.[59] Certainly, if your heart is the ark of God, as it should be, it will contain not only the rod that strikes, but also the manna that is sweet to the taste of your brother.[60] Nor should it contain a passion for acrimony, which is repulsive, but rather the zeal for charity which is profitable when it corrects. And thus the sting of correction should prick the wound of sinners, that the oil of meekness may caress it like a soothing lotion. Obviously, while I was busy promoting the edification of my brother, I exceeded the length that a letter should have, and so, contrary to epistolary practice, I inserted fitting titles to each of the various sections so that I might not promote disgust in the reader by my excessively long remarks.[61]

(36) And now, my dear father and lord, I throw myself at your feet and with tears humbly beg your pardon. I ask that you kindly forgive what I have said, and that in the sweetness of your charity you will not reject one who has presumed to taunt you so boldly, so long, however, as what I said above is accepted as having your welfare at heart. I do not refuse in offering satisfaction to bare my back to your rod, and in the future to submit with reverence to the paternal demands of your holiness. I hope that this correction of mine will not fail to bear fruit for you, since to your way of thinking, so grave and mature, and certainly so holy, what a younger man has dared to say may perhaps taste bitter; but within yourself you can clearly come to know what it must be like if someone hostile should speak harsh things about you.

(37) And so, venerable father, I ask that you always be

---

59. Cf. Cantin, *Sciences séculières* 350.
60. Cf. Num 17.10; Heb 9.4.
61. Here we have evidence that Damian himself, from time to time, inserted titles into his longer letters. But this statement does not guarantee that all titles found in the MSS of his letters were placed there by Damian.

ready to pray for me, a sinner. But since I have little hope of ever again seeing you personally in this life, I beg of God's goodness that when this time of combat is over, we will meet one another face to face, so that as veterans we may be enrolled as citizens in the same heavenly Jerusalem and may both enjoy together the reward of our good deeds. Blessed be the name of the Lord.

LETTER 45

Peter Damian to the clerics of the church of Florence. This letter berates the critics of monastic flagellation. Previously, he said, his discussion of the matter was for monks only, and did not have laymen or even clerics in mind. But now he is especially bitter that certain urban hermits, choosing what they please from monastic institutions, have derided the use of the discipline as a monstrous innovation. Damian disproves their contention by arguments from Scripture, from the canons, and from the example of the ancient fathers. There is a strong similarity between this letter and Letter 56, sent to a disgruntled monk, Petrus Cerebrosus, written in the summer of 1058. His most celebrated work on the subject, Letter 161, sent to the monks of Monte Cassino, was probably written between May and June 1069.

(About 1055)[1]

TO THE RELIGIOUS BRETHREN, the clerics of the holy church of Florence,[2] the monk Peter the sinner sends the service of sincere love.

(2) When a spiteful detractor indiscriminately reproaches him before those who are not even willing to listen, it is proper that an innocent man satisfy also those who do not ask for it. Nor is it unprofitable if, in good conscience, he explain the obvious truth for the same people to whom a false accuser has spread lies, so that a listener does not sin by believing falsehood and the good name of the accused does not suffer to the disadvantage of others. For what I wrote as a monk in the matter of monastic practice,[3] and especially concerning scourging oneself with the discipline,[4] I meant for

---

1. This letter seems to belong to the same period as Letter 44; Lucchesi, *Vita* 2.152, dates it as "likely after 1055." Woody, *Damiani* 50f., places it "before ca. 1060."
2. Lucchesi, *Vita* no. 57, discusses Damian's relationship to the diocese of Florence. See also Davidsohn, *Geschichte* 193f.
3. Very likely a reference to his Letter 18.
4. For a comprehensive bibliography on self-flagellation, see Reindel, *Briefe* 2.35, n. 3.

monks, and did not commission it to be brought to the attention of laymen or even clerics.

(3) But urban hermits,[5] that is, solitaries living in the town, monks who wander through all the world, have schemed to excerpt from my current writings only that which could beget scandal for those unacquainted with the secrets of monastic fervor. But brothers who live regularly according to the precepts of the *Rule* are my witnesses that I have written about deeds which they daily seek to perform. Nor has my reporting touched on anything but what ordinary and longstanding practice might customarily dictate. But those who have gained control over people by nominally professing to be monks, who by living in their holes preside, as it were, over tribunals or in the governor's mansion, publishing the laws of some imperial decree, who by cutting up and attacking others, claim only for themselves the right to administer justice, know nothing of what monks do in humble submission to the cross of Christ; and what others frequently do everyday, they consider as something marvelous.

(4) Look at this foreign teaching, they say, look at this novel practice of penance never heard of before in all the ages past. If this thing is once allowed, if it is sanctioned and observed, all the sacred canons will surely be destroyed, the precepts of the ancient fathers will disappear, and, as the Jew said,[6] the traditions of our fathers will be reduced to nothing. Such words, certainly, are totally foreign to the concept of charity and can be shown to stem from stupid and bestial madness. For according to the gospel, did not our Redeemer undergo scourging?[7] Did not Paul five times receive forty lashes less one?[8] Were not all the apostles beaten?[9] Did not the holy martyrs experience abuse and scourging?[10] Did not Moses command in the Law that the guilty should be punished by being

---

5. He probably has Teuzo in mind (cf. Letter 44) or, as Dressler, *Petrus Damiani* 84, contends, monks from the reform movement of John Gualbert.
6. Cf. Acts 6.14. Ryan, *Sources* 75, no. 136, sees in the "sacred canons" a reference to the penitentials.
7. Cf. John 19.1.
8. Cf. 2 Cor 11.24.
9. Cf. Acts 5.17–42.
10. Cf. Heb 11.36.

flogged?[11] Do we not read that St. Jerome and others were lashed at God's command?[12] Will Almighty God refuse to accept a penance offered freely, when at times he demanded the same thing from those who suffered unwillingly?

(5) But perhaps someone will object, that because it is known from the evidence of Scripture that the saints were flogged by others and did not flog themselves, we should not in violation of the norm that applied to them chastise ourselves with our own hands. But what now comes to mind, makes it easy to reply to their objection. Since the Lord commanded us to take up the cross by following him, we thus carry the cross in vain by our voluntary mortification unless, in keeping with his example, we are nailed to the wood of the cross by the persecutors. But since the time of persecution has passed, and there is no one to be found who would crucify us, it would now be useless to command us to carry the cross, since punishment is no longer inflicted on the combatant by the torturers. But since it is foolish and absurd to believe that the Lord would look down on this kind of self-imposed penance, which he himself deigned to undergo for our salvation, why should we marvel if a man in punishment for his sins becomes his own torturer, and to avoid judgment, appoints himself to be his own judge? As the Apostle says, "If we had judged ourselves, we should not thus fall under judgment."[13]

(6) For just as one is not to be accused of rashness if he fasts of his own accord, and not only by priestly command, so too one can not be thought to labor in vain if he chastises himself on his own, and not only at the hands of others.[14] If divine goodness did not despise the sack cloth worn by Ahab, a good-for-nothing king,[15] how kindly and with how much mercy will he look upon him who presents himself naked in the sight of God as one caught in the most atrocious crime.

11. Cf. Deut 25.2.
12. Jerome, *Epist.* 22.30, CSEL 54 (1910), 190.
13. 1 Cor 11.31.
14. Cf. Ryan, *Sources* 75, no. 137.
15. Cf. 1 Kgs 21.27.

He makes himself both accuser and torturer, the guilty one and the witness, the rigid judge as well as the executioner. He practices penance in an excellent way, who while punishing his flesh with blows, wins back by his sufferings the reward he had lost through carnal pleasure. This penance produces for him salutary bitterness where previously he had sinned through criminal pleasure. It makes little difference what punishment the flesh of the penitent is made to suffer, so long as the pleasure of former allurements is changed for the better by the vicarious suffering of the body he has put under restraint.

(7) But if to nonparticipants the practice of the discipline should seem to be something novel, and hence something reprehensible, and in the judgment of the malicious a destruction of the sacred canons, would we not have to contradict the Venerable Bede, who asserted that certain penitents, going beyond the authority of the ancient canons, bound themselves with iron fetters?[16] Should we rightly hold the lives of the holy fathers[17] in contempt when they assert that some of them did penance for their sins by standing in thornbushes for one and two weeks, others by rigidly extending their arms in the air from sunup to sundown,[18] and others by constantly hiding in empty caves? Should we also properly make sport of the Blessed Macarius, who, while repenting for even some small sin that he had committed, exposed his naked body for six months to the sharp stings of mosquitoes, which can even pierce wild boars?[19] Should we also despise the repentance of the people of Nineveh, who did not allow even their cattle to graze for three days?[20] Therefore, since these and many other

16. This reference is found in Bede, *Historia ecclesiastica* 5.21, ed. C. Plummer, *Venerabilis Bedae opera historica* 1.343.15. Cf. Ryan, *Sources* 75, no. 138, where he sought in vain for a penitential of Pseudo-Bede as the source of this statement.
17. For Damian's general knowledge of the *Vitas patrum*, see Della Santa, *Idea monastica* 174f.
18. Cf. L. Gougaud, *Dévotions et pratiques ascétiques du moyen âge* (Paris, 1925), 1f.
19. See Heraclides Eremita, *Paradisus*, c. 6 (PL 74.270D–271A); Palladius, *Historia Lausiaca*, c. 10 (PL 74.360B).
20. Jonah 3.7.

kinds of penance are not found in the sacred canons, are they to be considered detestable and judged to be contrary to the prescripts of the Fathers?[21] And so the frenzied tongue should be ashamed, and if it is unable to be eloquent, it should at least learn to be mute. If it cannot communicate in words, it might at least know how to avoid personal attack by its silence.

(8) But let this critic of the brothers,[22] this master of unknown doctrine tell me—him, I mean, who so arrogantly wields his intemperate rod over pupils that as yet he has been unable to attract any students—let him tell me, I say, when priests of the Church impose a penance on certain sinners that lasts for years, do they not at times fix a certain amount of money as a substitute for these years, so that they who are horrified at long fasts may redeem their sins by almsgiving? But since this commutation is not to be found in the ancient canons of the Fathers, should it be judged absurd and frivolous?[23] But if this should be allowed for laymen so that they might redeem their sins by almsgiving, lest in the case of sudden death,[24] which God forbid, they depart this life without receiving absolution for their sins, what should be prescribed for the monk who has perhaps received a long penance required by his sins, and who long ago renounced the money by which he might commute it? If because of human frailty it is decreed that a sin may be redeemed by giving a sum of money, is it proper to belittle punishing the flesh in atonement for sins of the flesh? Why should we be surprised if the flesh, when pampered, casts us into exile, but if, on the other hand, it is ill used it should lead us back to our fatherland?[25]

21. See Ryan, *Sources* 76, no. 139.
22. Here again Damian may have in mind either Teuzo or John Gualbert. On the latter, see the *Vita Iohannis Gualberti* . . . , ed. F. Baethgen, MGH SS 30/2 (1934), 1086.
23. Cf. Burchard, *Decretum* XIX 20, 22, 23 (PL 140.982C–983D). Damian refers to this practice also in Letter 96; cf. Ryan, *Sources* 76, no. 140 and 94, no. 180.
24. On this matter, see Woody, *Damiani* 275f., and his *Sagena piscatoris* 48, n. 70.
25. Cf. Burchard, *Decretum* XIX 23 (PL 140.983CD); Ryan, *Sources* 76, no. 141.

And likewise is it not proper that the flesh, by which we have sinned through longlasting harmful indulgence, should now be corrected by salutary chastisement? And is it not also proper that, in a manner of speaking, the same beast, now tamed, should bring the battered man to the physician for healing, whom it had at first senselessly and furiously kicked about? In addition, is it unusual if the land which had formerly brought forth thorns and thistles, when now improved after the thicket had rotted away, should afterwards fortunately become fertile? Therefore, the people who can only speak ill of others should be silenced, and those who are unable to correct their own faults, should at least stop abusing the virtue of others with their biting words. What they are unable to achieve in association with spiritual men, they should fear to deride and disparage in the presence of laymen.

(9) But you, my dear friends, sanctified by the religious life and enlightened by the brilliance of heavenly wisdom, stop the mouths of these hissing snakes, and by your influence prevent this pernicious poison from flowing freely to the detriment of others. And since, according to the Lord's words, "you are the salt of the earth,"[26] may the refinement of your prudent seriousness sweeten whatever acrimony my awkward and unlettered style might display. I was prepared to write more, but the hand of my scribe hurries along and the page is now complete; the messenger is now geared up to mount and is eager to be on his way.

26. Matt 5.13.

LETTER 46

Peter Damian to Pope Victor II. He accuses the pope of abetting injustice in the case of a certain Henry who, after entering monastic life, had been despoiled of his possessions. He reminds the pope of God's generosity to him and warns him that he will be the victim of God's anger unless he practices justice in his high office.

(Mid-February–28 July 1057)[1]

O THE LORD VICTOR, the bishop of the highest see, the monk Peter the sinner sends his proper service in Christ.

(2) The world is amazed, most gracious lord, that for such a long time your kindness has not had compassion on this miserable man, and that with zeal for justice it has not moved to punish this ruthless crime of robbery. While he was still living in the world he was completely and quietly in possession of all his property. But after seeking shelter under the wings of Christ, and after following Peter's example of giving up all things to follow in the footsteps of the Redeemer,[2] some cruel thief suddenly evicted him from his property and despoiled him of all that he owned, as if he had fled to the protection of some weak defender. In this case it is not just Henry[3] who has been injured, but Christ; Christ, I say, who is disadvantaged in the course of your pontificate. And "he who deals out justice to all who are injured,"[4] is himself denied justice in your exercise of jurisdiction.

(3) What if the Savior were to confront you in his own words and reproachfully pour out these complaints? "Without going back to the beginning of your career," he says, "I selected you for the priestly office from the common group

---

1. For the date, see Lucchesi, *Vita* no. 106f.
2. Cf. Matt 19.27.
3. Nothing more is known of this Henry.
4. Ps 145.7.

of clerics and, from among the ministers of the bishop, promoted you to the powers of the episcopal office. I made you, as it were, the father of the emperor and caused him to show favor to you in preference to almost all mortal men.[5] Into your hands I entrusted the keys of the Universal Church and placed you as my Vicar[6] over the Church which I redeemed by the shedding of my own blood. And if that were not enough, I added principality, and after the king was dead allowed you to exercise the rights of the whole Roman Empire then vacant.[7] Having granted you these great favors, I am now unable to find law or justice in your proceedings, and I withdraw from your court despised and unavenged."[8]

(4) Therefore, most gracious lord, if he "who will judge the living and the dead,"[9] were to accuse you in these words, what excuse could your holiness offer to these charges? What allegation in your defense could you find in justifying yourself before him who is not deceived by argument? So now let zeal for practicing justice inflame the holy confines of your heart, let vigor for ecclesiastical discipline now reach out to avenge itself by punishing crime, and disregarding the reluctance of evil men, restore Christ's rights as seen in this man whose property had been plundered. With priestly love extend justice to this miserable man, but show to the wicked the severity that characterizes royal punishment, so that he who granted you power over men may in his own case come to know you as the defender of justice and law.

(5) Excuse my words, venerable father. A man should not disdain another man's humble suggestions, since Almighty God himself said to men, "Come now and censure me."[10]

---

5. On his deathbed, the Emperor Henry III (d. 5 Oct. 1056) entrusted the care of his son to Pope Victor II (13 April 1055–28 July 1057). On this see Gregory VII, *Register* 1.19.32.

6. On the pope as the Vicar of Christ, see M. Maccarrone, *Vicarius Christi: Storia del titolo papale* (Lateranum N.S. 18, 1952), 53f., 70–75, 86f.

7. For Christ entrusting the empire to Victor II's care, see Neukirch 62; J. Rivière, "Saint Pierre Damien et les politiques du pape," *Bulletin de littérature ecclésiastique* 24 (1923), 360–366.

8. In these words, one can note the reproaches of the prophet Nathan addressed to David (2 Sam 12.7–8); see Lucchesi, *Vita* no. 106; Blum, "The Monitor of the Popes: St. Peter Damian," *Studi Gregoriani* 2 (1947), 464.

9. 2 Tim 4.1.   10. Isa 1.18.

LETTER 47

Peter Damian to an unidentified bishop V⟨ ⟩. A pastoral letter, written before his own consecration as cardinal bishop of Ostia, promoting episcopal vigilance over the education and deportment of priests of the diocese. He notes much clerical corruption and many violations of liturgical law, referring especially to the sacraments of the Eucharist and baptism, and suggests frequent episcopal visitation to instruct priests in their duties. He stresses the dignity of the priesthood, stating that no mortal man can perform greater deeds than a secular priest acting in his sacramental role.

(Before 1057)[1]

TO THE MOST REVEREND bishop, lord V⟨ ⟩,[2] Peter the sinner and monk.

(2) As I observe, most reverend sir, that you hold the highest office of the priesthood[3] in the Church, and as I confidently believe that you possess the priestly spirit, I have decided to acquaint you especially with the sorrow that fills my heart and causes me such pain over the subject of priests. Because of the laziness of bishops, there are priests who are now so deficient in education that not only do they not understand what they read, but can hardly stammer syllable by syllable through the parts of a clause. And so, what does he ask for the people in his prayers if, like a foreigner, he does not understand what he is saying? For it is written, "He who is ignorant will be ignored."[4] And since the Apostle prescribes that our service be that of a rational creature,[5] how can ser-

---

1. This letter seems to have been written before Damian was created cardinal (in August 1057 or March 1058). Lucchesi, *Vita* no. 60 dated it after this event, but in *Vita* 2.157 and 159 dated it before his appointment.
2. The name of the recipient cannot be identified.
3. Damian frequently uses *sacerdos* and *episcopus* interchangeably.
4. 1 Cor 14.38. For this citation, differing from the *Vulgate*, see Sabatier 3.711.
5. Cf. Rom 12.1.

vice be rational when he who offers sacrifice has no idea of what he is offering? And since Almighty God pays more attention to the desires of the mind in those who offer sacrifice than to the sound of their voice, what can he hope to obtain by his prayers if he does not know what he is asking for?

(3) What else will happen to them, do you think, but what overtook those priests whom the king of the Assyrians established in the cities of Samaria after the captivity of the Israelites, who were ignorant of the ceremonies of divine service? For since they knew not how to worship God according to the observances of the Law, they were killed by fierce lions. This is what Scripture says: "The king of Assyria was told that the deported peoples whom you had settled in the cities of Samaria did not know the established usage of the God of that country, and that the Lord sent lions among them which were preying upon them because they did not know the ceremonies of the God of that land."[6] And Peter says that "the devil, like a roaring lion prowls round looking for someone to devour."[7] And thus priests who are ignorant of God's Law are exposed to the teeth of lions, since the fury of evil spirits is ready to devour those who, while engaging in audacious practices in offering sacrifice, do not know how God should rightly be worshiped.

(4) And so they function in the office of priests without being aware of the mysteries of the priestly office, and through their ignorance there comes to pass what Scripture says: "Each of the nations made its own god, and they set them up within the hill shrines which the Samaritans had made, each nation in the settlements in which they lived."[8] So now, sad to say, through the ignorance of would-be priests who know not how to teach the people of God, it happens that some whose appetite is their god[9] and have their minds set on earthly things practice impurity; others venerate greed, which is idolatry;[10] others with sacrilegious devotion serve plunder, perjury, murder, and sorcery, and thus devote their

6. 2 Kgs 17.26.
8. 2 Kgs 17.29.
10. Cf. Eph 5.5.

7. 1 Pet 5.8.
9. Cf. Phil 3.19.

worship to various crimes as if they were statues and sculptured images of the gods. For each of these things in whose service he acts, makes him its slave, of which the Apostle says, "For this reason God has given them up to the vileness of their own desires and the consequent degradation of their bodies, because they have bartered away the truth of God for a lie, and have offered reverence and worship to created things instead of to the Creator."[11] By the faith which they profess they are included in the Church by its walls, but because of the wickedness of their lives they are excluded. "They profess to acknowledge God, but deny him by their actions."[12] They simulate faith by their words, but go right on practicing godlessness by their deeds. Hence it is said of them, "While these nations paid homage to God, they continued to serve their images."[13] Truth itself indeed convicted them when he said, "No one can serve two masters."[14]

(5) Since therefore the people remain uninformed and perish because of the ignorance of mad priests, it would be proper for a bishop to act severely in halting the ordination of such men so as not to heap the crimes of others on his own shoulders by his heedless hurry in this matter, especially since the Apostle says to Timothy, "Do not be over hasty in laying on hands in ordination, or you may find yourself responsible for other people's misdeeds."[15] For whoever promotes to sacred orders one who has committed a shameful act or who is ignorant of the Law of God, involves himself in this man's sins by giving him the opportunity of sinning, and burdens himself not only with the crimes he has already committed, but makes himself liable by anticipation for those he will commit in the future.

(6) There is something else that displeases me regarding secular priests, namely, that since they associate with laymen by living amid the citizens of a region, many of them are no different from their neighbors in their way of life and irregular morals. They normally involve themselves in secular af-

11. Rom 1.24–25.
12. Titus 1.16.
13. 2 Kgs 17.41.
14. Matt 6.24.
15. 1 Tim 5.22.

fairs, and show no restraint in taking part in idle and senseless conversation. Moreover, because of disputes and arguments they are often wanting in charity toward their neighbors, and while unable to control the flames of malice or earthy desire in their hearts, shamelessly involve themselves at the sacred altars, and do not abstain from offering the awesome sacrifice of the Mass, not aware that the sons of Aaron were consumed by fire from heaven because they presumed to offer an illicit fire in sacrifice to God. "Now Nadab and Abihu, sons of Aaron," says Holy Scripture, "took their censers, put fire in them, threw incense on the fire and presented before the Lord illicit fire which he had not commanded."[16] And then it added, "Fire came out from before the Lord and destroyed them; and so they died in the presence of the Lord."[17]

(7) Now when we prepare to offer God the sacrifice of this tremendous sacrament, we must be most careful not to carry illicit fire, that is, the flames of impurity or of any other vice, to ignite the victims that bring salvation. Rather that fire should burn in the censers of our souls, that flame of divine love should enkindle our heart which the Spirit of God pours into our being by invisible grace. Therefore those who are about to serve at the sacred altar should be warned not only to guard their heart from the ardent fire of passion, but to restrain their tongue, which is, as it were, the mediatrix between God and us, from light and idle talk. Peter indeed, who acknowledged that his guilty tongue had done wrong, refused to allow it to serve as a mediatrix between him and God.[18] But as he wept bitterly, he hoped to gain reconciliation by his tears, and begged pardon with his eyes by which he had not sinned. Therefore the saliva in our mouth should be virginal and pure, either by restricting it to undefiled silence, or by conversing discreetly, as it were, under the control of chaste speech.

(8) What a shameful scandal it is, moreover, that some are so negligent, so lazy and careless about the utensils used at

16. Lev 10.1. 17. Lev 10.2.
18. Cf. Matt 26.69–75.

the holy altar, that they indulgently allow the chalices made of pewter or of some baser metal to become horribly dirty and scurfy from long disuse; that they offer and preserve the Body of the Lord on filthy linens, and on that which any great person, who is only a worm, would consider most unbecoming to put to his own lips, they are not ashamed to place the Body of the Savior. What should I say, moreover, of the torn and decaying altar linens, of the various vessels necessary for ecclesiastical service, and then what of the priestly vestments? What finally should I say of the books, in which certainly we are unable to read even those things which we have already memorized without stumbling?

(9) Now all of these things, when we see them with our own eyes, cause the lighthearted to laugh, but provoke wiser men to tears. Hence priests of the highest dignity should greatly beware and should be terribly afraid lest the failings of those who are in the lower ranks be charged against those of higher grade who have the duty to correct them. No mortal man, as I see it, performs greater deeds in relation to God's sacraments than these very men who are secular priests. It is true, of course, that patriarchs and metropolitans and all bishops consecrate, produce sacred chrism, and perform other functions that pertain especially to their privileged status. But neither a bishop, nor chrism, nor anything else in the Church's sacraments is greater than the Body and Blood of the Savior. Priests, therefore, participate in the episcopal dignity in those things which in the Church are of the highest and most sublime value. And although all are commanded to be satisfied within their own limitations, these very men who in some matters are inferior, are in things of higher value found to be equal.

(10) No one, therefore, is guilty of sinning more gravely than a priest who, either by lack of knowledge or by his evil life, as far as it applies to him, defiles the sacrament of the life-giving sacrifice by his unworthy service. Certainly, if one speaks ill of or slanders a king or any other exalted person, or even attacks his property by robbery or destruction, he is easily forgiven if by proper satisfaction he corrects his of-

fense. But if he uses violence against him, if he daringly assaults him personally and attacks him like an enemy, since it is a criminal case and not a matter of money, nothing less is demanded of him than death, and there is no longer a question of restoring a disputed peace, but only of increasing the cost of the penalty. And thus it is one thing to offend against God according to the various types of human frailty, and quite another to sin in offering his most sacred Body and Blood. As it is one thing to disregard the published decrees of royal law, it is something else again to wound the king himself by wielding the sword against him with your own hand. The people of Israel often involved themselves in numerous crimes, but never did they so hardheartedly pollute themselves as when they crucified the Lord. Certainly, he who has no fear of taking the Lord's Body into his polluted hands is guilty of being partner to those who crucified Jesus. Such men should indeed be terrified by the verdict of the Apostle when he says, "For when men have once been enlightened, when they have had a taste of the heavenly gift and a share in the Holy Spirit, when they have experienced the goodness of God's word and the spiritual energies of the age to come, and after all this have fallen away, it is impossible to bring them again to repentance; for with their own hands they are again crucifying the Son of God and making a mockery of his death."[19]

(11) It is clear that Almighty God suffers greater injury from no one, and what is more, no one sins more seriously than a priest who says Mass unworthily despite the prohibition of the canons. By sinning in other ways we, as it were, offend against God in the things that belong to him; but by saying Mass unworthily we seem to have no fear of laying hands on his very person, since it is written, "If a man sins against another man, God can be reconciled with him; but if a man sins against God, who will intercede for him?"[20] So now let priests go on involving themselves in the sacrifice of the altar for temporal gain, let them grow rich from the offerings

19. Heb 6.4–6.   20. 1 Sam 2.25.

of the faithful out of love for themselves and their family, not, to be sure, that they might provide food for widows and orphans, not to minister to the needs of pilgrims, but that they might amass filthy profit for themselves and their kin. Let their descendants alone, I say, gratify themselves and their family by acquiring his heritage, so that afterwards they may with their very beings supply fuel for the devouring flames in eternity. How worthy of damnation are they whom we see feeding on the sins of the people,[21] not buying books from the wealth that they accumulated, not providing furnishings and equipment for their churches, but squandering everything on expenses in their own interest or that of their families, especially since these things were given to priests specifically because they have the duty to engage in prayer and supplication for the people and to expiate their sins? That is why Moses said to Eleazar and Ithamar, the sons of Aaron, "Why did you not eat the sin offering in the sacred place, which is the Holy of Holies? It was given to you to take away the guilt of the community by making expiation for them before the Lord."[22] But since the Lord suffered on the cross for the salvation of the world, he is now sacrificed on the altar to the advantage and profit of one single priest. Then he was crucified for all the people, but now the life-giving victim seems to be offered for the benefit of one little man. It is clear that these men are not the legitimate sons of the holy fathers who formerly were outstanding priests, but rather must be called bastards, and in the sight of God are deservedly not numbered among their heirs. According to Jeremiah, the former indeed "were nurtured in luxury," but the latter, sad to say, now grovel on dunghills.[23]

(12) He, to be sure, functions properly in the priesthood who does not oppose the rules set down by the Fathers, nor violates their plan of life, and hence Moses says, "The priest who shall rightly succeed his father, should present a cooked grain offering as a soothing odor to the Lord."[24] That priest

21. Cf. Hos 4.8.
23. Lam 4.5.
22. Lev 10.17.
24. Lev 6.21–22.

rightly succeeds his father, who by outstanding deeds demonstrates his noble descent from the holy fathers, and does not bring shame to the stock from which he springs by the ill fame of his bastardly way of life. Otherwise, whoever he might be that brings dishonor to the good name and nobility of his forefathers, or who by his wayward life shows himself to be illegitimate, ill-born, or outside the blood line, clearly proves that he should be expelled from the priesthood. Therefore of such as these it is said in the book of Esdras, "When search was made for their family record in the register, it could not be found, and so they were excluded from the priestly service,"[25] and at once were forbidden to eat of the sacred offerings. Therefore, just as they who preserve the nobility of the venerable fathers by the uprightness of their lives deservedly continue in the dignity of the priestly office, so also those who basely abandon the excellent deeds of the fathers who preceded us, are rightly deprived of their position of honor. They who have become unlike their fathers in reputation should, as priests, not remain in the office of their fathers, and for having dishonored their noble birth should in no way succeed to their rights. In the words of the prophet Hosea the Lord condemns them all, as if he were speaking to one person, when he says, "For having rejected knowledge, I will reject you from serving me as a priest. You have forgotten the teaching of your God, and I will forget your sons. The more priests there are, the more they sin against me; their dignity I will turn into dishonor. They feed on the sin of my people and batten on their iniquity. But people and priest shall be treated alike. I will punish them for their conduct and repay them for their deeds."[26]

(13) I do not wish to enumerate all the shameful deeds they have committed, either in offering the sacred mysteries or in the sacrament of man's rebirth, namely, in testing those who are to be baptized, in the profession of faith, and in the rites performed at the baptismal font. I say nothing of changing bread into life-giving hosts, which at times has become moldy

25. 1 Ezra 2.62.   26. Hos 4.6–9.

before it is consecrated at Mass; of not consuming the Holy Eucharist within eight days, but of frequently reserving it for three months to the dishonor of Almighty God. I make no mention of the fact that at times water is not mixed with the wine at Mass, and that thus, to some degree the people are separated from Christ by the false belief of this hidden schism.[27] One grows weary of prolonging the discussion of these and similar things, lest by pursuing them any further I appear to heap abuse on the Christian religion.

(14) Therefore, it is imperative that holy bishops remedy these evils designed to bring death to the Christian people,[28] and not allow the work of the apostles to be destroyed by these pseudo-priests who are now in our midst. Nor should they suffer the arduous effort of Christ to perish just so a few men might increase their holdings in an earthly business. In the meantime, my head is so full of these ideas that were I prepared to keep them to myself, I would find it impossible; my zeal provides the spark, but the pangs of conscience set them afire. What will happen to any bishop, worthy of damnation to the lowest pit of hell, who makes a profit from any of these fallen priests and restores to them the right to say Mass? He no longer just participates in the sins of another, but becomes their author. What is more, like Judas Iscariot,[29] he betrays the Savior into the hands of the wicked; for a vile sum of money he puts Christ up for sale, and for the love of money he hands over the author of life. He is at once guilty of all the crimes for which a wicked priest should be stripped of his sacerdotal dignity.

(15) But that my letter may get back to what I was saying above, it seems to me, if you will agree, that bishops must be advised to suspend from administering their office those who are unworthy and are guilty of shameful sins; but in the case of those who remain, they should appoint qualified men as

---

27. Damian refers to the interpretation of this mixture by Cyprian, *Epistula* 63.13, CSEL 3 (1871), 711f.
28. This statement might well be an indication that Damian was not yet a bishop when composing this letter.
29. Cf. Matt 26, Mark 14, Luke 22, John 18.

their representatives, whose duty it will be to visit and supervise them at frequent intervals. The king of Assyria also did something like this when he sent a priest to Samaria to instruct the other priests there. "Send back," he said, "one of the priests deported from Samaria to live there and teach the people the usage of the God of the country."[30] Now this priest, as Scripture goes on to say, lived at Bethel, and taught them how they should pay their homage to the Lord.[31] It is proper, therefore, that some important person manage affairs in Bethel, that is, "in the house of the Lord,"[32] one who will be able to instruct the others in the requirements of the priestly office. For we must fear what Moses said: "These are the rules for any man who through ignorance of the laws of sacrifice and of any of the commands of the Lord transgresses and does anything prohibited by them; if the anointed priest sins so as to cause the people to do wrong, for the sin he has committed he shall present to the Lord a young bull without blemish."[33] We must fearfully take note of that part of this quotation that says, "If the anointed priest sins so as to cause the people to do wrong," since a priest who transgresses by being ignorant of God's Law involves also the people in his sins, and those whose burden he could lighten if he were properly educated, by his ignorance he oppresses just as he does himself.

(16) And so, venerable sir, renowned for your way of life, outstanding for learning, and what is still more important, glowing with zeal and spiritual fervor, do not forget to delegate administration to other younger men, so that you are not hindered from frequent visitation of your diocese, doing what Solomon advises in Proverbs, "Bestir yourself, hurry and arouse your friend, give yourself no rest, allow yourself no sleep."[34] You should also not overlook what he says later on: "When you see a man being dragged to be killed, go to his rescue, do not fail to save those being hurried away to

---

30. 2 Kgs 17.27. 31. Cf. 2 Kgs 17.28.
32. Jerome, *Nom. hebr.* 3.18 (CC 72.62).
33. Lev 4.2–3. 34. Prov 6.3–4.

their death."[35] And then all excuse is excluded when he continues, "If you say, 'I am not strong enough,' God, who looks into the heart—be sure he will know."[36] As a distinguished pastor watch over the flock committed to your care, so that you remove slothful shepherds from their charge, and that with David you might break the jaws of attacking bears and lions,[37] or else like Abraham, after rescuing your brother Lot from captivity once the Amalekites had been slain, you might return in triumph to Melchizedek, the king of justice.[38]

35. Prov 24.11.
36. Prov 24.12.
37. Cf. 1 Sam 17.34–36.
38. Cf. Gen 14.14–16.

LETTER 48

Peter Damian to the cardinal bishops of the Lateran. Written shortly after his elevation to the cardinalate, this letter reveals how seriously Damian considered the office he was "compelled" to assume, on orders from Pope Stephen IX himself. This "open letter" to the other six cardinal bishops stresses the need for spiritual renewal in those who should be examples of virtue for the other bishops and their flocks. If this letter was actually received by his fellow cardinals, it may well be conceived as the instrument that contributed to their self-consciousness as eventual electors of the pope. Two years later this letter found its echo in the *narratio* of the Papal Election Decree of 1059, which almost certainly comes from the hand of Peter Damian.

(1057, Fall)[1]

TO THE VENERABLE and holy cardinal bishops in Christ, attached to the church of the Lateran, the unworthy Peter sends his goodwill and heartfelt devotion.[2]
(2) The guards on the towers and turrets of a castle, wishing to demonstrate their greater alertness, often call out to one another as they stand watch on a stormy night. Thus while each rouses the other, they surely maintain a greater vigilance in their role as lookouts. And so, I too, who was compelled—however it was done—to participate with those who fight for the strongholds of the Church's army, write

---

1. The dating of this letter depends on the date of Damian's elevation to the cardinalate. That he received this honor from Pope Stephen IX (2 August 1057–29 March 1058) is clear from his own testimony in Letter 72. Lucchesi, *Vita* no. 112, places Letter 48 in the fall of 1057; G. Cacciamani, "La nomina di S. Pier Damiano a vescovo e a cardinale di Ostia," *San Pier Damiano nel IX centenario della morte (1072–1972)* 1 (1972), 182, dates it for August 1057; others dispute the time. A Christmas date in 1057, depending on Damian's *Sermon* 61 (Petrus Damiani, *Sermones* 358) is not apt, since it was written, as Damian said, "in the name (*sub persona*) of the bishop of Rimini."
2. For the frequent use of this letter and its influence on the self-consciousness and independence of the college of cardinals, see Reindel, *Briefe* 2.53, n. 1.

these words to you, venerable fathers, and in my unpolished style make a great disturbance with my grating voice, not to waken you from your sleep, since you are vigilantly on guard, but rather to arouse myself, now meanly yawning under the influence of listless inactivity. Frequently we learn best while teaching,[3] and, as it were, at the sound of our own voice we are compelled to carry out what we advise to others, as Solomon notes when he says, "A workman's spirit plagues him because his mouth spurs him on."[4]

(3) And so, my dear friends, you will observe that the whole world, prone to evil, rushes headlong to its ruin on the slippery paths of vice, and the closer it approaches its end, which is already at hand, the more it daily heaps upon itself the burden of still graver crimes. Discipline that should characterize the Church is everywhere neglected, proper reverence is not shown to bishops, the decrees of canon law are despised, and only earthly interests are eagerly promoted as being worthy of God. Moreover, the legal order in contracting marriages is thrown into disorder, and, what an impious thing it is, those who superficially cloak themselves with the title of Christians live indeed like Jews. Where do we not find plundering? Where are we secure against theft? Who have any fear of perjury, of pandering, or of sacrilege? Who finally are horrified at committing the most heinous crimes? At the same time we repudiate the practice of virtue, and a plague of every kind of perversity has broken out like a wild beast on the attack. But let me not appear the stilted actor proclaiming a tragedy; it will be enough for me to quote the words of the Apostle, for like prophecies his words came forth when he said, "You must face the fact: the final age of this world is to be a time of troubles. Men will love nothing but self and money; they will be arrogant, proud, and blasphemous; with no respect for parents, no gratitude, no piety, no natural affection; never at peace, scandalmongers, intemperate and fierce, strangers to all goodness, traitors, adventurers, swollen

3. Cf. Seneca, *Epistulae morales* 17.8 and Ambrose, *De officiis* 1.3 (PL 16.24A).
4. Prov 16.26.

with self-importance. They will be men who put pleasure in the place of God, men who preserve the outward form of holiness, but are a standing denial of its reality."[5]

(4) Now amid these profound hazards that might shipwreck an endangered world, amid such yawning depths threatening damnation for the human race, the one and only harbor is obviously the Roman church; and, if I may put it so, the boat[6] of the poor little fisherman is ready to rescue from the swells and angry waves those who confidently resort to it, and bring them to peaceful and life-giving shores. For this reason the Roman church is endowed with greater privileges than those of all other churches throughout the world, and there can be no doubt that it was founded and endowed to possess sacred mysteries. Just to cite one of many items, the church of the Lateran, since it bears the name of the Savior who is indeed the head of all the elect, it is also the mother, the crown, and the summit of all churches in the world.[7]

(5) This church possesses seven cardinal bishops who alone, besides the pope, may go up to its sacred altar to celebrate the mysteries of the divine liturgy.[8] In all of this one clearly sees the prophetic words of Zechariah, "Here is the stone that I set before Jesus; a stone in which are seven eyes."[9] This stone is without doubt the rock of which the true Jesus spoke to Peter when he said, "On this rock I will build my Church."[10]

---

5. 2 Tim 3.1–5.
6. Damian here uniquely uses the word *sagena* to mean 'boat' and not net. This use occurs also in Letter 40, n. 314, Letter 72 (Reindel, *Briefe* 2.327), Letter 89 (Reindel, *Briefe* 2.571), Letter 144, and in the Papal Election Decree of 1059; see *Papstwahldekret*, ed. D. Jasper (*Beiträge zur Geschichte und Quellenkunde des MA*) 12 (1986), 100. Woody, Krause, Kempf, and Lucchesi see the use of this word by Damian as evidence of his co-authorship of the Election Decree, but Marchaud finds *sagena* used to denote the Church in earlier patristic literature.
7. Cf. *Constitutum Constantini* c. 13, ed. H. Fuhrmann, *MGH Fontes iuris* 10 (1968), 84. See also Ryan, *Sources* 53f., no. 97, showing that Damian knew the *Actus Sylvestri*, from which he might have derived his view of the Lateran.
8. On which, see E. Pasztor, "San Pier Damiani, il Cardinalato e la formazione della Curia Romana," *Studi Gregoriani* 10 (1975), 324.
9. Zech 3.9; on which see Laqua, *Traditionen* 203, n. 178.
10. Matt 16.18.

This rock has seven eyes, since Holy Church is resplendent with the same number of gifts of the Holy Spirit, with which it glows like a golden lampstand that cannot be extinguished, driving away the darkness of ignorance and illuminating the minds of men to contemplate the Sun of Justice. Of which the same prophet says, "I looked," he said, "and I saw a lampstand all of gold with its lamp at the top and with seven lights on it."[11] In the Apocalypse also the Blessed John did not hide the fact that he had learned of this mystery, and to him it was said, "Here is the secret meaning of the seven stars which you saw in my right hand, and of the seven lamps of gold: the seven stars are the angels of the seven churches, and the seven lamps are the seven churches."[12]

(6) And so this church, erected in honor of the Blessed Savior and built to be the peak and summit of all Christian religion is, if I might put it so, the church of churches and the holy of holies. It has on either side churches erected at various sites in honor of the blessed apostles Peter and Paul, but by association in its mystery they are united without distinction, because by standing in the middle it rises like the head above its members. With these like the outstretched arms of God's mercy, this highest and Universal Church embraces every area of the world. All who would be saved it fosters and protects in the bosom of its maternal love. Supported by this highest see, Jesus, the supreme pontiff, binds together his Church throughout the world in mystic unity, so that as there is but one priest, so too should we most properly believe that there is but one Church. And so it was said by the prophet, "Here is the man whose name is 'He who is to come'; he will shoot up from the ground beneath him and will build the temple to the Lord. It is he who will build the temple, he who will assume royal dignity, will be seated on his throne and govern, and he will be a priest upon his throne."[13] But since it is not my purpose to include here all the mystic allegory of the Church, I will let its explanation to

---

11. Zech 4.2.
12. Rev 1.20.
13. Zech 6.12–13.

others and turn my attention to a sequence of exhortations, as I had planned.

(7) Now we, my brothers, if I may dare to include myself in your number, we, I say, who are like seven eyes in the stone, who bear the likeness of stars, who share the dignity of angels in our office of proclamation, let us observe, brilliantly reflect, and announce the words of life to the people, not only with our lips but also by our deeds. The tongue, indeed, proclaims the word of the preacher, but his life commends it. Moreover, since various people from all the world come together at the Lateran palace, it is imperative that there, above all other places, one should always find the proper kind of life, that there a strict discipline of high morals should be observed. And so, like money that is continuously thrown into the furnace to remold the image on damaged coins, so too must men correct the baseness of their lives in the residence of the bishop. But if the matrix for the coins should become obscure or worn, and its impression is then made in metal, it does not produce money but counterfeit. Depravity in other men is never so damaging as that of bishops, since it is held up for imitation. For if he who is appointed the leader for the trip should himself fall from the cliff, it is sure that whoever follows his steps will plunge to the same death.

(8) And now, let us consider what that celebrated preacher had to say about this subject. "He who aspires to be a bishop, aspires to perform good deeds."[14] Here we see clearly that a bishop is nothing more than one who practices good deeds. He did not say that he aspires to high dignity or honor, but, "He who aspires to be a bishop, aspires to perform good deeds," as if he were saying, he who strives to be a bishop without practicing good works, foolishly wishes to assume the title without assuming the reality of the office. Therefore, the office of bishop does not consist in peaked caps of sable or of some other wild beast from overseas, not in blazing red garments, topped by collars of marten fur, not in flowing gold coverlets as ornamentation for their horses, and finally, not in

---

14. 1 Tim 3.1. For this variant from the *Vulgate*, see Sabatier 3.870.

the prancing lines of massed knights, nor in neighing horses champing at their spuming bits, but in uprightness of life and the practice of virtue. And then he continues, "The bishop must be above reproach."[15] He would wish the bishop to be so perfect, that almost preternaturally he might be called an apostle. For who, while he still breathes, can live so cautiously, can be so careful and circumspect in everything that he cannot now and then be blamed? Woe to those who live reprehensibly, and still more reprehensibly yearn for a place where they can live without reproach. To this class, indeed, belong those who, forgetful of their affection for kindred and homeland, follow the camps of kings through unknown and barbarous kingdoms of the earth. And to this end, ambition for perishable honors impels them, from which the promise of heavenly reward could not rescue them. Since they are not satisfied with what they have at home, they become wanderers in foreign lands; and so that, even if belatedly, they might hold the pastoral staff over others, they serve a harsh vassalage to royal lords. Indeed, it would have been an easier way if they had paid once and for all to buy the honors they had acquired, rather than submitting to such laborious hardship and distress. For when the prophet said of the just man that "he held back from every gift,"[16] who will defend him from the offering of bribes if he himself submits to the authority of another's service and, at the same time, wastes his substance on costly campaigns of long duration?

(9) It is clear that we should understand the prophet's statement in this way: we may speak of three kinds of gifts, namely, a gift of the hand, a gift of service, and a gift of the tongue. Obviously, a gift of the hand is money; a gift of service is the obedience required by vassalage; a gift of the tongue is flattering approbation.[17] And since the prophet says that one must hold back from each of these, one is found

---

15. 1 Tim 3.2. 16. Isa 33.15.
17. See John the Deacon, *Sancti Gregorii magni vita* 3.6 (PL 75.132f.), from Greg. I, *Hom. IV in evangelia* (PL 76.1091f.). Cf. Ryan, *Sources* 54, no. 98. See also Damian, Letter 69, where the same statement is repeated. For further discussion, see Reindel, *Briefe* 2.58, n. 25.

guilty of implicating himself in all of them if in striving to obtain honors he frequents the courts of powerful men of high estate. Moreover, since no small sum is expended in acquiring horses, equipment, and supplies of various kinds, he will without doubt be dependent on grants of money. There will also be little doubt that he must serve as a vassal to him whose subject he has become, exerting himself in an inferior role with much effort and travel. Finally, as he strives to please his lord and agree with his wishes in all things, he will often flatter him with all kinds of slavish applause. And what is more, whoever in giving and receiving ecclesiastical dignities is corrupted by only one of the banes we have mentioned, he will be judged guilty of supporting the heresy of simony.

(10) What excuse, therefore, do they offer for themselves if, even though they did not enter a verbal contract to buy or sell, by their deeds they were found guilty of being entangled in not one, but in all of these snares? And so they boast and pride themselves that they are not at fault because they did not pledge themselves to pay for the honors that they received. But tell me, my good cleric, whoever you may be, if when you bought a gold vessel or an estate, the dealer should require that you keep them, but instead of payment you should work in his interest, would it not afterwards be consistent for you to say that you obtained what you paid for at a just price, not indeed because you gave him money, but because you rendered him service? You might say, and you would perhaps be shameless in putting it so, "I paid more dearly in burdening myself with such effort and in expending so much of what I owned, than if once and for all I had handed out a fixed amount of money." In no way, therefore, can such men guarantee their innocence and be assured that they are free of the sin of simoniacal heresy, if even though they have not payed in sparkling coins, they have satisfied their debt for honors received by vassalage, just as if it were money. Let these adversary remarks suffice for those who deny that they are guilty of commercial deals, while at the same time they are burdened in their quest for power by hard and long service.

(11) But you, my dear friends, who were appointed by the authority of the Apostolic See to correct these and other abuses,[18] present yourselves as a model for upright living to others, not only to the faithful but also to bishops. In your life let them observe how one should act and what one should avoid; let no idle words escape our lips, let a barrier of discreet silence restrict our priestly tongue, let us not engage in jest, nor let unrestrained lightheartedness prompt us to hearty laughter. No more childish games, enough of this biting eloquence and refined style. Beware of sounding like a fool and of engaging in nonsense. For how can unsullied prayer be addressed to God from the lips of a bishop if they are soiled by the squalor of improper speech? Or how can the tongue be brought to mediate between God and men if because of its own guilt it deserves an angry judge? A defendant pleads in vain when his attorney himself is found guilty. Remember what was said to priests, "You are salt to the world."[19] But as Truth itself says, "And if salt becomes tasteless, how is its saltiness to be restored?"[20] With just a little salt, indeed, many things are sweetened, and by a small number of priests the totality of Christian people is instructed and informed. Just as the bishops are known to have obtained the primacy of the twelve apostles, so too priests in the Church represent the order of the seventy disciples.[21] This very thing is figuratively indicated by the encampment of the Israelites at Elim.[22] For twelve apostolic springs of water were flowing there, filling the parched hearts of men with the flood of God's word. Seventy palm trees flourished there, just the number of the disciples who, after the tyrannical slavery of the devil had been suppressed, would carry forth the palms of Christ's victory. The springs, to be sure, watered the palm trees, since the message of holy bishops is more than enough for other priests

---

18. On which, see Fois, *Cardinali* 94.
19. Matt 5.13. From here to the end of this paragraph there is an almost verbatim repetition from Letter 39.
20. Matt 5.13.
21. Cf. Fois, *Cardinali* 68f.
22. Cf. Exod 15.27; Num 33.9. See also Fois, *Cardinali* 70, n. 163.

in the Church to thrive without interruption in the hope of heavenly reward. Now these who in number are ten times seven, seem to indicate that the decalog is fulfilled by the sevenfold grace of the Holy Spirit.

(12) Therefore, my dear friends, since you should not only be bishops but the teachers of bishops,[23] it is imperative that your life should be a design, as it were a seal[24] made of the hardest steel that produces a rule of life for others. A seal made of steel[25] impresses its image on other metals without taking its form from them. When, therefore, the crowds arriving from all parts of the world rush in upon you, when people from various backgrounds shout to you, when each of them unduly wishes you to accommodate them, your appearance should always be the same, displaying a certain festive serenity, lest unthinkably, childish lightheartedness should emerge in any way. Mature dignity should distinguish the bishop's face, so that the weak audience is not frightened at his excessive sternness. Our good humor should be so appealing to others that our seriousness does not turn into wantonness and rudeness. If someone begins to laugh or engage in levity, immediately as he comes into our presence he should break off in the middle of a word, and with a finger to his lips, take alarm and be silent. And so, indeed, by deservedly becoming Peter's partners, we will receive the keys of the Church while presenting ourselves as a true model of living and a seal to the rest of the faithful.

23. The words *sacerdos* and *episcopus*, meaning "bishop," are frequently used interchangeably in Damian's letters; see Dressler, *Petrus Damiani* 117, n. 167.
24. On the use of the word "seal" in medieval sacramental theology, see N. M. Häring, "Charakter, signum und signaculum. Der Weg von Petrus Damiani bis zur eigentlichen Aufnahme in die Sakramentenlehre im 12.Jh." *Scholastik* 31 (1956), 41–69.
25. Adamant, meaning steel or diamond; see Isidore, *Etym.* 12.1.14 and 16.13.2–3.

LETTER 49

Peter Damian to the archdeacon Hildebrand, to Stephen, cardinal priest of St. Chrysogonus, to archbishop Alfanus of Salerno, and to Abbott Desiderins of Monte Cassino. He explains the wonders of creation, especially the significance of the sabbath. This he takes to mean Christ, in whom the soul, freed from the cares of this world, can take its rest, as the Creator did on the first sabbath. In this life the indwelling of the soul in Christ and Christ in the soul is the symbol of a future, mutual, and eternal indwelling.

(Autumn 1057 or somewhat later)[1]

O THE APOSTOLIC SEE'S Hildebrandine twins,[2] the monk Peter the sinner in the enduring bond of charity.

(2) It is well-known, my dear friends, that the richly endowed would not possess their abundant wealth if the poor had not given them the trifling gifts and offerings from their small estates. And frequently one enjoys some simple but delicious dish from a poor man, which at once refreshes a queasy stomach that in its recent discomfort was nauseated by rich broths. But who am I, with my unrefined speech and poor talents, that I should dare to address such famous and learned men, since moreover along with myself they are disciples, not of philosophers, but of fishermen?[3] And especially since Paul says, "I owe a duty to the educated just as much as to the uneducated."[4] But since recently, out of love for quiet

---

1. The dating of this letter follows Lucchesi, *Vita* no. 215.
2. In MSS V1, C1, and V5 the recipients are identified as Hildebrand and Stephen. In MS C2, the only case where it duplicates a letter in MS C1, the recipients are given as Alfanus and Desiderius. For a fuller discussion of the recipients and the relevant bibliography, see Reindel, *Briefe* 2.62–63, n. 1.
3. For this phrase, used also in Damian's *Sermo* 6 (Petrus Damiani, *Sermones* 34), see Blum, *St. Peter Damian* 129, and Cantin, *Sciences séculières* 345.
4. Rom 1.14.

I was separated from you physically,[5] although not in affection, and had decided to experience a spiritual sabbath,[6] I should like to discuss this sabbath briefly with you prudent men. And so, as I celebrate my sabbath, I shall explain what it means to me.

(3) In all the pages of the Old Law I find no precept so strictly proposed as this one, so frequently commanded, or put forth with so many admonitions, and that not only with great frequency among the orders and ceremonies of the Law, but also repeatedly in the pronouncements of the prophets. "You must keep the sabbath," it says. "The man who does not observe the sabbath day, his soul shall perish from the midst of his people."[7] And how should we understand the sabbath, except that it means Christ?[8] In this sabbath, to be sure, we take our rest, since we place our hope in him alone and love him with all our heart's affection, and despising all desire for temporal goods, we stop performing all servile work. Both of these ideas are included in one and the same command: to observe the sabbath and to obey the voice of the angel that leads the way. "I myself," he says, "will send an angel before you to guard you as you go and to bring you to the place that I have prepared. Give him reverence and listen to all that he says. Offer him no defiance; he would not pardon such a fault, for my name is in him. If you listen carefully to his voice and do all that I say, I shall be enemy to your enemies and will afflict those who afflict you, and my angel will go before you."[9]

(4) And so it is that on the first of the tablets given to Moses, where only three commandments were written down, this was the third. For after it was written there, "You shall have no gods except me," and "You shall not utter the name

---

5. It is impossible to be precise about the absence to which Damian refers.
6. For an insight into the "spiritual sabbath" here mentioned, see M. Della Santa, "Il sabato giudaico nell' interpretazione di S. Pier Damiano," *Vita monastica* 10 (1956), 68–73.
7. Exod 31.14.
8. For a similar interpretation, see Augustine, *De Genesi ad litteram*, ed. J. Zycha, CSEL 28.1 (1894), 4.11.107f.
9. Exod 23.20–23

of the Lord your God to misuse it," at once was added, "Remember the sabbath day and keep it holy."[10] On the second tablet, where one finds the other seven commandments pertaining to other things and not to the substance of God, it begins like this: "Honor your father and your mother."[11] Of this the Apostle says that it is the first commandment given with a promise,[12] and it was placed first in rank on the second tablet, for otherwise it would have to be called the fourth and not the first in holding out the promise of a long life. For elsewhere it says, "Honor your father and your mother, that you may have a long life on the earth."[13]

(5) Since Christ is signified by the sabbath, the commandment concerning the sabbath is properly placed on the tablet that pertains only to faith in God. For at the very birth of the world, when Scripture set the limit for every day with its "morning came and evening came," arriving at the sabbath it speaks of neither of these, to show, as it were, that it was wholly without beginning or end. The historical narrative runs so: "Evening came and morning came, the sixth day. Thus heaven and earth were completed with all their array;"[14] and immediately it says, "On the seventh day God completed the work he had been doing. He rested on the seventh day after all the work he had been doing."[15] Unlike the other days, he said nothing in introducing the creation of the sabbath, but, as already noted, suddenly allowed it to make its appearance; and by saying nothing of its morning and evening showed that somehow it has no beginning or end.[16] Moses introduces the sabbath about the way he spoke of the priest Melchizedek, of whom the Apostle stated to the Hebrews, "He is the king of Salem, that is king of peace; he has no father, mother, or ancestry, and his life has no beginning or ending; he is like the Son of God. He remains a priest forever."[17]

10. Exod 20.3–8.
11. Deut 5.16.
12. Eph 6.2.
13. Exod 20.12.
14. Gen 1.31–2.1.
15. Gen 2.2.
16. This is a commonplace interpretation in patristic literature; see, e.g., Augustine, *De Genesi ad litteram* 4.18.116f.
17. Heb 7.2–3.

(6) And it is right that things having one allegorical meaning should not conflict in the way they are written. And this is true in both cases, for as Melchizedek is called the king of Salem, the king of peace, so also the sabbath is interpreted to mean rest.[18] Therefore these two, which by their names mean peace or rest, properly concur in their significance in symbolizing him who is the highest peace. "For he is the peace between us and has made the two into one."[19] And it was proper that the Creator of all things should rest on this sabbath, because the Almighty Father found not one thing that might offend him in Christ Jesus, the mediator between God and men.[20] Finally, he deservedly rested in him of whom he spoke within earshot of the disciples, saying, "This is my Son, the Beloved; my favor rests in him."[21] He sweetly took his rest in him, indeed, at the sight of whose singular purity he took pleasure. Therefore, the Almighty Father rested on this sabbath as in a sanctuary and commanded us to rest. And so he says in Leviticus, "You must keep my sabbaths and reverence my sanctuary."[22] For he who is a sabbath is also a sanctuary, "in whom the complete fullness of divinity dwells corporately"[23] and of whom the same Apostle says, "God was in Christ, reconciling the world to himself."[24] And in the gospel, Truth says the same thing, "I pray not only for these, but for those also who, through their words, will believe in me, that they may all be one, Father, as you are in me and I am in you, that they also may be one in us."[25] And again, "With me in them and you in me, that they may be completely one."[26]

(7) But in a few words I should like to explain how man may be made complete, how he may be made perfect, using the order of things that can be found in the narrative on the creation of the world. For since man is called a microcosm, that is, a little world,[27] it is necessary that in striving to achieve

---

18. See Jerome, *Nom. hebr.* 15.2 (CC 72.77), 75.29 (CC 72.154), 78.14 (CC 72.157), 81.17 (CC 72.161).
19. Eph 2.14.
20. Cf. 1 Tim 2.5.
21. Matt 3.17.
22. Lev 19.30.
23. Col 2.9.
24. 2 Cor 5.19.
25. John 17.20–21.
26. John 17.23.
27. See Damian, Letter 28, n. 63, where the same idea occurs. See also

full growth he imitate the model provided by the earth; that as this visible and physical world is perfected by the mass and multitude of its parts, so also our inner man gradually arrives at his fullness by the increase of virtue. The Apostle says of this spiritual fullness, "Until we all become the perfect man, fully mature with the fullness of Christ himself."[28] Come, therefore, God said, "Let there be light."[29] It was said of man that there should be light in him, when he was illumined by the light of faith. For indeed faith is the first light of the soul.[30] Hence the Apostle once said to the faithful, "You were darkness once, but now you are light in the Lord."[31] And this is the first commandment of the Law, "Listen, O Israel; the Lord your God is one God."[32] The first day arrived for man when he first came to the faith.

(8) On the second day God made the vault, that is, the heavens, and divided the waters so that some would flow below and others would remain above.[33] And what is this vault, if it is not the force of the Scriptures? Hence we read that on the day of judgment the heavens will be rolled up like a scroll.[34] What is meant by the lower waters, if not the multitude of men? And what are those above, if not the choirs of angels? For the angels of the Scriptures do not have a heaven above them, but one below them, for they have no need to hear the word of God read to them, for they clearly see God himself as present and are always aflame with his love. Therefore when man by means of the vault, that is, by means of the document of heavenly eloquence, began to separate the inferior from the superior waters, that is, to separate the carnal from the spiritual, and the things of earth from those of

---

M.-T. D'Alverny, "L'homme comme symbole. Le microcosme," *Settimane di studio del Centro Italiano di studi sull'alto medioevo* 23 (1976), 123–183.
    28. Eph 4.13.   29. Gen 1.3.
    30. Isidore, *Quaestiones* 1.1.5 (PL 83.210A).
    31. Eph 5.8.
    32. Deut 6.4; for this variant from the *Vulgate*, see Sabatier 1.340.
    33. Cf. Gen 1.6–8.
    34. Cf. Isa 34.4. See also Isidore, *Quaestiones* 1.1.6 (PL 83.210AB). Throughout the remainder of this letter Isidore, *Quaestiones* 1.1.6–17 continues to be Damian's source.

heaven, then the second day occurred for him, for he was possessed not only of the light of faith but was now beginning to discriminate one thing from another.

(9) Then God said, "Let the waters under heaven come together into one place, and let dry land appear."[35] Once a division was made, as I said, between earthly and heavenly things, it was necessary for man's mind to effect a more refined division among earthly things. And so, as the sea was separated from the dry land, he distinguished wicked men, who eagerly seek the brackish wisdom of this world, from the just, who thirst for the source of faith. For unbelieving or carnal men are agitated by the bitter flood of temptation and swell up in a storm of desires and a tempest of avarice. But the saints, that is, the just, like the dry land thirst for God and like the fertile earth strive to produce the fresh fruit of good works. Therefore, on that same day God commanded that "the earth produce vegetation, seedbearing plants, and fruit trees bearing fruit."[36] Therefore, whoever carefully studies these events and intensely meditates on them, for him undoubtedly the third day has now arrived. So let everyone separate himself from the bitter salt water of those whose taste is carnal, becoming dry land, let him thirst with all his being for God, the fountain of life, and bring forth plants bearing good fruit, that the third day may dawn for him.

(10) After these things were created and put in order for his benefit, the soul of man after dispersing and laying to rest the darkness of vice, begins to shine with the brightness of virtue. And so it was said that on the fourth day the lights in the vault of heaven were made.[37] Why is it that first the earth produced plants and that then the lights were created, unless it means that with the appearance of the buds of good works, the light rises in the soul in greater abundance so that it might follow in the footsteps of its Redeemer? Therefore, let the earth increase the growth of spiritual fruit in the human soul that it might be illumined by the brilliant rays of inner

---

35. Gen 1.9.   36. Gen 1.11–12.
37. Cf. Gen 1.14.

light, and while enjoying the light of the fourth day it may be carried aloft on spiritual wings to contemplate the things of heaven.

(11) Then on the fifth day fish were created, symbolizing those who receive the sacrament of baptism, and birds also which signify those who climb aloft on the wings of virtue to contemplate heavenly things.[38] Therefore everyone who is possessed of the fifth day with its birds, after despising the love of this world, disdains, as it were, to tread the unclean earth, and by the grace of contemplation advances himself to desire the glory of heaven. Now, indeed, he no longer walks on the earth but flies through the air, because in despising all earthly things he thirsts for heavenly possessions, saying, "My soul has thirsted for the living God; when shall I go to see the face of God?"[39] And so as a perfect man, he is rightly made in the image of his Creator[40] in that he possesses the dignity of such spiritual gifts, that now he is commanded not only to observe the standard of ordinary holiness but to strive, insofar as that is possible, to imitate the example of God himself, as the Apostle says, "Try, then, to imitate God, as children of his that he loves, and follow Christ by loving as he loved you."[41] There was indeed a difference between Paul, who imitated Christ, and those whom he urged to imitate himself. "Take me for your model," he says, "as I take Christ."[42]

(12) And then on the sixth day man was created in the likeness of his Creator.[43] Truly, what was then achieved at the beginning of human existence is now performed by the sacrament of interior renewal. Man, moreover, receives a certain sovereignty over all the living things of earth, water, and air, and a kind of preeminence of greater excellence, because every perfect man, accomplished in virtue, knows how to judge all things rightly, as the Apostle says, "A spiritual man, on the other hand, is able to judge everything, but he is not

---

38. Cf. Gen 1.20–21.
40. Cf. Gen 1.26.
42. 1 Cor 11.1.
39. Ps 41.3.
41. Eph 5.1–2.
43. Cf. Gen 1.26–27.

to be judged by other men."⁴⁴ And so Almighty God established the perfect man, who was dead to the world but who lived for him, as his throne, and through him often published his just decrees. For this reason also the order of angels, through whom Almighty God frequently makes his decisions known, is called a throne, because the supreme judge presides on them, when through them he proclaims the decrees of his justice. Hence God ordained that the perfect man should be his throne that he might sweetly rest on him. Accordingly the prophet says, "On whom should my spirit rest, but on the humble and gentle man who trembles at my word?"⁴⁵

(13) We should note that at each day it was said, "Evening came and morning came"; namely, the evening meant the very perfecting of good works, while morning indicated the light of the soul. For when a good deed is brought to perfection, the light of spiritual grace then rises in the soul of the achiever, so that while externally performing his shining deed he is illumined within by the grace of the Spirit.

(14) And thus we arrive at the sabbath on which God, after completing his work, rested and commanded man to take his rest.⁴⁶ In this way man becomes the sabbath of God and God the sabbath of man, since he rests in God and God in him. "Make your home in me," he says, "as I make mine in you."⁴⁷ For us he is time without time and place without place. He is without place, indeed, because he is not confined; without time, because he never ends. He is surely time for us, when he says, "Are there not twelve hours in the day?"⁴⁸ That he is the day with twelve hours we know from the like number of apostles.⁴⁹ That he is place is undoubtedly expressed by the prophet, who after stating, "But yourself, you never change, and your years are unending," at once added, "Your servants' sons will have a permanent home there,"⁵⁰ no doubt, in you.

---

44. 1 Cor 2.15.
45. Isa 66.2.
46. Cf. Gen 2.1–3.
47. John 15.4.
48. John 11.9.
49. Cf. Bede, *De temporum ratione* c. 3, CC 123B (1977), 275f.
50. Ps 101.28–29.

(15) Now God made heaven and earth and it is not said that he rested; he made the seed bearing plants of earth and the lights of heaven, and it is not said that he rested; he made all that are fed on the earth and all that move in the waters, and with all these we never read that he rested. But after forming man in his own image the quiet sabbath suddenly dawned and then the maker of the universe took his rest, that he might say through the prophet, "Heaven is my throne and earth my footstool,"[51] on which he took his rest, not in the creation of all other things, but only after creating man. And that you might wonder the more at the special dignity of this day, Scripture says, "God blessed the seventh day and made it holy, because on that day he had rested after all his work;[52] which we do not find him doing on the other days. What does it mean to make holy the sabbath for God, but to construct for him a temple in the soul of the holy and perfect man? To which the Apostle says, "You are the temple of God, and the Holy Spirit is living in you."[53]

(16) Moreover, reason demands that whatever we have said of the sabbath we must also say of the temple, because while God is the temple of man, man is also the temple of God, as John says in the Apocalypse: "I saw there no temple in the city, for the Lord God Almighty and the Lamb were themselves the temple."[54] And so God becomes the temple of man and man becomes the temple of God. This temple of man is a spiritual paradise, that is, a holy mind, a perfect mind, a pure mind expressly fashioned in the image of its maker. This mind, I say, or this rational soul is rightly called a paradise,[55] watered by the streams of heavenly gifts, and as fruitful trees and plants are adorned with green, so it too flourishes with a growth of holy virtues.

(17) Now the spring or river that is there said to flow from the place of pleasure to irrigate paradise,[56] and which is divided into four branches, is the mind's reason from which, as

51. Isa 66.1.
52. Gen 2.3.
53. 1 Cor 3.16.
54. Rev 21.22.
55. Cf. Ambrose, *De paradiso*, ed. C. Schenkl, CSEL 32.1 (1897), 1.6.267.
56. Cf. Gen 2.10.

from its original source, flow the four virtues, namely, justice, fortitude, prudence, and temperance, like so many healing streams that render the soil of our heart fertile.[57] The tree of life, however, is wisdom, the mother of all that is good, of which also Solomon says, "She is the tree of life for those who hold her fast, those who cling to her live happy lives."[58] But the tree of the knowledge of good and evil is the transgression[59] of public law and the experience of misery. But since it is not my purpose to explain everything in turn, these few remarks should suffice in examining that which pertains to our subject.

(18) It should be noted, however, that the confusion of hell is found in every soul at odds with God, while in the holy, pure, and perfect soul there exists the beauty of paradise. But the hateful and avaricious soul, preoccupied only with worldly affairs, and aflame with the fire of lust—does this not seem to you to be hell, in which the devil lives and where the fires of concupiscence never cease to burn? From that soul, moreover, emerges a sulphurous stench of passion, and from its utter darkness overwhelming thoughts pour forth like swirls of dense smoke. For while it loves one thing, it fears another; in some things it rejoices, and others it hates; another it passionately desires. It is an unhappy soul, always suspicious and uneasy, curious, at once anxious and alarmed, torn asunder by its demanding interests, and ripped to shreds by the teeth of conflicting passions. This sorry soul has indeed become a Gehenna, a Tartarus, a hell, in which the torments of disquiet afflict it and the blazing fury of vice lays it waste. But the soul that is bathed in the light of its Creator and is adorned with the green garlands of spiritual virtues, that finally the fountain of wisdom waters with the four streams that flow from it, and makes fertile with the dew of heavenly grace that brings forth fruit of good works, this surely is paradise; this is the garden of delights[60] of which the

---

57. Ambrose, *De paradiso* 3.14.273.
58. Prov 3.18.
59. Ambrose, *De paradiso* 12.59.319.
60. Peter Damian, *Rhythmus sanctae Mariae virginis* c. 19, ed. M. Lokrantz, *L'opera poetica,* 79.

Lord speaks through Isaiah, "I will pour my spirit on your descendants and my blessing on your children, and they shall grow among the plants like willows beside the running waters."[61] For then it will be effectively fulfilled what was promised by the prophet Hosea, "I will be as the dew; Israel shall bloom like the lily, and his root shall shoot forth like that of Lebanon. His branches shall spread and his glory shall be like the olive tree and his smell like that of Lebanon. They shall come back to sit in his shade, they shall live upon wheat and they shall blossom like a vine, his memorial shall be like Lebanon."[62] As we read of the sabbath, Almighty God sanctifies and blesses this soul and in it is delighted to take his rest. It is, indeed, a sabbath, the temple, and the sanctuary of its Creator.

(19) Moreover, as he afflicted Egypt with a plague of flies,[63] while the people of Israel received the sabbath as a reward, so the reprobate soul is always eager to gad about amid the noisy business of this world, while the holy soul takes its sole delight in the quiet of its Redeemer. This is why it was at Riblah and not elsewhere that the king of Babylon slaughtered the sons of Zedekiah, and then put out his eyes.[64] Clearly, while Sacred Scripture tells the story of Zedekiah's capture, it hints at the course of spiritual captivity. For the king of Babylon is the ancient enemy, the lord of internal confusion, who first slaughters the sons before the very eyes of the beholder, because he often kills good works in this way, so that the captive may grieve at the sight of his loss. Often a soul will grieve, and yet, overcome by the pleasures of the flesh, loses through this love the good that he bore, considers what he suffers to be a loss, and does not lift a finger of virtue against the king of Babylon. But while he looks on, he is struck by a foul deed, that is, at times he is so overcome by sin that he is deprived of the light of reason itself. And so after first killing the sons, the king of Babylon put out Zedekiah's eyes, because the evil spirit first steals good works and

61. Isa 44.3–4.
62. Hos 14.6–8.
63. Cf. Exod 8.21–32.
64. Cf. 2 Kgs 25.6–7.

then takes away the light of reason. And it was proper that Zedekiah should undergo all this at Riblah. Riblah, indeed, is understood to mean these many things.[65] He is rightly deprived of the light of reason who shuns the rigors of holy silence and is carried away by worldly interests. It is proper that he should become blind at Riblah, since after despising the one, the impatient soul is debauched in seeking after many things. Consequently, the soul of the true Israelite enjoys its sabbath by removing itself from the bustle of worldly affairs and becoming occupied with reading and prayer. The Egyptian soul, on the other hand, is overwhelmed by the swarm of infesting flies as it takes its delight in the restless affairs of this world.

(20) What is more wearisome in this life than to burn with earthly desires? What is more quiet and sweet than to seek nothing at all of this world? Solomon says, "Dead flies spoil a perfumed oil,"[66] because unnecessary thoughts, that are constantly coming and going in the mind occupied with carnal things, lose for him the sweetness which the Spirit inwardly provides for everyone. Hence when Truth in a marvelous act of love comes to a heart, he first casts out from it the ferment of carnal thoughts and then arranges within it the gifts of virtue. The sacred gospel narrative gives us a good indication of this when, in speaking of the Lord's invitation to awaken the official's daughter, it adds at once, "But when the people had been turned out he went inside and took the little girl by the hand, and she got up."[67] The crowd is put out so that the girl might revive, because if the troublesome horde of worldly cares is not first expelled from within the heart, the soul that is inwardly dead does not arise. For while the soul dissipates itself in countless thoughts about earthly desires, it is never able to concentrate in self-examination. No one, indeed, fully understands wisdom, which is God, unless he strives to withdraw himself from the agitation that accompanies the affairs of the flesh. Whence in another place it is said, "To write

---

65. Jerome, *Nom. hebr.* 55.11 (CC 72.128).
66. Eccl 10.1.　　　　　　　　67. Matt 9.25.

wisdom in a time of leisure, and the man who is less active grows wise."⁶⁸

(21) Therefore, since we cannot be Israelites without observing the sabbath, let us celebrate a sabbath of spiritual leisure so that, like the Egyptians, we are not disturbed by a worrisome swarm of flies. Now since by the gift of God's goodness we have already come into possession of the land of Israel, it is not right that we be ignorant of the culture of the Israelites, lest by not learning their ceremonies we be exposed to the fierce teeth of invisible lions. For as sacred history in the Book of Kings relates, the king of the Assyrians was told, "The nations, they said, you deported and settled in the towns of Samaria do not know how to worship the god of the country. And the Lord has sent lions against them; and now these are killing them because they do not know how to worship the god of the country."⁶⁹ But anyone enrolled in the religious life who serves God in handsome outward attire, thus indicating that he has not given up the high fashion of secular living, should somehow be considered ignorant of the cult and worship of the one God as he tries, so to speak, to serve many gods. Hence, of such also it is said, "For when they worshiped the Lord they served their own gods at the same time with the rites of the nations."⁷⁰ In some way a man demonstrably worships both the Lord and the gods of the nations if, as he goes about his business in the sacred state in which he lives, he still does not abandon worldly affairs and the ways of carnal living. "No one," says the Lord, "can serve two masters."⁷¹ Does it not seem to be more tolerable for one to live according to the flesh, or to engage in giving service to the world, than to worship the devil according to the rite of the nations? For the same prophet who says, "All the gods of the nations are demons,"⁷² also states, "Accursed are they who stray from your commandments."⁷³ And the Apostle who asks, "Has the temple of God a common ground with

---

68. Sir 38.25; for this variant from the *Vulgate*, see Sabatier 2.480.
69. 2 Kgs 17.26.   70. 2 Kgs 17.33.
71. Matt 6.24.   72. Ps 95.5.
73. Ps 118.21.

idols?"⁷⁴ also says, "People who are interested in unspiritual things can never be pleasing to God."⁷⁵ And again, "No one in the army of God gets himself mixed up in worldly affairs so that he may be at the disposal of him who enlisted him."⁷⁶ The evil spirit, moreover, who is the source of idols, is called the prince of this world.⁷⁷ And James says, "Anyone who chooses the world for his friend turns himself into God's enemy."⁷⁸ What does it matter if a wicked man, in flaring up as an enemy of God, does so by offering sacrilegious worship or by leading an evil life?

(22) As I stated before, it will not be to our profit to begin living in the land of Israel unless we worship the one and only God of Israel without consorting with the gods of the gentiles. What is this land of which I speak unless it be that referred to by the Syrian Naaman, when he spoke to Elisha? "I beg you," he said, "allow me your servant to be given as much earth as two mules may carry."⁷⁹ In an allegorical sense, what does the Syrian Naaman signify but the human race? For as formerly Naaman was a leper, as soon as he had washed seven times in the waters of the Jordan he was cleansed of all the filth of leprosy;⁸⁰ so a worldly people, after receiving the seven gifts of the Dove that descended upon the Lord in the Jordan,⁸¹ cast off the infection of sin in the bath of holy baptism. What is symbolized by the earth for which Naaman begged if not the incarnation of the Redeemer? Mystically, this is the promised land where, it is said, milk and honey flowed. Milk, indeed, flows from the flesh, while honey comes from the upper parts. Since, therefore, the milk of humanity and the honey of divinity are recognized as present in the one mediator between God and men, the mystery of his incarnation is properly symbolized by the land where milk and honey flow. In asking for as much earth as two mules could carry, what else did he ask for but the writings of the two apostles, Peter and Paul? Hence, one of them says, "The

---

74. 2 Cor 6.16.
76. 2 Tim 2.4.
78. Jas 4.4.
80. Cf. 2 Kgs 5.14.
75. Rom 8.8.
77. Cf. John 14.30.
79. 2 Kgs 5.17.
81. Cf. Luke 3.22.

same person whose action had made Peter the Apostle of the circumcised had given me a similar mission to the pagans."[82] And because it is necessary, not only for the apostles, but also for all preachers to be knowledgeable and to work, the Lord sent two disciples into the village that was facing them,[83] and as Luke relates, he sent them in pairs "into every town and place he himself was to visit."[84]

(23) That Naaman, therefore, requested as much holy soil as two mules can carry, seems to indicate the human race earnestly begging for the teaching of the apostles concerning the Lord's incarnation, that these pack animals might bring earth to the world from which an altar could be made for offering sacrifice in the sight of the Creator. Hence, the Lord commands the sons of Israel, "You are to make me an altar of earth."[85] Now to erect an earthen altar to God is to hope in the incarnation of our Redeemer. And then, to be sure, the gift is accepted by our God when our humility places whatever we do on this altar, that is, upon our faith in the Lord's incarnation. We place our offering on an altar of earth if we strengthen our deeds by faith in the Lord's incarnation. Of this altar Isaiah says, "That day there will be an altar to the Lord in the center of the land of Egypt and, close to the frontier, a pillar to the Lord. And it will be both sign and witness of the Lord of hosts in the land of Egypt."[86] That Naaman, moreover, asked earth of the prophet only for the purpose of building an altar to the Lord is shown by what he at once added: "Because your servant will no longer offer holocaust or sacrifice to any god except the Lord."[87]

(24) In this land, therefore, let us also worship God, not according to our law, but his, so that he may not be able to say of us as he said of them, "They do not know how to worship the God of the country."[88] He decides to worship God according to his own law who, to all appearances, obeys God's commands; but in his actions he looks primarily to his own

---

82. Gal 2.8.
83. Cf. Matt 21.2.
84. Luke 10.1.
85. Exod 20.24.
86. Isa 19.19–20.
87. 2 Kgs 5.17.
88. 2 Kgs 17.26.

advantage and, while outwardly living according to Christian principles, disguises himself as an honest man, but interiorly strives to be prosperous in this life. We worship God, however, according to his laws and ceremonies if, when we know his will in some matter, we put aside completely our own interests and make every effort to comply; if we are not much concerned about amassing wealth, but care a great deal about how simple, how pure, and lastly, how sincere our conscience is within us; if we have no interest in how the tall horses on which we sit prance and arch their necks as if they were mad, but how we ourselves may be worthy to have God as our rider; if we do not set our hearts on some dead metal, but hide the living stone[89] in the jewel box of our heart; if jeweled trinkets do not adorn our attire, but if pearls of virtue sparkle in our souls; if in our hearts should glow the glass of purity and the gold of saving wisdom, that it might now be like the city of which John spoke in the Apocalypse, "The wall was built of diamond, and the city of pure gold, like polished glass; the foundations of the city were faced with all kinds of precious stones."[90]

(25) The soul, therefore, that has these qualities is without doubt a paradise; it is a garden of delights where God has his home. While it enjoys the contemplation of its Creator it is restored to the dignity in which the first man was made. Hence, when in Leviticus the Lord was about to say, "I will set up my dwelling among you, and I will not cast you off. I will live in your midst; I will be your God and you shall be my people," he first made this point, "You shall eat the oldest of last year's harvest, and still throw out the old to make room for the new."[91] In the oldest we may understand the first man seeing God in paradise; but the old is the people of Israel observing the rite of circumcision and sacrifice and the commands ordering various ceremonies. Then, indeed, do we spiritually eat the oldest of last year's harvest when, like our first parents we look upon the face of God; but we totally

89. Cf. 1 Pet 2.4–5.
90. Rev 21.18–19.
91. Lev 26.10–11.

throw out the old to make room for the new when, at the dawning of the grace of the gospel, we no longer observe the Mosaic Law. Therefore, if we seek to possess with God the glory of paradise, it is necessary that we first present ourselves to him as his dwelling, so that, while he lives in us and we in him, we so strive to celebrate the sabbath, not in ungenerous idleness but in diligent quiet, that we may deserve to pass on to the Lord's day that will have no end.

(26) May Almighty God, my dear friends, who has made you outstanding in the sight of men, grant that in his eyes you may also be true promoters of his Law.

LETTER 50

Peter Damian to Stephen, one of his fellow monks, who had left the cenobitic life to become a hermit in Damian's congregation. This letter may well be considered his exposition of the *Rule* contained in Letter 18. It is an extended description of the eremitic life in general, and of the laws and customs of his institute.

(1057; 2d edition, 1065)[1]

O MY DEAR BROTHER Stephen,[2] a hermit out of love for heavenly glory, Peter the least servant of the cross of Christ,[3] sends greetings in the same mystery.

(2) I have received your worthwhile request, my dear son, by which you ask to be instructed in the rule of the eremitic life[4] through something I might write for your advice. After leaving the less strict way of the monastery, you at once fervently confined yourself in the narrow prison of your cell. This is not a request that one might turn aside, nor is it an idle or empty undertaking, and if carried out properly, will also be of great service to those who shall come after us. But for me, who do not surpass others living this form of life, I find it rash to speak up before others like a guide, or like one

---

1. This letter has been variously dated from 1050–1057, with Woody, *Damiani* 197, placing it as late as 1063. But a consensus of scholars seems to hold that a first edition appeared in 1057, a second edition in 1065. See Lucchesi, *Clavis* 80f., and his *Vita* 2.158. For a complete discussion of this problem and of the relationship of Letter 50 to later Camaldolese legislation, especially in the work of Paolo Giustiniani, *Regula vite eremitice* (1520), the first printed edition of Letter 50, see Reindel, *Briefe* 2.77–79, n. 1–3.

2. Della Santa, *Idea monastica* 18f., notes that this letter (Reindel, *Briefe* 2.130 at note 126) is addressed to "my brothers," and not to Stephen alone.

3. Fonte Avellana and its daughter houses were dedicated to the Holy Cross.

4. Damian also refers to the "rule of the eremitic life" in his *Vita Rodulphi et Dominici Loricati* (Letter 109). Also in MS V1 this letter bears the title *Heremitica regula*.

who leads the way. It is surely preposterous for one to address others as if he were holding the teacher's rod over them, if his own life demonstrates that he belongs to those who are still in need of chastisement. But after suppressing your own will and deciding to obey God in all things, you are indeed worthy of having your request carefully fulfilled in all fraternal charity.

(3) Wherefore, while constrained in my desire to satisfy your wishes and yet not daring to overstep the bounds of my own ability, I think it safe and proper not to set forth the rules of this order. But it will suffice for me simply to explain what I see taking place in our congregation, and on which I am well informed. Nor will I discuss in general how hermits should live, but what should be done in our own hermitage, speaking specifically of both this place and its personnel. I have no doubt that this will not be without profit to those who read these words with love, since precept, to be sure, shows us the way to the heights of perfection, while example urges us on.

Praise of the Eremitic Life

(4) It is true, my brother, that, as it is said, you established the distinctive quality of this subject when you laudably chose to reach God not by just any way, but by this golden road. Nor did human prudence compel you to this action, but without doubt it was the Spirit of God who prompted you. This is indeed the high road, preeminent among others leading to higher things, that even now allows the traveler to enjoy his heavenly homeland, refreshes him who must still engage in work, and comforts him with restful peace. Those who walk this road are not pricked by worrisome thorns or impeded by the mire of worldly affairs. This road, moreover, is both wide and narrow, but in such a way that whoever follows it possessed of a desire for heaven, is not harmfully impeded because of its narrowness, nor diverted from the straight line of virtue because of its width. For even though it might often appear restricted and difficult for beginners, it is afterwards not deserted because of weakness and inconstancy unless,

which God forbid, faith is wanting. But to those who have grown accustomed to it, or are nearing or have achieved perfection, the eremitic life seems to be an easy and somehow a broad road. They never grow weary of carrying the cross in Jesus' footsteps as they suppress their own desires and war against the temptations arising from their own thoughts. You have taken a wife, my dear brother, who, unlike the wives of Jacob who were either denied motherhood by barrenness or whose beauty was marred by bleary eyes, is indeed both fruitful like Lea and beautiful like Rachel.[5] This is clearly the case so that your sight is sharpened that you may see God, and that many others might imitate the example of your noble fervor.

(5) Here is indeed the wife of whom it is said that "she is clothed in bravery and beauty."[6] In the solitary life it is one's duty to be so engaged in bravely performing great deeds, that one always takes pains to display the beauty of a heart that is pure. Here is the wife, I say, of whom it was also said, that "she performs mighty deeds and her fingers grasp the spindle,"[7] because one who lives satisfactorily in this life extends himself with such fervor in achieving great things, that he is careful not to overlook matters of small importance. This certainly could be said to the credit of the two sisters of Lazarus,[8] that while Mary was seated at the Lord's feet and listened to his words, Martha served the same Lord with various choice foods of virtue.

(6) But why do I dwell any longer on describing the benefits of this holy way of life? To sum it all up, there are many ways that lead to God. There are many states of life among the faithful, but in all of these there is none so direct, so certain, so unencumbered and so free of all stumbling blocks, since this way removes almost all occasions for committing sin. It

---

5. Cf. Gen 29.17; 29.37. For the interpretation of Lea and Rachel, see Jerome, *Nom. hebr.* 8.7 (CC 72.68), 9.25 (CC 72.70), 36.17 (CC 72.104), 63.1 (CC 72.138). In his Letter 153, Damian sees Lea as the symbol of the active life, and Rachel symbolizing the contemplative life.
6. Prov 31.25.   7. Prov 31.19.
8. Cf. Luke 10.39–40.

also heaps up a vast increase of virtue by which we are pleasing to God, so that, as it were, it deprives us of the ability to sin and compels us to perform good works. If one does not refuse to investigate, he will be able to find this subject more fully explained in my other slight works. And so, to this holy and, as I believe, this life-giving form of living we can aptly apply the words of Solomon, "Many daughters have gathered wealth, but you excel them all."[9]

On the Originators of This Life, and That There Are Two Kinds of Hermits

(7) Now good order demands that before taking up the branches of my discourse, I should carefully investigate the origin of its roots and clearly explain who might have originated this institution.[10] I think it is proper first to examine the source, so that afterwards we may safely drink from the stream.

(8) To start at the beginning, in the Old Testament Elijah began this type of life, but Elisha extended it as the number of disciples grew larger. In New Testament times, however, Paul and Anthony, not unlike them, followed one another with like results, since, if we can believe the record, Paul lived alone in the desert while Anthony brought many disciples to take up this life.[11] Although this too is not unknown, that just as he began publishing the Law, Moses[12] led the people for forty years through the wilderness, our Redeemer too spent the same number of days in the desert just as the grace of the gospel made its appearance, on the evidence of Mark who after telling of his baptism, then added, "Thereupon the Spirit sent him away into the wilderness, and there he remained for forty days and forty nights, was tempted by Satan, and lived among the wild beasts."[13] John the Baptist was also

---

9. Prov 31.29.
10. On possible sources of Damian's discussion of the origins of the eremitical life, see Della Santa, *Idea monastica* 188, n. 112.
11. On the disciples of St. Anthony, see *Vita Antonii*, ed. G. J. M. Bartelink, *Vite dei Santi* (1974), c. 16, 40.
12. Cf. Exod 16.35.   13. Mark 1.12–13.

no ordinary promoter of this profession, deciding with God's help to live in the wilderness without eating food supplied by men.[14]

(9) Wherefore it is clear from both the very beginning of this institution and from the succession of those who followed, that the order of hermits has two divisions, of whom some live in cells while others move about in the wilderness refusing to live in fixed abodes. Those who wander about through the desert are known as anchorites, while those who remain in cells[15] are called hermits, from whom the name common to them became specific. Even though today the brothers are proud to adopt this name, still, for the sake of humility, they prefer to call themselves penitents. The descendants of Jonadab[16] were then the first anchorites who, as Jeremiah reports, drank no wine or spiritous beverage. Moreover, they lived in tents and settled down only when it became dark. In the psalm[17] it is further said of them that they were the first to endure captivity at that time of persecution, since they were forced to enter the cities by the Chaldaean army that invaded Judaea. They therefore considered towns as prisons, and thought of solitude in the wilderness as a sweet and peaceful place to dwell. But today, since anchorites are rare or nonexistent, we give them only our respect, and turn our whole attention in this discussion to hermits.

On the Battles That Novices Must Fight

(10) Whoever, then, enters a cell to fight with the devil and is incited by heartfelt fervor to engage in the arena of spiritual combat, should direct his complete attention to suppressing even momentary carnal delights, so that he might live as one dead to self and to the world. He should prepare his spirit to bear misfortune and misery, should vow to die for

---

14. Cf. Mark 1.4–6.
15. See Pierucci, *Struttura* 133.
16. Cf. Jer 35.6. In this citation, however, Jeremiah speaks only of wine. Other spiritous drinks are referred to in Deut 29.6, Judg 13.4, and also in Luke 1.15.
17. Cf. Ps 136.

Christ, gird himself spiritually with various weapons of virtue, suggest to himself all sorts of harsh and difficult situations, so that when they occur, he is not unprepared and weakly goes down to defeat, but is able to bear everything calmly. Indeed, just as a river is extremely small as it originates at its source, but in its downhill progress becomes broader as other streams empty into its flow, so too the man who practices the interior life begins his spiritual journey in a dry and narrow way, but gradually gains strength by his growth in virtue as by a concurrence of streams from all sides.

(11) Therefore, whoever wishes to check the river's flow must try to dam the current as it exits from its source, so that when it is not yet a rushing torrent but only a stream, it may more easily be obstructed. Also he who plans to travel to the royal court, starts out with only a few companions; but along the way the group grows larger as others join the party. Hence if someone should wish to ambush the travelers, he will lie in wait near the house from which they started so that they will not escape the sudden attack because of the great number of those who later joined them. Then, in truth, do we start our trip to visit our king, when as untried and new beginners we swear our oaths and join the spiritual army. But because we are not yet surrounded by a host of those who are trying to live by the spirit, have not yet grown strong by reason of virtues acquired in leading a perfect life, our ancient enemy will then prepare an ambush before the entrance from which we are to emerge and there arrange his sly tricks, his black arts and snares, his deceptive devices, and every evil artifice his cunning can invent. This he does to block the narrow stream of good works and eliminate the traveler before he is supported by an increase of his companions.

(12) Yet amid this growing hailstorm of missiles, this whirlwind of violent battles, the knight of Christ will not freeze with fear, will not weaken and crack at the effort, but armed with the shield of unconquered faith by which he is able to bear the sharp attacks of the treacherous foe about him, will trust more certainly in a helping God inspiring him nearby.

Nor will he ever doubt that if he escapes unharmed from the first onslaught of temptation, he will shortly afterwards be strong and brave in overcoming his adversaries who flee and fall about him. For this reason the conspiring spirit spews forth all the venom of his wickedness at novices; so too he pours out every poison his tricky and deceptive cunning can devise, because he is aware that if he then loses the opportunity of this evil attempt, he will later have no chance to do harm. Moreover, if he is unable to cause his victim to stumble, he will later shamefully end up in failure; and if he cannot win his battle with a novice, he will fall before one who is well-trained.

That a Hermit Must Be Especially Careful about Three Things

(13) We should take note that while all who strive for eternal life should be endowed with every virtue of the spirit, for him who tries to live the solitary life, three external conditions are especially fitting, and before all else should be brought to his special attention; namely, quiet, silence,[18] and fasting. Other tools for arriving at perfection should be used now and then out of dedication or habit, but these three should be practiced with constant and familiar devotion. As it is the function of a priest to occupy himself with offering sacrifice, of a learned man to preach, so too is it the duty of a hermit to live in quiet, in fasting, and in silence.[19] Hence it was not in vain that the ancient founders of this way of life should have said, "Remain in your cell, hold your tongue, and curb your stomach, and all will go well with you."[20] The stomach, indeed, should be controlled so that by immoderate eating it does not infect the other members of the body with vice. The tongue, too, should be restrained, because when it is relaxed and undisciplined it empties the soul of the vigor of

18. See L. Gougaud, "Anciennes coûtumes claustrales," *Moines et Monastères* 8 (1930), 14–23; P. Salmon, "Le silence religieux. Pratique et théorie," *Mélanges bénédictins* (1947), 11–57.
19. On the traditional roles found in the Church, see Laqua, *Traditionen* 90–103.
20. For reference to possible sources of this statement in the *Vitas patrum*, see Reindel, *Briefe* 2.86, n. 22.

God's grace and weakens our salutary firmness. But in such matters moderation and discretion should be observed, lest what we do thoughtlessly we timidly put aside as a burden we are unable to bear. As I have promised above, I will briefly explain the rule of life[21] that is observed in this hermitage, that as you bring this rule to your attention and use it as a measure for your life, either exceeding it or failing to reach its standard, by returning to it with careful purpose, you will not be in a position to err.

On Fasting Throughout the Year

(14) From the thirteenth [the Ides] of September[22] to Easter it is the custom here to fast five days a week. But from the octave of Easter until Pentecost we observe the fast only four days a week, with this difference that besides Sunday, which all agree is preeminent, the brothers eat twice a day on Tuesday and Thursday. In this period one is permitted to live somewhat more relaxed, even though by authority of the sacred canons the monks are not forbidden to fast.[23] But from the octave of Pentecost until the birthday of St. John,[24] a stew[25] is allowed the brothers on Tuesdays at 3:00 P.M., and this meal is repeated on Thursdays. From the feast of St. John, moreover, until the thirteenth of September, a meal is served twice a day on Tuesdays and Thursdays, but on the remaining four days the fast is observed as usual, except that if it is noticed that someone of the brothers is sick,[26] we tenderly care for him, doing everything that is necessary.

21. Capitani, *L'istituto eremitico* 162 notes that what follows in no way contradicts other norms or regulations found in Damian's papers.
22. G. Zimmermann, "Ordensleben und Lebensstandard" . . . *Beiträge zur Geschichte des alten Mönchtums und des Benediktinerordens* 32 (1973), 243f., no. 12 remarks that originally the great fast began on the Ides of September, but that gradually this date was replaced by the feast of the Exaltation of the Cross (14 September).
23. On these "sacred canons," see Zimmerman, "Ordensleben" 44f.
24. On 24 June.
25. In the *Benedicti regula* c. 39.1.108 and c. 39.3.109 the author of the *Rule* refers to a cooked meal (*cocta pulmentaria*). See also Du Cange 6.563f., citing Peter Damian, Letters 109 and 119.
26. For milder treatment of the sick, cf. *Benedicti regula* c. 36.104f.

On Feast Days

(15) On the feast days having twelve readings from Scripture which fall between the thirteenth of September and Easter the brothers eat only once a day, except for the solemnities[27] of All Saints, St. Martin, and St. Andrew, the Christmas week, and the feast of Epiphany and Candlemas Day. On these days, as is our custom, we eat twice a day. But on other feast days we are satisfied with one meal a day.

(16) We should note, however, that not all the feasts observed in the monastery are celebrated in the hermitage.[28] Those that are had here are usually transferred, so that they are celebrated either on a Tuesday or a Thursday, except, of course, the principal feasts which because of their greater dignity cannot be changed. On many of these festivities which are not of great significance, either during Lent or during the course of the year, the cellarer gives a bit of extra food, but rarely, to those who live near the church, when there are twelve readings from Scripture, and it is approved by the prior. On the other hand, those who live in scattered cells, are not able to go out, and are content with three readings, they observe the fast as usual. By fasting we mean eating bread with salt and water. But when something else is added, in the hermitage we do not call that fasting. During the two Lenten seasons that precede Christmas and Easter some of the brothers here observe the fast the whole week, and daily, except for Sundays, live on bread and water. There are also some brothers who during both Lenten periods abstain from all cooked food, not only on feastdays but also on Sundays. At first I sought to forbid this on Sundays because of the importance of the holy Resurrection, but later at the urgent request

---

27. These solemnities fall on 1 November, 11 November, 30 November, 6 January, and 2 February. For the use of the Greek term (*ipopanti*) for Candlemas Day, see Blum, *St. Peter Damian* 108, n. 12.

28. It is not clear from this statement whether Damian is speaking of monastery and hermitage in general, or whether at Fonte Avellana, as in Camaldoli, the two types of life were found together. It would also appear that fewer feast days were celebrated by the hermits.

of the brothers I was constrained to allow it. Their food consists of fruit and edible roots, of stewed or boiled legumes.

(17) Nor should I fail to say that at the beginning of each Lenten season all the monks and also the lay brothers observe a strict three day fast, so that those who are unable to abstain totally from food, are satisfied with only bread and water.

On Stewed Food

(18) It is customary[29] for the brothers to have two stewed dishes on Sundays throughout the year, except for the two Lenten seasons mentioned above, during which on all Sundays and saints' days they are satisfied with only one. On other days, when they moderate their fast and live less strictly, if they eat twice a day, two dishes of stew are prepared for them, one at lunch and the other at dinner. But if there is only one meal, stew is served only once. Since, however, as we will recall, a stew is usually served twice on Sundays, this was permitted contrary to the eremitic rule because only very rarely do we receive gifts from people outside the hermitage. On the other hand, where a religious house is frequently visited by the faithful out of devotion, the second serving of stew is omitted.

(19) And so it is that in the hermitage we built with God's help on the slopes of Mt. Suavicino,[30] more than one stew a day is unheard of throughout the whole year. For some time we abstained from drinking wine, so that neither the lay brothers nor those who came here from outside the hermitage drank anything but water, even on Easter; wine was had only for the sacrifice of the Mass. But because those who were here enrolled began to grow ill, and because some wishing to enter the eremitic life seemed to be appalled at this severe practice, I condescended to allow for this fraternal, or more correctly, this common weakness by granting a dispensation, permitting wine to be drunk here if used with moderation

---

29. One may here compare these fasting regulations with those in Damian, Letter 18.
30. On the founding of Suavicino, see John of Lodi, *Vita* c. 7 (PL 144.125A); Reindel, *Briefe* 2.91, n. 44.

and sobriety. For if we could not, like John,[31] live in total abstinence, we should at least, with Timothy,[32] the disciple of Paul, remember to care sparingly and humbly for our weak stomach, and if we were unable to abstain completely, we should at least try to be temperate in its use. Yet in the two Lenten seasons we mentioned above, the custom prevails that neither monks nor lay brothers are allowed to take wine or eat fish, with the exception of the four feast days, namely, those of St. Andrew[33] and St. Benedict,[34] Palm Sunday and Holy Thursday, on which holy days they use wine and fish out of joy in celebrating these high solemnities. On Holy Saturday and on the Vigil of Christmas, so that their duties in the church might be lightened, those who wish eat the full measure of bread, but both lay brothers and monks totally abstain from other food. Only three octaves are annually celebrated here, during which no one is compelled to fast, namely, at Easter, Pentecost, and Christmas. But for some, because they are not so accustomed, it is difficult to eat twice a day for a whole week, and because at times they humbly so request, it is compassionately allowed them to fast a bit, for both ecclesiastical tradition and the authority of the Fathers determined that one fast during the octave of Pentecost. But during the octaves of all other feasts we carry out ecclesiastical rites in keeping with the monastic rule,[35] but we do not alter the customary fast.

On Servants or Lay Brothers

(20) That the whole household of God be maintained with regular discipline and care, and that every member work corporately at the duties proper to him, even the lay brothers[36]

31. Cf. Luke 1.15. 32. Cf. 1 Tim 5.23.
33. On 30 November. 34. On 21 March.
35. On the vows taken by his hermits in keeping with the *Rule* of St. Benedict, see Blum, *St. Peter Damian* 91.
36. Damian here uses the term *famuli*, which I translate as 'lay brothers.' They may be considered as 'servants,' but in the title, taken from MS V1, they seem to be the equivalent of *conversi* or *laici*, the more common terms for 'lay brothers.' On which see Reindel, *Briefe* 2.93, n. 49; 106, n. 82. In any case, the term is unclear. But see Hallinger, "Woher kommen die Laienbrüder?" *Analecta sacri ordinis Cisterciensis* 12 (1956), 1–104, esp. 32–37.

who give their service to this hermitage will not depart from the rule of life assigned to them. Customarily they fast three days a week throughout the year. But in the two Lenten seasons they fast four days a week, excepting those who are required to travel some distance. Wherever they may travel, however, they are always forbidden to eat meat, and like the monks are never allowed personal property. Many of them, moreover, rise early to attend the chanting of the night office along with the brothers who live near the church. When they enter here, they take this promise: "I, Brother 〈   〉, promise to persevere in obedience all the days of my life in this hermitage, built to the honor of God and the Holy Cross, out of reverence for our Lord Jesus Christ and the good of my soul. But should I at any time attempt to flee or depart from here, it is permitted the servants of God who shall live here to search for me with all the authority that is theirs, and to use force or violence to bring me back to their service."[37] To a written copy of this promise they shall prefix the sign of the cross, and after it is read by one of the brothers to all those present, they shall place it on the altar. Monks, however, take no other vows except those which are customarily taken in monasteries, with only the name of the hermitage added. Likewise, for both monks and lay brothers who wish to enter here, everything harsh and difficult is at once set before them, namely, the poverty of our clothing or its very absence, the meanness of our food, giving up one's own will, the severe and exacting correction, continuous reproach and reprimand, ever present work and fatigue. I will not continue to enumerate these and other things like them, since we are aware that the same conditions are found in monasteries that follow the rule.

On the Quantity of Bread

(21) The measure of bread[38] in the hermitage is the same as in the monastery, with this difference: on days when there are one or two meals, if a brother wishes to eat the total

---

37. On which see Blum, *St. Peter Damian* 94.
38. On the weight of the bread, using the Roman pound (=327 grams)

amount he will not be blamed; but on days of fasting, he always weights what he is about to eat, since every brother has a set of scales in his cell. The amount is arrived at in this fashion: by adding a half loaf to a quarter, half of the whole loaf weighs a half when the quarter is removed intact. And that there can be no doubt about measuring in this way, nine African hen's eggs weigh the same as three goose eggs. But this will suffice on the subject of fasting or of the weighing of food.

(22) On the topic of other spiritual exercises, I fear writing about the constant and continuous fervor one finds here, the eagerness, the frequency of work and of prayer by night, lest I appear to brag while living with these men, but not taking part in what they do. This much I can say, that there is no little earnestness here in genuflections, in strokes of the discipline, and in other practices of this kind, which, my dear brothers, since you can more clearly learn about them by speaking to those who are so engaged, there is no need here to put them all down in writing.

On the Manner of Reciting the Psalms

(23) On the reciting of the psalms,[39] it is customary here when two live together in a cell, that daily they complete two psalters, one for the living and one for the dead. The psalter for the living is recited along with the additions which the blessed Romuald prescribed, which I do not hesitate to include, in case some novice should complain that I have omitted items that he should know about. After reciting five psalms, they should then add, "Praise be to you,[40] O Trinity, one equal Godhead before all ages, now and forever. Pray for us, all you saints of God, that we may be worthy of the promises of our Lord and God, Jesus Christ. Our Father. . . ."

---

in accord with the *Benedicti regula* c. 39.4.109, see Reindel, *Briefe* 2.94, n. 52.

39. See B. Calati, "Devotio-Poenitentia in S. Pier Damiano," *Fonte Avellana nel suo millenario* (1982), 143f. on the influence of Benedict of Aniane on Fonte Avellana.

40. See F. J. Mone, *Lateinische Hymnen des MA* (1853; 1964), 11, no. 8.

When these prayers are finished, we then continue, "Our help is in the name of the Lord, who made heaven and earth."[41] After reciting the next five psalms, one then says, "You, God, the uncreated Father, you the only-begotten Son, and you the Holy Spirit, the Paraclete, holy and undivided Trinity, we acknowledge with all our heart and speech, we praise you and bless you, to you be glory forever. Amen. O Lord God, come to my assistance; O Lord, make haste to help me. Let my enemies, who seek my life, be dismayed and brought to shame. You are my help and my salvation, O Lord, do not delay.[42] Glory be to the Father and to the Son and to the Holy Spirit."

(24) After each five psalms these prayers are always added alternatively until the psalter is finished, with the inclusion of the three canticles said on Sunday and those said throughout the week. We should also not forget to recite the prayers contained at the conclusion of the psalter, namely, the "We praise you, O God,"[43] "Now, O Lord, dismiss your servant," the two Creeds, "Glory to God in the highest," the "Our Father" with the profession of the Catholic faith, and lastly the litanies and their prayers to bring all these to a proper conclusion. The psalter for the dead, however, is recited with nine readings, three for each fifty psalms. But if a brother lives alone, he will, of course, daily complete the whole psalter for the living, but of that of the dead he will recite either the whole or a half as his strength will allow. The chanting of the canonical hours takes place here in its entirety and in the same manner exactly as in the monastery.

On Silence in the Cells

(25) Among other things, I must not overlook this item, that it is our custom to maintain continuous silence[44] in the cells, just as in the oratory, nor is it there allowed that anyone speak to another even for the purpose of confession, except

---

41. Ps 123.8.   42. Ps 69.2–37.
43. Damian here incorporates the *Te Deum* among the daily prayers of his hermits; on which, see M. Huglo, "Te Deum," NCE 13 (1967), 954–955.
44. On silence, see *Benedicti regula* c. 6, 41f.; Blum, *St. Peter Damian* 121.

if the prior sees fit to permit the novices to speak to their instructors for a short period of time. But if they have need to speak, they should make known what is necessary as they walk to the church. I know from experience that it is a great disturbance to the soul when random conversation is allowed in the cell. For when some lighthearted brothers visit one another under the guise of confession, after briefly completing what they set out to do, they soon allow themselves to discuss frivolous and useless matters once their wanton tongue is given its freedom, and suddenly forgetting why they came, they then speak disparagingly of their brothers, or even of the prior, and sink their teeth, if I may put it so, with biting slander into those whom they should love with purity and sincerity. Then they pass on to secular affairs, and in the cell argue about what is going on in the towns. The news has not yet reached the ears of the people before it resounds through most of the hideouts in the mountains. To this you may add that when the superior is absent, the more secure they are from censure the more freely they pour out words that flow from their lips. And so it happens that those who came together to be absolved from sin, depart from one another more contaminated by still more sins of the tongue.

On Various Practices of Regular Observance

(26) It is also a significant part of the penitential life that at all times, both summer and winter, the brothers wear neither shoes nor stockings[45] in the cell, but that it is customary to go barefooted and barelegged, except for those suffering from grave infirmity. It is a part of the monastic *Rule*,[46] that those who are sent on a trip should not eat outside the monastery if they plan to return the same day. Added to this practice we also prescribe that if one is outside the hermitage for one or two days, he should always return fasting, except for principal feastdays, so that he does not overlook the penitential life even when away.

---

45. Cf. Isidore, *Etym.* 19.34.5, who defines *ocreae*, the Latin word used here, as *tibialia calciamenta*.
46. Cf. *Benedicti regula* c. 51.1.133.

(27) Concerning other monastic practices, whatever is done in strict monasteries that observe the *Rule*, is also cautiously and carefully carried out here, that is, in the matter of prompt obedience, that whatever is commanded is humbly and fervently fulfilled; of not giving or receiving without the prior's permission; of not possessing personal property; that when they are in the cloister adjacent to the church[47] they observe silence both on feastdays and at all unsuitable hours; that they not neglect regular custom in the chapter, in the oratory, or in the refectory; that they not speak with guests; that either going to or coming from their cells to the church they not abandon the rule of silence, and many other similar items.[48] These I will not further enumerate so as to avoid boring redundancy.

On Loving Care for the Dead

(28) I would not wish to pass over in silence, that when a brother of ours dies,[49] all those who live here fast seven days for him, take the discipline seven times, each with a thousand strokes, perform seven hundred genuflections, recite, moreover, thirty psalters in the usual way, and every priest personally celebrates seven masses, in addition to the masses said for him in the presence of the whole community for thirty continuous days. No one is allowed to alter this regulation in our hermitage, and this custom regarding the dead shall be forever maintained strictly and inviolably.

(29) But if anyone, for example, a novice, for any reason is unable to complete the penance here imposed, or is prevented by death, as soon as it becomes evident to the brothers, the entire penance, equally divided among them, will be accepted with great fervor, and however much it is, shall be gladly performed in a short space of time, observing all the various forms of penance.

---

47. For building arrangements at Fonte Avellana, see Pierucci, *Struttura* 131–139.
48. Cf. *Benedicti regula* c. 6.41f., c. 38.5.107, c. 42.114f., c. 52.2.124, and c. 53.23f. and 138f.
49. On which, see *Excerpta ex veteribus liturgicis codicibus Fontavellanensibus* (PL 151.920–931).

(30) These few words will suffice on how we presently live in this hermitage, so that from what has been briefly noted, one can understand what should be thought of those things I have passed over in silence.

That Everyone Should Carefully Examine Himself and Then Act According to His Ability

(31) And so, my dear brother, you should carefully note what I have shown you about the way of life our brothers lead. Gauge your strength in the balance of strict self-examination, so that whether you rise or fall in your estimation, you cannot lose your way completely through the tortuous turns as you constantly observe the signposts on this oft-trodden road. A painter, you know, places the picture to be copied before the sheet of parchment he is using, reducing everything to the size of the painting he holds in his hand, and composes his piece according to the lines of the borrowed work. You too should use the powers which the giver of heavenly gifts has bestowed on you and put them to work, that you may know how much you will be compelled by necessity to lessen your effort, or how much through an increase of grace you can enlarge it. For while some easily spend the whole week in fasting, others find it difficult to fast for two days, but in so doing each gains equal merit; the stronger who performs greater deeds, and the weaker one, who by doing what he can, does not fail to do what is less.

(32) Therefore, it is difficult to set a definitive and general rule for fasting, lest we appear to force the stronger ones to lessen their resolve to overachieve, or to prevent the weaker from applying their strength in attempting greater things. "For everyone has the gift God granted him, one this gift and another that."[50] We read of many of our ancient Fathers[51] who even while living together in common did not observe a common rule of life. So everyone must gauge his own strength,

---

50. 1 Cor 7.7; on the variants from the *Vulgate*, see Sabatier 3.678.
51. Here one is reminded of early Eastern monachism, in which fast rules of communal living were not yet fixed; see Rufinus, *Historia monachorum* c. 21f. (PL 21.443B–445B).

not foolishly deceiving himself and not cheating by pretending to be weak, but checking himself as far as he is able by the law of sobriety and the rigor of abstinence.

On How Strictly Some of the More Perfect Brothers Live

(33) There are, moreover, some brothers here who follow a greatly different way of life from what I have written here and bind themselves severely to live by a much stricter law. Some, indeed, never drink wine or use wine vinegar in any way; others do not take eggs, milk, cheese, or lard. Many look down on a bed of matted reeds as something too soft, and are satisfied to rest on papyrus leaves, so that they also completely refuse to lie on straw. Others lightly regard the harshest hairshirts as soft and delicate garments and wear iron corselets next to their skin. We have one brother here, who during the whole year is content to eat half the measure of bread, not only on ordinary days, but also on holy days and Sundays. For about a year and a half this same brother did not touch food five days a week, and was content to eat only on Sundays and Thursdays. But now he eats one cooked meal at 3:00 P.M. on Sunday and Thursday and completely bypasses the second.

(34) There is also a brother, who out of love for continence and sobriety determined to abstain not only from fruit, but also from onions and leeks and all green vegetables. One brother every day during the two Lenten seasons lives on two handfuls of chick-peas, always on Thursdays eating only bread and now and then on Tuesdays. He also constantly wears an iron chain about his waist so as not to exceed this manner of frugal repast.

(35) One of our old men confided to me that when he dined alone in his cell he did not eat his food quickly as his hunger demanded, but by hesitating and delaying, now and then, and that, one at a time, put crumbs rather than pieces of bread into his mouth, and thus by experiencing severe necessity he tormented himself while nourishing his body. Thus his very food did not relax him but became instead a torture, and eating could rather be called exhaustion, since it did not

offer refreshing delight but painful punishment. "I reprimanded our young people for still being soft, and corrected them, moreover, with sharp reproach because they ate a quarter loaf of whole wheat bread a day, and at last succeeded in getting them to reduce that amount by half."[52]

(36) Now this old man at that time wore an undergarment of iron, and from Sunday to Thursday took no food at all, and on the other three days of the week lived only on bread. We have another brother here, a young man who is still a novice, who customarily recites a whole psalter with arms outstretched,[53] lowering his tired arms after fifty psalms, but raising them again before he is even finished reciting the next psalm. There is another old man, already stooped with age, who chants two psalters with arms constantly extended, one of them with its canticles and litanies and many prayers, the other for the dead with nine readings from Scripture.

(37) I will speak of another, but who will know whether he should believe my statement or not? But one can make light of it if human audacity reproves a person whom the highest Truth does not charge with lying. This same old man, named Dominic,[54] often spends a whole day and a night meditatively reciting the psalter nine times, and while so doing almost continuously beats his naked body with scourges held in both hands. It should be noted that while he is so engaged he does not sleep day or night, but at times is on his knees and rests his head on the ground, and thus naked, he snatches a little sleep, and with that he is satisfied. At one time as we were engaged in friendly conversation, he confided to me that often as he recited these nine psalters, he could never complete a tenth. I know of a brother who admitted that while chanting he performed as many genuflections as there are

---

52. This sentence seems to reflect the words of the "old man," quoted here by Damian.

53. On this occasion Damian seems to indicate that the brother prayed with his arms raised to heaven. Elsewhere (Letter 109) it appears that the arms were extended in the form of a cross.

54. It is uncertain whether this account about Dominic was in the original version of Letter 50. See Lucchesi, *Clavis* 66.

verses in a psalter and a psalter is said to contain about four thousand verses, as they assert who took pains to count them.

(38) But I shall not continue with this any further, for I am afraid to offend those about whom I speak; and to live with those in whose effort I do not take part, makes me feel ashamed like an indolent man who is describing another's fervor. So I deem it proper to let these practices to strong and more perfect men, and with some amount of discretion to moderate those milder commands that were described above. I do this so that while the more vigorous are eager to drive through the high seas of virtue with powerful strokes of the oar, the weaker sort are not compelled to hug the shore and remain behind with their swift craft stuck in a sandbank.

Here the Practice of Severe Fasting Is Moderated

(39) Yet lest what I write appear to waver as if freed from our rule of law, I believe that every brother who remains in his cell can, with God's help, easily fast on bread and water three days a week the whole year long, both in summer and in winter, unless he is so sick that he must remain in bed. And since fasting on Saturday is also in authentic canonical tradition, it would not appear difficult for a brother also to defer his meal on Saturdays to 3:00 P.M., but that he eat only once that day, at which meal he is not forbidden to have wine and a cooked dish indulgently granted in this our disposition. This is the norm in summertime. But you know that from the thirteenth of September until the joyous feast of Easter we fast four days a week, but if one should at times experience some disability on Saturdays, he will be allowed, also in winter, to temper his normal fast a bit by eating boiled legumes or edible roots, or also fruit. But if he partakes of one of these, he should not eat one of the others unless real necessity should dictate. Finally, however, with the less courageous in mind, if it should be truly necessary, whatever is allowed in summertime may also be permitted with discretion on Saturdays during the winter time.

(40) Also on feastdays which are celebrated in the winter season, about which I stated that we usually eat only once a

day, it is also allowed to take food twice a day as is customarily done among cenobites. During the two Lenten periods, moreover, which precede Christmas and Easter, they may have a cooked meal on Tuesdays and Thursdays, and on Sundays and principal feasts, including Thursdays, they may also drink wine.[55] In Lent the brothers should be satisfied with one cooked meal when they eat only once; but when they take food twice a day, they shall have one for lunch and another for dinner. But during the rest of the year they may always have two. On Sundays and greater feasts, moreover, if supplies allow, I would not deny also a third.

Here the Care of the Sick Is Left to the Disposition of the Prior

(41) I leave the care of the sick to the decision of the prior, in that he should judge the potential of each one, and if he sees that it would be of benefit to any one, he will provide them with what they need. I am wholly in accord with what we read of the blessed Romuald, who often said to his disciples, "So long as any brother does not abandon his cell, he is even permitted with discretion to eat meat if it appears to be unavoidably necessary." And he also added, "This is almost like leaving the hermitage and returning to the monastery, or like abandoning the monastic life and going back to the world."[56] Hence it is necessary that whoever is at the head of this eremitic fraternity should carefully examine the strength of each of the brothers and should supply what is needed according to each one's ability. And, indeed, the best situation is had if all are strong enough to live according to the same regular norms; but if one or more perhaps are ill and do not have what they need, the prior's loving solicitude should quietly and secretly provide for them, so that those who are healthy should continue their rigorous discipline without becoming envious. Nor is it necessary that what is done for one

---

55. On the use of wine, see Damian, Letter 18 at n. 21 and Letter 10 *passim*.
56. On this relaxation of the rules regarding the use of meat, see Reindel, *Briefe* 2.105, n. 80.

should suddenly become the norm for all, since the same brother who today is in need of compassionate treatment may next week perhaps be much stronger and not require special care. For the Blessed Romuald himself, as his disciples used to say, changed the weekly regimen in such a way that the brothers spent one week from Sunday to Sunday fasting on bread and water, and during the next he allowed them a cooked meal on Thursday. The solicitude of the prior should also extend to the lay brothers,[57] determining how much they should fast.

On the Norms of Sleep

(42) In the matter of sleep, moreover, in some cases it is necessary to use moderate discretion rather than harsh severity. Surely it is better to grant the body sleep with a certain tempered liberality, and afterwards to engage fervently in praising God, than to be dissolutely yawning the whole day and almost falling asleep. During the time of our recent predecessors it was not customary to sleep for a short period during the day. But now during summertime we take a siesta; for as I learned by experience, whatever progress is lost by sleeping during the day is offset by rising earlier at night and by more easily taking part in divine services.

(43) But it should be noted that before gathering for night choir, either if it is still completely dark, or if the office for any reason appears to be difficult, one is allowed to go back to bed; but after the night office this is totally forbidden. And so, that this regular observance may more easily be maintained, I have ordered that daily the signal[58] for the night office shall be given for the first time. Then, after the psalter is finished in its usual way, the signal will be repeated and we will perform the night office, so that about daybreak when we are particularly subject to drowsiness, we will stand and engage in chanting the canonical hours. God forbid that we should give in to sleep or laziness at the hour when our Re-

---

57. I have translated *conversi* as 'lay brothers,' but Damian's exact meaning is unclear; see *supra* n. 36.
58. See Blum, *St. Peter Damian* 124, n. 60.

deemer rose after destroying the reign of death, lest we be asleep when the physical sun is rising and our inner man should await the never setting light, and lest those mocking words should appear to apply to us, "His disciples came by night and stole the body while we were asleep."[59]

(44) We must, therefore, be on our guard not to yield to sleep at improper times, even for a moment. For if sleep should frequently creep up on us when we are seated or even standing, afterwards when we should wish to take our rest, sleep will be impossible. And thus sleep begets wakefulness, and wakefulness sleep, for he who is sleeping, is afterwards reluctantly awakened; and again he who stays awake for an extended period must necessarily go to sleep. Something like this often happens to those who are indiscreet in eating. Some are silly enough to complain endlessly that they cannot eat supper, but certainly their loss of appetite comes from eating too much for lunch. For if they had not exceeded the bounds of frugality at lunch, they would not have to turn up their noses at the evening meal. Therefore, if one is to eat his evening meal and soon afterwards go to sleep, he should eat frugally at lunch and not give in to idle napping. But I must not fail to mention that there are some who hurry to anticipate their recitation of the psalms while it is still light, that they might sleep more quietly at night and loudly snore away in deep slumber till they have had their fill. Such are strictly forbidden to begin the psalms before they have said compline at the proper time.

On Various Categories of Eremitic Discipline

(45) Each brother will daily chant one psalter,[60] but if he wishes to add a psalter for the dead, it is left to his discretion whether he chants the entire psalter, a half, or even a third, or omits it altogether. In doing so he must remember to observe the rules of psalmody, both for the living and for the dead, just as it is done in monasteries. On the four days on

---

59. Matt 28.13.
60. Cf. *Benedicti regula* c. 18.23.80.

which I have required fasting, they will observe silence, unless perhaps some necessity should dictate otherwise. But in the cells themselves they may never speak to anyone, unless they remain there in total seclusion, or also, if they live near the church. Nor should a brother ever presume to eat in his cell with another brother, whether from his own community or from some other, or to invite others to eat where it is not even allowed to confess to another brother in the vernacular.

(46) If two brothers live together in a cell,[61] one is always the superior and the other obeys in accord with the commands of the common prior. But if one of them is a novice, they have permission to converse once or twice a week after vespers; but after he ceases being a novice, they shall from then on put an end to their conversation. Going to and from their cells, as I said above, they shall always maintain silence. When the signal is given for the brothers to assemble, on hearing the signal, and as he grooms himself, no one is permitted to remain in his cell longer than it takes to recite five psalms.

(47) A dutiful brother will be careful not to damage or thoughtlessly handle things that are assigned to his necessary use, or any other equipment such as garments, tools, dishes, or similar things. He should be especially cautious in handling our Sacred Books, so that he never puts his hands on the letters, never allows them to be soiled by smoke or to reek of odors from the fire. He should place the things that are needed every day close by, so that when he is required to use them he need not frequently get up to fetch them. Excessive moving about is also to be avoided, so as not to walk aimlessly in his cell. Whoever wishes, moreover, may wear shoes in his cell.

(48) I do not require any of the brothers to engage in prostrations, the use of the discipline, or slapping his hand on the ground, or in praying with arms extended, or in other practices of holy fervor,[62] but rather think that these things are

---

61. See John of Lodi, *Vita* c. 4 (PL 144.120CD).
62. For the translation of *metanea*, *disciplina*, and *palmatae*, see John of Lodi, *Vita* c. 5 (PL 144.122f.); Blum, *St. Peter Damian* 115; Reindel, *Briefe* 2.109, n. 87–90.

not adapted to all the brothers, and so it seems more proper and more liberal that in these matters one be given an option rather than prescribe them by definitive legislation. Each month they should shave their heads,[63] excepting the two Lenten seasons, during which they should also not wash their heads. If they are in good health they may not bathe.[64] I have ordained these things with such a measure of mild discretion after removing all rigor and austerity, so that a brother who is solicitous for his salvation will not dread this live-giving order, and still if he performs these tasks he may be fully confident in the mercy of Almighty God. Consequently, this rule must remain in force after my death, for while I am alive I will not, with God's help, allow the customs here established to be diminished.

On the Practice of Obedience

(49) One must be especially careful not to depreciate the obligation of obedience under the guise of leading a hermit's life; rather he should bind himself the more firmly under the law of obedience to the degree that he is aware how greatly this way of life exceeds the rule of the cenobites. For it frequently happens that a brother is directed to leave one cell for another and is not allowed to take with him any of the equipment that he had made with his own hands. Often as we seek to live quietly in seclusion, we are forced to leave here to perform our work. At times the keys to the doors of the cells are removed, and for a long period of time are not returned except on Sundays. Now and then when planning to follow a strict regimen in eating, we are forced to live more mildly; and on the other hand, when we would wish to eat we are compelled to fast. Often a brother is commanded to travel some distance, guiding the pack animals, and frequently he is sent to the market to buy or sell. Now these and all other tasks which are commanded by the prior should be carried out with such patience and humility, as if they were ordained

---

63. Damian is here a bit more strict than other monastic legislators. See Reindel, *Briefe* 2.110.
64. On bathing, see Zimmermann, *Ordensleben* 172f.

by God himself. Indeed, obedience recommends our good deeds and atones for the sins of negligence.

(50) Therefore, if our seclusion and penitential life are to bear fruit, they should always be seasoned with the salt of salutary obedience; and whatever branches of good works our life should produce, they must always proceed from the root of obedience.

That Only a Few Items Have Been Described, Because the Cell Itself Is a Better Teacher of Those Who Continuously Live Here

(51) I have not described in detail all the precepts of this institute, but have purposely omitted many items which in the course of time came to mind. For whatever is said in the *Rule of St. Benedict,* in the life of the Fathers or in their regulations and collations, everything, I think, pertains to our discipline, and to put them all together here seems to me superfluous. To this I might add, that the cell itself and living here for any length of time are an efficacious instructor of one who perseveres in this life, and in time clarifies situations which it is impossible to explain in words. Hence, out of many things I have selectively and briefly discussed only a few, for greater knowledge of this holy discipline I have left to experience in the cell. If only a brother will persevere in his cell, it will more fully instruct him in our entire mode of living.

On the Struggle with Our Own Thoughts

(52) Now let me say a few words about what goes on in our mind, so that I might inform him who struggles with his own thoughts in this spiritual combat how to use certain invincible weapons in this fight with the devil. In the first place, then, my son, when you prepare for hand to hand combat with the hidden enemy, try to secure your mind by carefully guarding it against the surprise attack of every suggestion; and just as you promptly cast into the fire all filth and dirt falling from your hands when you work, so you should commend your mental activity to God. And since he is a consuming fire, hand over to him for burning all the outcroppings of your heart,

always remembering this saying of the Apostle, "Cast all your cares on him, for you are his charge."[65] And also recall the words of the prophet, "Commit your thoughts to the Lord, and he will sustain you."[66] Neither of these two things should be wanting to you as you valiantly take up the fight: first, that you vigilantly resist the entry of all tempting ideas, and that you try to eliminate them if they have already entered. For it is easier to break up a hostile group in the forecourt than to throw them out if they have already gained access. It is safer to stand guard at the door than to force them to retreat once they have entered the house.

(53) So you should view temptation as if it were a serpent. If a serpent is promptly driven away from the door, all will be well, no harm is done, and nothing inside is polluted. But if once it gains admission, even though afterwards we use every effort to get rid of it, at least something of its poison or of its scaly skin, no matter how small, will remain. Therefore, be always on guard at the outset to withstand budding temptation, armed and ready for battle, and dash the small beginnings of your thoughts on the rock which is Christ.[67] Often take advice from one who knows by experience. Frequently I allowed temptation to enter just as if I were thinking it over, at first just making a deal with myself that I would get rid of it as soon as possible. But even though afterwards I expelled this suggestion by confessing it, though I punished myself by doing penance, I do not know how long it was till I was free of some of the after effects of this pollution; and rightly so, for if at first we voluntarily deceive ourselves with idle imaginings, we will later be disturbed by the sharp pricks of a biting conscience.

On Overcoming Gluttony

(54) And since gluttony is the first vice that is likely to attack beginners with the weapons of its allurements, you should zealously strike at this beast, armed with the sword of contin-

---

65. 1 Pet 5.7.
66. Ps 54.23.
67. Cf. 1 Cor 10.4.

ence. It will suggest that you eat more than you should;[68] with the bridle to your body in hand, never allow yourself to be completely satisfied. Perhaps it will prompt you to desire fancier food; you should recall where food goes after it has served its purpose. If we properly pay attention to both of these, it would be almost as mad to long for luxurious food as it is to imagine toilet tissue[69] along with the food falling into the cesspit. Now both notions are equally laughable, for just as this image does not any more effectively clean away the filth of evacuation, so too man's stomach does not distinguish fine food from the coarser kind. The mouth, moreover, along with gluttony experiences the flavor of food, but neither can enjoy it for long, for when food is chewed it quickly passes into the stomach. And so in turn, gluttony by which we taste food, experiences the flavor only momentarily, and in the stomach where taste is absent, it is preserved over a lengthy period. But the devil looks about for food that we will consider more tempting. After placing it before us, he advises us to hold on to it that he might enhance our gluttony, that is, while we are not disposed to give it to anyone else, and as we await the proper time for eating, our mind in the meanwhile becomes a place for meditating on drunkenness and on overflowing kettles of food.

(55) So that you might be rid of the cause of this vexation, throw aside whatever is a disservice, and at once your thoughts will rise, freed of the burden that oppresses them. Some people who have no desire for more dainty food, relax the check on their eating by using impetuous liberty under the pretence of increased fasting or of fasting they will later increase. But it is clear that this kind of intemperate eating burdens the body without increasing its strength, dulls the senses, induces sluggishness and begets drowsiness, and while flatulence causes them frequently to belch and break wind, their bloated condition, or as I might put it, their healthy listlessness makes it impossible to concentrate on prayer or chanting. Therefore,

68. See Blum, *St. Peter Damian* 87f.
69. For the Latin word *anitergia* used here, cf. DuCange 1.256.

if you are looking for energy from taking food, never eat to excess, since what is good for the body is also conducive to bodily strength.

(56) Also be content with few and poor garments. Accustom yourself, then, to putting on light and very little clothing. That which calls for much difficulty in the beginning becomes almost natural as you grow accustomed to it, and the inconvenience of cold weather is more easily borne. The poor condition of his clothing and the scarceness of food completely expel avarice from the heart of a monk. Why should I desire that which food and clothing cannot provide? And so barefootedness, scanty clothing, a hard bed, rough hair shirts, drinking water, eating stew, and similar things, while as beginners we dread them with a certain amount of fear, once we have endured them through long practice, we consider them quite easy and tolerable. For frequent use softens harshness and habit recommends severity.

On Discernment of Thoughts

(57) You should usually also not burden yourself by ever stating as certain what you are going to attempt or do, but rather, if you are trying to please God, you should plan your actions conditionally and suspend judgment in view of the will of God. Therefore design what you are about to do publicly, so that you carefully keep in mind God's will according to his disposition. Thus if your effort breaks down in the face of some intervening difficulty, your purpose will at once take note of the decrees of divine providence. Amid the flood of thoughts that try to overwhelm you, consider your mind to be some sort of net that will hold proper ideas as if they were fish, allowing idle notions to flow through and escape like so many abominable crawling creatures. Try to understand your thoughts and give close attention, not only to whatever might come to mind, but also to their source. Listen to what I say: It often happens that the wicked enemy conjures up past sins that you might again take pleasure in them; frequently the divine spirit does the same, that in tears you might experience compunction; and since one and the same thing ends up in

different results, almost always an uncautious mind will be unaware of what is happening. Often good thoughts that plan works of devotion are inspired by the good spirit, and the crafty devil pretends to be their author so that good will not emerge, because by this deception the mind thinks they were suggested by the evil spirit. At other times when we are reciting the psalms, we are violently attacked by the devil with thoughts about some duty to be performed. Thus while our mind thinks it is planning something good, we allow our eyes to wander and do not understand what we are reciting.

(58) We should not forget that when we chant, we are offering to God a sacrifice of praise. But pestilent spirits, like harpies, fly about this sacrifice, and by inducing evil thoughts befoul it as if they were attacking it with a kind of excrement, or certainly disrupt it, as if by infesting it with temptations they can hinder us from praying. But as sacrifices cannot placate God if they are stolen from us, so also those which have been defiled cannot be pleasing to the author of purity. Hence we must be equally on our guard not to abandon our sacrifice by finding pleasure in temptations, or by allowing the enemy to attack and contaminate it by the contagion of filthy thoughts. Whether you are engaged in meditating on the Scriptures, or are intent on performing any task, frequently have recourse to prayer, and while bodily prostrate on the ground, raise your mind to heaven. This is done so that temptation may leave us alone, and that unseemly drowsiness, caused by lengthy sitting, may not burden our eyes. But do not lie there too long, because then the devil, as the mind is at ease, is quick to attack us more fiercely with his temptations and to furnish phantasmagoric imaginings mixed with sleep. For as soon as the hidden enemy sees our eyelids begin to droop, he at once fires an arrow of evil thoughts into the weary soul. It is then that the cunning spirit finds an opportunity of harming us when, by watching our eyes, he catches us lowering our guard. Frequently as you pray, extend your arms in the form of a cross, so that as you attempt to express the figure of this life-giving symbol, you may more readily find forgiveness from him who was crucified.

LETTER 50

That in Every Mental Conflict You Should Think of the Grave

(59) In every struggle with titillating pleasure, try always to evoke the memory of the grave. Should anger perhaps savage the mind, turn your eyes at once to the grave. You will soon put aside all bitterness, for wherever human fury tries to reach, the foreseeing mind has already anticipated it. Should the spirit of pride make you haughty, turn your thoughts to the grave. For at that point we will certainly suppress our stiff-necked conceit when we recall that we are but dust and ashes, since it is written, "What have you to be proud of, dust and ashes?"[70] Should you burn with the flames of envy, also look to the grave and learn that we who so quickly leave this life, uselessly envy others their temporal goods. Should you be aflame with lustful desires, let the grave teach you how quickly the virility of the human body fades away, and how extravagant it is for our corruptible flesh to lie on a bed of pleasure, when resting in a house of horrors can be momentarily expected.

(60) When the sensual desire to eat excessively entices you, meditate at once on the grave; for as we cause our bodies to grow fat by delicate and tender nourishment, we undoubtedly provide food for worms. And thus the more we eat, the more there are that can feast on us, and when we sensually feed our stomach, we nourish our ungrateful guests with luxurious food.

(61) Should you be incited to avarice, hasten at once to the grave and there be eager to learn that it is vain for us to accumulate great riches in this mortal life, since the road we travel will in a brief moment come to an end. Does drowsiness or a tendency to sleep disturb you, let the grave remind you now to be on the lookout for eternal reward, where you will surely find your rest without need for further compensation. For as you await the eternal rest of the joys of heaven, you will be only too glad to contend for the moment with your own sluggishness and sloth.

70. Eccl 10.9.

(62) When you think about the glamor of splendid clothes, turn your eyes to the grave and remind yourself how foolish they are who eagerly adorn this worthless bit of dust with ostentatious garments. Such people cover clay with gold and clothe filth in elegant attire, because they do not understand the true adornment of the spiritual man. Should vain glory perhaps attempt to exalt you, look to the grave and be aware how all human glory is terminated. "All mankind is grass and all its glory is like flowering grass."[71] Does your tongue long to abandon itself in idle or scurrilous words? Let the grave come to mind, and as it restrains you from serious sins, so too let it keep you from idle or lighthearted chatter. There you will skillfully learn how worthwhile it is to turn away from all the vain things of this life. And, lest I hold you any longer with a lengthy recital of other items, may real concern not abandon you at the moment of conflict, so that you may promptly turn your attention to meditation on the grave. As you stand there remembering that you are unclean and lowly dust, you should not arrogantly lift your head against your Creator. For as you are aware that you will surely die, you will show the vices that assail you that you are now just as good as dead. Be also on your guard when you are alerted to the presence of evil thoughts, that with thumb extended you quickly make the sign of the cross over your heart. For as the symbol of the holy cross[72] is printed on your body, the inner man is at once incited to use all its strength to fight against these vicious thoughts. And thus the mind, unfurling as it were the banner of triumph, will manfully engage its enemies and will drive them away from your house while they are still detained at the door.

Private Confession

(63) But if ever you should sin in thought or in deed while you are in your cell, because of which your stricken conscience should ever so little disturb you, and you are unable to go to

---

71. Isa 40.6; for this variant from the *Vulgate*, see Sabatier 2.529.
72. See P. Palazzini, "Teologia pedagogia e Devotio Crucis," *Fonte Avellana nel suo millenario* (1982), 113.

confession or break the rule of rigorous silence, you should in the meantime confess to our Lord Jesus Christ and pledge yourself to future confession in these words: "Lord Jesus Christ,[73] eternal pontiff and servant of the saints, priest of the true tabernacle according to the order of Melchisedech, who offered the holy and spotless lamb of your own body as a life-giving victim to God the Father and as a sweet sacrifice for our sins, and thus once a year, not without shedding your blood, entered the Holy of Holies, that is, into heaven itself to appear before the Father, I confess to you that I committed this sin which cannot be hidden from the eyes of your majesty. And so, because of this and because of my other innumerable grave sins, I am unworthy to lift my unhappy eyes to heaven or to enter your Holy Church, or even to speak your blessed and glorious name with my polluted lips. Wherefore, with tears I beg your boundless mercy, who deigned to die for sinners like me, that in your clemency you forgive my sin and grant that I may experience true and fruitful sorrow."

Another Form of Confession

(64) But if you should still ask how you might confess when you are alone at the first hour of the morning or at the close of the day, you could say the following: "I, miserable and unhappy man, confess to God and to you, holy and glorious Virgin Mary, and to all the saints of God, that through my own fault I have sinned grievously by pride, suggestion, pleasure, consent, in thought, word, and deed. Wherefore, I beseech you, most loving mother of God, and all you saints and chosen ones of God, in your goodness to pray for me, a miserable sinner. With all your intercession may Almighty God have mercy on me, forgive all my sins, deliver me from all evil, preserve, encourage, and strengthen me in every good work, and may God free me from the chains of all my sins, and may Christ, the Son of God, bring me to life everlasting. Amen."

73. Cf. Heb 5.10, 6.20, 8.2.

That Tears and Contemplation Are Most Helpful in Lightening the Eremitic Life

(65) By all means and with every effort you should try to achieve the gift of tears[74] and the perfection of contemplation. This will not only be profitable in acquiring a higher place in the kingdom of heaven, but it will also provide that in the life you now lead, all dread of stern austerity will be dissipated, and that every severity and affliction that seems so bitter will be turned into sweetness. When love takes the place of fear, and freedom slavery, then necessity is turned into desire, and by the unspeakable fire of charity, whatever until then seemed harsh and unfeeling will become sweet and agreeable. Moreover, when the people of Israel were living in the vast wilderness,[75] when, too, they could not then return to Egypt and, still shackled with their sins, had not yet entered the promised land, they were forced to bear the irksomeness of work and of travelling and the lack of many necessities of life. So too, anyone who has already despised the benighted lack of restraint of this world, but still does not aspire to the heights of perfection because he is held fast by cowardice and listlessness, is compelled to bear many difficulties from hardship and labor. And thus as he stands between both conditions, he does not receive the least consolation from the good things of this life, and is not yet worthy to enjoy the light of heavenly contemplation. He has obviously turned away his eyes from the world he has abandoned, and is not yet able to see the light that he seeks. He no longer has secular pleasures with which he can be happy, and does not savor the spiritual joy toward which he does not hurry with genuine fervor.

(66) Wherefore, you must use every effort to reach perfection, or you will have to put up with many calamities and temptations. It is surely a burden to do military service at the royal court, but after attaining the favor of the king, you find yourself standing familiarly at his side, frequently entering his

---

74. On the "gift of tears," see Blum, *St. Peter Damian* 79f.
75. Cf. Exod 14f.

chamber, present at his audiences, conversing with him and taking part in his private councils. Then all this military effort becomes sweet and pleasant, and this restless job is thought to be quite peaceful and agreeable, in that you work without effort, are unworried in your task, and move about without disturbance.

(67) Be quick, therefore, to destroy all affection for sin, so that when you are admitted to the king's chamber, you may join him as one of the family, and your mental powers may the more freely be directed to the author of light, where the darkness of your imagination and idle thoughts will be no obstacle. It often happens when we are besieged by many temptations, that by turning our thoughts to God's goodness we are suddenly caught up in contemplation. And thus, peering into his lodging, as it were, we behold the magnificent glory of the king through hidden cracks while, as our body remains outside, we endure gusty winds and raging rainstorms. So too it seems that only our eyes are allowed to enjoy the delights of the king, while our other members are exposed to the wild and furious tempest. Therefore, that the burdens of our journey may be lightened, we must turn our eyes to our peaceful home in heaven. Then everything we undertake becomes easy if we always keep before our eyes the goal toward which we are hurrying. This too is of no little value in lifting the weight of eremitical severity from our shoulders, if for a time we should punish ourselves by taking less food, enduring thirst and certain other practices that go against the flesh. For when afterwards we return to what we normally do, the customary rule will seem to be an indulgent relief, and after eating a bit, our body will consider it a great blessing that something was added to that with which it was formerly satisfied.

How One Can Acquire the Gift of Tears

(68) Now, since I have been saying that we should often be moved to tears, let me briefly indicate how one can attain this gift, insofar as its author will allow. If you should wish to experience copious tears and not just dry eyed sorrow, you

must not only avoid the bustle of worldly affairs, but also frequently refrain from speaking with your brothers. Cut off all cares and worries over what is happening about you, and be quick to remove them as so much rubble and as obstacles blocking the vent through which the fountain may gush forth. As water coming from the depths gathers in an underground cavern, but does not spout forth because of some obstruction, so too in the human heart, if we take into account the depths of God's wisdom, sorrow is born, but does not emerge in a flood of tears. If the impediment of worldly cares stands in the way, sadness is indeed the source of tears, but that the artery of this fountain may vent profusely, take care to remove the obstacles of all secular interests. And I will not pass over what I have often learned from experience: the very zeal for spiritual things, the direction of those committed to our charge, the correction of sinners, engaging in preaching; these and similar matters, even though they are sacred and certainly commanded by God's authority, are without doubt recognized impediments to tears.

(69) Hence, if you wish in your holy purpose to arrive at the gift of tears, you must restrain yourself not only in worldly affairs, but at times place a curb on taking part in certain spiritual practices. Also rid your heart of malice, anger, and hate, and other vicious plagues, lest while your accusing conscience forcefully reprimands you, your spirit should be deprived of the moisture from this internal dew and grow weak because of arid fear, as Scripture says, "Men will wither away with terror."[76] A reputation for sanctity and a conscience that is witness to our innocence water a pure spirit with streams of heavenly grace, and melt it to tears, soften the hardness of an uncultivated heart, and open the way for profuse weeping. Therefore let your conscience be pure, clean, and bright, let it be sincere, unleavened, and undefiled by any stain of spiritual wantonness, so that when compunction of heart is at the point of breakthrough, the obstacle of an accusing conscience will not stand in the way, nor will the cold of deserving fear

76. Luke 21.26.

enclose an anxious heart, and the water of our tears will not flow because it has been turned to ice, even though fear of sin at times will produce the tears of compunction.

(70) But it is one thing to have servile fear, quite another to possess spiritual grace by which we offer plump victims to God on the altar of a contrite heart, and burn a rich sacrifice that gives off a pleasant and salutary odor. But if this grace of the Holy Spirit is lacking, even though one tries to lift up his mind to heavenly glory, even though he should recall the pains of hell or his past sins, or even remember the mysteries of the Lord's passion, tears will not break forth on their account if sins demanding our attention harden our innermost heart. Like a prudent and busy farmer you should constantly till your soil, furrow the field of your heart and of your body with the plow of holy discipline, harrow the hard earth and strive to pull up the weeds of sin, and thus you will be prepared each day, with eyes intent on heaven, to await the downpour of rain from above. For the supreme judge, that hidden supervisor, "who stands outside our wall, peeping in at the windows, glancing through the lattice,"[77] even though for a time he may withhold the water his providence bestows, if he thus observes you diligently at work and on your guard, he will soon water his field with a generous rain of his own grace. And thus the land will be adorned with various blossoms of virtue, so that what once lay uncultivated and sterile will be rich and fruitful with an abundant harvest of grain.

That One Should Persevere in the Kind of Life He Once Took Up, and That Sin Does not Permit Us to Grow in Virtue

(71) Wherefore, persevere in the type of life you once began and doggedly carry on, lest, which God forbid, you appear to be false to your own self by playing a theatrical role. Do not follow the example of Icarus,[78] a poor flier who at first reached good altitude, but then by losing his wings and beginning his fall, plunged into the depths of the sea because of his incon-

---
77. Cant 2.9.
78. On Icarus, see Hyginus, *Fabula* 40; Isidore, *Etym.* 13.16.8.

stancy and unbridled freedom, lest perhaps, as it is said, your faltering changeableness may cause you to show different colors. Rather let your seriousness demonstrate that you are always the same. Be true, therefore, to what you have begun and adhere to the line of your accustomed life style, lest by varying your mode of living you appear as someone always new. Rather let the normal practice of the established rule strengthen the base of holy constancy, so that the observance of longstanding custom may sweeten what human frailty would abhor as something totally harsh and bitter. At all times show that you are conspicuous for virtue and clothed, if I may put it so, in the uniform of sanctity to which no patch of vice whatever has been sewn. It would seem disgraceful and ridiculous if you were clad in purple garments, silk stockings, and gilded shoes, and only your cap of shabby ram skin among all this finery showed that you were a peasant.

(72) This is what I am trying to say: since by your rigid fasting, your observance of silence, and the roughness of your garments you imitate Anthony, you should not play Democritus[79] by your lighthearted laughter or the urbanity of your elegant speech. "Can there be a pact between the temple of God and the idols of the heathen? Can light consort with darkness? Can God agree with Belial?"[80] "A little leaven leavens all the dough."[81] Therefore, may the field of your spirit be filled with a rich crop of virtue, so that through negligence thorns and briars may never grow wild. On the one hand, may your upright life edify those who observe you, and on the other, by committing sin may it not, like a battering ram, cause the building to totter. Therefore, be dignified when you walk, proper in your speech, slow to anger, and quick to forgive those who repent. In all things be an example of the highest virtue and, as one might say, always demonstrate that you are well-turned and well-rounded; so that as you are now pounded

---

79. In Isidore, *Etym.* 8.9.2, Democritus appears as a magician; in 17.1.1 as an author writing about rustic affairs.
80. 2 Cor 6.14–16.   81. 1 Cor 5.6.

by the hammer of discipline and polished with the file of penance and spiritual combat, afterwards without ringing and clanging you may be set into the rank of fired stones.

On How the Prior of the Hermitage Should Conduct Himself

(73) Since, therefore, in keeping my writing brief I have in one way or another described how a hermit should live, it now becomes my task at the end of this work to add a few words also on the quality of the prior[82] of the hermits. We should not consider this order of things distorted, if he, who is to be first by reason of his office, should, as the *Rule* is explained, be placed last, since he must first live the same *Rule* before he becomes the superior, and as he presides over government must show himself to be the least of all. Be careful, therefore, that the prior of the hermits is not chosen from the monastic order, even though he appear prudent and learned or even well-informed about regular discipline. For this reason a brother should be chosen who is deeply religious, who from the very beginning has learned to struggle with evils of the spirit; one who can infer from his own knowledge the battle that others must wage, and as one who is familiar with combat, will recognize in his own conscience what he might hear from one who confides in him.

(74) Therefore, prior, if I may address you as one with whom I am well acquainted, since by your office you are above others, you should also, if possible, surpass them by the way you live. It is truly a vivid and powerful sermon for your disciples, if in providing food for others the provider remains steadfast in rigorous fasting. He preaches best about nighttime prayer who, after a long period spent in chanting, gives the signal to awaken the brothers. It is most eloquent to recommend silence if we ourselves curb our tongue. He who demeans himself by wearing torn clothes can profitably speak of poor garments. He who in fine attire stands out like a rich

---

82. See A. Giabbani, *L'eremo, vita e spiritualità eremitica nel monachesimo camaldolese primitivo* (1945), 48 and 121; *Benedicti regula* c. 2.21–29.

man, preaches in vain with John about camel's hair.[83] One who avenges an injury is not very persuasive when speaking of patience. One who is eager to hoard money will hardly put out the fires of avarice in the hearts of others. He who seizes every opportunity for travel holds a sorry discussion on the rule of staying at home. But one who spends long years in his cell, makes of his whole body a tongue that will praise stability, and when his mouth is silent, his mute members are eloquent because they call out in more varied ways.

(75) Let your life, moreover, serve as a witness, for it must speak of your hidden good deeds for the edification of the brothers and be able to cleanse your reputation of any devious suspicion. Conduct your flock to level ground, but while there the prudent shepherd will point out to them the mountains, so that as they ascribe it to your administration when they live somewhat more relaxed, and to the authority of the Fathers when they hear of stricter measures, they will more easily be prepared to climb to the heights of perfection. He should be ashamed to allow them to live dull and obscure lives in the lowlands, when it comes to their attention that others before them often nobly moved about in the highlands. To those who proceed along the proper way show yourself to be their equal, but be zealous in using vigorous discipline on those who stray. If you would in conscience remain pure and innocent, do not lay aside the rod of reprimand. But you should so resort to words of correction that the sweetness of brotherly love is evident in your demeanor. As the hawk simply flies away from the hand of the hunter on its way to catch birds, so you should speak with indignation, without you yourself experiencing indignation. An arrow, indeed, wounds the person who is struck by it, but the bow that delivered it knows nothing of blood. It should be noted, however, that a fragile disposition to persevere in the hermitage is easily broken, even though only an occasion for slight injury occurs. For a heavy load will be laid aside with just minor deliberation, if only our shoulders that bear it can somehow be persuaded.

---

83. Cf. Matt 3.4; Mark 1.6.

(76) It is easy, therefore, for one to leave the community when daily everyone suffers from lack of food and only rarely is told to take all that he wants. Hence one must use moderation in applying strict rules, lest the added harshness of severe correction overwhelm those who are weakened by private penance. Whenever you are citing an example of someone who is performing heroically, withhold his name if he belongs to the community; but if he is someone outside our hermitage, you may say who it is. It is more effective to use recent examples[84] rather than older ones, and it causes great shame and embarrassment if, in striving to lead a holy life, our hermits find themselves inferior to holy men living at the same period. Seeing that only high-mindedness strengthened these other men, latter-day weakness does not excuse those who come after.

That One Who Leaves the World Should Be Converted in the Hermitage

(77) When one wishes to convert to the eremitical life after living in the world,[85] do not, in keeping with what I said above, advise him to act like a novice in a monastery, but if his dedication appears true and sincere, introduce him to life in the hermitage that he is seeking. Sorry to say, many monasteries have become so lax, that those who leave them are found to be worse than those recently rescued from the waves after shipwreck in the world. Certainly, one can easily impress on clean metal the device that makes it money; but after the coin has been falsified, it is difficult to convert it to honest currency.

(78) The doors should, therefore, be opened to one coming from the world, so that as he arrives he can be stamped like a clean piece of metal. When he enters his cell, he should not at once be allowed to practice every customary regulation, but he should seek for these things over a longer period of time; for what is difficult to find, one values more dearly. Later,

---

84. Here, certainly, we have the reason why Damian frequently cites examples of contemporary eremitical heroes.
85. For an extended discussion of this concept in the literature, see Reindel, *Briefe* 2.127, n. 116.

however, all restrictions on his holy purpose should be relaxed, and he may undertake any heavy task his heart might suggest, so that in this first spiritual fervor he might attempt to move on a higher path, which later he may be ashamed to abandon. What once he undertook when he was a novice he should keep before his eyes as a model, so that if he never comes to higher things, he would blush to forsake at least those which he then tried to do.

How One Should Be Advised Who Comes to the Hermitage from the Monastery

(79) If, before entering the hermitage, an applicant formerly followed the monastic life,[86] one should with modest disapproval criticize certain useless practices of monastic discipline, such as the unnecessary clamor of bells, the excessive singing of hymns, the ornamental décor, and other similar things.[87] Indeed, one should properly belittle them, disparage without condemning them, referring to the words of the Apostle, "In Christ Jesus circumcision is nothing, uncircumcision is nothing; the only thing that counts is new creation."[88] And again, "The Most High does not live in houses made by men."[89] And this saying written to the Hebrews, "The training of the body does bring limited benefit, but the benefits of patience are without limit."[90] Therefore, using this and similar evidence, depreciate the monastic order by moderately taking it to task, so that as the structure of his former life is destroyed in the mind of the listener, the edifice of solitary living that is here described may be built up, and that for the future he may bravely equip himself to stand firm, where up to now he thought of himself as lying idle.

(80) But if after long struggles in carrying out his tasks, after subduing the desires of his tortured flesh he still sees himself beating down certain sins like so many enemies, he

---

86. For withdrawal from the monastery to the hermitage, see Blum, *St. Peter Damian* 127; Pierucci, *La vita eremitica* 76f.
87. See J. Leclercq, *S. Pierre Damien* 55f.
88. Gal 6.15.   89. Acts 7.48.
90. 1 Tim 4.8.

will begin to despise the intemperate deeds of the past and hold in higher esteem the means that are now at hand. We should then praise the work of the cenobites and refer to the glory of God whatever they do in their form of life, and cite the sacrifices that flow from salutary obedience, so that as we commend the profession of the common life, we may abolish any arrogant opinion of solitary living that unawares, perhaps, has risen among us. Nor should we grow haughty as though we were privileged to lead a more perfect life,[91] since perhaps our style of living does not equal that of some at a lower level whose humility causes them to arrive at greater achievements. We should be advised when perhaps we have something urgent to do, that like some cenobites we should not therefore hurry up our chanting of the psalms, and thus perversely try to abandon chanting for other duties, as if trying to swim away from the sea to reach the shore. The crafty devil incites spiritual anxiety, but the prince of peace seeks out the quiet and humble soul where it takes its rest. While we are chanting, we should answer the adversary spirit who suggests marvelous deeds: "While I am occupied here, I have a task to perform," and then remain quiet. If afterwards you find it necessary, you may speak of it.

(81) But if he still insists on attacking you and remains obstinate, put your curse on both what he suggests and on him who made the suggestion. Also use threats that will terrify him by saying, "Let me alone, you miserable creature, and remember the fearful day of judgment when you will rightly be damned to burn forever in the avenging flames." This sort of terror is most useful in winning the battle and in putting the clever devil to flight. For this reason, after reciting the prayers of exorcism,[92] by ecclesiastical tradition one always added, "He who is to come to judge the living and the dead, and to try the world by fire"; that when the evil spirit is struck down by such a fearful attack, he may in terror be driven

---

91. See J. Leclercq, *S. Pierre Damien* 62, 143.
92. See *Excerpta de veteribus liturgicis codicibus Fontavellanensibus* (PL 151.912ff.).

from this creature of God. Therefore, skillfully instruct your comrades to use these and similar weapons, and as their leader teach them always to fight together against their enemy.

On How Patient the Prior Ought to Be

(82) Obviously, since you should be possessed of all virtues, placed as you are over others to exemplify these virtues, strive earnestly to be patient, and through patience to overcome all obstacles. Let patience show that you are as hard as stone, even as impossible to cut as a diamond. For a diamond cuts a figure on other stones, but at the same time totally resists being cut by any other hard substance.[93] Your spirit, moreover, will not be stamped with the form of any alien stone if it is not disturbed by any foe that attacks it. Rather, it will impress its character on others, for when something untoward occurs, with sweetness of heart and tranquility of mind it will convert this evil into something profitable. Only rarely or not at all should you assemble a chapter of all the hermits where, after prostration, you should not accuse yourself of faults, but of your own accord with truly humble authority beg to be subjected to the discipline. If you perceive that your own feelings have been hurt, or those of any other brother who opposes you, do not rest, as the case might be, until you have tried to heal the wound either by correction, or appeasement, or even by accepting a penance. I have spoken at length about the office of prior, because I have no doubt that under the guidance of God's grace every advancement of his subjects on the way to perfection depends on his leadership. What the stomach is to the human body, so approximately is the prior to this congregation of spiritual brothers. As vigor and strength spread to all members of the body from the receptacle of the stomach, so too from the well-administered office of the presiding prior[94] the whole body of those who live here is nourished in the bond of charity.

---

93. Cf. Isidore, *Etym.* 16.13.2.
94. Pierucci, *La vita eremitica* 69, notes that Damian's *prior* is indeed the same as the Benedictine abbot, and not the monastic prior.

Here the Writer Excuses Himself over the Charge of Laxness

(83) My brothers, I beg that those who lead a stricter life than that I have here described, will not accuse me of laxness, and will not with perhaps greater severity than is deserving beat me till I am black and blue for having mitigated the austerity of this hermitage. For while the Israelites had mercy on those wicked men after the Benjaminites had been defeated,[95] and grieved with many tears that one tribe had been lost to Israel, lamenting over them and weeping bitterly, what are we to do when we see other eremitical orders within the Church's jurisdiction so diminished in numbers, that there is little doubt that in some regions they have completely disappeared. Benjamin, therefore, was to be spared, that is, the strongest and most renowned fighters in all Israel, so that merciful and moderate action might allow them to increase and grow in the next generation, when extreme severity or rather human frailty would have annihilated them. And so, the number of tribes remained intact, since restrained severity was able to preserve what seemingly had been wiped out. We should also not forget that the holy apostles who had been sent to preach the cross of Christ to all nations as the young faith was just beginning, decided that certain gentiles observe only this command: "to abstain from meat that had been offered to idols, from blood and from anything that had been strangled, and from fornication."[96] While imposing minimal standards, I did not forbid greater penance, so that those who might be deterred by the severity of a new way of life should at length be able to undertake bolder deeds, enticed by milder precepts; and beginning like suckling babes with small and easy tasks, they might later when coming of age manfully fulfill the stiffer commands of God's Law.

(84) I, moreover, who made children's rattles for babes in the spiritual life and, if I might express it so, constructed cradles for hermits still in their nursing days, as I led those who were frail like me over level ground, in no way did I

---

95. Cf. Judg 21.3.   96. Acts 21.25.

forbid those who were prepared for the trip to climb to difficult heights. This I did so that those who were still weak might be nourished by the milk I provided, without turning the strong and healthy away from heavier and more solid food. I trust through the goodness of God's mercy that whoever carries out what is written in this little work and eagerly attempts to make progress, will not suffer harm from the second death,[97] nor have his name erased from the book of life; but that the Lamb who beholds him taking up his cross to follow him, may assign him to the heavenly Jerusalem and with certainty make him his heir. Amen. Blessed be the name of the Lord.

97. Cf. Rev 20.14–15.

LETTER 51

Peter Damian to the Duchess Beatrice of Tuscany. He rejoices over the report from her husband, Duke Godfrey, that they had agreed to live in continence. In thus imitating Abraham and Sarah, they should also follow their example in personally extending hospitality to the poor. He proposed noble models of generosity to the Church—"grant land and you will snatch heaven away"—and advised her to look to the lives of holy queens and empresses, from whom she might learn the practice of virtue proper to her calling.

(1057)[1]

TO THE MOST EXCELLENT duchess Beatrice,[2] the monk Peter the sinner sends the constancy of daily prayer.

(2) I certainly rejoice and stand in the greatest admiration of the disposition of Almighty God on your behalf and of that of your most glorious husband.[3] While placing you at the summit of earthly dignity and allowing you, moreover, to bring forth a harvest of good works, what else has he done but display to the world the miracle of the productive fir tree? The grapevine is indeed small but fruitful; the fir tree, however, is tall but bears no fruit. The former, indeed, by the abundance of the grapes that it bears, compensates for its less stately stature. The latter, however, while placing nothing on the table, is useful in erecting buildings, and where it fails in producing delicacies, it serves the needs of construction. But where these two qualities concur, namely, where the tree is both tall and fruitful, the more rarely this occurs, the more likely it is that we should consider it a miracle.

(3) And so, this outstanding gift of twofold grace is found

---

1. On the dating of this letter, see Neukirch 97; Lucchesi, *Vita* no. 203; and Dressler, *Petrus Damiani* 164, n. 369.
2. On Beatrice, see M. G. Bertolini, "Beatrice," *Dizionario biografico degli italiani* 7 (1965), 352–363.
3. Cf. K. Reindel, "Gottfried II," NDB (1964), 662.

in you, namely, a humble and holy devotion to God, and, regarding the world, the exalted heights of power, so that you might properly be called tall-growing grapevines and fruit-bearing fir trees. With regard to the mystery of mutual continence, however, which, as God is my witness, you are observing with one another,[4] I must say that for some time I have been inclined to have two views, namely, that your husband joyfully offered this gift of chastity, but that you, because you wished to have children, did not gladly go along. But when your exalted husband recently informed me at the tomb of the blessed prince of the apostles[5] about your holy desire and your purpose to observe perpetual chastity, I exclaimed, "I was glad when these words were said to me,"[6] and shouted with joy. Now you are free of that ancient curse in which it was said to the first woman, "You will be in the power of your husband and he shall be your master."[7]

(4) It is evident that Sarah had purposed to live in chastity from that time on when, as sacred history reports, "Sarah was past the age of childbearing."[8] And in addition she said, "After reaching an advanced age and my husband grew old, shall I give myself up to pleasure?"[9] And so from these words it is obvious that she had by that time purposed to live in chastity. And after these events God said to Abraham, "Pay attention to everything that Sarah will say to you."[10] Notice that as a result of her chastity, she to whom Abraham had previously given orders he was now commanded to obey, so that now he was to listen to her in everything, whereas formerly he had controlled her as her master.

(5) In addition, from these same patriarchs you should learn a salutary lesson that you should never fail to be gracious to guests. On this matter, after the Apostle had said, "Always love your fellow Christians and remember to show

---

4. On continent marriage, see J. Wenner, "Josephsehe," LThK 5 (1960), 1140–1141; Dressler, *Petrus Damiani* 164, n. 369.
5. See Lucchesi, *Vita* nos. 175, 203, for Damian's presence in Rome during the spring of 1057, when Pope Stephen IX held several synods.
6. Ps 121.1.   7. Gen 3.16.
8. Gen 18.11.   9. Gen 18.12.
10. Gen 21.12.

hospitality," he then added specifically, "There are some who by so doing have entertained angels as their guests."[11] For as sacred history reports, "When the three men approached Abraham, he hurried into the tent to Sarah and said to her, 'Take three measures of flour quickly, knead it and make some cakes.' And then it continued, 'Then Abraham ran to the cattle and chose a fine tender calf, etc.'"[12] Clearly we should note from these words of Holy Writ that in being gracious to his guests Abraham did not give orders to the slave girl Hagar, did not charge the servants, and did not command any of his household slaves to do this, but personally he and his wife carried out this task of hospitality. So at once the account continues, "He took butter and milk and the calf he had prepared, set it before them, and waited on them himself under the tree."[13] He and his wife served the guests and did not decide to delegate this duty of graciousness to less worthy persons.

(6) To be sure, the wife of the emperor Theodosius[14] also followed their example, of whom the *Historia tripartita* reports, and I add its very words, "She showed special regard for the lame and infirm," it says, "not employing slaves or other servants, but doing so herself, going to their homes and serving each as he had need."[15] And then it continues, "So too, going through the hospitals belonging to the churches, she waited on the sick with her own hands, cleaning their pots, tasting the soup, handing them spoons, breaking their bread and serving them food, diluting their wine with water, and performing all the other duties regularly taken care of by slaves and servants."[16] Woe to us who are lazy, idle, and proud, who can scarcely force ourselves to throw a pittance and the leftovers from our table into the laps of the poor. But if perhaps some flatterer were present, and in the interest of

---

11. Heb 13.1–2.   12. Gen 18.6–7.
13. Gen 18.8.
14. This is Galla, the second wife of the emperor. See A. Lippold, *Theodosius der Grosse und seine Zeit* (1980), 37.
15. Cassiodorus, *Historia tripartita* 9.31.546f.
16. *Ibid.*, 547.

royal dignity would tell her to desist from her zealous service, she would say, "It is the duty of empire to distribute gold; but on my part, I perform this service in the name of the empire which has bestowed all good things on me."[17] Nor was she satisfied to stand alone in performing these hospitable deeds, but also urged her husband the emperor to engage in the same acts of sacred devotion. And these are her very words: "Husband," she said, "you should always remember what you were and what you soon will be. If you always give these matters some thought, you will not be ungrateful to your benefactor, but will govern the empire you have received according to law, and will appease the author of all these things."[18] Therefore we can say of this woman that, completely unlike the first woman, she spoke in a different way and was quite the opposite in her actions. For the latter first ate the forbidden fruit and then persuaded her husband to do the same.[19] But this woman set an example which her husband might imitate and offered him words of holy advice. By her words and actions the other caused her husband to be expelled from paradise, while the latter called him back by her words and deeds.

(7) Wherefore, my lady, do not, like many powerful persons in the world, grow wealthy by confiscating the goods of the Church, but strive rather to enrich impoverished churches by grants from your own possessions. Grant land and you will snatch heaven away. Possessions that pass away should be commuted into claims on eternal inheritance. Let me tell you what was related to me by Henry, the venerable abbot of the monastery dedicated to the holy virgins Flora and Lucilla, situated in the territory of Arezzo.[20] "Do you see the basilica standing close by," he asked? (We were just on our way to look at it.) "This church used to be popularly called the

---

17. *Ibid.*, 547. 18. *Ibid.*, 547.
19. Cf. Gen 3.6.
20. On the monastery of Sts. Flora and Lucilla in Arezzo, cf. *ItPont* 3.161f. Damian composed two sermons for the feast day of these saints (Petrus Damiani, *Sermones* 34 and 35, 204–213). On Abbot Henry, see G. Lucchesi, "Il sermonario di S. Pier Damiani come monumento storico agiografico e liturgico," *Studi Gregoriani* 10 (1975), 7–68, esp. 20, n. 23.

church of Mary the Poor.[21] One day it happened that Guilla, the mother of the esteemed Marquis Hugh, was passing this way and accidentally heard what this church was called. Upon learning this, the noble and distinguished lady became quite angry and said in thorough disgust, 'God forbid that we should call her poor who gave birth to the dispenser of heavenly glory. God forbid, I say, that on earth she should be deemed worthy of the word "poor," when in heaven, raised above the angels, she possesses eternal riches.' And presently she continued, 'Does this property belong to me?' Someone replied that in this area she owned a rural estate, comprising according to ancient custom, nine manorial holdings, but that later, according to modern usage, it was divided into more units. 'This estate,' she said, 'shall belong in perpetuity to this church, and from now on let no one dare to call her poor.'"[22]

(8) Always emulate such noble deeds, and let not your family descent, but rather your holy lineage prompt you to action. It is surely frivolous to boast of the renown of our ancestors, but glorious to attain to the victories of our holy predecessors. Roman history relates that Helena, the mother of the Emperor Constantine, had been an innkeeper's daughter. And so Eutropius says in so many words, "When Constantius died, Constantine his son by an ignoble marriage, was made emperor in Britain."[23] With this assertion the blessed Ambrose also agrees in his letters.[24] But by the excellence of her remarkable deeds she so altered the quality of her ignoble birth that numerous basilicas throughout the world bear her name.[25] And what empresses descended from ancestors of the highest nobility could not achieve, the innkeeper's daughter was able

21. Cf. *ItPont* 3.160.
22. On Guilla and her monastic building program see Reindel, *Briefe* 2.135–136, n. 14.
23. Eutropius, *Breviarium ab urbe condita* 10.2.2 (MG auct. ant. 2 [1879], 170).
24. Ambrose, *De obitu Theodosii* c. 42 (CSEL 73.393), where Helena is called *stabularia*. Cf. also Jerome, *Interpretatio chronicae Eusebii Pamphili* (PL 27.665–666), where Helena is referred to as a *concubina*.
25. See F. Werner, "Helena," *Lexikon der christlichen Ikonographie* 6 (1974), 485–490.

to do, if I might put it so, by the lineage derived from her noble life.

(9) I beg you, therefore, most worthy lady, and humbly suggest that you walk in the footsteps of holy princesses, take as your model their way of life, that by keeping them in mind you may learn what you should accept and what you should avoid. You should not so much delight in the high quality of birth as in the adornment of spiritual virtues, so that as you excel in earthly dignity among men, you may in the sight of God—a thing much more glorious—be inscribed in the register of saintly women.

LETTER 52

Peter Damian writes to the two Roman clerics, B. and St., on behalf of the lame abbot of St. Apollinaris who, besides his personal affliction, has also feared the ruin of his monastery. He begs the two clerics not for gold or silver, but for mercy and humanity in the interest of the poor abbot.

(After 1057)[1]

TO THE HOLY and most reverend priests of the Holy See, B. and St., the monk Peter the sinner, their dutiful servant.[2]

(2) I would not have you ignorant, my most dear brothers and lords, that this modern Jacob,[3] namely, the abbot of the monastery of St. Apollinaris,[4] managed to climb to our mountaintop. And what is more, this man, who is accustomed to move slowly in level and unobstructed valleys, spurred on by fear and propelled as it were by wings,[5] was determined with all haste to fly up the rocky walls of the mountains. He who could scarcely crawl when the ground was even because of his lameness, wandered with leaps and bounds over the mountain's craggy ridges.

(3) Wherefore I beg for your fraternal concern, that as both of you, like Peter and John,[6] compel the lame man to walk, you should graciously offer him, not gold or silver

---

1. For the date here assigned, see Lucchesi, *Vita* no. 215.
2. Lucchesi, *Vita* no. 215, identifies the recipients as Boniface and Stephen, cardinal priests of Albano and St. Chrysogonus; but the identification is not altogether certain.
3. Cf. Gen 32.27–31.
4. On San Apollinare Nuovo in Ravenna, see *ItPont* 5.83f.; V. Federici, *Regesto di S. Apollinare Nuovo* (Regesta Chartartum Italiae, 1907), 21, 22–25, 27, with reference to an abbot John and a prior named Peter.
5. Cf. Vergil, *Aeneid* 1.301.
6. Cf. Acts 3.3–8.

which perhaps you do not possess, but the compassion with which you are abundantly endowed. May his feet and arches grow strong, so that he need not fear the ruin of his monastery or the destruction of his home. May all go well with him for having scaled the heights of this difficult mountain, and may he yet enter the temple to give thanks to God, leaping and praising God on his way.

LETTER 53

Peter Damian to John, the prior of the hermitage of Suavicinum. This fragment is found in Letter 109 cited by Damian to illustrate the life of Dominicus Loricatus. In this letter he exhorts the brethren at Suavicinum to pray with arms extended.

(1057–1058)[1]

... We[2] have here a certain young brother who admitted to me that while chanting the psalter from beginning to end he held his arms aloft, so that often his hands touched the beamed ceiling of his cell. This he did with the proviso that, after completing each fifty psalms, he would lower his arms for a moment, and would then immediately elevate them. We have another, a stooped old man of advanced years, who, as I secretly told you, is Dominic. Once he found a scrap of writing where it said, that "if one should chant the herein mentioned twelve psalms twenty-four times with hands extended in the form of a cross, one would regularly be able to compensate for one year of penance." At once he began to carry out what was said there, and daily, in one turn, chanted the twelve psalms with his arms extended in the form of a cross twenty-six times, as was said, without pausing at all. ...

1. The dating follows Della Santa, *Idea monastica* 218f. Neukirch 96 dates the letter for 1050–1058, while Lucchesi, *Clavis* 66, places it after the spring of 1061.
2. For notes on this fragment, see *infra*, Letter 109, where it is part of a longer letter.

LETTER 54

Peter Damian to his secretary, the young hermit, Ariprandus. Responding to the latter's request that one of his writings be addressed also to him, Damian advises him on the difficult task of gladly accepting correction. He considered this attitude so important, that anyone who refused correction could not long survive at Fonte Avellana. The young should be reprimanded even when reproof was undeserved, so that their humility might be tested and that they be thus prepared to accept reprimand when it was fully called for. No religious institute can endure without spiritual correction. A lengthy section of this letter discusses St. Paul's public rebuke of St. Peter, despite the latter's preeminence, as a model for every human institution.

(1057–1058)[1]

TO MY MOST DEAR BROTHER, Ariprandus,[2] the monk Peter the sinner sends the fondness of paternal love.

(2) You have urged me, my dear son, to write something for you, and beg that since at my dictation you have frequently written to others, something should also be composed for you. But how can I more properly begin writing to a scribe than by referring to the mystic dignity of writing itself. Now in your case, that which writes are three fingers and one hand; but he for whom you write is the one God in three persons. Since, therefore, from several letters you make up one continuous word, you should always direct your purpose to that one, whose mystery, by a certain resemblance, you behold in yourself. And since while you were still in school along with other boys and your ruddy young face had not yet grown a beard, not even the slightest down, the fervor of the Holy Spirit had encouraged you, not to become a

---

1. The dating follows Della Santa, *Idea monastica* 220.
2. Ariprandus was also the recipient of Letters 55 and 117. Damian frequently employed him as his scribe; cf. Reindel, *Studien* 1.52f.

monk, but rather to take up the vocation of being a hermit,[3] you should be on your guard lest under the pretext of your still untested youth, you break the rule of this holy institute and weaken the rigor and severity of this blessed way of life. You should not wish to change the normal practices sacredly observed here, nor presume to introduce novelties of foreign invention. For he who is the Lord of the angels in heaven followed the manner of living on earth as he found it. Nor did he disdain to live according to earthly customs, even though he had come to bring that which was heavenly.

(3) But to pass over countless other items, why did he allow his head and his feet to be anointed[4] by the hands of a woman, if it had not been customary in Palestine and the region of Judaea for the inhabitants there to be frequently anointed?[5] And so he said, "But when you fast, anoint your head."[6] And why should we wonder that during his life the Lord observed the custom of his homeland, since he did not ignore the sacred obsequies used at his burial? For as John relates, "Joseph of Arimathaea and Nicodemus took the body of Jesus and wrapped it, with the spices, in strips of linen cloth according to Jewish burial customs."[7] Since, therefore, he who is wisdom itself, through whom all things were made, did not refuse to observe the traditions of men even in those things that seemed to have hardly any significance, how presumptuous it would be for one to break the rule of discipline which he knows was handed down by the holy fathers?

(4) And so, among the other important items of this holy way of life which, indeed, you see observed by others and which you yourself through the bounty of God's mercy are already impeccably carrying out, be careful of one thing in particular, namely, that you never take offense at correction, never grow ashamed on any account to be reproved, even by those younger than you. This is a thing so adapted to this

---

3. Damian speaks in similar fashion in Letter 152. See also John Cassian, *Conlationes viginti quattuor,* ed. M. Petschenig, CSEL 13 (1886), 3.1.68.
4. Cf. Matt 26.7; Mark 14.3; Luke 7.37; John 12.3.
5. See G. T. Kennedy, "Anointing," NCE 1 (1967): 565–566.
6. Matt 6.17.   7. John 19.40.

holy place and so inborn, that should anyone refuse to be corrected, he would not be able to live in our midst.[8] For this purpose a man leaves the world and submits to the authority of regular discipline that he might cleanse away by the polish of sharp correction the mildew he had contracted in the alluring world. To this point wisdom spoke in Proverbs, "If only you would respond to my reproof, I would give you my spirit."[9] He did not say, to my flattery, but, "If only you would respond to my reproof." And thus he said of certain men who refused to be corrected, "They shall rise in the morning and shall not find me, because they considered discipline hateful and have not chosen to fear the Lord, and have spurned all my reproof."[10] For that reason he gives this warning, "My son, do not spurn the Lord's correction or take offense at his reproof; for those whom he loves the Lord reproves, and like a father takes delight in his son."[11]

(5) Rightly, therefore, this correction is said to belong to the Lord and not to men, since for the love of Christ chastisement is imposed on a fellowman by his neighbor. He strays far from the way of wisdom who does not bow his proud head to divine rebuke. And so the same Solomon says, "He who loves correction loves wisdom; he who hates reproof is a fool."[12] Wherefore in the book of Proverbs the same fool complains, "Why did I hate correction and set my heart against reproof? I did not listen to the voice of my teachers or pay attention to my masters."[13] On the other hand, one who calmly accepts correction is not removed from the register of the wise. And so it is written, "Whoever listens to reproof in his life shall enjoy the society of the wise. He who refuses correction is his own worst enemy."[14] Now stepfathers spoil their stepchildren, but fathers very often use hard blows on their own offspring. The former spare those whom they hate, but the latter instruct and punish those whom they love. Con-

---

8. On accepting correction, see *Benedicti regula* c. 33.8.99, c. 48.20.129, c. 65.19.170.
9. Prov 1.23.
10. Prov 1.28–30.
11. Prov 3.11–12.
12. Prov 12.1.
13. Prov 5.12–13.
14. Prov 15.31–32.

sequently it is written, "A father who spares the rod hates his own son, but one who loves him keeps him in order."[15] And elsewhere, "Open reproof is better than love concealed. The blows a friend gives are better than the perfidious kisses of an enemy."[16] And again it is written, "Chastise your son while there is still hope for him, but be careful not to flog him to death."[17] A father truly flogs his son to death when he sees him doing something wicked, and then not only does not reprimand him, but even delights in his actions that ought to be punished, and does not fear to compliment him with pleasant words, when he ought to beat him within an inch of his life.

(6) Therefore, whoever is wise will deem austere punishment dealt him to be medicine for the wounds of his soul. And so it is written, "Reprove a wise man, and he will understand the correction."[18] And again, "A reproof is of more benefit to a man of discernment than a beating to a stupid man."[19] And it is also said of this man of discernment, "To be patient shows great understanding, but quick temper is the height of folly."[20] One who is impatient shows what a great fool he is, because the more often he is harmed by others because of his ill temper, the more savagely he rages against them in his daily quarrels. And so we read, "An evil man is always looking for arguments, but a cruel angel is sent against him."[21] A cruel angel is sent against one who looks for an argument, because it is right that a cruel occupant should invade the mind in which cruelty dwells, since, as the apostle says, "Anger is possessed of a devil."[22] Hence, just as the wise man taught that a cruel angel would be sent against the impatient man, he at once added, "Better face a she bear robbed of her cubs than a stupid man who trusts in his folly."[23] Of this stupid and impatient man it is written, "Never make friends with an angry man nor keep company with a bad

15. Prov 13.24.
16. Prov 27.5–6.
17. Prov 19.18.
18. Prov 19.25.
19. Prov 17.10.
20. Prov 14.29.
21. Prov 17.11.
22. This citation is not found in the *Vulgate*, but is perhaps echoed in Eph 2.3, 4.31, and Jas 1.20.
23. Prov 17.12.

tempered one; be careful not to learn his ways or you will put yourself in danger of sinning."[24] Moreover, just as a sick man who does not take his medicine will die, so too one who cannot be corrected is unable to free himself from the ills that afflict his soul. To this point Solomon says again, "Do not withhold discipline from a boy; take the stick to him, it will not kill him. If you take the stick to him yourself, you will keep him from going to hell."[25]

(7) Would you like to hear what threatens those who refuse to be corrected, who disdain reprimand by their elders? "A man," he says, "who stubbornly despises correction is subject to sudden death, and well-being will not be his lot."[26] And a little further on he continues, "Correct your son, and he will be a comfort to you and bring delight to your soul."[27] When a horse is still unbroken, one strikes it on the underpart of the foot so that later it will allow nails to be driven into its hooves on the iron footrest. A garland made of limber grapevines is put on a young bull, so that after becoming accustomed to this training, it will later not be in a mood to refuse the yoke. And so, every young brother should also be rebuked, even when he has not done wrong, so that afterwards he will calmly bear the discipline of real correction. On the other hand, it is written of one who is not corrected, "Pamper a slave from boyhood, and in the end he will prove ungrateful."[28] And the wise man says of such a slave, "An ass is tamed by fodder and switch and burden, but a slave by bread and discipline and hard work."[29]

(8) My dear son, I have not amassed for you so many citations from Scripture that they might serve to censure your upright disposition and your actions, but rather to counsel those of your generation by the opportunity that you provide. You did not bring me a bowl filled with the water of Jericho, into which, like Elisha, I might sprinkle the salt of heavenly wisdom and thus cleanse it of its bitterness.[30] Nor did you

24. Prov 22.24–25.
25. Prov 23.13–14.
26. Prov 29.1.
27. Prov 29.17.
28. Prov 29.21.
29. Sir 33.25.
30. Cf. 2 Kgs 2.20–22.

present yourself as a pot filled with wild gourds called colocynth, whose bitter taste was made sweet by the finely ground meal of God's word, and thus became edible to the sons of the prophets.[31] You did not appear as a reed in the wilderness, shaken by the wind,[32] but rather as one which produced honey by which John, the precursor of the Lord, was nourished.[33] You have conducted yourself, my brother, as a beehive filled with overflowing honey. You have shown me that you are a field, not to be weeded by the hoe, but teeming with scythes at the cutting; not overgrown with thorns and brambles, but as one turning to gold by the beauty of its abundant harvest.

(9) On the other hand, the wise man says of the negligent man and the fool, "I passed by the field of an idle man, and see, it was all overgrown with thistles."[34] Clearly, for ill-tempered men corrections are like swords. But if they wish these swords to be turned into sickles, the prickly thorns of their vices with which they bristle, must be changed into standing grain. Hence, after the prophet had first said of our Savior that "he will be judge between nations and arbiter among many peoples," at once he continued, "They shall beat their swords into plowshares and their spears into pruning knives."[35] This is certainly the correct order of things, for first the sinner is reproved, and then swords are made into plowshares and spears into pruning knives. For when an impatient man, made meeker by discipline, is broken up like a level field by the plowshare of correction, and then is planted with the gentle seed of holy preaching, it is thus finally filled with an abundant harvest of good works. For such a man swords are made into plowshares and spears are turned into pruning knives. For he who first allows himself to be reprimanded, as if pierced by a sword, will then willingly accept the plowshare of sacred doctrine that he may bear fruit, and await the pruning knife of the heavenly harvesting that he might fill the larder of God's granary.

31. Cf. 2 Kgs 4.39–41.
33. Cf. Matt 3.4.
35. Isa 2.4.
32. Cf. Matt 11.7.
34. Prov 24.30–31.

(10) Surely, every spiritual group that does not with brotherly solicitude use frequent correction, mystically suffers want like the people of Israel, who at the beginning of Saul's reign had no blacksmiths. For Scripture says that "no blacksmith was to be found in the whole of Israel."[36] Moreover, as iron by its strength overcomes all other metals, so also the hammer of correction checks the vices of those who sin, and by its blows breaks, as it were, the obduracy of an inflexible heart. And so Isaiah says of the leader of all spiritual blacksmiths, "It was I who created the smith to fan the coals in the fire and forge implements each for its purpose."[37] Of iron also Ecclesiastes says, "When the axe is blunt and not as it formerly was, but rather dull, it is sharpened only with much labor; so too, after much effort, we become wise."[38] Now the Philistines carry off all blacksmiths from the land of Israel when the evil spirits, under the guise of false piety, remove all zeal for correction from the lips of the brothers. And so it was further said, "For the Philistines took care that the Hebrews made no swords or spears."[39] And a little further on, "So the blades of the plowshares and the mattocks, of the tridents and axes were dull and the goads needed sharpening."[40] Since the Philistines fear swords, they take away the blacksmiths, so that while the making of weapons is restricted, there is also no one available to make other tools needed for working, as the Apostle indeed notes, "The sword of the spirit is the word of God."[41] Because the evil spirits fear this sword, they remove blacksmiths from the land of Israel, so as to deny the use of the discipline to those who should rebuke the erring for their faults. And so it comes to pass that because of this dissolute negligence, in many monasteries the servants of God not only do not hear the preaching of the word of God, but also fail to practice useful trades. For since the strict discipline of authority does not reprove them, while occupied with their own whims, they never learn to write, and never become proficient in any suitable trade or

36. 1 Sam 13.19.
37. Isa 54.16.
38. Eccl 10.10.
39. 1 Sam 13.19.
40. 1 Sam 13.21.
41. Eph 6.17.

manual skill, even though the Apostle says, "The man who does not work, shall not eat."[42]

(11) And still, since these tasks must be performed, they employ laymen, even evil ones, because these skills cannot be found in their own community. And so it was said in Holy Writ, "The Israelites had to go down to the Philistines for their plowshares, mattocks, axes, and sickles to be sharpened."[43] The Israelites did not go up to the Philistines, but went down to have the tools that they needed sharpened, since monks lower themselves to the level of laymen to get something that will serve their use. Do you not see that if the practice of correction is removed from a monastery, vigorous discipline is totally weakened? And all religious life is ruined, because when each one follows his own free choice, he violates the practice of spiritual observance by returning to things that are secular. Hence, whoever burns with fervor for regular life should freely accept correction, and even when it is undeserved, will delight in being reprimanded, not that his conscience torments him for having sinned, but because he hopes that others will profit when they hear of it; so that while he who is pure and innocent is reproved, others who have fallen or who are perhaps likely to fall may be reformed.

(12) As I write these things, I am reminded that Paul, as he wrote to the Galatians, rebuked his fellow apostle Peter.[44] And yet, in his own mind, he agreed with him whom seemingly he reproved by disagreeing with him. "When Peter came to Antioch," he said, "I opposed him to his face, because he was clearly in the wrong. For until a certain person came from James he was taking his meals with gentile Christians; but when they came, he drew back and began to hold aloof, because he was afraid of the advocates of circumcision."[45] And then he added, "The other Jewish Christians

---

42. 2 Thess 3.10. For Damian's deviation from the *Vulgate*, cf. *Beuron* 25 (1975–1982), 368f.
43. 1 Sam 13.20.
44. For the interpretation of the meeting of Peter and Paul in Antioch, see G. Cacciamani, *I Ss. Apostoli Pietro e Paulo negli scritti di S. Pierdamiano*, Atti dei Convegni di Cesena e Ravenna (1966–1967) 1 (1969), 604f.
45. Gal 2.11–12.

played along with his pretense, so that even Barnabas was carried away by this false show."⁴⁶ What harsh words these are on the surface, and if you take them only syllable by syllable, how completely foreign they are to the dignity of the head of the apostles. Is Peter blameworthy, he to whom all the kingdoms of the earth were committed for censure and correction?⁴⁷ Is he to be opposed to his face, when it is at his command that the gates of the kingdom of heaven are opened to Christ's faithful? Is he to be called the model of pretence, when he is the first among the preachers of truth? And to heighten the injury still more, carefully note what follows: "But when I saw that their conduct did not square with the truth of the gospel, I said to Cephas before the whole congregation, If you a Jew born and bred, live like a gentile, and not like a Jew, how can you insist that gentiles must live like Jews?"⁴⁸

(13) What is the meaning of this, Blessed Paul, that you abuse your superior with such rebukes, that you heap on him such reproof? How can you dare shame him in the sight of all, when by special right he was granted the privilege of presiding over the Universal Church throughout the world? Have you perhaps forgotten what your common master taught you? "If your brother," he says, "commits a sin against you, go and take the matter up with him, strictly between yourselves. But if he will not listen, take two or three others with you."⁴⁹ Yet you did not meet with him alone, nor speak to him privately before witnesses, but rebuked him openly before all; and what is still worse, you wrote that you had done this so that it came to the notice of all posterity. Have you also forgotten what you advised Timothy? "Never be harsh with an elder; appeal to him as if he were your father."⁵⁰

(14) But because Paul publicly reprimanded Blessed Peter in the presence of all, Peter appeared outwardly to be his opponent, yet in conscience he carried out his wishes.⁵¹ When those who had converted from the Jewish faith were present,

---

46. Gal 2.13.
48. Gal 2.14.
50. 1 Tim 5.1.
47. Cf. Matt 16.19.
49. Matt 18.15–16.
51. Cf. Gal 2.11–20.

Peter never dared to sit at table with gentile converts lest the former be scandalized, and on that account promptly abandon their faith which was still immature. And so, he who was accustomed to eat with gentile Christians, left their company when certain persons came from James, fearing that if Jewish Christians should see him eating with gentiles, they might be in danger of losing their faith. Now that in all of this Peter agreed with Paul, namely, that gentiles should not be compelled to observe Jewish rites, there can be no doubt if one should read the Acts of the Apostles.

(15) Moreover, it was undoubtedly Peter who is now accused by Paul of being some sort of transgressor, who first among all the apostles was the author of the following statement: "Why do you now provoke God by laying on the shoulders of these converts a yoke which neither we nor our Fathers were able to bear? No, we believe that it is by the grace of the Lord Jesus that we are saved, and so are they."[52] And so Peter wished especially to be charged in the presence of all; he rejoiced at being embarrassed by disparaging invective, so that what he had done unwillingly he would refrain from doing after he had been rebuked, and that he find company in what he feared doing alone. Paul, therefore, when he opposed him was really in agreement with Peter and undoubtedly concurred with him in his heart while externally accusing him. Otherwise how could Paul condemn in another what he had done when faced with a similar necessity? For it was on account of Jewish Christians, who contended that the Law must be observed and the ancient rites maintained, that he circumcised Timothy, who was the son of a gentile. And he himself, fulfilling his vow, shaved his head and offered sacrifice according to the ceremonies of the ancient rite.[53]

(16) Thus, while appearing to rebuke Peter, he was in agreement with him, rather than his adversary. As Porphyrius thought,[54] he did not proudly campaign against him, but

---

52. Acts 15.10–11. For Damian's variant from the *Vulgate*, see Sabatier 3.551.
53. Cf. Acts 16.3; 21.24–26.
54. See Jerome, *Epistula* 112 c. 11, 2.380; Jerome, *Ad Galatas* 1.2 (PL 26.341AB); cf. also *supra* n. 44.

served him in all humility. This rebuke by Paul, then, was given in the service of obedience, and was not a disciplinary correction; it was not bold invective, but a harmonious meeting of wills.

(17) You too, dear brother, when on occasion you receive correction, even if your conscience does not accuse you for having sinned, freely accept the charge against you and humbly admit before your brothers that you are guilty. This will then be for them a model that they can imitate, and for you it will provide an increase in virtue. Remember what Solomon says: "It is better to be rebuked by a wise man than to be deceived by the praise of fools."[55] Your will should be such that if someone perhaps harshly rebukes you, you should agree with it internally. And when in some matter you are sharply assailed, you should rather appear to be pleased than show yourself opposed. Your action will therefore be a shining example to those present, and for those who are absent your renown will be held in benediction. As I said before, be like a field that overflows with its harvest, redolent with heady spices, so that Almighty God may also be delighted with you and say, "Oh, the smell of my son is like the smell of teeming fields."[56] And since you are called Ariprandus, and the Latin *ares* means 'virtue,'[57] like a bountiful field you may bear fruit a hundredfold, and be able to set before God a meal of your virtues.

---

55. Eccl 7.6.   56. Gen 27.27.
57. Cf. *Mittellateinisches Wörterbuch* 1 (1967), 927.

LETTER 55

Peter Damian to his brethren, Rodulfus and Ariprandus. A most personal letter to his closest confidants, in which he tells of his long illness. For seven weeks he was in bed with fever. Up and around too soon, he seemed for three or four days to be recovering, when a relapse set in, and for the next three weeks he was near death. He was anointed, and funeral preparations were under way. But through divine intervention, as he reported, he recovered after his brethren had given food to a hundred poor people. Through all his sickness he praised God for giving him patience and fortitude to bear his sufferings.

(1058, summer)[1]

O MY BROTHERS, Rodulfus[2] and Ariprandus,[3] the monk Peter the sinner sends sentiments of his dearest affection.

(2) It is the quality of cordial friendship that a brother tells his brother both good news and bad, so that as one's heart faithfully feels compassion for the bearer of such a message when misfortune strikes, it can likewise rejoice with him when all goes well. So I will tell you the whole blessed story of my calamities so that you may grieve with me as I was forcibly struck down by divine blows, and may be delighted as I was also mercifully released by the power of the same good God.

---

1. Dating: Lucchesi, *Vita*, nos. 109, 122–128. Neukirch 96, however, dates the letter for 1054–1057, while Woody, *Damiani* 224, for the end of June 1064.

2. Damian founded the monastery of Camporeggiano on property given by Rodulfus (C. Pierucci and A. Polverari, *Carte di Fonte Avellana* 1 [*Thesaurus ecclesiarum Italiae* 9.1, 1972], Carte no. 11.) (cf. *ItPont* 4.90f.). According to J. Leclerq, "Documents sur S. Pierre Damien," *Rivista di storia della chiesa in Italia* 11 (1957), 106–113, Rodulfus entered Fonte Avellana in 1057, and already in 1058 became bishop of Gubbio; cf. Schwarz, *Bistümer* 245. Damian wrote Letter 62 to him, and after his death, probably in 1064, also wrote his vita (= Letter 109).

3. Ariprandus was a hermit in Fonte Avellana, to whom Damian addressed Letters 54 and 117; cf. also Letter 54, n. 2.

"The Lord did indeed chasten me, but he did not surrender me to death."[4] I had often prayed that he let me feel the full rigor of heavenly discipline, and that he might chastise the wanton arrogance of my body with some grievous sickness. In this case divine mercy did not despise my petition, but listened to my prayers beyond all expectation, complying with my wishes, and that with interest. For he gave me a sorrowful Pentecost, not a Paschal one, and if I might put it so, he granted me a jubilee, not resounding with the blare of priestly trumpets,[5] but one that tearfully cried out with sighs and groans.

(3) That Sunday I went to bed with a fever, and after seven weeks, with the help of God, I got up, also on a Sunday, on *Quinquagesima*, the Sunday before Lent.[6] But as the doctors said, I was not careful to observe their diet regulations, and I was deluded by three or four days of apparent good health, when suddenly I suffered a relapse and for the next twenty days I was continuously plagued by the same affliction. And so it was that after a jubilee of storm rather than of peace, my seventy days of captivity were fulfilled. Moreover, as I burned with a high fever from the disease that was called *oxea*, as I spat up blood mixed with phlegm and displayed such obvious signs of approaching death that the doctors at my bedside almost gave up all hope, Almighty God granted me the grace of never complaining and of wholeheartedly accepting everything that happened.

(4) I give thanks to you, O merciful God, I said, since while I deserved to be snatched away for punishment under the rubble of my sins, you saw fit to consume me with the fire of your fatherly chastisement, and to cleanse away the blight from my soul as by the blows of a hammer. But let not my will prevail, O Lord,[7] which is always evil and contrary, but rather yours which all the powers of heaven and all men

---

4. Ps 117.18.   5. Cf. Lev 25.9.
6. He took sick either in Acereta or in Gamugna. In 1058 Pentecost fell on 7 June. He refers to his illness also in Letter 122.
7. Cf. Luke 22.42.

should humbly adore. Burn, amputate, cut through, and examine all the folds and lurking places of my wounds. Let not the slightest corruption remain hidden within me which might escape your curing lancet. And while I calmly bear these blows of the heavenly discipline, let me not, which God forbid, ascribe this attitude to my patience. For as you, O Lord, mete out punishment, you so adjust your blows that as I endure the heights of pain and anguish, as I suffer such convulsions that I am almost forced to die, I suddenly detect the force of this intense pain diminishing, and the hand that beats me withheld with a certain relaxing gentleness, as if one took a fourfold lash, ready to strike, and then out of kindness, removed one of the thongs from the whip.

(5) Thus it is not I, but you, most merciful One, who are the author of this patience, you who dispense your blows with such moderation. For even though at the time when I was disheartened by excessive weakness, I was compelled to scribble with my quill these sad and lugubrious works: "I am burning, I am dying, I am being killed," this was only the groaning of the flesh, and not the complaint of a protesting spirit. One thing, moreover, I beg of you, most loving Lord, that you soon put an end to my life, and not allow me to live any longer in my usual tepidity and worthlessness. But if it please the inscrutable will of your majesty that I drag on longer in this fleshly house of correction, grant me, I ask, a stronger impulse of your love, or a more bounteous grace of compunction, or certainly, an increase of every virtue which up to now I have not enjoyed. Otherwise, may it never please your goodness that I die before the gift of virtue, which I have not yet achieved, increase in me to some extent, no matter how small it be.

(6) As I often repeated these and similar prayers, preparations were going forward for my burial.[8] I was anointed with holy oil, and like one at the point of death, I was laid out on a bed in sackcloth and ashes. Just as when the shell of

---

8. On these preparations for death, see *Liber tramitis aevi Odilonis abbatis*, ed. P. Dinter, *Corpus consuetudinum monasticarum* 10 (1980), 195.272–278.

an egg is broken, and by rotating the knife, the yolk emerges, so too my soul, torn from an enveloping body, was on the point of departing.

(7) In the meantime, there was a brother in the hermitage whose name was Leo,[9] a man far advanced in years, but highly respected for his strict manner of living and for the purity of his guileless spirit. Now in a dream a man in bright and magnificent garments appeared to him, and Leo asked him what he should do. The brother told the man that he was indeed asleep, but that he was very sad because his prior was about to die. And the visitor said, "Tell Peter Damian, of whom you speak, that he should have no faith in the doctors. He should only give food to a hundred poor persons and without a doubt he will promptly recover from his sickness." When the hermit, because of his interest in the better life to come, said, "My lord, will he go to heaven?" he replied, "He will soon be in heaven, but tell him that as soon as he gives food to the poor, he will at once enjoy good health." When the brother awoke, he at once walked over to the church, but because it was not yet dawn, he could not enter. And still in wonder over the vision, he did not return to his cell.

(8) To make a long story short, the brother reported the vision to his brethren, who in their charity gave the alms to the needy with great eagerness, and from their abundance also gave them money, and so the next day my illness disappeared and I recovered. Thus the return of good health proved the genuineness of the vision. But as we were completely out of fish, and because of my sick stomach I could not take food, the brothers began to urge me and strongly insist that for three days at least I should eat some meat to overcome my weakened condition. And if I were to assent to their pleading and should impose on them any weighty penance that I chose, they promised to accept it readily and devoutly. But I related to them the humorous story of deception

9. This Leo seems to have lived at Gamugna, but cannot be identified with any of the other Leos of whom Damian writes. This is perhaps the only time in his letters that Damian is referred to as *Petrus Damiani*.

that involved Count Pharulfus of Orvieto[10] who was said to own a hundred thousand manorial holdings.

(9) Now as it was told me, when the count sat down to eat, a certain monk was also sitting there. Since they had no fish, he began begging the monk that, because of the real necessity, he should eat meat. At first the monk refused, but then little by little he relented, and at length gave in to the badgering requests. In the meantime a boar, its thick skin roasted to a crisp, was set before them, and the stupid monk was falsely persuaded by the enticing words of the guests that this was not meat and could be eaten with good conscience. And so it happened to him, just as Solomon had said of the foolish man deceived by the woman of easy virtue: "Persuasively she led him on, she pressed him with seductive words. Like a simple fool he followed her, like an ox on its way to the slaughterhouse, as ignorant as a playful lamb, not knowing that it was being led to the noose until the arrow pierced its vitals, and like a bird hurrying into the trap, not aware that he was risking his life."[11]

(10) In this way also the brother was persuaded by deceitful and enticing words, and like a tender bird was caught in the snares of the fowler. Then as he coyly began to blush, and fearfully observing the eyes of those who watched him from all sides, he first began to lick the surface of the meat, and then, once he took the liberty of eating, relaxed all restraint to his eager appetite. When at length he had eaten his fill and had satisfied his desire for the delicious meat, the waiter brought in a pike of great size, and with that all eyes of the guests were on him. As the monk sat marvelling at the fish and let his eyes avidly feast on it, the count said, "You have eaten meat like a layman, why like a monk do you keep your eye on that fish? Surely, if you were at liberty to do so, you might properly chant this verse, 'Gilead is mine and mine is Manasseh.'[12] Moreover, if you had abstained from eating meat, we would have taken pains to serve you this fish. But

10. On Count Pharulfus of Orvieto, see Reindel, *Briefe* 2.151, n. 9.
11. Prov 7.21–23.   12. Ps 59.9 and 107.9.

since you have satisfied your base appetite with meat, this fish will not pass your lips after you so carnally stuffed yourself." The monk was properly made to suffer this shame and disgrace because he had weakened the force of his noble resolve by listening to the bad advice of his flatterers. Rightly he had to bear the confusion of his obvious humiliation because he failed to curb the seductive and tantalizing appetite of the flesh.

(11) So I say, perhaps the Lord will do the same to me, my brothers, if, after I agreed to eat meat which you might procure, he should deign to favor me with a gift of fish. And thus I would be sorry that through gluttonous impatience I had violated my vow just as it happened that through the goodness of God a supply of fish was now at hand. No more said than done. Three days after I had made this remark, so many fish were brought me from Guido, the Count of Imola,[13] and from the city of Faenza that I had plenty to eat for many days to come. And so from the story of how Pharulfus deceived the monk, I was able to avoid the disgrace of being put to shame. It is much more tolerable to be despised by men than to be demoralized in the presence of God's majesty.

(12) As a friend, my dear brothers, I have revealed these matters to you, my friends and confederates, and with intimate familiarity have explained the course of my affliction as if I were speaking to my blood brothers. Because of your holy prayers, Almighty God has indeed made me whole in spirit, but has afflicted my body as my wickedness deserved. And so, as I experience the merciful Judge provoked to heavy blows in this life, may I be worthy to find him serene in the life to come. My dear brothers, after God I commit this brainchild of mine to your confidence, for whatever good should emerge from the purpose for which it was sent, should be especially ascribed only to you.

---

13. Count Guido of Imola was the recipient of a letter from Pope Gregory VII in 1073 (cf. Gregory VII, *Register* 1.10.16f.). For further literature on Guido, cf. Reindel, *Briefe* 2.152f., n.11.

LETTER 56

Peter Damian to the monk Petrus Cerebrosus. After admonishing him for using wild and insulting language, Damian takes up Peter's additional charge that self-flagellation is absurd and unsuited to present Church discipline. With many arguments and *exempla* Damian demonstrates that this practice is not new, but was frequently used in most well-regulated monasteries. He urges that self-inflicted discipline substitutes in time of peace for the oppression suffered by the Church in sterner ages, when Christ and his apostles and martyrs suffered at the hands of others. In the new conclusion to this letter, found in only four manuscripts, Damian recalls the difficulty Cerebrosus is having with his abbot, but refuses to enter the controversy. He seems to agree, however, that the abbot has the right to chastise a disobedient subject.

(1058, summer)[1]

TO THE MONK PETRUS CEREBROSUS,[2] the monk Peter the sinner sends greetings.

(2) He who thinks that acrimony is the equivalent of eloquence is mistaken because he is deceived by their similarity. For as the wise man says, "The foolish speak of senseless things, but the words of the wise are weighed in the balance."[3] And just as an unbroken horse wheels about in circles and takes every kind of impassable and difficult road, so the tongues of fools indiscriminately and lightly prate of both proper and frivolous things, whichever might be at

---

1. The dating follows Lucchesi, *Vita* no. 128; however see Neukirch 199, who opts for 1043–1060; Dressler, *Petrus Damiani* 239, for the summer of 1060; and Woody, *Damiani* 226, for August–November 1064.

2. Gaetani thought that the Peter addressed here was the same as the recipient of Letter 9, with which Neukirch 117, n. 1 disagreed. But Lucchesi, *Vita* no. 128, returned to Gaetani's position; cf. Reindel, *Briefe* 1.125, n. 1. Leclercq, *S. Pierre Damien* 102, conjectured that the recipient's name might be fictitious. The name *cerebrosus* means 'mad' or 'insane.'

3. Sir 21.28.

hand. But the prudent man thinks over what he is about to say, and like a cautious traveller, in all his utterances carefully watches where he might place his foot. The former in his impatience blabs whatever might be secret; the latter, if usefulness demands, keeps the secret safe by using the key of silence. And the wise man says the same: "Fools blurt whatever is on their mind, while the words of the wise remain their own secret."[4]

(3) You have recently discharged much bitterness against me, my brother, speaking and writing what indeed might seem to be madness emerging from an unsound brain, and fury from a mind deprived of reason. Passing over other items, that with biting hatred your violent temper spewed forth, with the help of Almighty God, I will reply in the matter of self-inflicted discipline[5] which the brothers customarily undertake, on which for some time you have left your slanderous mark.

(4) Now this type of discipline was by no means recently invented by modern ingenuity, but stems rather from the authority of Sacred Scripture. For we know that our Lord and Savior was scourged by the governor's troops,[6] that the blessed apostles were beaten in the council by order of the chief priests,[7] and we read of many saintly martyrs who were fearfully whipped with rods and lashes. Paul, too, boasted that three times he was beaten with rods, and that five times he received forty strokes less one.[8] So that is the way it was.

(5) In Deuteronomy, Moses commanded, "If the guilty man is sentenced to be flogged, the judge shall cause him to lie down and be beaten in his presence."[9] And then he added, "The number of strokes shall correspond to the gravity of the offense, so that they give him forty strokes, but not more; for if he is more cruelly beaten, your brother may die before your

---

4. Sir 21.29.
5. On the use of the discipline, see Letter 45, n. 4, and Reindel, *Briefe* 2.35, n. 3.
6. Cf. Matt 27.26; Mark 15.15.
7. Cf. Acts 5.40.
8. Cf. 2 Cor 11.24–25.
9. Deut 25.2.

eyes."[10] But that which was then a rule of law for this people, is for us a mysterious allegory. The number forty, indeed, means the span of human life. Thus it was that Israel wandered forty years in the wilderness, and so too Moses and Elijah and the Lord himself extended their fast for that many days.[11] As the Lord also lay dead in the tomb for forty hours, he was likewise in the company of his disciples for that many days after his resurrection,[12] so that the good master might teach us, his members, that by walking in the footsteps of our leader, we should be dead to the world and dwell like strangers in this life. In the law, moreover, it was mystically commanded that when a guilty man was scourged, it was forbidden to go beyond forty strokes, because whoever does perfect penance in this life will not afterwards be made to suffer punishment for his sins.

(6) Also the number three relates to the faith, because of the mystery of the blessed Trinity, while the number five, referring to our five senses, concerns its implementation. And since in sinning, everyone either errs in faith or fails in its execution, it was proper that Paul who had sinned in both regards, was beaten three times with rods and five times flogged with forty blows to achieve perfect expiation.[13] In saying "less one," the Jewish judges meant no doubt to lessen the number forty by one blow, so that by not coming up to the legal count, they would not go beyond the prescription of the law in his regard. And since they stayed on this side of that number, they would not go beyond it.

(7) Therefore, since not only the authority of the Old Law, but also the grace of the gospel recommends the use of scourging, sometimes by command, and at others by example, so that we read of both the holy apostles being flogged in the council and of the blessed martyrs frequently being lashed—for all Ancient Scripture was written for our instruction[14]—what is so absurd or so improper if now in times of

---

10. Deut 25.2–3. On the variant from the *Vulgate*, cf. *Biblia sacra* 3.474.
11. Cf. Exod 34.29; 1 Kgs 19.8; Matt 4.2. On the symbolism here involved, see Bede, *De templo* I, ed. D. Hurst, CC 119A (1969), 172f.
12. Cf. Acts 1.3.   13. Cf. 2 Cor 11.24–25.
14. Cf. Rom 15.4.

peace Holy Church should follow the practice it formerly used in times of war? For the Apostle says again, "I bruise my own body and make it know its master."[15] And elsewhere, "The saints had to face jeers and flogging."[16] Moreover, since now the hand of the executioner is withheld from being laid on the martyrs, what objection can be raised if fervent devotion should inflict upon itself that which makes one worthy of being a partner of the blessed martyrs? For when I freely scourge myself with my own hands in the sight of God, I demonstrate the same genuine and devout desire, just as if the executioner were here in all his fury. For if out of love for Christ the punishment is so dear to me when the persecutor is not present, how ready I would be to accept it if he were on the scene? If I should wish to suffer martyrdom for Christ and do not have the opportunity because the time of battle is over, by afflicting myself with blows, I at least show my heart's fervent desire.

(8) Indeed, if the persecutor should flog me, I would be beating myself, because I would of my own accord be offering myself to be scourged. Now if one carefully reads the Scriptures, one finds that Christ, the king of martyrs, was handed over not only by Judas, but also by his Father and by himself. For the Apostle says of the Father, "He did not spare his own Son, but gave him up for us all."[17] And elsewhere he said of the Son, "He loved me and gave himself up for me."[18] Therefore, if I punish myself with my own hands, or if the executioner applies the blows, I become the actual author of this ordeal if I voluntarily present myself to be tested. Moreover, since the tambourine is made of dry skin, in the words of the prophet, he truly praises God on the tambourine[19] who, when weakened by fasting, scourges his body with the discipline.

(9) Obviously, also the sacred canons at times order those

---

15. 1 Cor 9.27.
16. Heb 11.36. On this variant text, cf. Gregory I, *Liber regulae pastoralis* 3.6 (PL 77.57B).
17. Rom 8.32.   18. Gal 2.20.
19. Cf. Ps 150.4.

who have sinned to be flogged.[20] Thus, many holy pontiffs commanded that some penitents first be scourged in their presence, and then sentenced them to further penance.[21] And before our own time this disciplinary norm was by no means unknown in most holy monasteries, even though it was not often used.[22] Accordingly, it was the custom to commute a year of penance into a thousand blows of the discipline. But you denounce not so much the regulation of using the discipline, but rather its prolonged application. You do not forbid one to administer the discipline while reciting one psalm, but stand in horror at someone taking the discipline while chanting the entire psalter.

(10) But tell me, brother, if I may speak with your good leave, do you detest the disciplinary practices that customarily occur in chapter? Do you also, perhaps, condemn the custom whereby a brother who has admitted some slight offense is often required to undergo twenty blows, or at most fifty? But since this amount of discipline is hardly oppressive and easy to bear, and is regularly administered in the order, it is clear that you do not oppose or condemn the practice lest you appear to challenge the common custom of our holy order.

(11) But now let us get to the point. If, as we said, it is permissible to impose fifty lashes, why not also sixty, or if I may dare to go so far, why not up to a hundred? And if one is allowed to approach a hundred blows in this offering of loving devotion, why not also two hundred, why not three hundred, four hundred, or five hundred? Or why can we not go on to a thousand and beyond? For it is really absurd to freely accept a minimal part of a thing and to condemn a greater measure. And it is most foolish to believe that we should be allowed to begin something good, but not permitted to intensify it. Is it indeed possible that if a small amount

---

20. Cf. Burchard, *Decretum* 19.5 (PL 140.968D); *Capitula Italica* c. 7 (MG Capit. 1 [1881], 336); Ryan, *Sources* 71, no. 124.
21. Ryan, *Sources* 71, no. 125, refers to Gregory I, *Reg.* 11.53 (JE 1845); John the Deacon, *S. Gregorii magni vita* 4.31 (PL 75.194D).
22. See *Benedicti regula* c. 2.28.26; c. 28.1.91; c. 30.3.94.

of discipline is purifying, its increase will pollute us in the sight of God? For if fasting for a day is something good, fasting for two or three days is better.

(12) And so it is with spending the night in prayer, with chanting, working, and obeying, and so too with constant meditation on the Scriptures. The more extended any devout practice, the more worthy it is to be rewarded with commensurate glory. Does it apply only to this type of devotion, that the more it is increased, the more harshly it should be judged? You will say, "Why should I punish the flesh?" And I reply, "Why should I afflict the spirit?" For the psalmist says, "I am greatly distressed and lash out at my spirit."[23] I flog both flesh and spirit, for I admit that I have sinned both in the flesh and in the spirit. I chastise the latter by disciplining my thoughts; the former, together with other penitential practices, also by the use of scourging, so that as the flesh enjoyed leading me into sin, when punished it will lead me back to forgiveness.[24]

(13) A man wears an iron corselet next to his flesh, he encircles his arms and legs with iron fetters; with great energy he performs prostrations, and he frequently slaps the ground with his hands.[25] Why does he engage in these and similar practices if not through them to punish his body so that he might find rest for his soul? Whatever means he may use as a penance in chastising and discouraging his flesh, by it he is surely[26] cleansed from the filth he has contracted through sin.

(14) Listen to what I happened to learn just three days after your frantic temper flared up against me, not out of spite, I should say, but in your simplicity. Two brothers[27] traveling from the area around the city of Pola, as you know,

---

23. Ps 76.7.
24. See Ryan, *Sources* 71f., no. 126, with reference to Burchard, *Decretum* 19.23 (PL 140.983D) and Regino, *De synodalibus causis* 2.453.
25. See Blum, *St. Peter Damian* 115 and 157.
26. At this point the letter breaks off in the edition of Gaetani, reprinted in PL 144. But the continuation, translated here, is found in ten MSS, not available to the first editor.
27. In Letter 109 Damian also speaks of these two young monks, one from Spoleto, the other, named Michael, from Pola in the duchy of Venice.

came to our hermitage[28] and were kindly received. One of them, named Michael, on the very day he arrived, coming in to make his confession, related the events of his past life. "I was born of a military family," he said, "and my mother chose a wife for me, putting on a splendid and pompous display, but was unable to force me into marriage. Afterwards when I had the opportunity, I became a monk, and early on girded myself with an iron belt, but not without stipulating the following condition to this self-imposed practice. Lord Jesus, I said, when I find a monastery where I will certainly be saved, may this belt break as a clear token of your mercy. And suddenly, scarcely an hour ago as I was meditating on a certain page of the *Rule,* I experienced a slight feeling of compunction that led to tears, and at that very moment, as you can see, the belt broke into two pieces." And since this happened to him scarcely three hours after he had entered our hermitage, he rejoiced in the Lord with all his heart over the answer to his prayers.

(15) Go on then, brother, and poke fun at what you consider to be pious absurdities, since Almighty God listens to those whom you deem foolish and stupid, just as he would those who are close to him. Perhaps he will still acknowledge you and your wise friends. But as my letter comes to an end, I have written enough about the disciplinary practices of monks, that should not be derided but held in honor.

(16) In the matter of the bad relations that exist between you and your abbot, it seems to me that I should refrain from comment, lest I be stung by the opinion of Solomon when he says, "A foolish passerby who meddles in another's quarrel is like a man who seizes a dog by the ears."[29] And undoubtedly you should beware of the statement that reads, "Melancholy does harm to a man's spirit like a moth in one's clothing and a termite in wood."[30] But this I know: as a bishop is permitted to excommunicate a cleric who has seriously sinned, an abbot

---

28. Also in Letter 109 the hermitage is identified as Gamugna. On Damian's residence there, see Lucchesi, *Vita* no. 128.
29. Prov 26.17.   30. Prov 25.20.

may do the same to a disobedient monk.³¹ For just as an actual father may disinherit a rebellious son, so may a spiritual father in a display of strict justice expel a disobedient subject from the Church. Hence the Apostle says, "We had earthly fathers and paid due respect to them; should we not submit even more readily to our spiritual father, and so attain life?"³² And just a bit before that he said, "Can anyone be a son, who is not disciplined by his father? But if you escape the discipline in which all sons share, you must be bastards and no true sons."³³ And still further on he says, "Remember your leaders, those who spoke God's message to you; and reflecting upon the outcome of their life and work, follow the example of their faith."³⁴

(17) Wherefore, dear brother, put a stop to vilifying and abusing your father, end this blasphemous attack on brothers who, in weeping for their sins, apply the scourge to themselves, in keeping with what Solomon said, "Do not forbid anyone from doing a favor when he can, and if you are able, help him yourself."³⁵ Take care of yourself, but in such a way as not to ridicule others but rather by loving them, so that in whatever you do for the love of God and in those things that you cherish, you may always practice fraternal charity.

---

31. Burchard, *Decretum* 2.175 (PL 140.654B) and *passim* gives cases of clerical excommunication. For monks, cf. *Benedicti regula* c. 23.86f.
32. Heb 12.9. 33. Heb 12.7–8.
34. Heb 13.27. 35. Prov 3.27.

LETTER 57

Peter Damian to Gerard, bishop of Florence, now Pope Nicholas II elect, and to Hildebrand. About a year after his elevation to the cardinalate, Damian begs to be relieved of his office and of the administration of the diocese of Gubbio. He pleads ill health and advanced years and his desire to retire to his "beloved solitude" at Fonte Avellana. In citing several historical precedents, he contends that abdication from a bishopric is not uncanonical. His "holy Satan" Hildebrand is held responsible for his previous elevation. Because of greetings sent to Cardinal Stephen of St. Chrysogonus at the end of the letter, it appears that a copy, under separate cover, may also have been sent to him.

(June–December 1058)[1]

O THE BELOVED GERARD, bishop of the city of Florence and the bishop elect[2] of the Apostolic See, and to Hildebrand, the rod of Assyria,[3] the monk Peter the sinner sends his service.[4]

(2) Those who engaged in the study of natural history tell the story that it is the nature of lynxes that when looking back at something, they at once forget him who has just passed before them.[5] It happens all the time, that when something is out of sight it is also out of mind. And since this beast excels all other wild animals in the sharpness of its vision, so that it can penetrate stone walls, it has this defect that once it removes its eyes from something, this object is no longer re-

---

1. For the dating, see Krause, *Papstwahldekret* 65f.; Woody, *Damiani* 198–202; Lucchesi, *Vita* n. 122–124, 126.

2. In the oldest MSS the name of the pope-elect is not mentioned, but more recent MSS provide this informaiton; on which, see Reindel, *Studien* 3.351–355 and *idem, Korrespondenten* 216.

3. Cf. Isa 10.5, 30.31. In Letter 99 Damian also used this title for Cadalus of Parma, the antipope Honorius II.

4. Lucchesi, *Vita* no. 122, conjectured that this letter was never sent, but that several parts of it were used in later writings (Letters 72, 73, 75).

5. On the lynx, see Jerome, *Epistula* 9, c. 2.1.34.

membered. I would say that there is some likeness between you and these animals, unless I were restrained out of reverence for your greatness. Yet it makes me marvel that such sharp prudence, and what is more glorious, that such sincere and fervent charity which receives me affectionately when I am present never deigns when I am absent either to write to me, or to send a verbal greeting. Moreover, since I have not been found worthy to hear from you in writing, if I were dealing with others I would say that what the Apostle calls a letter of love is not written in the fleshy tablets of your heart,[6] but erased, as they say, from the lowliest wax tablet. But as I watch what I say, I must nevertheless consider to whom I speak. Wherefore, I dare not indulge in freedom of speech, I put my finger to my lips, and so the complaint expressed up to this point, of which my soul is filled, I will briefly explain.

(3) Blessed be the divine will of the omnipotent Creator, that recently I visited you, weighed down with the burden of two episcopal sees,[7] one to govern and the other to visit, that I crossed over the rocky summits of the Alps, and then after putting down the troublesome burden, relieved and free, I retreated to my beloved solitude like a fugitive who had come home.[8] It would be pleasing, therefore, in something of a mental fancy, to move my feet after their long bruising in the stocks, to raise my neck weighed down with heavy chains, and joyfully to sing that prophetical refrain, "You undo my fetters, O Lord; I will offer you the thanksgiving sacrifice."[9] You know, indeed, and are quite certain that these burdens were thrust upon me and not assumed; and, if I might put it so, I did not enter the net but was violently ensnared. Wherefore, given the proper occasion, I disposed of this weight to which previously I did not willingly submit. And since you are the

---

6. Cf. 2 Cor 3.2–3.
7. The reference here to two bishoprics is unclear; see Reindel, *Briefe* 2.164, n. 6.
8. His "beloved solitude" is usually Fonte Avellana, but here it would seem to be Gamugna; on which see Lucchesi, *Vita* 1.160ff.
9. Ps 115.16–17.

Apostolic See, you are the Roman Church,[10] it seems correct to me, in laying down and returning that which I am unable to bear, not to approach some building of stone but rather to appeal to those in whom the sacramental power of the Church resides. In the time of the Jewish persecution, wherever the apostles were, there too was the primitive Church. Now, however, as Simon, that ancient counterfeiter,[11] restores his hammers and anvil, as he usurps the city of Rome as his workshop for his moniers engaged in nefarious traffic; wherever Peter flees, leading you with him, there, without doubt, he demonstrates to all that the Roman Church resides.[12] Hence as I propose to abdicate ecclesiastical government into your hands, I have made no mistake when I restore to the Roman Church, which you are, what belonged to it. And that I may acknowledge that I pleaded guilty to you for this surrender, a hundred years of penance should consequently be imposed on me, using such remedies as were instituted by monastic regulation. But if this seems too light, you should also add to it, going so far, if it be your pleasure, as to chain me in prison. After such an aberration in roaming and harmful liberty, what remains but to compel me to submit to the censure of imprisonment and silence.

(4) But here, perhaps, that smooth tyrant who always compassionated me with the concern of a Nero, who caressed me with blows, who certainly, if I may put it so, flattered me with his eagle's tongue, will complain as he sputters, "See now, he is looking for a refuge, and under the guise of penance he hopes to escape from Rome. From his disobedience he schemes to win his ease, and while others are falling in battle he seeks out the coolness of ignoble shade." But I will answer my holy Satan,[13] using the words employed by the sons of Ruben and Gad in replying to their leader Moses: "We our-

---

10. See Ryan, *Sources* 61, no. 106, for the significance of Damian's rhetorical remarks.
11. Damian here uses the word *trapezita* in a pejorative sense as forger or counterfeiter; on which see Woody, *Damiani* 264–273.
12. Cf. Ryan, *Sources* 61, no. 106.
13. In all of these references lurks the figure of Hildebrand, the archdeacon and curial, in the service of the future Pope Nicholas II.

selves," they said, "will take up arms to lead the sons of Israel until we have brought them to the place appointed for them; our young children and all we have will stay in the fortified towns, safe from the inhabitants of the country. We will not return to our homes until every one of the sons of Israel has taken possession of his inheritance. For we shall have no inheritance with them on the other bank of the Jordan, since our inheritance has fallen to us here, east of the Jordan."[14] Thus, indeed, am I prepared to accompany you and take up arms; but after the battle, once you are victorious behind Christ our leader, I shall soon depart. This is what Barzillai the Gileadite, who had gone down from Rogelim, said to David the king: "Your servant will just cross the Jordan with you. Allow your servant to go back to die in my own town."[15]

(5) But perhaps I will hear the objection[16] that once authority has been accepted, it is not permissible for one to lay it down. To this I will briefly speak my mind: There are many that have not deserted the rights enjoyed by bishops and are found to be on the Judge's left,[17] just as we read of those that have renounced their rights with a proper intention, and yet have every reason to hope that they will eternally enjoy Christ's company. I do not say these things so that one might lightly desert the episcopate, but only in the case where some great necessity intervenes.

(6) The Blessed Valerius,[18] indeed, while providing for a successor, enthroned the great Augustine as bishop of the church of Hippo. When Lucidus,[19] the bishop of Ficoclae, became aware that his death was imminent, he betook himself to the shelter of a cenobite order and exchanged the trap-

14. Num 32.17–19.
15. 2 Sam 19.36–37. Damian has shortened the *Vulgate* version.
16. The following section (Reindel, *Briefe* 2.167.14 to 170.9) is repeated almost verbatim in Damian, Letter 72.
17. Cf. Matt 25.41.
18. Cf. E. Hendrikx, "Augustinus," LThK 1 (1957), 1095. As bishop of Hippo, Valerius consecrated Augustine his coadjutor in 395, and a year later Augustine succeeded the old man in the see of Hippo.
19. Ficoclae (= Cervia); cf. M.-H. Laurent, "Cervia," DHGE 12 (1953), 181f.; Ughelli, *Italia sacra* 2, 468.

pings of episcopal dignity for the monastic garb. And that you might know what this conversion bestowed on him, when he was at the point of death, as the authentic record of his collected letters relates, the grace of the Holy Spirit was reflected on his happy face. Before he died, moreover, the blessed apostle Andrew appeared to him and told him the hour at which he would pass away.

(7) What shall I say of Blessed Adalbert the martyr?[20] Because he deserted the authority of the church of Bohemia and became a monk, he was found worthy to wear the triumphant crown of martyrdom. As I purposely pass over others in silence, a certain holy penitent comes to mind, but for the moment I forget his name.[21] Before finishing seven years of service he gave up his episcopal office. An angel at length came to him and commanded him to return to his see. But he refused until, at the warning of the angel, the Blessed Remigius[22] suddenly appeared. And so, lest perhaps he become the victim of deception, fearing even things that seemed safe, he yielded to human command while at first refusing to budge at the word of an angel.

(8) The bishop of Sabina[23] also deserted his pontifical throne after turning his back on the episcopal dignity, and then built the monastery of Farfa. Ancient tradition which honors the deeds of his sanctity bears witness to the nobility of this man of Christ, and present devotion is also at hand to hold his memory in benediction. Many there were, before and after his time, who remained in that see till the end of their days, but never did they produce such bounteous fruit for the Lord.

---

20. Cf. Iohannes Canaparius, *Sancti Adalberti vita*, ed. J. Karwasinska (*Monumenta Poloniae historica*) N.S. 4.1 (1962), c. 8.12f. and c. 30.44–47.

21. The reference is to St. Genebaldus of Lodi; on which see Damian, Letter 72.

22. Cf. Hinkmar of Reims, *Vita Remigii episcopi Remensis* c. 16, ed. B. Krusch, MGH SS rer. Merov. 3 (1896), 303f.

23. Laurentius Illuminator, on whom cf. I. Tassi, "Farfa," DHGE 16 (1967), 547–553. On the problem of his origin in Syria and his coming to Farfa, see Reindel, *Briefe* 2.169–70 n. 25.

(9) Nor do I forget you, Blessed Bonitus,[24] who only for the reason that you happened to receive your see from the hand of the king, namely, from a layman, despised your church, and suddenly retired to a life of solitude. What, I ask, would he have done had he borne the torments with which our bishops are afflicted? What if hosts of shield and lance-bearing men should march *en masse* behind him as he rode ahead? What if armed companies prepared for battle should crowd around him like the leader of a pagan army? And he for whom it is much more proper to proceed reverently with a chanting choir, is forced to hear on all sides the clash of resounding arms. Thus it is that, as a bishop, which is proper, he is not accompanied by various ranks of clerics, but rather by courts and fighting men armed with flashing weapons. We may wonder also how this comes about, since some take part in such activities unwillingly. And still, those whom they support they purchase dearly with the goods and properties of the Church, whether they are willing or not. Daily there are royal banquets, daily they engage in pomp and splendor, daily they hold nuptial celebrations, and resources that ought to relieve the poor are used to refresh the carriers of red banners. Despite the fact that a bishop should be the steward and almoner of the poor, strangers belch at his table that groans with delicious food, while those to whom all this belongs are totally excluded and grow weak from need and hunger.

(10) Among all these evils, moreover, this one thing stands out and seems almost to equal the wickedness of the devil himself, that with property wasted on military affairs, tithes and the people themselves are annexed to every earthly piece of property, and that as a benefice for laymen. Indeed, this dishonest liberality both deprives the needy of their sustenance and also deters the people of the diocese from paying their tithes. This one thing takes from them bodily support and also is the cause of danger to their souls. All of which, no doubt, is heaped on the head of the evil administrator;

---

24. On Bonitus, bishop of Clermont-Ferrand, who died in Lyon in 706, see F. Prinz, *Frühes Mönchtum in Frankenreich* (1965), 506.

and if his own vanity leads him in this direction, no ancient necessity will constrain him. I could add many other items concerning the many tribulations of bishops unless I were restrained by the rule of epistolary terseness.

(11) But what a crime it is! The Apostolic See alone so afflicts me that it turns me away from saying all these things. In this see, in which we are accustomed to admire the reverend majesty of its bishop, we now behold that despicable person, Mincius.[25] Such affliction was experienced by that venerable man, Peter the bishop of Apsara,[26] who gave up his episcopal office, and travelling by sea from the kingdom of Slavonia to Italy, landed at the port of Ancona. In his lament, as he explained to me how the whole kingdom had held him in reverence, and as he told of the weariness caused by lack of rest, among other things he related one event about which I must tell you. There was a certain man, he said, degenerate in morals but distinguished by titles of greatness, who married a close blood relative. What happened then? Even though it was forbidden, he persisted; when excommunicated he continued on as usual and considered the entire force of ecclesiastical censures to be nothing but tales of childish nonsense. But as a certain sign of divine anger, it happened that when bread from the nuptial table was thrown into the street for the dogs to eat, they refused to touch it. Oh, how we must fear the severity of God's displeasure. As he continued to stand firm in his resolve and refused to accept with humility the commands of the bishop, unwilling to provide for his own salvation, he was struck by lightning and died while sleeping in his bedroom. Thus he who in life had despised the remedy for his wound, in death experienced the sentence of divine anger. I have told these things to show what a man of holy authority he was who renounced his episcopal see.

(12) But while I relate these things, something else comes

---

25. John Mincius, bishop of Velletri, consecrated antipope by the archpriest of Ostia. See Dressler, *Petrus Damiani* 119, n. 172; Schmidt, *Alexander II* 78f. See also Damian, Letter 58 in Reindel, *Briefe* 2.191, n. 3.

26. In Damian, Letter 72 he is called Gaudentius of Apsara; on which see Reindel, *Briefe* 2.172, n. 28.

to mind which you, venerable Hildebrand, recently told me. And although it does not seem to be of great moment for the matter I have in hand, still by putting it in writing lest it be swallowed up in the whirlpool of forgotten things, I will nevertheless make it fast with small stakes as one does for something likely to be tossed about. As I remember you telling it, to use his own words, this is what the bishop of Novara[27] related to you. "When I was visiting a certain bishop in Germany," he said, "and it was time for dinner and he had nothing with which he could prepare a proper meal for me, he became excited and anxiously looked about to see how he could take care of me on my journey. The more the need increased, the deeper was his concern, and now in real trouble, he hardly knew what to do. Suddenly a flock of cranes flew overhead, making a figure as they flew together and composing themselves in equal lines drawn up in two groups under one leader. With fervent faith the bishop then firmly and resolutely said, 'Lord, command one of these cranes to fall down for us that your servant might provide hospitality from your blessed gift.' How marvelously quick was God to hear that prayer. Hardly had the words left his lips when suddenly a good sized crane fell to the ground at our feet and thus was faith, which is fruitful through love,[28] fulfilled." When you had finished this story, I earnestly asked you, "Was this bishop a spiritual man?" How you found out I do not know, but you answered that he was a man who lived for bodily pleasure, so that it was clear that it was not the uprightness of his life but faith joined to charity that obtained this wonder.

(13) You also added, as you had it from Leo[29] the bishop of the Apostolic See, that there was another bishop whose life was carnal and ill-advised, who, beyond all that he deserved, had received such grace from God that he frequently worked signs and wonders, going so far, with a great show of author-

---

27. On the bishops of Novara from 1040–1077, see Schwartz, *Bistümer* 123f.
28. Cf. Gal 5.6.
29. Pope Leo IX († 19 April 1054).

ity, as to drive out devils from the bodies of the possessed. Among other wonders, this one happened with Leo of blessed memory present, in the case of a person possessed by the devil. When the bishop had commanded the wicked spirit to depart, the devil replied in words filled with hostile pride until, adjured terribly in the name of Christ, he could no longer resist. When he violently shook the head of the miserable man in all directions and in horrible fright made his hair stand on end, and opened his mouth several times in the act of vomiting, the bishop at once objected, "You will never get out through his mouth," he said, "as you are trying to do; you will be completely frustrated in what you are attempting. I command you to leave through his rear, for I will not permit you to go out through his mouth. Unclean dweller, you will go out through filthy passageways and, as is proper, you will leave foul footprints behind you." Hardly had he finished speaking, when the evil spirit was ejected by a movement of the bowels.

(14) There was also another bishop, as you related, who was very thirsty and ordered wine to be brought to him. The waiter had just poured all that was in the flask into the cup and brought it to the bishop, when an insistent poor man begged him to give it to him, saying that he was so dry that if he did not have a drink he would die. But the waiter declined, saying that there was nothing more in the flask and that it was impossible to find more wine in the house. The brave bishop caught in this dilemma, since on the one hand he could hardly put off satisfying his thirst, and on the other, judging that if he drank the wine it would be a wicked thing in the face of the other's dire need, denied himself and helped his brother in his necessity. He therefore ordered the wine to be given to the pauper. But now as all hope of getting a drink had passed, the bishop's thirst increased the more. Then he ordered the waiter to have another look at the wine flask, hoping perhaps that he might find some drop of consolation, no matter how small. But the waiter continued to shake his head, insisting that there was nothing left, and finally without hope, but rather compelled by the command,

he complied. In astonishment he found the flask that he had emptied now filled with wine.

(15) I heard another story about a certain abbot who, led by a desire for delicacy, had ordered a lamprey to be brought to him. When the servants said that this kind of fish was hard to come by in this region, one of them remarked that he had seen one of them for sale priced at no less than twenty shillings at Pavia.[30] The abbot commanded the money to be paid. Under the diligent eye of the cooks the fish was elegantly prepared and brought to the abbot. Before he could touch it, however, a poor man appeared at the door and earnestly begged that the very dish brought to the abbot be given to him. Without hesitation, the man of God at once gave the poor man the whole fish just as it was. Suddenly the poor man was seen to ascend with the plate filled with fish, and, holding his hands poised as if he were carrying a gift, he went up into the heavens in full view of all. Hence it is clearly proven that what is given to the needy, is given to God, and what we hide in the bosom of the poor, we deposit in heaven.

(16) This, moreover, which I now include, although not a miracle, is still a proper topic for edification with which I associate everything that I write. A certain bishop ordered a lamprey prepared for him. A little later while devoutly standing at the holy altar celebrating Mass, the memory of the lamprey suddenly tempted him with feelings of extreme desire. But since he was an exceptional man, who was ashamed that he could suffer such feelings in the sight of the hidden but omnipotent Viewer, after finishing the service went back and commanded that the fish that had so aroused his appetite be given to the poor. And thus, indeed, the little dog of voluptuousness that lives any way it can under the table of our body, when it impudently breaks into the holy of holies, deserves to die from the blows of penance.

(17) A certain poor householder had only one coin in his pocket with which he wanted to buy something to eat along with his bread. He was shrivelled and lean for lack of better

---

30. See C. Brambilla, *Monete di Pavia* (1883), 181f.

food, and as he was thinking about his purchase for some time, a poor man approached him begging alms. Taken by surprise, he found himself in a real dilemma. For if he gave the alms, he feared for his poor body; if he kept his coin, he worried about the fault he would commit in denying the alms. Finally his spirit won out over the flesh, and imitating the widow in the gospel,[31] in the person of this poor man he gave all he had to God, to whom he was indebted for all good things. He went home and the bread which he usually had was served. His table was indeed poor, but his conscience was rich in the hope of good things to come. The harm to his body was compensated by his gain in love of God. When suddenly a man who was completely unknown to him and whom he had never seen before, quickly and urgently put in his hand twenty shillings worth of pennies[32] tied up in a cloth, saying that they were sent by his lord. Just as if the latter were expecting him, he quickly departed. When the poor man in his surprise wanted to question him, he disappeared.

(18) I do not cite the names of these people because the order in which a thing happens has more readily remained in my memory, while on the other hand, I admit that the names, with other affairs intervening, have been forgotten. Nor do I greatly try to be considered a collector of names so long as the sequence and order of events are not lost. However the deeds themselves of which I write, since in passing I did not happen to hear whether they were completely credible, I do not hold to be so. Therefore, lest my narrative arranged without names cause fastidious readers to turn up their nose, I shall in the meantime refrain from telling these stories. And certainly it is more salutary that, putting all of this aside, I return to myself to bemoan myself and always keep myself in focus. For now, indeed, my eyes grow dim and more often than not are likely to be clouded by mucus.[33] Wrinkles are appearing and my gums give signs of the ruin

---

31. Cf. Mark 12.42–44; Luke 21.2–4.
32. See A. Suble, "Denar," *Wörterbuch der Münzkunde*, ed. F. von Schrötter (1930), 126–131.
33. Cf. Isidore, *Etym.* 4.5.7.

of my teeth. My head, moreover, which up to now was sprinkled with grey hair, now grows snowy white like a swan. My voice becomes hoarse and my strength is failing, and, alas, for me only the root of vice completely ignores old age. Every day I conjure up death before my eyes and try to place myself before the tribunal of the fearful Judge. Now in imagination wicked spirits with fierce faces appear before my mind and in frightening form terribly attack me as I gasp my last breath; and now bright, white, holy angels are seen as if trying to help me.

(19) It came to my attention, moreover, that a short time ago something happened which, while it often comes to mind, never ceases to increase my fear. A certain penitent dressed like a pilgrim was wandering in our area. When asked what fault compelled him to live in exile, he replied, "I was out cutting wood with my fellow villager when suddenly a serpent as big as the branch of a tree, bearing two heads on its scaly necks crept up with its slithering motion. When it saw us walking there, it attacked us with flashing eyes and three-pronged tongues[34] darting from its mouths. At once my companion unsheathed his sword and cut off one head, but then the blade fell from his hands. At once the serpent, implacably aroused to a wild fury, rose up and lifting its one remaining head, snatched his tormenter in its teeth, and holding him thus, wrapped its sinuous coils around him, and avenging itself with all its might, carried the man whole into its underground lair. While he was being carried away, the only thing my companion could do was beg me and cry out to me to come and help him or hurry and give him the sword that was in my hand. But unhappy and ignoble man that I am, and guilty of the avenging flames, thinking that it was better that only he be devoured by serpents—Oh, what a murderer I am—I began to tremble and, in the urgency of the moment, knowing what I should do with my hands but not with my feet, I prepared to run. Therefore I endure this exile imposed on me by the priests and am forced to admit sadly that I am truly the cause of his death."

34. Cf. Pliny, *Naturalis historia* 11.65.

(20) The history of this woeful calamity so shook my whole being and caused me so to tremble and filled my heart with such fear that I am unable to express my feelings in writing or in words. Often I meditate upon this theme that they are there, man and beast, together in that hole. No one intervenes, no rescue appears, no compassion enters the beast's wild heart, especially since in addition to its mad appetite it is prepared to avenge itself for the harm that it suffered. What a sight this was, I ask you? What the thoughts of this poor man could have been after he became the prey of this enemy, when hope of escaping no longer existed, but rather forced to become food for cruel teeth, he would soon satisfy the beast's wild appetite, I am unable to appreciate. Often I picture in my mind the image of this fearful scene, and at the same time with awesome reflection I behold that dragon, the source of all cruelty, and how he snatches and devours souls, frequently repeating the verse sung by the prophet: "Let him not at any time," he says, "seize my soul like a lion, while there is no one to free me, no one to save me."[35] What lengthy material for fearful reflection this short passage presents to those of sound mind!

(21) About a year ago, moreover, in a village not far from here, it was reported that a certain farmer got up a little after dawn and saw a great dragon.[36] Thinking that it was a log, he sat down on it. Suddenly the beast moved, and raising its head seized the man in its cruel mouth and with wild hunger swallowed him alive. This should strike great fear in our hearts and cause us to be more concerned for the dreadful judgments of God in our regard. Frequently we see these things happening to men who lead good and honest lives, while, on the other hand, we notice carnal and disorderly men, as we said above, who also are famed for their miracles.

(22) But lest I dwell on this topic too long, a certain pilgrim who was returning from Jerusalem, told how the following happened to him and his companions. As they were worn out

35. Ps 7.3.
36. Cf. Isidore, *Etym.* 12.4.4.

from the efforts of their journey and were resting one night by the road, a terrible lion pounced on the sleeping men. A priest, a man of good reputation and upright life, who was returning from his fourth visit to the tomb of our Lord, was resting with his companions all around him. When the wild animal struck, it touched none of those that it first came upon, but leaping over them and ignoring them as if they were bits of wood lying there, it distinctly sought out only the priest, rushed to attack him, and brought his prey to the other lions which were not far away. Within earshot of his companions who heard him screaming and groaning terribly, the lions quickly devoured him and then followed the path the pilgrims took leading up to a tower toward which they climbed in terror. To those, indeed, whose judgment is weak this seems to be a very terrible thing, that those who deserve reward are chastised and that heavenly punishment should come to those who are worthy of grace.

(23) In a similar vein, this story too seems to be a worthy subject for fear, something I learned from the account of a pious abbot from the diocese of Pisa. He said that in a certain German town it happened last summer that there was a servant of God, a man of holy life and reputation, who lived in a cell near a monastery. It was revealed to him that if the people did not at once desist from their wickedness and do penance, within thirty days their whole city would go up in flames.[37] He not only notified the bishop of the city of his mysterious vision, but immediately took pains to announce the fact to all the people. But they continued to go their evil ways, thinking that the man of God was crazy, and completely mocking the threats and warnings of God, refused to correct their lives. At the same time the man of God ordered that the precious possessions of the monastery be put in a secret place where they would be safe from the fire.

(24) But why delay the story? Finally the unhappy day ar-

---

37. On the recluse, Paternus, and the great fire in Paderborn on 10 April 1058, cf. Marianus Scottus, *Chronicon*, ed. G. Waitz, MGH S55 (1844), 558; cf. also Neukirch 98 and A. D. von den Brincken, DA (1961), 91–238, esp. 193.

rived and fire broke out in seven regions of the city. The monks anxiously rushed to the cell of the servant of God and begged him to hurry and leave in the face of the imminent danger. But he refused to go, leaving everything to God's judgment, waiting there for whatever God was pleased to do. The fire leaped furiously into the sky, engulfing everything in its path, and destroyed not only all the city but also the monastery, and, sad to say, the servant of God and all his cell. Indeed, this judgment of God is rather to be feared than examined. For what insight of the human mind is able to penetrate the depths of divine decisions, since God is "so much to be feared for his deeds among mankind."[38] Who could believe that he, who through a revelation had merited to know about the destruction of the doomed city, was ignorant of the fact that he too was about to be a victim of the horrible flames? When I think about these events and others like them and consider them in deep meditation, I know not what is still in store for me; I grow numb and tremble in all my being; and then I am reduced to tears, and if at times my hard heart does not permit me to weep, my mind at least is overcome with grief. I often consider how it could be to come under the power of hungry dragons, to be among hostile enemies, to experience living death, to dwell in fire. This, too, I dwell on, how among all other elements this one was chosen to torture the wicked, that while a flying hot ember, if it lights on any part of the body, cannot be tolerated for a moment, avenging flames will devour miserable men as they leave this world, and for all eternity the open mouth of hell will devour them. On this I could say much more if I were not restrained from lingering on this subject by the rule of epistolary briefness. But still in reference to this topic something now comes to mind which will not be out of place to include at this point.

(25) Two men of the best families of Faenza died some time ago and in a vision appeared together to a certain deacon, dressed in iron garb, which after the manner of a priest's cassock, reached to the heels. When the deacon inquired of

38. Ps 65.5.

them, "Did you always serve God when you were in this world?" they responded, "We, who now suffer eternal fire in hell, never served the Lord." Clearly—and this adds to the burden of my solicitude—the brother of whom I just spoke, as may be inferred, was in the same condition when he beheld this warning revelation; he was then perhaps involved in some grave fault when this decisive moment arrived. When we find ourselves in a crisis we will then be tried; and even though we are now pure, in a moment we may be defiled.

(26) This story too comes to mind, which I happened to hear when once I was in the city of Benevento. The prince of that city had a chaplain, a man of holy life, who was always diligent in celebrating divine services, especially in saying Mass. Every day as he was engaged in the sacred mysteries, an angel of the Lord usually appeared and, as the prince looked on, took the sacrament of the Body of the Lord from the minister's hands. But, O the uncertain and hazardous condition of this disastrous life! He who was so pure that he enjoyed the services of angels suddenly fell into the pit of shameful passion. And what more should I add? The time came for divine services and the priest was compelled by the circumstances of the moment to go on. But with his conscience tormenting him, he was terribly disturbed. He vested, approached the altar, trembled and panted, but still presumed to celebrate. Then, as usually happened, the angel came and while the prince observed, wrung out a sponge filled with water over the head of the priest and thoroughly washed his whole body. When Mass was over he again wrung out the sponge and once more poured forth over all his members the grime and filth that he had previously removed from his body. When the prince saw this happening he was astounded and waiting till everyone was gone, he met with the priest. When the priest was asked if he had recently committed some grave sin, in horror at such a thought, he at first denied the charge. But then, conscious of his crime and forced by the authority of the prince, he at last confessed that on the previous night he had sinned with one of the prince's maids.

(27) In the same city I met a monk whose name was Madelmus, who lived in a cell near a monastery[39] and was known as a hermit or solitary. He told me that on Holy Saturday, the day before the feast of the resurrection of the Lord, he lit about fourteen lamps in the church which he customarily attended. After putting in some water, he then poured oil into all of them but one. When all the others had been cared for, there was one that remained untrimmed for lack of oil. He requested more oil from the abbot but none was given him. Finally, not doubting for a moment, he filled the lamp with water, lit it, and at once it began to glow along with the others, burning through the whole night. While it is natural for water always to extinguish fire, this water caused the lamp to burn brightly. When the abbot was called as a witness, he wondered at this miracle and became afraid, and in confusion admitted that he had not supplied the oil. This monk, moreover, was said to have worked other wonders. But woe to him who walks securely with eyes closed and does not attend to the snares of the wily enemy. For later this monk fell into the depths of uncleanness, and he who had up to then been held in great reverence by the prince and the citizens was publicly beaten with rods, and it is said that in a disgraceful spectacle he was shamefully shorn.[40]

(28) Now, I have narrated these events that it might become quite evident that many ambushes lie in wait for those who walk the paths of this mortal life, that the hidden enemy conceals many stumbling blocks, scatters many traps, and daily places many snares and toils to hinder our progress. Let those who would be bishops tell me, "Offer yourself to be a ruler over people." But since I am unable to protect even myself amid so many swords and arrows, how can I free others from the devious meshes of crafty devices that lie hidden before

---

39. He does not name the monastery, but in Letter 83, Damian speaks of the monastery "of Blessed Peter the Apostle located within the walls of the city of Benevento." In 1073 a Madelmus was abbot of St. Sophia in Benevento; cf. *ItPont* 9.84, no. 8.

40. On cutting a monk's hair as a punishment, cf. Fructuosus, *Regula monachorum* c. 16 (PL 87.1107A).

them? I must therefore put down the burden that I am unable to bear: it is better to throw off the weight than to die of a broken back to the detriment of the Lord, whose servant I am. Now as evidence it will suffice to quote only this passage from St. Jerome,[41] which I remember reading not more than an hour ago. While treating of an idle pastor of a church, he had this to say: "At once," he said, "he heard the bruising reply of the angry master. 'You wicked servant, why did you not put my money in the bank, so that on my return I could have drawn it out with interest?'"[42] And explaining this, the same doctor continued, "That is, deposit at the altar that which you were unable to bear. For while you, the lazy manager, were holding the money, you were occupying the place of another who could have doubled the sum." I agree with the counsel of this holy man, I gladly accept it, and reject the burden that I was compelled to bear. Moreover, as a lazy manager I deposit at the altar the money that I was unable to double.

(29) Once, indeed, there was a time, but now that time is past, when I was able to maintain a blush of modesty, the badge of mortification, a proper severity, and the reputation for priestly dignity. And speaking only for myself, you must have noticed that as soon as I visit you, there are at once witticisms, jokes, pleasantries, humorous remarks, banter, and a host of questions; a whole plague of useless words breaks loose which show that we act not as priests but rather as orators and rhetoricians, or, which is worse, as clowns. For as soon as we join in conversation, a certain excessive allurement for words gradually takes over our speech, which improperly softens the rigor of the spirit, and causes our steady severity to dissolve into peals of laughter and shameful jokes. And so it is that the mind, spread out beyond itself grows confused, the sharp edge of the heart is dulled, the light of God's love is extinguished, and fear in others and reverence for the priesthood are lost. And what is still more dangerous, the

41. Jerome, *Epistula* 14, c. 8.1.57.
42. Luke 19.23.

norm of right living that was established as an example for others is not observed.[43]

(30) But if I, either through shame or fear despise myself for having indulged in these things, let me be judged as inhuman and inflexible like the stone tigers which the Hyrcanians produce.[44] But now I had better stop writing. I blush with shame if more scandalous absurdities should be added, namely hunting, snaring, the rage for gambling or for chess, which indeed make a farce of the whole priesthood; they especially arrange together on a spit the eyes, the hand, and the tongue, and thus seasoned, that they may taste the sweeter, they are served as food at the tables of devils.

(31) And now, if I should recall what happened to me in connection with the bishop of Florence,[45] it would, I think, serve the purposes of edification. Once when I was his companion on a trip, and around evening we had come to a hospice, I went into a priest's cell and he resided in a large house with many people coming and going. When morning came, my attendant told me that the bishop had been playing chess.[46] This news pierced my heart like an arrow and inflicted an angry wound. At a time that seemed right for the occasion I confronted the man and sharply rebuked him. I began by saying, "With a powerful hand I am ready with the rod, and I am waiting to inflict blows if anyone is prepared to offer me his back." He replied, "If guilt is inferred, one should not refuse a penance." "Is it right," I asked, "and was it a part of your office to spend the evening playing frivolously at chess and to defile with sacrilegious wantonness the hands that offer the Body of the Lord and the tongue that intercedes between God and man, especially since canonical

---

43. The above paragraph is undoubtedly an explanation of the scurrility of which Damian accuses himself in several of his letters.
44. Cf. Pliny, *Naturalis historia* 8.25; Isidore, *Etym.* 12.2.7.
45. This bishop, despite attempts by Neukirch, Davidsohn, and Borino, remains unidentified.
46. On these references to the game of chess, among the earliest in Western literature, see Von der Lasa, "Die Einführung des Schachspiels in Europa und ein Brief des Peter Damiani von 1061," *Schachzeitung* 25 (1870), 163–169, 198–202; G. Lucchesi, *Scritti minori* (1983), 104.

authority has decided that bishops who gamble are to be deposed?[47] And what advantage does one derive when authority decides to condemn, even if there is no external judgment in the case?" For his part, however, the bishop put up a defense by citing the difference in terms. "Chess is one thing," he said, "and dice is another. And while authority prohibits dice, by its silence it permits chess." To which I replied, "Written law," I said, "does not mention chess, but includes both games under the name of dice."

(32) Wherefore, while playing at dice is prohibited and by name nothing is said of chess, it is clearly evident that both types are included in the one word and are condemned by the authority of a single judgment. Then the bishop who was meek in spirit and sharp in wit, after I had given my reasons, acquiesced, agreed by solemn promise never to repeat the fault, and asked that a penance be assigned to him. Then I commanded that he recite the psalter three times with accompanying meditation, and that he wash the feet of twelve poor people and give the same number of coins for their relief. The reason behind these actions is this: that as his fault was committed for the most part by the hands and in speech, by washing the feet of the poor, he especially cleansed his own hands from the contagion; and by putting his lips to the feet of strangers, he restored peace with the Lord whom he had offended by jokes that he should bemoan. I have told of this event so that one may learn from another's reform how improper, how absurd, and finally how defiling is this wantonness in a bishop.

(33) Wherefore, my dear friends, to get back to the subject over which I proposed to write this piece, for the future do not be hard on me, so that I must again desert the haven of quiet to which, with the help of Christ who steers through you, I have returned, and be forced again to fight the foaming waves and swells, and plow through rough waters and the Scyllaean whirlpool.[48] For although I am a miserable sinner

---

47. Cf. Pseudo-Cyprian, *De aleatoribus*, ed. W. Hartel, CSEL 3, Appendix (1871), 92–104.
48. Cf. Isidore, *Etym.* 11.3.32.

LETTER 57   389

and he was holy, still since in a way my case is a great deal like that of Samuel,[49] a similar conclusion may be reached about both. He indeed abandoned the dignity of leadership, but still anointed David as king. I too, following his example, wish with the help of God to install[50] the head of the Apostolic See, and then immediately retire from my own episcopal office.

(34) So now, my dear friends, while extending my remarks to you I have offended against the rule of epistolary brevity. But if someone wishes to accuse me of redundant verbosity, let him rather charge it to my charitable impatience over your silence; and one should know that briefness in verbosity is present when the writer expands his piece in such a way that he still does not exhaust the content of a heart that is full to overflowing. At the end of this letter I also include greetings to Stephen,[51] whom I consider to be among my best friends, and beg that he not neglect to remember me. May he rescue poor Peter from the hands of Hildebrand, at whose command Herod's prison flew open to the great Peter.[52]

49. Cf. 1 Sam 16.13.
50. Pope Mark (336) bestowed this right on the bishop of Ostia; cf. *Liber pontificalis* 35.1.202.
51. On the possible reference here to the cardinal priest of St. Chrysogonus, see Reindel, *Briefe* 2.62–63, n. 1.
52. Cf. Acts 12.7–10.

LETTER 58

Peter Damian to Henry, the archbishop of Ravenna. In answering a letter bearing Henry's seal, Damian gives his opinion of the two men who were contending for the Apostolic See, the interloper Benedict X, and the candidate of the cardinal bishops, Nicholas II, the former bishop Gerard of Florence. His judgment of the former is frank and devastating; the latter comes off with high praise. Damian acknowledges the request of Henry to keep his opinion private, but refuses to go along with the suggestion, asking, in fact, that this letter be made public, and that, in the face of possible dire consequences.

(1058, second half)[1]

TO THE MOST REVEREND Archbishop H.,[2] the monk Peter the sinner sends the service of the obedience he owes.

(2) As soon as I saw the letter bearing the seal of your holiness,[3] venerable father, I promptly took it in hand, opened it with pleasure, and read it with much interest. Therein I at once clearly learned of your kindly and paternal affection for me, and the assured promise regarding the request that I had previously laid before you. But regarding the matter that you added at the end of your letter, that I write to you giving my opinion of the man who now occupies the Apostolic See, and of him who was elected to that see; even though you could earlier have gotten this information from various clerics of your own diocese, in view of your command, I shall also put in writing my conclusions about the differences between these two men.

---

1. The dating follows Lucchesi, *Vita* nos. 118, 127.
2. The recipient is generally identified as Archbishop Henry of Ravenna, in office since 1052.
3. On letter seals, see Carl Erdmann, "Untersuchungen zu den Briefen Heinrichs IV," AUF 16 (1939), 184–253, esp. 187f. and 190–193.

(3) The former,[4] it seems to me, is a simonist, unable to clear himself of this crime; for in the face of the outcry, the objections, and the terrible anathemas of all of us cardinal bishops of that city, he was enthroned at night with armed mobs rushing about in a furious uproar.[5] Thereafter he managed to acquire the tainted patronage of wealthy men, disbursed money to the people in every ward, alley, and lane of the city, broke into the ancient treasury of Saint Peter, and thus having made the whole city into a workshop of the evil forger, Simon, hardly any other sound was heard, so to speak, but the clang of hammers on the anvil.[6] And what a crime and monstrous portent! Peter, as we know, who had condemned Simon and all his trafficking to everlasting hell,[7] was forced to pay from his own resources for all of Simon's mongering. But that he concealed this crime in every way he could and used the excuse that he was dragged into it and was forcibly compelled to act as he did, even though I am not certain of the facts, still I do not altogether deny it. For he is so obtuse and lazy, and is a man of so little talent, that one might believe that he would not know how to plan these events himself. But yet he is guilty, because he willingly wallowed in this dirty mess into which he was early violently thrown, and delighted to carry on in this adultery which unwillingly he had previously committed.

(4) But that I may not, as they say, drag out my remarks about this intricate promotion, while we bishops were variously going into hiding, a priest of the diocese of Ostia—if only he were able to read correctly a single page syllable by

---

4. On the debate over the identity of the antipope Benedict X, and on the future of the diocese of Velletri from which he came, see Reindel, *Briefe* 2.191, n. 3.

5. On the election of Benedict X in Rome on 5 April 1058, seven days after the death of Stephen IX in Florence on 29 March 1058, cf. *Chronica monasterii Casinensis*, ed. H. Hoffmann, MGH SS 34 (1980), 2.99, 356, for which the present letter is the source. For full bibliographical treatment, see Reindel, *Briefe* 2.192, n. 4.

6. For similar patronage, see D. B. Zema, "The Houses of Tuscany and Pierleone in the Crisis of Rome in the Eleventh Century," *Traditio* 2 (1944), 155–175, esp. 163, 171f.

7. Cf. Acts 8.9f.

syllable—was seized upon by the followers of satan and forced to promote him to the apostolic office.[8] And notice, since the decrees sanctioned by the canons are known to you, that if the whole catalog of objections which could be brought against him were suppressed, this alone would suffice to render his action totally invalid. For if a priest is undoubtedly to be deposed for usurping the rights of his bishop, how can a man remain in office when his consecrator has been sentenced to the loss of his priestly dignity just because of him? To this I may add that Pope Stephen of blessed memory,[9] after the bishops and the citizens of Rome, the clergy and the people, had gathered in the church, ordained under severe penalty of excommunication that if he were to die before Hildebrand, subdeacon of the Roman church, who had been sent on mission by common consent, should return from the court of the empress, no one should elect a pope, but that the Apostolic See should remain vacant until his return. But lest my lengthy remarks, which God forbid, tire your holiness, busy as you are with many other affairs, and exceed the bounds of epistolary brevity, let this suffice.

(5) But that I may further satisfy your request in my reply, it seems to me that the pontiff-elect is well educated, a man of brisk intelligence, chaste above all suspicion, and generous in giving alms. I will not say more so as not to appear amenable to everything he has done, but only as an advocate for specific items. Regarding his opponent, on the other hand, if he were able to explain fully for me—I will not say just one psalm, but even one line of a homily—I would no longer mutter a word against him; I would take his hand and kiss his feet and, if you should say so, would call him not merely apostolic, but verily an apostle.

(6) Yet as to your written request that my reply to you be kept secret—advice given me out of paternal affection, so

---

8. This was in keeping with Roman custom that designated the archpriest of Ostia or Velletri to officiate if the bishop of Ostia were absent. Yet Damian considered this action to be uncanonical. Cf. Woody, *Sagena piscatoris* 37.

9. On the death of Stephen in Florence, see F. J. Schmale, "Etienne IX," DHGE 15 (1963), 1198–1203.

that I perhaps do not encounter difficulties for having freely spoken my mind—God forbid that in such matters as these hard and delicate subjects be evaded, and by overlooking the incest practiced on such a noble mother, I should hide in the shadows like a degenerate son. Rather, I request that this letter be made public,[10] so that through your efforts all will come to know what should be thought about this danger to the whole world.

(7) I will say nothing further, venerable father, concerning your blessing which I requested, except that whatever is given to my messenger, be placed in the hands of him who sent him.

10. Here we have evidence that Damian wished his letters to be "published." See Reindel, *Korrespondenten* 212f. on conflicting evidence in this matter.

LETTER 59

Peter Damian to Alfanus, archbishop of Salerno. After thanking his friend for his many favors, he continued with a discussion of the sublime dignity and responsibility of the episcopal office to which Alfanus had been elevated. His theme develops as an elaboration of the consecration rites current in the Old Testament.

(After 1058)[1]

O THE VENERABLE Archbishop A⟨lfanus⟩,[2] the monk Peter the sinner sends sentiments of his deepest devotion.

(2) Since the patriarch Jacob said to his son Joseph, "The blessings of your father have been strengthened by the blessings of his fathers,"[3] in like manner I can say that the blessings of my father have been reinforced by the blessings, not of the fathers, but of my father himself. There have been so many blessings that have come to me as a result of your liberality, that one prepared for the other and, as Scripture says, those that went before reinforced those that followed. Moreover, if David was deserving of thanks when he presented the elders of Judah with gifts from the spoils he had taken from the Amalekites, saying, "This is a present for you out of the spoil taken from the Lord's enemies,"[4] how much greater should be my gratitude since I have received not bloodstained gifts from the possessions of God's enemies, but those that had been sanctified by coming from the Lord's sanctuary.

(3) Indeed, to use the topic of physical gifts to direct our attention to the mystery of spiritual blessings, since the Apos-

---

1. The dating follows Lucchesi, *Vita* 2.150f.
2. It appears quite certain that Alfanus, archbishop of Salerno and former monk of Monte Cassino is here addressed. Cf. G. Lentini, "Alfano," *Dizionario degli italiani* 2 (1960), 253–257.
3. Gen 49.26. 4. 1 Sam 30.26.

tle was most happy to announce, "You have been called to receive a blessing as your inheritance,"[5] what a great dignity has been granted you, that is, the most exalted bishops in the Church, not only to possess the blessing bestowed on you, but that you should be able also to give it to others. And this blessing is not just an ordinary one, but that of being a bishop, by which it is your right to consecrate bishops. And since it is something both awesome and frightening to be even a priest of inferior status, for whom the Law prescribes that he bear the sins of the people,[6] how terrifying and fearfully unsettling it is now to exceed all others in ecclesiastical dignity, and also to be required in the presence of all to give an account in the court of the awe inspiring judge.

(4) Therefore, we must carefully provide that he whom the highest officer in the priesthood elevates to receive the episcopal dignity in the Church be conspicuous for his exceptional and praiseworthy manner of life. And since, by accepting this sublime office, he stands head and shoulders above others, so too must he exceed others by the eminence of his life and the brilliance of his spiritual deeds. And so Moses said, "The pontiff, that is, the high priest among his fellows, who has had the anointing oil poured on his head, whose hands have received priestly consecration, and who has been clothed in sacred vestments, shall neither uncover his head nor tear his clothes. He shall not enter the place where any man's dead body lies; not even for his father or his mother shall he render himself unclean. He shall not go out of the sanctuary for fear that he dishonor the sanctuary of the Lord, because the consecration of the anointing oil of his God is upon him."[7] The head of a bishop[8] is indeed anointed with oil when his soul is nourished by the fullness of the Holy Spirit. The same oil also consecrates his hands, when the determination to act uprightly, which a bishop has set as his goal, is likewise visibly demonstrated in his actions.

---

5. 1 Pet 3.9.   6. Cf. Num 18.1.
7. Lev 21.10–12.,
8. The Latin word *sacerdos* used here and throughout the letter must be understood as bishop, since only a bishop's head is anointed.

(5) It is clearly the role of a holy bishop both to devote his thoughts to sacred things, and to make evident in his deeds what he has internally perceived. Otherwise, of what value is it to think of something that is good if one does not constantly take pains to put it into action.

(6) A bishop must therefore see to it that his head is consecrated by views that reflect his holy purpose, and that his hands be anointed with spiritual chrism by evident proofs of good works. He is also said to be clothed in sacred garments, because it is proper that a bishop be always attired in the vestments of piety and justice, as it is written, "Let thy priests be clothed with justice."[9] He is commanded not to uncover his head, that is, that he not open his heart to the desires of this world, but should always keep it detached for the purpose of attaining the kingdom of heaven. He is likewise enjoined not to tear his clothes, namely, that he should always carry on, clad in the garment of integrity and of a proper mode of life, lest, which God forbid, he sever it and clothe himself instead with wicked deeds.

(7) He was forbidden, moreover, to enter the place where someone lay dead, which meant that he should carefully refrain from evil acts which cause the death of the soul, and with constant solicitude be on his guard against deadly pursuits. Of which the Apostle says, that "Christ rescued us from the deadness of our former selves and fit us for the service of the living God."[10] He was also instructed not to render himself unclean, not even for his father or his mother, that is, that he not defile himself by involvement in the affairs of this world or by his desire for this mortal life. And thus it was well said, "He should not leave the holy place for fear that he dishonor my sanctuary."[11] A bishop goes out from the holy place when by neglecting the cure of souls, he wanders about seeking earthly pleasure. He leaves the holy place when, by turning his back on ecclesiastical discipline, he involves himself excessively in things of passing value. And then the text

9. Ps 131.9.
10. Heb 9.14.
11. Lev 21.12.

aptly continues, "For fear that he dishonor my sanctuary."[12] The sanctuary is dishonored when a bishop, consumed by earthly desires and dissolutely occupied with secular affairs, boldly dares to approach the holy altar. And then we witness what the prophet said: "Then it will be the same for priest and people."[13] Wherefore, that the Church of Christ may continue to flourish in all its purity, and not be soiled by the moral filth of unworthy ministers, it is also aptly stated, "He shall marry a woman who is still a virgin. He shall not marry a widow, a divorced woman, a woman who has lost her virginity, or a prostitute, but only a virgin from his father's kin; he shall not mingle the descendants of his father's kin with the lowborn of his tribe, for I am the Lord who hallows him."[14]

(8) We can properly understand a bishop's wife to be his life and manner of living which indeed should be virginal, kept immune and untouched by the defiling pleasures of an unclean spirit that violates the temple of the soul. It should not be a widow, but one happily married to the heavenly bridegroom. A divorced woman, a woman who has lost her virginity, or also a prostitute is forbidden, so that if his life be soiled by the foul contagion of lust and sensual vice, it will be fatally divorced from the bridegroom of the soul. The Apostle divorced this unclean wife when he said, "What formerly I considered to be assets I have written off as sheer loss because of Christ, for whose sake I lost everything and count it as so much dung."[15] He seemed to be saying, the spoiled and meretricious wife whom I had married while practicing Judaism, I have divorced and abandoned, and have cast her off like dung once the divorce became effective. Such a bishop's wife will not bring forth children who offer sacrifice to God, but rather such who will incur the wrath and severity of God's punishments. So it was that God spoke to the prophet Hosea: "Go, take a wanton for your wife and get children of her wantonness; for like a wanton this land is unfaithful to the Lord."[16] As Scripture asserts, "he went and took Gomer, the

12. Lev 21.12.
13. Isa 14.2.
14. Lev 21.13–15.
15. Phil 3.7–8.
16. Hos 1.2.

daughter of Diblaim, and she conceived and bore him a son. And the Lord said to Hosea, 'Call him Jezreel.' "[17] This name, even though it seems to mean 'fortunate,' in that it can be translated, 'seed of God,'[18] it nevertheless means 'the vengeance and the fury of God,' since the text at once continues, "For in a little while I will punish the line of Jehu for the blood shed in Jezreel and put an end to the kingdom of Israel. On that day I will break Israel's bow in the Vale of Jezreel."[19] But that here we should not understand Jezreel to mean salvation or good fortune, but rather the anger of God, is also hinted at in the words that follow immediately: "She conceived again and bore a daughter, and the Lord said, 'Call her "without mercy," for I will never again show love to the house of Israel, but shall totally forget her.' "[20] When she bore a third child, he said, "Call him 'not my people,' for you are not my people, and I will not be your God."[21]

(9) We obviously learn from these names given the children of this wanton woman, that every man who leads an impure life as if he were married to such a wife and delights in her wickedly soothing caresses, will never beget children of her who are pleasing to God, because it is impossible to bear sweet fruit from bitter roots. "For an evil tree cannot bear good fruit."[22] Therefore, a bishop must beware of marrying a soiled or meretricious wife, but should always display the integrity of a chaste and pure manner of living. From such a life he will be able to beget legitimate children, not bastards, as he endeavors, with God's grace, to produce the noble fruit of good works. And so it behooves a bishop to marry a priestly wife from whom he might procreate offspring who will reflect their father's character. Thus it was properly stated in Scripture, "He shall not mingle the descendents of his father's kin with the lowborn of his tribe."[23] Now a bishop joins the descendents of his father's kin with the lowborn of

---

17. Hos 1.3–4.
18. Jerome, *Nom. hebr.* 28.11 (CC 72.95).
19. Hos 1.4–5.
20. Hos 1.6.
21. Hos 1.9.
22. Matt 7.18.
23. Lev 21.15.

his tribe, when by his mean way of life he hardly differs from the crowd by failing to display the quality of outstanding deeds. Finally, when he walks along the broad and spacious way of worldly pursuits, he does not dissociate himself by the excellence of a spiritual life from the common actions of the crowd. But that a bishop might beget offspring worthy of its noble lineage, he must not abandon the path trodden by his forefathers, namely that of holy bishops who preceded him, lest by his ignoble life he dishonor that outstanding ancestry and lose the privilege of the episcopal office in which he had functioned unworthily.

(10) Consequently, when one reads the following in the book of Ezra, "From among the descendents of the priests the line of Hobaiah, of Hakkoz, and Berzillai, who married one of the daughters of Berzillai the Gileadite and took their name," the text then continues, "These searched for their family record in the register and could not find it, and so they were excluded from the priesthood."[24] Obviously, those who do not find their family record in the register are to be excluded from the priesthood, since they who are perceived to have dishonored the noble lineage of their forefathers by the tawdriness of a worldly life, should properly be expelled from the priesthood with all the force that canon law can muster. A bishop of the Church must therefore be noble, and as the Lord's minister he should blush if he were to become a slave of sin. He of whom the Apostle spoke has raised us to this noble status, "for he rescued us from the domain of darkness and brought us away into the kingdom of his dear Son,"[25] and his blood has cleansed us from the servitude of sin. Of him John also said, "He loved us and freed us from our sins with his life's blood."[26]

(11) That a bishop might surpass all others in possessing such purity, he should strive to bear the stigmata of Christ's blood, as the Apostle says, "I bear the marks of Jesus forever branded on my body."[27] Hence also in the Old Law it was

24. 1 Ezra 2.61–62.
26. Rev 1.5.
25. Col 1.13.
27. Gal 6.17.

ordered that blood from the slaughtered ram be put on the lobe of the high priest's right ear and also on his right hand, and on his right foot.[28] But that my explanation may move forward more quickly, the bishop bears the blood of the slaughtered ram on his ear, when he takes great delight in attending to the mystery of Christ's passion. The same blood is also applied to his right hand, when the attentive listener carries out in deeds what he has come to understand. The right foot is also marked with the same blood, when the life of a bishop is armed against the efforts of the devil with meditation on the passion of Christ, so that as he received the power to tread on serpents and scorpions, he need not fear their bite or the poison from their weakened fury; or certainly, because the foot is the terminal part of the body, by this is meant the highest level of good works, namely, that in every good deed that we undertake, we should also persevere in bringing it to a happy conclusion. And so it was that the voice of God spoke to the people of Israel, "If you will hear the voice of the Lord your God by carrying out and observing his commandments, then the Lord your God will raise you high above all the nations of the earth."[29] In these words we have the clear meaning of what is symbolized by the various parts of the body. "If you will hear," he said, "the voice of the Lord your God," here we have the blood of the sacrificial ram, like a ruby on the ear of the bishop. The words that follow, "that you carry out," indicate the hand of him who performs. And the last phrase, "and observe his commandments," signifies perseverance in good works. No one will benefit from beginning a good deed unless he also takes care to bring it to completion.

(12) It should be noted that only the right ear, hand, and foot of the high priest were to be daubed with blood, so that always and in everything that he does he might hew to the line of faith and right living; that his feet never wander from the path and that he may never lose his way by making a false turn. Or more clearly, he should always consider the mystery

---

28. Cf. Lev 8.23.   29. Deut 28.1.

of the Lord's passion as the right way, and despise all the pleasures of this world as totally sinister and without value. For since the bishop is the leader and the standardbearer of the Lord's army, he must go forward adorned with the symbols of Christ's passion, and be able to carry the banner of Christ's blood and cross before the ranks of the Church's troops that follow after him. This the prophet Zechariah prefigured when he said, "On that day shall be inscribed on the bridle of every war horse, 'Holy to the Lord.'"[30] Before the coming of the Savior, moreover, what was the human race, if not an untamed horse that madcap liberty caused to dash about in the open fields of its own pleasures? But our Redeemer put a bit in its mouth when he interposed the holy gospel by which all the vices of wanton passion were held in check. On this bridle, "Holy to the Lord," that is, the cross, was inscribed, since every precept of the holy gospel is alive with the cross, inviting us to bear the cross in the footsteps of Christ.

(13) The same meaning may be attached to the thin plate of gold which the high priest wore on his head as an ornament of honor, on which was engraved the four-lettered name of the Lord.[31] Just as the four letters were there engraved, so too are there four arms of the cross, embracing the four parts of the earth. This the high priest wore as an ornament of honor and glory, for the Apostle also says, "God forbid that I should boast of anything but the cross of our Lord Jesus Christ."[32] For this reason the bishop should wear the plate of gold on his head, that he may always be reminded of the cross of Christ. He should also employ the horse's bridle, emblazoned, "Holy to the Lord," that he might crucify his flesh with its vices and evil desires. Then, indeed, does the bishop wear on his head the golden plate and use the bridle that is holy to the Lord, if he directs his attention to the cross of

---

30. Zech 14.20.
31. Cf. Exod 28.36. See also Hrabanus Maurus, *De universo* 1.1 (PL 111.15C); E. C. B. MacLaurin, "YHWH, the Origin of the Tetragrammaton," Vetus Testamentum 12 (1962), 439–463.
32. Gal 6.14.

Christ and restrains his body like a wild horse from freely engaging in vice and wantonness. For this reason Scripture speaks of this twofold mystery of carrying the cross, when it reports that both Elijah and John the Baptist wore leather belts around their waist.[33] Of our Savior, moreover, John says in the Apocalypse, "For he wore a golden girdle round his breast."[34] We know also that a man's heart lies between the two breasts. Consequently, the bride speaks in Canticles, "My beloved lies between my breasts,"[35] that is, he rests always in my heart. What is the meaning of girding the waist or loins where lust especially has its origin, with leather belts which are made of dead animals, but checking at all times the seductive impulses and desires of carnal passion by tormenting the body? And what is the significance of wearing a golden girdle round the breast, but the constant and careful control of annoying imagination and assailing thoughts? We gird our waist with leather belts when we restrain our lusting flesh by continuous fasting. We have a golden girdle round the breast, when we engage in implacable combat against the attack of molesting thoughts.

(14) And then will happen what follows in the passage cited above. Just after saying that "Holy to the Lord" was to be engraved on the horse's bridle, the prophet continued, "And the pots in the house of the Lord shall be like the bowls before the altar. Every pot in Jerusalem and Judah shall be holy to the Lord of Hosts."[36] In the gospel the Lord commanded that pots be turned into bowls and that a golden girdle be worn round the breast, when he said, "Do not let your minds be dulled by dissipation and drunkenness and worldly cares."[37] By pots we should understand dissipation and drunkenness, and by wearing a girdle round the breast, worldly cares. Their hearts were truly like pots, when the Israelites longed for the fish they had had in Egypt; when growing tired of manna, they were hungry for melons and yearned for onions

---

33. Cf. 2 Kgs 1.8; Matt 3.4.
34. Rev 1.13. 35. Cant 1.12.
36. Zech 14.20–21. 37. Luke 21.34.

and garlic.³⁸ Were they not like pots when they impetuously cried out that "we had sat round the fleshpots"?³⁹ Such hearts are indeed like pots wherein gluttony rules, and in which one may cook various delicacies and diverse kinds of food on the fires of lust. But these pots are turned into bowls that are placed before the altar and made holy to the Lord, when we engrave on the horse's bridle "Holy to the Lord," and when also we wear a golden girdle round our spiritual breast. Then, indeed, are the fleshpots turned into golden bowls, filled with incense, the prayers of the saints.⁴⁰ And these bowls are placed before the altar, while when they were just pots, they stood about in the fumes of the kitchen.

(15) The heart of a bishop is like a golden bowl, filled with the odors of spiritual incense, when it is carefully bent on prayer and good works. And one may say that this bowl is placed before the altar, since in all his thoughts he never ceases to offer sacrifice to God. Then, indeed, is this pot dedicated to the Lord, when by the laying on of hands he pours over into others the graces of consecration which he received for himself as a gift from the giver of all good things.

(16) But now, in excessively extending my remarks, I have almost forgotten to whom I was speaking, and have exceeded the normal bounds of a letter. So let this suffice, except only that as I began with a blessing, let me also conclude in like manner. May the right hand of God, venerable father, fill you with his blessings and bring you to the kingdom of heaven, accompanied by the flock committed to your care.

38. Cf. Num 11.5. 39. Exod 16.3.
40. Cf. Rev 5.8.

LETTER 60

Peter Damian to Pope Nicholas II. After congratulating the pope on the high esteem in which he is held in the area of Fonte Avellana, he pleads the cause of the people of Ancona, excommunicated by him because of the political obstinacy of a few leaders. He decries the use of spiritual weapons that indiscriminately destroy the souls of the innocent, and begs Nicholas to take advice in the matter from the counsel of Hildebrand, Humbert, and Boniface, the "sharp eyes" in his curia. His own criticism, he remarks, is excusable in the sight of God.

(1059, March)[1]

TO THE LORD NICHOLAS, the blessed bishop of the highest see,[2] the monk Peter the sinner sends the obedience of his devoted service.

(2) Since the news of your good fortune has spread throughout this region, great joy has filled my heart, and with my whole being I thank the Lord who is the author of these gifts, so that as I internally rejoice, my tongue must also exult in these words of divine jubilation, "Glory to God in highest heaven, and on earth peace to men of good will."[3]

(3) Yet, venerable lord, I deeply grieve over the people of Ancona[4] who are dying each day, and am gravely shaken by the confused and indiscriminate danger befalling both the innocent and the sinner alike. Indeed, every day we see them physically dying, and because of your decision, the sword of Peter is on the attack, causing the death of their souls. We, indeed, take our rest; but the naked sword of the Apostolic See does not sleep, felling countless thousands of men in one cruel and deadly slaughter, not carried out, to be sure, on

---

1. The dating follows Lucchesi, *Vita* no. 131.
2. Pope Nicholas II (24 January 1059–27 July 1061).
3. Luke 2.14. For Damian's variant from the *Vulgate*, see Sabatier 3.267.
4. On Ancona, see M. Natalucci, *Ancona* 227 (1960).

their bodies that are destined to die, but, sorry to say, and that intolerably, on their souls that are destined to live forever. I dare say that after my lord rose to the apostolic office, we who are commissioned to see to his well-being, considered no other act of his to be so dreadful. These people wished to be your subjects, they wished to hand over their city to you, and humbly subjugate themselves and their belongings to your service. Yet because their sins stood in the way, not only were the gates of your mercy not opened to them, but once the sentence was handed down, they were on the contrary excluded from the kingdom of God and from the confines of the Church like rebels obstinately refusing to obey. God forbid that my lord, who is the teacher of all Christian compassion, should allow the sword to slaughter this vast number of souls in such sweeping fashion, when the right arm of any tyrant[5] is suddenly restrained by fear once it has caused the death of two or three persons. For when Abner, too, at the very height of the battle called out to Joab, "Must the slaughter go on forever?" the latter at once replied, "As the Lord lives, if you had said a word this morning, the people would have given up the pursuit of their brethren."[6]

(4) God forbid, I say, that while wishing to please one person,[7] such a great number of those should perish, for whom Christ's blood was shed. You, indeed, hold the office of him who, even though he was weak and poor, did not fear to raise his voice against exalted leaders and magistrates, when he said, "We must obey God rather than men."[8] And again, "If it is right in God's eyes for us to obey you rather than God, judge for yourselves."[9] Wherefore, if it please my lord, sit down with sir Hildebrand,[10] a man of clear and sound judg-

5. For a commentary, with bibliography, on the political situation here alluded to see Reindel, *Briefe* 2.204, n. 4.
6. 2 Sam 2.26–27.
7. Almost certainly, a reference to Duke Godfrey of Lorraine, who was also the prefect of Ancona.
8. Acts 5.29.
9. Acts 4.19.
10. Hildebrand was probably appointed archdeacon about the time of this letter.

ment, and also with the most reverend bishops, Humbert[11] and Boniface,[12] men who are your acute and sharp-sighted eyes. Discuss with them, then, these highly confidential matters, and decide upon the remedy you might employ to put an end to the death and destruction of so many souls that are perishing. Use moderation in the way the Apostolic See normally passes sentence, and restrain the application of ecclesiastical punishment, so that those whom spiteful cruelty seeks to disperse, may be embraced by priestly mercy.

(5) Excuse my words, dear father, and do not take note of the noise made by my bold tongue, but rather observe the hidden secrets of a devoted heart. Nor should you be annoyed at your servant's humble censure, since Almighty God himself said to men, "Come now, and reprove me."[13]

---

11. On Humbert, see J. T. Gilchrist, "Cardinal Humbert of Silva Candida (d. 1061)," *Annuale mediaevale* (1962), 29–42.
12. On Boniface, cardinal bishop of Albano, see Z. Zefarana, "Bonifazio," *Dizionario biografico degli italiani* 12 (1970), 113f.
13. Isa 1.18.

INDICES

INDEX OF PROPER NAMES

Aaron, 106, 133, 255
Abigail, 219
Abihu, 106, 255
Abimelech, 135
Abishai, 218
Abner, 36
Abraham, 49, 67, 103, 105, 262, 336
Abruzzi, 9
Absalom, 136, 218
Acacius, 176, 178
Accaron, 136
Acereta, monastery, 356
Achan, 104
Achilles, baths, 159
Adalbert, St., 373
Adam, 65, 66
Adnès, P., 235
Agathora, 86
Ahab, 46, 217
Ahaziah, 68, 69
Alexander II, pope, 4, 60, 65
Alexander, patr., 198
Albizo, abbot, 71, 222
Alfanus of Salerno, 64, 272, 394
Allophyli, see Philistines
Alps, 222
Amalekites, 262
Amiziah, 69
Ambrose, St., 51, 264, 280, 281
Amelrich of Ravenna, 64
Amicus of Rambona, 187
Amore, A., 158
Amnon, 136
Ananias, 103
Anastasius II, pope, 176, 177
Anatolius, patr., 152, 154
Ancona, 404
Ancyra, council, 25, 27
Annas, 134

Anthimus I, patr., 149
Anthony, St., 93
Apostolic canons, 25, 197
Apostolic See, 185, 270, 371, 375, 389, 392
Arduin of Fano, 98
Arduin of Rimini, 188
Arianism, 208
Arians, 51, 170, 171, 185
Ariprandus, 344, 355
Arles, council, 89
Arras, synod, 188
Athanasius, bp., 198
Atto, bp. of Florence, 237
Augustine, St., 51, 67, 114, 116-118, 123, 130, 132, 139-141, 150-152, 167, 172, 273, 274, 372
Auxilius, 97, 148, 149, 153
Azariah, 37, 69

Balaam, 124, 125, 126
Balak, 125
Balboni, D., 187
Baldassari, S., 162
Bareille, G., 36
Barnabas, 105
Bartoccetti, V., 98
Basil, 28, 30
Beatrice of Tuscany, 235
Bede, 41, 114, 247, 279, 363
Beelzebub, 136
Benedict, St., 92, 93
Benedict of Aniane, 301
Benedict X, pope, 390, 391
Benevento, 384, 385
Benjamin, 75, 108, 232
Bloch, Marc, 135
Blum, O. J., 25, 226, 227, 234, 236, 252, 272, 297, 299, 300, 302, 310, 312, 316, 322, 330, 366

409

410   INDEX

Boaz, 162
Boniface, card., 341
Bonitus, St., 374
Bonosus, bp., 175, 200
Book of Gomorrah, 3, 5–53
Boswell, J., 4
Brambilla, C., 378
Bultot, R., 240
Burchard, 6, 15, 18, 20, 25, 28–30, 33, 45, 46, 77, 79, 82, 84–87, 89–91, 119, 121, 174, 181, 190, 194, 202, 248, 365, 368
Burchi, P., 188

Cabrol, F., 215
Cacciamani, G., 263, 351
Caiaphas, 133, 134, 135
Cain, 65, 66
Campana, A., 216
Camporeggiano, mon., 355
Cantin, A., 239, 241, 242, 272
Capecelatro, A., 56
Capitani, O., 167, 181, 225, 286
Carletti, C., 187
Carlyle, R. W. and A. J., 219
Carthage, council, 171
Cassiodorus, 159, 337
Cathari, 169
Cavigioli, J., 17, 140
Cecilian, bp., 172
Chalcedon, council, 61, 85
Charybdis, 224
Chess, 387, 388
Chirat, H., 176
Cicero, 80
Classe, 220
Clement II, pope, 180, 205
Collectio Dionysio-Hadriana, 25, 27, 82, 84, 89, 120, 139, 169, 171–173, 176–178, 191, 194, 195, 200, 201–202, 205
Conrad II, emp., 54
Constantine, emp., 339
Constantinople, 159
Cyprian, 260

Dagon, 45
D'Alverny, M. T., 276
Dareine, C., 98
Dassmann, E., 51

David, 36, 40, 57, 68, 101, 119, 127, 162, 207, 208, 218, 366
Davidsohn, R., 155, 244
DeClercq, V. C., 170
Decretum Gelasianum, 105
Della Santa, M., 71, 74, 93, 227, 231, 236, 247, 273, 289, 292, 343, 344
Democritus, 326
Desiderius, abbot, 272
Diogenes Laertius, 222
Dominicus Loricatus, 231, 307
Donatists, 51, 171, 174
Donatus, St., mon., 158
Dresdner, A., 6
Dressler, F., 7, 56, 57, 93, 112, 203, 218, 245, 271, 336, 361
DuCange, C., 296, 316
Duchesne, L., 155

Ebal, Mount, 63
Eleazar, 258
Eleuchadius, 156
Eli, 49, 161, 183
Eliezer, 134
Elijah, 142, 217, 235, 292
Elim, 105
Elisha, 142, 285, 292
Elkanah, 161
Elze, R., 63
Enoch, 65, 66
Erdmann, C., 390
Esau, 103, 136
Esdras, 259
Eusebius of Caesarea, 134
Eutropius, 339
Ezekiel, 179

Faenza, 156, 240, 360
Fano, 98
Farfa, mon., 373
Faul, D., 171
Felix I, pope, 178, 194
Fiesole, 159
Firmanus of Fermo, 187
Firminger, W. K., 148, 153
Flavian, patr., 152
Fleckenstein, J., 112
Florence, 155, 244
Fois, M., 270

INDEX

Fonte Avellana, 71, 94, 118, 231, 289, 297, 301, 304, 355, 369, 370
Formosus, pope, 197
Fornasari, G., 135
Friedberg, E., 63
Fructuosus of Braga, 385
Fuhrmann, H., 25, 30, 79, 82, 93, 150, 265
Fulbert of Chartres, 205

Gaetani, C., 4, 16
Galla, empress, 337
Gamugna, mon., 356, 367, 370
Gandulf, 188
Gaudentius of Apsara, 375
Gebhard of Ravenna, 186
Gehazi, 122
Gelasius I, pope, 83, 89, 166
Genebaldus of Lodi, 373
Gerard of Florence, 155, 158, 237
Giabbani, A., 327
Gibelli, A., 59
Gilchrist, J., 121, 124, 164, 169, 170, 173, 191, 406
Gislerius of Osimo, 63, 73, 219
Giustiniani, P., 289
Godfrey II, 335, 405
Gomorian, 36
Gomorrah, 8, 33, 39, 42, 43
Gordini, G. D., 187
Gougaud, L., 247, 295
Granata, A., 58, 143, 144
Gregory I, pope, 9, 66, 86, 87, 129, 166, 182, 196, 199, 223, 268, 364, 365
Gregory VI, pope, 59, 98
Grierson, P., 188
Grillantini, C., 76
Guido of Imola, 360
Guido of Numana, 73, 74
Guido of Pomposa, 187
Guinizo, monk, 239

Häring, N. M., 117, 271
Hallinger, K., 299
Hamilton, B., 223
Hannah, 161
Hantsch, H., 92
Hefele, C. J.-Leclerq, H., 176, 207

Heinemann, L. von, 111
Helena, 339
Henry, abbot, 338
Henry, abp. of Ravenna, 111, 112, 212, 214, 390
Henry III, emp., 112, 180, 218, 251
Heraclides, hermit, 247
Hermann of Reichenau, 112
Herod, 123, 135
Hilarion, 93
Hildebrand, archd., 272, 369, 371, 389, 392, 404, 405
Hinkmar of Reims, 373
Hophni, 183
Hopper, V. F., 145
Horace, 241
Hosea, 259
Hrabanus Maurus, 401
Hubert of Rimini, 187, 188
Humbert of Silva Candida, 56, 111, 214, 406
Humbertus Bobiensis, 54
Hyginus, 325

Icarus, 325
Immaculate Conception of Mary, 162
Imola, 158
Importunus, 9, 10
Innocent I, pope, 90, 170, 172, 173, 176, 183, 190, 191, 193, 195, 200, 201
Isaac, 132
Isaiah, 39, 107, 207, 279
Ishmael, 134
Isidore of Seville, 24, 40, 92, 99, 104, 145, 182, 218, 222, 224, 228, 271, 276, 303, 325, 326, 332, 379, 381, 388
Ithamar, 258

Jacob, 67, 103, 162
Jadin, L., 187
James, apos., 11, 78, 285, 353
Jared, 66
Jechoniah, 67
Jeremiah, 32, 156, 157

INDEX

Jerome, 36, 51, 65, 67, 92, 99, 109, 130, 135, 233, 246, 261, 275, 283, 291, 339, 353, 386, 398
Jerusalem, 153
Joab, 36, 37, 40
Joash, 69
Job, 235
John XIX, pope, 186
John, abp. of Ravenna, 196
John Cassian, 345
John Chrysostom, 33
John Gualbert, 245
John of Cesena, 53
John of Lodi, 215, 298, 312
John of Suavicinum, 343
John the Baptist, 100, 115, 117, 292, 402
John the Deacon, 9, 86, 87, 96, 166, 181, 210, 268, 365
John the Evangelist, 44, 48, 50, 116, 117, 130, 192, 266, 287, 345, 402
Jonadab, 293
Jonah, 49
Joram, 68
Joseph, 67, 68
Joseph, son of Jacob, 49
Josephus, 134, 135
Joshua, 104
Judah, 108
Judas, 103, 123, 152, 167, 177, 209
Jude, 44
Justinian, emp., 216

Kahn, Cynthia, vii
Kenan, 65
Klinck, R., 99
Koch, C., 219
Koch, G., 219

Lamech, 65, 66
Laqua, H. P., 55, 80, 98, 112, 136, 186, 187, 199, 203, 206, 212, 213, 218, 265, 295
Lasa, Von der, 387
Lateran, 265, 267
Laurentius Illuminator, 373
Lea, 291
Leclercq, J., 226, 330, 331, 355, 361

Lentini, G., 394
Leo I, pope, 24, 82, 83, 152, 174, 181, 205, 223
Leo IX, pope, 3, 4, 61, 73, 74, 111, 112, 180, 186, 204, 205, 213, 376
Leo of Preggio, 230
Leo of Sitria, 228
Leo the hermit, 358
Levites, 100, 101
Liber gratissimus, 111–214
Liberius, pope, 148
Lindemans, S. P., 148
Little, L. K., 7
Lokrantz, M., 111, 112, 281
Lot, 13, 49, 103
Lucchesi, G., 3, 54, 55, 59, 61, 71–73, 75, 111, 113, 218–221, 240, 244, 2515, 263, 289, 307, 335, 336, 338, 343, 355, 361, 367, 370, 387, 390, 404
Lucidus, bp. of Ficoclae (Cervia), 372
Luke, evangelist, 102, 115
Lupus, hermit, 230

Mabillon, J., 59, 112
Macarius, 247
Maccarrone, M., 203, 251
Macedonians, 192
McGonagle, D. J., vii
MacLaurin, E. C. B., 401
Madelmus, 385
Mahalalel, 65, 66
Mai, A., 215
Mainz, council of, 85, 86
Manasses, 136
Mandonnet, P., 105
Manichaeans, 51
Marianus Scottus, 382
Marinus, 156, 157
Mark, evangelist, 19, 106
Mark, pope, 389
Martha, 291
Martin, Storacus, 226
Mary, 67, 68, 321
Mary, sister of Lazarus, 291
Mary the Poor, church, 339
Massa Sorbituli, 59
Matthew, evangelist, 66, 68

INDEX 413

Maurus, bp., 75
Melchizedek, 120, 262, 274, 275
Mephibosheth, 57
Methuselah, 66
Miccoli, G., 77, 82, 98, 102, 105, 189, 213
Michael, archang., 207
Michel, A., 25
Midianites, 108
Mincius, bp. of Velletri, 375
Mitterelli, J. B.-A. Costadoni, 56, 76, 222
Moab, 125
Mone, F. J., 301
Moses, 43, 52, 101, 127, 133, 144, 258, 273, 292, 362

Naaman, 285, 286
Nabal, 219
Naboth, 46, 217
Nadab, 106, 255
Natalucci, M., 404
Nebuchadnezzar, 135
Neophytes, 181
Neukirch, F., 6, 56, 61, 64, 73, 113, 215, 218, 251, 335, 343, 355, 361, 382
Nicaea I, council, 169
Nicholas II, pope, 155, 213, 369, 371, 404
Nicholas, deacon, 183
Novatians, 77, 92, 159, 169, 174, 192, 195
Novatus, 169

Obed, 162
Ochozias, 136
O'Connor, E. D., 162
Ocri, 55
Odalricus, bp., 216
Onan, 8, 9
Oportunus, 9
Osimo, 61, 76

Paderborn, 382
Palazzini, P., 73, 76, 79, 88, 216, 226, 320
Palladius, 247
Papias, 99
Parmenianus, 150

Paschasius Radbertus, 118, 123, 128, 130, 137, 140, 142, 148, 163, 164
Passivus, 9
Pasztor, E., 265
Paternus, 382
Paul, apost., 11, 14, 19, 31, 43, 44, 49, 62, 63, 68, 114, 115, 119, 121, 124, 125, 131, 138, 141, 146–148, 150, 151, 177, 179, 185, 191, 192, 199, 223, 238, 252, 254, 264, 272, 274, 276, 278, 351, 353, 354, 362, 363
Paul of Samosata, 173
Paul, hermit, 93
Paulianists, 173, 185, 192, 195
Paulicians, 173
Pavia, money of, 188, 378
Payer, P. S., 4
Pelargus, 159
Perugia, 238
Peter, apost., 25, 43, 63, 109, 122, 166, 192, 194, 203, 204, 255, 271, 286, 351, 353, 389
Petrus Cerebrosus, 361
Peter Damian, 3, 5, 36, 54, 56, 59, 61, 64, 71, 73, 80, 92, 94, 98, 104, 111, 112, 118, 212, 215, 216, 218, 221, 227, 242, 244, 250, 252, 263, 272, 289, 335, 341, 343, 344, 354, 358, 361, 369, 390, 394, 404
Peter, martyr, 198
Pharaoh, 46, 129, 135
Phares, 162
Pharulfus of Orvieto, 359, 360
Philip, apost., 192
Philistines, 45, 350, 351
Phinehas, 183
Photinian, 176
Photinus, 176
Physiologus, 228
Pierucci, C., 51, 72, 94, 231, 293, 304, 330, 332
Pisa, diocese, 382
Pliny, 380
Poggiaspalla, F., 98
Pola, 366
Polychronius of Jerusalem, 153
Pontine Islands, 149

Porphyrius, 353
Prete, S., 98
Prinz, F., 374
Pseudo-Augustine, 133
Pseudo-Isidore, 139, 150
Pseudo-Stephanus, 79

Rachel, 291
Rahab, 162
Rahner, H., 176
Raimbaldus, bp. of Fiesole, 154, 155
Ravenna, 114, 200
Regino of Prüm, 29, 83, 84, 87, 89
Reindel, K., 64, 72, 74, 92, 111, 112, 148, 153, 197, 216, 218, 221, 224, 228, 230, 231, 238, 241, 244, 263, 265, 268, 272, 289, 295, 298, 299, 301, 309, 312, 313, 329, 335, 339, 344, 359, 360, 362, 370, 372, 373, 375, 389, 391, 393
Remigius of Reims, 373
Resnick, I. M., 225
Rimini, 112
Rivière, J., 251
Robert of Sinigaglia, 59
Robinson, I. S., 80
Robinson, J., 133
Robison, E. G., 111
Rodulfus, hermit, 355
Rome, 73, 371
Romuald, St., 223, 301, 309, 310
Romuald of Camerino, 187
Romulus, St., 155, 158
Rozo, 155
Rufinus, 135, 199, 305
Rufus, bp., 200
Rusticus of Narbonne, 82
Ruth, 162
Ryan, J. J., 6, 9, 16, 20, 25, 27, 29, 41, 56, 77, 79, 82, 83–91, 119, 120, 139, 148, 150, 153, 154, 166, 169, 171–174, 176–178, 181, 183, 190, 191, 195, 197, 201, 202, 205, 207, 245–248, 268, 365, 366, 371

Sabatier, P., 17, 23, 35, 42, 43, 62, 101, 122, 129, 137, 217, 241, 252, 267, 276, 284, 353, 404
Sacred Heart, 114
St. Apollinaris in Classe, 218
Samaritani, A., 71
Samson, 45, 160, 168
Samuel, 100, 183
San Apollinare nuovo, 341
Sapphira, 103
Sarah, 135, 336
Saul, 127, 219
Savioli, A., 156
Schmidt, T., 186, 375
Schmale, F. J., 65, 392
Schwaiger, G., 153
Schwarz, G., 54, 59, 74, 112, 154, 155, 188, 355, 376
Scylla, 224
Seekel, F., 114, 116–118, 123, 124, 128, 130, 132, 133, 137, 139, 140, 141, 148, 150, 151, 153, 154, 163, 167, 182, 199
Seneca, 264
Seth, 66
Shealtiel, 67
Sheerin, D., 49
Silverius I, pope, 149, 150
Simon, high priest, 134
Simon the Magician, 112, 122, 207, 211, 371, 391
Simonists, 112
Siricius, pope, 30
Sixtus III, pope, 153
Sodom, 8, 31, 34, 39, 42, 43, 49
Solomon, 101, 103, 115, 162, 261, 281, 295, 354, 359
Soule, W. J. A., vii
Spinelli, G., 186
Steindorff, E., 113
Stephen IX, pope, 263, 336, 392
Stephen, card., 64, 272, 341
Stephen, deacon, 105, 183
Stephen, hermit, 289
Strabo, Walafrid, 15
Suavicino, 298
Suble, A., 379
Sulpicius Severus, 45
Symmachus, pope, 153

Tamassia, N., 79
Te Deum, 302
Teuzo, 221, 224, 241, 245
Theodolus, 153
Theodore, 25
Theodosius, emp., 337
Timothy, 11
Toledo, council, 84
Trier, council, 84
Tripartite History, 159

Ubertus of Sarsina, 54
Ughelli, F., 187
Urbicus, abbot, 86
Uriah, 162
Uzziah, 37, 68, 69

Valentinian I, emp., 153
Valerius Gratus, 134
Valerius, bp. of Hippo, 372
Verberie, council, 88
Vergil, 104, 341
Ventum est, 190

Vernarecci, A., 59, 60
Vicar of Christ, 251
Victor II, pope, 250
Vigilius I, pope, 149
Vitaletti, G., 51, 94

Walther, H., 228
Wasserschleben, F. W. H., 20
Weyer, P. H., 169
Wilmart, A., 186
Woody, K. M., 75, 204, 218, 232, 237, 244, 248, 289, 355, 361, 371, 392

Xenocrates, 222

Zechariah, 265
Zedekiah, 282
Zefarana, Z., 406
Zema, D. B., 391
Ziba, 57
Zimmermann, G., 296, 313
Zipporah, 108

INDEX OF SACRED SCRIPTURE

(Books of the Old Testament)

Genesis
1.6–8: 276
1.9: 277
1.11: 163
1.11–12: 277
1.14: 277
1.20–21: 278
1.22: 163
1.26: 278
1.26–27: 278
1.31–2.1: 274
2.1–3: 279
2.2: 274
2.3: 280
2.10: 280
3.6: 338
3.16: 336
4.13: 77
4.15: 65
5.1–18: 66
12.4: 105
13.5–12: 103
14.10–12: 103
14.14–16: 262
18.6–8: 337
18.11–12: 336
19: 8
19.9–11: 13
19.11: 14
19.18–19: 13
19.24: 52
20.6–7: 136
21.12: 336
26.15–18: 203
27: 103
27.23: 132
27.27: 354
27.27–29: 132
29.17: 291
29.37: 291
30: 162
32.2: 104
37: 49
38: 162
38.9–10: 9
41: 135
49.26: 394

Exodus
4.24: 108
4.25: 108
5.21: 56
8.19: 129
8.21–32: 282
13.2: 136
14f.: 322
15.27: 270
16.3: 403
16.35: 292
20.3–8: 274
20.12: 62, 274
20.24: 286
20.25: 109
21.6: 136
22.28: 136
23.5: 45
23.20–23: 273
24.14: 213
25.40: 101
28.36: 401
29.28–44: 135
31.13: 141
31.14: 273
34.29: 363

Leviticus
4.2–3: 261
6.21–22: 258
8.23: 400
10.1–2: 107, 255
10.17: 258
14.1–32: 17
19.30: 275
20.9: 62
20.13: 9
21.10–12: 395
21.12: 396
21.12–15: 397
21.15: 398
22.4: 36
25.9: 356
26.10–11: 287
26.19: 32, 210

Numbers
1.49–50: 100
1.52: 100
1.53: 101
3.41: 99
3.45: 99
5.2: 36
6.23–27: 141
6.27: 133
11.5: 403
11.16–17: 143
11.25: 143
11.26: 144
17.10: 242
18.1: 395
19.22: 191
22.7: 125
22.16–17: 125

INDEX

Numbers (continued)
23.20: 126
24.2: 127
24.2–3: 125
24.3–4: 125
31.8: 126
31.16: 126
32.17–19: 372
33.9: 105, 270

Deuteronomy
5.16: 274
6.4: 276
25.2: 246, 362
25.2–3: 363
27.13: 63
28.1: 400
29.6: 293
32.32: 42
32.41: 43
32.42: 43

Joshua
2.1: 162
7.24–25: 104

Judges
3.15: 232
3.15–20: 75
13.4: 293
14.8: 168
15.17–18: 168
16: 45, 160
20.8–11: 108
20.16: 75
20.18: 109
20.18–25: 108
21.3: 333

Ruth
4.17: 162

1 Samuel
1.1: 100
2.4: 49
2.20–21: 161
2.25: 257
3.1: 183
13.19: 350
13.20: 351

13.21: 350
16.13: 389
17.26: 207
17.34–36: 262
19.20–21: 128
19.21–22: 128
19.23: 132
24.7: 136, 219
25.10: 219
26.9: 136, 219
30.26: 394
31.4–6: 60

2 Samuel
2.26–27: 405
3.28–29: 36
12.7–8: 251
13: 136
16.1–4: 57
16.7: 218
16.10: 219
19.36–37: 372
23.15–16: 208

1 Kings
13.18–19: 160
13.20: 161
13.28: 157
16.32–33: 46
19.8: 363
19.18: 235
21.13–14: 46
21.19: 217
21.27: 46, 246
21.28–29: 46
22.27: 149

2 Kings
1: 136
1.8: 402
2.9: 142
2.20–22: 348
4.39–41: 349
5: 122
5.14: 285
5.17: 285, 286
8.25: 68
10: 129
15.1: 69
17: 52

17.26: 253, 284, 286
17.27–28: 261
17.29: 253
17.33: 284
17.41: 254
21.3: 136
23: 207
25.6–7: 282

1 Chronicles
10.4–6: 60

2 Chronicles
8.14: 101
26.10: 37

Ezra
2.61–62: 399
2.62: 259

1 Maccabees
2.48: 91

Job
5.14: 14
39.34: 235

Psalms
1.3: 58
7.3: 381
10.4: 152
11.9: 14
14.1: 62
32.9: 29
40.9: 45
41.3: 278
44.8: 119, 231
50.16: 40
54.23: 315
59.9: 359
62.12: 203
63.11: 91
65.5: 127, 283
67.5: 12
67.22: 178
69.2–37: 302
82.14: 14
83.12: 220
95.5: 284
100.7: 178

101.28–29: 279
105.1: 187
107.9: 359
111.7: 48
115.16–17: 209, 370
117.18: 356
118.21: 294
118.22: 68, 109
121.1: 336
123.8: 302
131.9: 118, 396
136: 293
145.7: 250
150.4: 364

Proverbs
1.23: 346
1.28–30: 346
3.11–12: 346
3.18: 281
3.27: 368
5.12–13: 346
6.3–4: 261
7.21–23: 359
12.1: 346
13.24: 347
14.29: 347
15.8: 39
15.31–32: 346
16.26: 264
17.10: 347
17.11–12: 347
19.18: 347
19.25: 347
22.24–25: 348
23.13–14: 348
24.11–12: 262
24.30–31: 349
25.20: 367
26.11: 78
26.17: 367
27.5–6: 347
29.1: 348
29.17: 348
29.21: 348
31.19: 291
31.25: 291
31.29: 292

Ecclesiastes
1.7: 115
7.6: 354
10.1: 283
10.9: 319
10.10: 350

Song of Songs
1.12: 402
2.9: 325

Wisdom
1.5: 150
1.6: 137, 138

Sirach
21.28: 361
21.29: 362
33.25: 348
37.12: 64
37.15: 64
38.25: 284

Isaiah
1.10–15: 39
1.15: 40
1.18: 97, 251, 406
1.22: 80
2.4: 349
6.5: 107
10.5: 369
11.2: 241
14.2: 397
14.12: 207
16.3: 210
19.19–20: 286
19.25: 99
24.2: 80
30.31: 369
33.15: 268
34.4: 276
40.6: 320
44.3–4: 282
54.16: 350
56.4–5: 47
66.1: 280
66.2: 129, 241, 279
66.16: 42

Jeremiah
2.14: 34
4.10: 80
9.1: 33
14.17: 33
35.6: 293
48.10: 50

Lamentations
1.6: 34
1.10: 32
1.20: 32
2.1: 34
2.11: 34
2.16: 35
3.24: 99
4.1: 80
4.5: 33, 258
4.6: 34

Ezekiel
3.18: 50
18.20: 180
18.21: 77
18.28: 77
22.18: 80
30.21: 46
32.26: 52
33.11: 77
36.22: 132
37.4: 211
43.8: 132

Daniel
3: 135
13.42: 132
14.26: 206

Hosea
1.2: 397
1.3–6: 398
1.9: 398
4.6–9: 259
4.8: 258
4.9: 80
14.6–8: 282

Jonah
 2.4–5: 49
 3.7: 247

Zephaniah
 1.18: 42

Haggai
 1.6: 103

Zechaniah
 3.9: 265
 4.2: 266

6.12–13: 266
14.20: 401
14.20–21: 402

Malachi
 1.3: 136
 3.6: 127

Books of the New Testament

Matthew
 1.5: 162
 1.6: 162
 1.8: 68
 1.12: 67
 1.16: 67
 1.17: 67
 3.1: 100
 3.4: 328, 349, 402
 3.11: 177
 3.16: 119
 3.17: 275
 5.13: 105, 249, 270
 5.45: 124
 6.17: 345
 6.19: 109
 6.21: 110
 6.24: 254, 284
 7.2: 22
 7.5: 17
 7.6: 156
 7.18: 398
 7.22–23: 137
 8.4: 17
 9.25: 283
 10.5–7: 152
 11.7: 349
 11.29: 129, 241
 12.30: 103
 12.32: 194
 13.25–29: 203
 13.29: 204
 15.14: 17
 16.6: 105
 16.18: 265
 16.19: 352
 18.6: 6

 18.7: 60
 18.15: 221
 18.15–16: 352
 18.16: 28
 19.11: 49
 19.27: 250
 21.2: 286
 21.12: 206
 23.2–3: 142, 177
 25.41: 372
 26: 260
 26.7: 345
 26.14–25: 103
 26.69–75: 255
 27.3–6: 209
 27.26: 362
 27.51–52: 123
 28.13: 311
 28.19: 117
 28.20: 110

Mark
 1.4: 100
 1.4–6: 293
 1.6: 328
 1.10: 119
 1.12–13: 292
 6.8–9: 106
 12.41–44: 154
 12.42–44: 379
 14: 260
 14.3: 345
 14.10–20: 103
 15.15: 233, 362

Luke
 1.15: 293, 299
 2.14: 404
 3.2: 100
 3.22: 285
 5.4: 17
 6.39: 17
 6.41–42: 17
 7.37: 345
 9.1–2: 115
 9.10: 115
 9.62: 78
 10.1: 144, 286
 10.4: 106
 10.39–40: 291
 11.17–18: 23
 11.20: 160
 11.23: 103
 11.24–26: 79
 12.13–15: 102
 12.34: 110
 12.48: 11
 12.49: 107
 15.12: 102
 19.23: 386
 21.1–4: 154
 21.2–4: 379
 21.26: 324
 21.34: 402
 22: 260
 22.1–21: 103
 22.42: 356
 22.51: 122

John
 1.16: 115
 1.32: 119

INDEX

1.33: 117, 120, 121
3.5: 62
3.8: 128, 137
3.34: 115
4.2: 117
6.51: 36, 215
6.53: 184
6.59: 36
6.63: 131
6.64: 162
6.70: 152
8.7: 108
10.1: 130
10.8: 206
10.9: 13
11.9: 279
11.25: 45
11.41–42: 138
11.50–51: 134
11.51: 133
12.3: 345
12.6: 152
12.24–25: 215
13.10: 151
13.18–26: 103
13.26: 167
13.27: 123
14.23: 129
14.30: 285
15.1: 151, 215
15.3: 150, 151
15.4: 279
15.5: 148
17.20–21, 23: 275
18: 260
18.10: 122
19.1: 233, 245
19.40: 345
20.22: 146

Acts
1.3: 363
1.5: 120
2.1: 105
2.3: 146
3.3–8: 341
4.19: 405
4.32–35: 102
4.36–37: 105
5: 122

5.1–10: 103
5.1–11: 204
5.17–42: 245
5.29: 405
5.40: 233, 362
6: 105
6.5–6: 183
6.14: 245
7.48: 330
7.59: 105
8: 192
8.9f.: 391
8.14–17: 116
8.20: 122, 204, 206
9.21: 97
12.7–10: 389
15.9: 151
15.10–11: 353
16.3: 353
19.2–6: 192
20.26–27: 50
21.24–26: 353
21.25: 333

Romans
1.14: 272
1.24: 12, 41
1.24–25: 254
1.26–28: 12
1.28: 14
1.32: 14
2.5: 36
2.7: 63
8.8: 295
8.9: 146, 185
8.32: 364
9.22: 29
9.28: 224
10.2: 179
10.8: 151
10.8–10: 151
12.1: 252
14.4: 237
15.4: 106, 199, 219, 363

1 Corinthians
1.17: 19
2.11: 125
2.15: 137, 279

3.6: 177
3.11: 109
3.16: 280
4.1: 118
4.15: 19
5.6: 326
5.9: 162
7.7: 305
9.17: 150
9.27: 364
10.4: 315
11.1: 278
11.31: 246
11.16: 223
11.29: 124, 131, 132, 167
12.4–6: 115
12.11: 115
12.12–13: 147
12.18: 147
12.23: 148
14.38: 252
15.9: 97
16.22: 63

2 Corinthians
3.2–3: 370
3.6: 96
4.7: 114
5.19: 275
6.2: 72
6.14–16: 326
6.16: 285
11.4: 121
11.24: 233, 245
11.24–25: 362, 363

Galatians
2.8: 286
2.11: 97
2.11–12: 351
2.11–20: 352
2.13–14: 352
2.20: 139, 364
3.13–14: 138
4.19: 19
5.6: 376
5.9: 238

Galatians (continued)
6.14: 401
6.15: 330
6.17: 399

Ephesians
1.3: 117
1.5: 118
2.3: 347
2.14: 275
2.20: 68
4.5: 121
4.13: 118, 276
4.24: 118
4.31: 347
5.1–2: 278
5.5: 11, 253
5.14: 44
5.25–26: 151
6.2: 62, 274
6.17: 350

Philippians
1.15: 141
1.18: 141
2.21: 81
3.7–8: 397
3.19: 253

Colossians
1.3: 399
2.3: 114
2.9: 275

1 Thessalonians
2.19: 19
4.4–5: 49

2 Thessalonians
3.10: 351

1 Timothy
1.9–10: 11
2.5: 275
3.1: 267
3.2: 268

4.8: 240, 330
5.1: 352
5.11–12: 91
5.22: 254
5.23: 299

2 Timothy
2.4: 285
2.14: 223
2.16: 223
2.23–24: 222
3.1–5: 265
4.1: 251

Titus
1.15: 31, 167
1.16: 254

Hebrews
2.9: 167
4.13: 57
5.10: 321
6.4–6: 257
6.20: 120, 321
7.2–3: 275
7.23–24: 62
8.2: 101, 321
8.3: 110
8.5: 101
9.4: 242
9.14: 396
9.24–25: 116
10.27: 107
10.31: 42
10.38: 147
11.36: 245, 364
12.7–9: 368
13.1–2: 337
13.27: 368

James
1.20: 347
2.10: 238
4.4: 79, 285
4.17: 11
5.20: 78

1 Peter
2.25: 62
2.3: 118
2.4–5: 287
2.5: 109
2.21: 151
3.9: 395
5.7: 315
5.8: 104, 253
5.13: 19

2 Peter
2.6: 43
2.9–10: 43
2.13–14: 43
2.22: 78

1 John
2.19: 51
4.1: 95
4.8: 104
4.16: 104

Jude
6–7: 44

Revelation
1.5: 399
1.13: 402
1.16: 50
1.20: 266
3.4–5: 48
3.17: 34
3.20: 95
5.5: 114
5.8: 403
12.4–7: 207
14.3: 48
14.4: 48
18.7: 34, 41
20.14–15: 334
21.18–19: 287
21.22: 280
21.27: 44
22.17: 50

www.ingramcontent.com/pod-product-compliance
Lightning Source LLC
Chambersburg PA
CBHW032023290426

44110CB00012B/637